D0170792

Verbal Behavior and Learning:

PROBLEMS AND PROCESSES

PROCEEDINGS OF THE SECOND CONFERENCE
SPONSORED BY THE OFFICE OF
NAVAL RESEARCH AND NEW YORK UNIVERSITY

McGRAW-HILL SERIES IN PSYCHOLOGY
HARRY F. HARLOW, *Consulting Editor*

John F. Dashiell was Consulting Editor of this series from its inception
in 1931 until January 1, 1950. Clifford T. Morgan was Consulting Editor
of this series from January 1, 1950 until January 1, 1959.

Verbal Behavior and Learning:

PROBLEMS and PROCESSES

Edited by

Charles N. Cofer and Barbara S. Musgrave

PROCEEDINGS OF THE SECOND CONFERENCE SPONSORED BY THE OFFICE
OF NAVAL RESEARCH AND NEW YORK UNIVERSITY

Participants

Roger W. Brown
Glenn L. Bryan
James Deese
Albert E. Goss
James J. Jenkins
George Mandler
Arthur W. Melton
George A. Miller
Bennet B. Murdock, Jr.
Charles N. Cofer

Clyde E. Noble
Lloyd R. Peterson
Leo Postman
Wallace A. Russell
Roger N. Shepard
Arthur W. Staats
Benton J. Underwood
Delos D. Wickens
Barbara S. Musgrave

McGRAW-HILL BOOK COMPANY

New York San Francisco Toronto London

LB1051
.C675
1961

Verbal Behavior and Learning: Problems and Processes

Copyright © 1963 by McGraw-Hill, Inc. All Rights Reserved.
Printed in the United States of America. This book, or parts thereof,
may not be reproduced in any form without permission of the
publishers. *Library of Congress Catalog Card Number 62-20183*

III

11551

INDIANA-
PURDUE
LIBRARY

WITHDRAWN

FORT WAYNE

PREFACE

This book presents the Proceedings of the Second Conference on Verbal Learning and Verbal Behavior, sponsored by the U.S. Office of Naval Research and New York University. The conference was held in June, 1961, at the Frank Jay Gould House, Ardsley-on-Hudson, New York. In the paragraphs which follow, I wish to report how this second conference was organized, how it proceeded in its discussions, what these proceedings represent, and to make grateful acknowledgement to those who made the conference possible.

In April, 1960, Denzel D. Smith, then of the U.S. Office of Naval Research, and Glenn L. Bryan, of that office, suggested to me that I set up a second conference along the lines of the first one which had been held in 1959. Both Dr. Smith and Dr. Bryan felt that the first conference had been valuable in providing for an interchange among students of verbal learning and verbal behavior and that a second meeting, following closely on the first, would capitalize on the gains made in the first conference. While new topics, it was recognized, should be used in the new conference, the participants should remain much the same. I agreed to organize a second conference and proceeded to write to the participants of the first one, asking about their willingness to participate again, soliciting topics to be discussed, and obtaining nominations of individuals (both past conferees and new people) for specific assignments. Of the 14 participants in the first conference, 11 agreed to participate again. W. A. Bousfield, C. E. Osgood, and D. D. Smith withdrew because of prior commitments and similar reasons.

A large number of topics and names were submitted by the group, but in two or three exchanges of correspondence agreement was reached on topics and participants. I then invited the new participants to join with us. Again, because of prior commitments, three people declined, but the final roster of nineteen participants was soon established and topics were assigned.

The conference procedure was the same as the one used before. Eight papers were prepared and distributed ahead of time. One conference session was devoted to each paper. The session for a paper was led by the discussant of the paper. Typically, he made some comments about the paper and a general discussion ensued. Extensive notes were taken of the general discussion by Dr. Barbara Musgrave, the Recorder, and by the writer. In a final session, Dr. D. D. Wickens summarized the major points on which the conference had focussed.

In these proceedings, Chapters 2 through 9 present, in each case, a paper prepared ahead of time, the discussant's remarks, and a summary of the conference discussion. The prepared papers appear here, with minor exceptions, as they were distributed to the participants. Some of the discussants wrote their remarks ahead of time and made no further revision. Other discussants wrote their remarks after the conference. The summaries of the discussions were prepared, for the most part, by the writer from his and Dr. Musgrave's notes. They were reviewed by the other participants, especially Dr. Musgrave. The first chapter is a summary of the conference, prepared by the writer from all the materials available. Dr. Wickens's remarks are not only a summary but also a review of points receiving heavy emphasis and an evaluation of agreements and disagreements. They form Chapter 10 in the volume.

Bibliographies of papers cited follow the papers in which citations occurred. Additional references, mentioned in the course of general discussion but in neither the prepared nor the discussants' papers, will be found following the summaries of conference discussion.

Acknowledgments are due to Mr. Aaron Finesot and Miss Jane Stroup of New York University's Office of Special Services to Business and Industry for making available the university's Frank Jay Gould House for the meeting. To Mr. Carol E. Spette, resident manager of Gould House, his wife, and his superlative staff we are once again indebted for taking such good care of our housekeeping and culinary needs that the routines of living did not in any way interfere with our deliberations.

The conference was jointly sponsored by the Psychological Sciences Division of the Office of Naval Research, U.S. Navy Department, and the Department of Psychology, New York University. It was partly supported under Contract No. Nonr–285(47).

Charles N. Cofer

CONTENTS

ix

Chapter 1

INTRODUCTION AND SUMMARY

The topics treated in this second conference represent, to a major extent, unfinished business of the first conference. A reading of the proceedings of the first conference will reveal, at several points, concern with matters such as meaningfulness, familiarity, syntax, immediate memory, and one-trial learning. Few of these topics were treated explicitly in the first meeting, but they all received direct treatment in the present conference. Other topics treated here did not figure in the earlier deliberations as directly as those just mentioned, but again, the record of the first conference shows some concern with mediational mechanisms and the selectivity which subjects often show in the responses they give to specific situations. The treatments in this second conference of stimulus selection, mediated associations, and purpose and associative selectivity are relevant to these concerns touched on a year and a half ago. Recognition processes, the remaining subject in the second conference, are regarded as basic to many other issues.

There is, then, a good deal of continuity between the conferences. Taken together, they give a picture of substantial scope of the fields of verbal learning and verbal behavior and of their interrelationships. A summary of the major concerns of each session follows.

Bennet B. Murdock, Jr.
An Analysis of the Recognition Process

Murdock's paper is concerned with recognition as a means of measuring retention. Several kinds of recognition procedures may be distinguished, and Murdock's discussion is focussed on one of them, the multiple-choice type of test. He constructed tests of this kind, as well as a recall test, in order to study hypotheses about the recognition process. Analyses of test performance revealed that there were individual differences in the subjects' knowledge of the material, that their knowledge is not characterizable as an all-or-none matter, that the alternatives do not have equal probabilities of being selected as correct, and that the subject behaves as if he first eliminates alternatives he regards as wrong and then randomly selects his answer from the remaining alternatives.

1

Postulating that there is a fixed value for the probability that a given distractor would be eliminated as incorrect, Murdock was able to show that recognition test performance declines as the number of alternatives per item increases. These findings led Murdock to emphasize, in the measurement of recognition, the critical role the distractors play. Further, he said, recognition and recall are not equivalent measures. Knowledge by the subject of the list membership of an item probably accounts for the fact that scores on recognition tests are higher than they are for recall.

In his discussion, Deese emphasized the complexity of the problem of recognition, stressing the highly probable existence of interactions among the alternatives. He went on to develop certain implications of Murdock's paper, among them the notion that, in contradiction to what he has said on other occasions, subjects probably do edit their recalls of clustered or associatively related words.

The discussion which followed sought variables in terms of which recognition could be described in relation to the differences between recognition and recall scores. One factor which was mentioned is that in recognition procedures the alternatives are provided for the subject, whereas in recall the subject must provide the alternatives. However, recall processes were suggested as occurring during recognition procedures. Other models proposed in this connection were one based on the notion of a signal (correct response) to noise (distractors) ratio and one based on a trace concept. Emphasis on response processes during recognition was felt by some participants to be erroneous, since recognition can be a passive process; data were presented which were interpreted as inconsistent with an S-R analysis of recognition, but not all participants were persuaded by this information. Computer simulation of recognition performance was suggested as an approach to the problem, but a number of questions and objections were raised to this mode of analysis.

Benton J. Underwood
Stimulus Selection in Verbal Learning

It is apparently often true that in learning situations the stimuli which are presented and controlled by the experimenter are not identical to those to which the subject responds. This is the problem to which Underwood's paper is addressed, in the contexts of paired-associate and serial learning. Data from several experiments, both new and old, with paired-associates show that subjects tend to select some aspects of the stimulus to which to respond, rather than the total stimulus complex. With serial learning, on the other hand, several experiments have failed to indicate what the functional stimulus is. These experiments studied transfer between paired-associates and serial learning. Among the possibilities for which little or no support has been forthcoming are the preceding item, two or more prior items, the numerical position of the item, its spatial position, and its temporal position. In paired-associate learning, the subject utilizes the minimally differentiating aspect of the stimulus as the functional stimulus, a utilization which may vary with stimulus meaningfulness. Relations between stimulus selection in rote learning and processes in concept formation were suggested.

Shepard, in his discussion, argued that much of what Underwood said, while true, is perhaps not compatible with prevailing S-R concepts. These concepts, he said, are deficient especially in the case in which the behavior of individual subjects on particular trials is in question. However, the greater the meaningfulness or integration of the stimuli, the better S-R principles work. It is where selective attention to stimulus attributes may operate that the need for non-S-R principles is evident. In the latter case one cannot meaningfully speak, for example, of the strengthening of a connection between the stimulus and the response by reinforcement; generalization will not be uniform around the reinforced "stimulus." Where the subject's attention is "forced" to be selective to consistent attributes, as in concept learning, S-R principles can be shown to work. Shepard gave various examples of learning curves displayed by subjects in learning situations. Presumably, attentional factors underlie the variations the curves display. Shepard went on to describe, as a further problem for S-R theory, the tactic of stimulus recoding and even response coding (rules, hypotheses); what is being reinforced in such cases? This and other evidence suggest that hypotheses, plans, strategies, etc., must be added to, or perhaps must supplant, the notion of the strengthening or weakening of S-R bonds. Shepard went on to urge the use of computer simulation in the analysis of assumptions and their interactions in verbal learning.

The general discussion in this session concerned the significance and utility of computer simulation, the value of S-R analyses, and the problem of the assessment of strategies utilized by subjects in learning situations.

Clyde E. Noble
Meaningfulness and Familiarity

In his paper, Noble reviews the history of earlier attempts to measure properties of words which are related to meaningfulness (m) and discusses the background and rationale underlying his measure of m. The operations involved in obtaining m values are respecified, and evidence concerning the high reliability of m and its validity (as shown by its relations to 10 other variables) is summarized. Noble's m has been criticized by a number of writers, and Noble here replies to these criticisms, many of which have arisen from misunderstanding or misinterpretation of what he has said.

That meaningfulness and familiarity are independent concepts is a viewpoint which Noble develops in his paper, although he recognizes that measures of these two factors are often highly intercorrelated. But familiarity (f) refers to ratings of the frequency with which a word is experienced, whether it has any associations or not, whereas meaningfulness refers to the number of its associations. A word may be familiar and not meaningful, but a word cannot be highly meaningful without being familiar. Familiarity is a variable which enters into serial learning, but its role in paired-associate learning is somewhat uncertain. Noble has data indicating that its important effect in this learning situation is through the stimulus term rather than the response term; m has its influence via the response term. He reviews possible reasons for the discrepancies among experimental findings in these matters.

Goss devoted his discussion of Noble's paper to the variables and processes which underlie the relationships between meaningfulness and other variables to which it is related. How may these relations of meaningfulness to other matters be accounted for? Goss's analysis is a theoretical one, directed to the actual and potential stimulus-response elements which are involved—their properties, antecedents, and consequences—with especial attention to paired-associate learning. Methodological points were the chief concerns of the general discussion of this session.

Roger Brown and Colin Fraser
The Acquisition of Syntax

This paper is concerned primarily with certain empirical observations about language behavior in children, especially observations concerning their use of grammar. The development of grammatical usage appears to involve little understood processes which seem to have an analogic character: On the basis of his experience the child (or the learner of a second language) is able to extend his utterances to correct use of words and sentences he has not experienced or on which he has received no training. A number of experiments with contrived linguistic materials show that young children do, in fact, have rules for word inflection (as in pluralization) and sentence construction. The paper is devoted, for the most part, however, to a description of systematic collections of the speech of two- to three-year-old children and the attempt to discover in this body of material the grammar which underlies it. Detailed descriptions of the methods and outcomes are provided. The grammar used by the youngest children is not that of adult English, at least at first glance, but what it seems to be is an adult grammar with certain parts missing. Further study of this point revealed consistencies among the children in the ways they "reduce" English. Studies of direct attempts of such children to imitate adult speech revealed similar consistent reductions. The interpretation suggested is that very young children speak a sort of telegraphic English which retains words which, among other things, carry the most information, occupy terminal positions in the sentence, and are stressed in pronunciation. Limitations of memory span and an unlearned "recency principle" are factors productive of this telegraphic English.

In his comments on this paper, Cofer stressed the desirability and importance of an experimental program designed to uncover the functional stimuli which control the inflectional and sentence construction skills manifested by young children. Possible experiments were outlined. He went on to suggest, citing certain data in doing so, that adult human memory may be derived from a reduced or telegraphic version of the material being retained. That is to say what the adult subject actually remembers is a sort of shorthand version from which he constructs the coherent recall which is actually recorded in an experiment.

Much of the discussion in this session concerned Cofer's suggested experiments, about the value of which there was disagreement. Problems related to factors in language learning of young children, such as those suggested by the terms imitation, reinforcement, and concept formation, received attention. There was discussion of the nature of linguistic contexts.

James J. Jenkins
Mediated Associations: Paradigms and Situations

Jenkins's paper begins with the statement that mediational phenomena are well established but that there has been disagreement as to the nature of the mediating mechanism. However, he believes that it is less important to debate the disagreement than it is to study the procedures used to predict mediational effects and the conditions of which mediational effects are a function. His paper is addressed to the problem of appropriate conditions.

He reviews experiments on three-stage mediation paradigms, most of which show positive results, and then describes various experiments designed to study mediation in four-stage paradigms. None of these has shown mediation to occur. Various explanations for these failures are advanced, and relevant evidence is brought to bear upon them. Of particular interest is a comparison of the paradigms and situations under which "semantic conditioning" may be found with an instrumental response as opposed to paradigms which yield conditioning with a classical procedure. A number of experimental follow-ups are needed to determine whether four-stage mediational effects can be obtained. Especially emphasized are the use of reinforcement for specific mediational responses, reinforcing the act of mediating, and looking into the characteristics of tasks and situations which appear to vary in the extent to which they yield associative arousal and hence mediational effects.

Mandler, discussing this paper, expressed some concern over the application of group norms to individual subjects and also thought more attention should be paid to data from individual subjects than is usually the practice in experiments on mediational processes. His comments further suggested that some of Jenkins's suggestions imply that in mediational studies attention and "strategies" are involved on the part of the subject to an extent much greater than is assumed in the usual interpretations of such phenomena. He went on to argue that perhaps the subject's behavior is logical, or partially so, rather than automatic, and he presented data from experiments showing that when logical relations are present in a learning situation, subjects learn better than they do when this is not the case. Mandler suggested that many mediational experiments may, in fact, be concept learning experiments.

Various arguments were offered in opposition to Mandler's objections to the use of associative group norms in experiments on verbal problems. The processes to which such operations as extinction and reinforcement pertain in mediational situations were seen as difficult to define and to specify, and the problem of interference in the mediational paradigms received attention. Criticisms were directed at Mandler's "logical" paradigms.

Wallace A. Russell
Purpose and the Problem of Associative Selectivity

The fact that verbal behavior often shows apparent selectivity has led to the postulation of such concepts as set, selector mechanisms, intentions, and other parallel notions. Professor Russell's paper is directed to the analysis of this problem; the term set is rather vague and in any case describes the phenomenon of selectivity rather than suggesting any mechanisms. Russell uses the general term purpose in his discussion and suggests that it may designate processes independent of both habit and of drive (as an energizing factor). As to possible mechanisms which may underlie purpose, Russell suggests and discusses several possibilities, such as mediational processes, the fractional goal response and its consequent stimuli, changes in the range of stimuli to which the organism is sensitive, attention cathexis, and the notions of tactics, strategies, and plans. A number of research suggestions arise from these considerations.

In commenting on Russell's paper, Staats preferred to avoid the notion of purpose and to give an analysis of apparently goal-directed behavior in terms of control by external stimuli or by the individual's verbal response sequences and sequences of motor behavior. Such an S-R analysis, he argued, makes considerations of ends or goals irrelevant. Experiments on the operant conditioning of word classes show the nature of selectivity in the case of verbal behavior. Words may function in classes, when, according to S-R acquisition variables, they have been organized into hierarchies developed around a common word or meaning response, or when they have been associated with one another in various ways, including serial orders. These processes account for the operant conditioning of word classes, indicating that the study of language behavior demands an integration of word-association principles and mediation principles, as well as operant conditioning principles.

A number of objections were raised in the discussion to Staats's attempt to deal with purpose in S-R terms and to his application of the operant conditioning paradigm to certain features of language acquisition. A major concern developed as to the applicability of S-R analyses to processes such as sets, *Aufgaben,* and rules. Among the concerns was that commitment to S-R notions might lead to the neglect of significant properties of behavior and of variables to which it is related; it was doubted by some that S-R principles have sufficient breadth to cope with purposive or goal-determined dispositions. Several participants seemed to feel that Staats's analysis had ignored important matters, for example, the instructions in various experiments and the subject's "purpose" of obtaining rewards.

Leo Postman
One-trial Learning

The formation of associations can be conceived as a gradual process, with increments to associative strength occurring on each trial, or it can be conceived as an all-or-none phenomenon, occurring in one trial. The incremental view has long held sway, but experimental results have been obtained since 1957 which have been interpreted as offering support to the all-or-none conception. Postman, in reviewing this problem, points out that many facts of acquisition are consistent with either formulation, but that others, especially the facts of proactive and retroactive interference, are not. Further, the lack of perfect correlation among measures of association may be a problem for all-or-none theory. Relevant experiments are analyzed critically, and Postman presents new evidence based on experiments of his own. This evidence supports the incremental model. Methodological defects in certain experiments, together with conflicting evidence, lead Postman to conclude that at the present time the all-or-none model has not been supported. Miller's discussion, on the other hand, raised problems relating to the strategy people use in verbal learning, and Miller was able to point to successful predictions and ordering of available data that certain theories of the learning of a list had achieved, even though they postulate all-or-none formation of associations. Processes relating to strategies or tactics in verbal learning are involved in such theories. Miller here implies that the formation of specific associations is only one, and perhaps a minor one, of all the processes involved in verbal learning.

The discussion in this session was concerned with the characteristics and adequacy of the model which Miller had described. The problem of the measures to be used and of the extent of their intercorrelation was discussed, some participants holding that a one-trial conception need not require perfect intercorrelation of the measures of verbal learning. Several participants expressed concern over the definition of terms and processes used in computer simulation models, apparently feeling that words like attention or strategy obscured important details. S-R theory, however, came in for criticism from several participants because of its lack of explicitness.

Lloyd R. Peterson
Immediate Memory: Data and Theory

In this paper, Professor Peterson distinguishes among three aspects of memory. There is the stimulus trace, which is brief and serves for short-time storage. Two kinds of associative mechanisms, cue learning and background conditioning, function in both short-time and long-term storage. Cue learning refers to responses associated to cues introduced by the experimenter, such as those developed between pair members in paired-associate learning. Background conditioning refers to general situational or to subject variables over which little control can be exercised but which enter into associative relations with the subject's responses. Pertinent evidence is reviewed concerning all three of these aspects of memory.

Melton pointed out that earlier conceptions of memory had assumed only one process, not two or more, as is suggested in Peterson's analysis. Hebb suggested a duplex model and Peterson's is a triplex conception. Much of Melton's discussion was devoted to the problem of whether there are different kinds of traces involved in various aspects of memory, or alternatively, whether there is one kind of trace, which, subject to different influences, may show a variety of decay functions.

The discussion concentrated on the differences between cue learning and background conditioning, and a number of proposals were made for experiments which could untangle these processes and delimit their relative effects. The interpretation of the decay functions discussed by

Peterson was a source of concern, and the role of interference and of the background factors in decay was a subject of some debate.

Delos D. Wickens
Conference Summary

In summarizing the work of this conference, Professor Wickens pointed first to the expression in it of two viewpoints, one characterizable as S-R, the other as non-S-R. He thought S-R workers move along lines dictated by theory and do so as parsimoniously as possible. The non-S-R workers, on the other hand, are more likely to enter a problem area and develop theory on the basis of their findings; they often choose problems which arise in other disciplines, such as linguistics or engineering. The S-R psychologists are oriented to think physiologically, in the tradition of the Chicago school of functionalist psychology; this is not so true of the non-S-R theorists, who see much value in computer analogues and computer language as the source of and means of expression for concepts. Wickens finds it healthy that there are such divergencies of viewpoint in the verbal learning–verbal behavior area. He would look to the non-S-R approach to open up new areas to inquiry, with careful evaluation from the S-R side.

Topics which Wickens found pervasive throughout the conference were those of the functional stimulus and context cues, and he thought it a hopeful sign that both topics were acceptable as concepts, since this may mean that useful work will follow their acceptance.

Wickens suggested, further, that in terms of papers and discussions in this conference, we are near solutions to the problems of one-trial learning and of the effects of m and f on learning. Not so near solution, but with directions for future research rather clear, are immediate memory and mediating response. In other cases, however, the problem area is in the formative stage. This characterization Wickens applied to recognition, language learning, and set.

The discussion of Wickens's summary centered on the S-R–non-S-R divergence, with some clarifying comments on the orientation of S-R workers on the one hand, and on the use of computers on the other.

Chapter 2

AN ANALYSIS OF THE RECOGNITION PROCESS

Bennet B. Murdock, Jr.[1]

UNIVERSITY OF VERMONT

The emphasis in the present paper will be on recognition as a method of measuring retention. All we shall attempt to do is to suggest some possible hypotheses about the nature of the recognition process, state them quantitatively, test them, and then explore some further implications of the most promising hypothesis. The perceptual aspect of recognition as manifested, for instance, in the recognition of ambiguous stimuli (see Binder and Feldman, 1960) is beyond the scope of the present paper and will not be considered here. No attempt will be made to survey either studies comparing recognition and recall as methods of measuring retention (Postman and Rau, 1957) or studies assessing the reliability and validity of multiple-choice tests (Kinney and Eurich, 1932).

Recognition is one of the traditional methods of measuring retention, and it tests the individual's ability to identify previously learned material. Three different types of recognition tests may be distinguished. The first, essentially a variant of the method of single stimuli, requires the individual to make a binary choice (usually "yes" or "no") about a single stimulus item (Seward, 1928). Although not usually cast in this form, a true-false test question is essentially a recognition test of this type. The second type of recognition test requires the individual to select the one "correct" stimulus from a group of several stimuli (Postman and Rau, 1957). This, of course, is the familiar multiple-choice type of test. The third type of recognition test requires the individual to select all correct stimuli from a larger number of stimuli (Luh, 1922). This is essentially a test of knowledge of list membership and is often used in

[1] This work was supported by a research grant, M-3330, from the National Institutes of Health.

tests of serial learning and free recall. For all three types, recognition may be measured by accuracy, latency, or both.

There is no reason to believe that these three types of recognition tests involve fundamentally different processes. In general, the individual must select the correct response from zero, several, or many possible alternatives. In this paper we would like to concentrate primarily on the second of these three types of recognition, the multiple-choice type of test. As Cronbach and Merwin (1955) say, "theory regarding the multiple-choice item and its construction has been almost non-existent" (p. 337).

Tests employing multiple-choice items are, of course, coming into widespread usage in educational and vocational testing. Also, multiple-choice items have been used to test retention in rote learning studies (see, for instance, Postman and Rau, 1957). In either case, in using a multiple-choice item, what you are testing is the ability of the individual to select the one correct answer from (usually) four or five alternatives. The ability tested is most clearly related to retention when the material covered by the test item is factual in nature and when it can be assumed or demonstrated that the material had, at some previous time, been apprehended by the individual. An analysis of the recognition process, then, necessitates an analysis of how the individual identifies the correct answer in a multiple-choice item.

To study this problem we constructed a multiple-choice test which we labeled "General Information." To make it as much a test of retention as possible, the test was constructed so as to cover factual information to which, it was hoped, the average college undergraduate would have been exposed. The original test consisted of 24 questions in each of 20 different categories (fine arts, botany and zoology, chemistry, astronomy and mathematics, world literature, English and American literature, geography, American history, world history, classical civilization, philosophy and religion, physics and weights and measures, government and political science, psychology, elementary French vocabulary, inventors and explorers, colleges and universities, sports, entertainment, and advertising). The test was first constructed as a recall test necessitating one- or, occasionally, two-word answers. We tried to make the questions as simple, direct, and brief as possible; a typical question would be, "What is the first book of the Old Testament?"

This recall form was first administered verbally to 15 subjects tested individually. These subjects were students enrolled in the course in general psychology at the University of Vermont. Of the 480 questions on the test there were 207 questions (including, believe it or not, the sample question given above) which were correctly answered by not less than 5 and not more than 10 of the 15 subjects tested. We then selected 200 of these 207 questions and made them into three different forms of a paper-and-pencil test designed for group testing. Each form used the same 200 questions.

The first form, a recall test, used the questions in identical form except that spaces were provided for subjects to write their answers. The second and third forms were recognition tests using four alternatives. The correct answer was one of the four alternatives, and its position among the other three was determined by a table of random numbers. The three distractors for each question were selected to be reasonable alternatives and, whenever possible, were selected from incorrect answers given in the original administration. The same distractors were used in both forms.

The second form, a ranking form, required the subjects to rank each of the four alternatives to each question from 1 to 4, 1 being the most likely answer and 4 the least likely answer. The third form, an X0 form (see Coombs, Milholland, and Womer, 1956), required the subjects on each question to eliminate (cross out) as many incorrect alternatives as possible. Thus, on the X0 form the subjects were to cross out anywhere from zero to three alternatives, being careful, however, not to cross out the correct answer. Nothing was said on either recognition form about guessing. The three forms were administered to 56, 55, and 86 subjects respectively, all students from the general psychology course.

These three forms can be used to evaluate various hypotheses about test performance. The first hypothesis to be tested is that each question has the same probability of being answered correctly and that the subjects do not differ in their ability to answer the questions correctly. If this were so, any obtained differences would be due to chance. According to this hypothesis, scores on the recall form should be described by the binomial $(p + q)^n$, with p the probability of getting each question correct and n the number of questions (i.e., 200). Using as an estimate of p the value of .498 (the mean proportion of correct answers on the recall form), the expected variance would be approximately 50; the obtained variance for the 56 subjects was 784. This gave an F ratio greater than 15, significant at well beyond the .001 level of confidence. If it were considered that some questions had a probability higher than .498 and others a probability lower than .498, this could only decrease the expected variance and make the F even larger. Thus, this first hypothesis is clearly incorrect; there were, in effect, real individual differences among the subjects.

The second hypothesis to be tested is that performance on each question is an all-or-none affair; the subjects either know the answer or they do not. If this were so, the number of correct answers on the second, third, and fourth choice in the ranking form should comprise a rectangular distribution. This rectangular distribution was not obtained. The mean number of correct second, third, and fourth choices was 27.6, 17.1, and 12.7 questions, respectively. An analysis of variance gave an F ratio of 163, significant at well beyond the .001 level, and the two adjacent differences were each significant by t tests at the .001 level. Thus, the all-or-none hypothesis is untenable; the second choices were more often correct than the third choices, and the third choices were more often correct than the fourth choices.

The third hypothesis to be tested is that, on a recognition test, each alternative in a question has the same probability of being selected as correct. Thus, if the subject's first choice was not correct, the probability of being correct on the second choice would be the same, and so on, until the fourth choice when, of course, the subject would have to be correct. If this hypothesis were correct the results of the ranking form could be described by the geometric distribution pq^{n-1} with n the ordinal choice number (i.e., 1, 2, 3, 4). Because of the problem of averaging geometric distributions with different p values, we obtained a separate estimate of p for each subject; the estimate was simply the proportion of correct first choices. Having obtained the predicted number of correct second, third, and fourth choices for each subject, we then averaged and obtained expected values of 39.4, 12.0, and 5.9 questions, respectively. As given above, the obtained mean number of correct answers was 27.6, 17.1, and 12.7 questions, respectively. By t tests it was found that there were significantly too few correct second choices and significantly too many correct third and fourth choices, all at beyond the .001 level. Therefore, each alternative does not have the same probability of being selected as correct.

The fourth (and final) hypothesis to be tested is that, on each question, the subject eliminates anywhere from zero to $n - 1$ of the n alternatives as being incorrect, then randomly selects the correct answer from the remaining alternatives. On the X0 form the mean number of 3, 2, 1, and 0 alternatives crossed out was 152.3, 16.4, 5.9, and 25.3 questions, respectively. However, in some cases the correct answer was one of the alternatives crossed out; the mean number of times this happened was 27.6, 3.7, and 0.6 questions for 3, 2, and 1 alternatives, respectively. Because of guessing, the above values probably represent underestimates of the true values. The standard correction for guessing was used and the obtained values were increased by factors of $\frac{1}{3}$, $\frac{1}{2}$, and 1, respectively. Thus, the corrected values for the number of correct answers wrongly crossed out became 36.8, 5.6, and 1.2 for 3, 2, and 1 alternatives, respectively.

There remains the problem of allocating those cases where the correct alternative was crossed out to one of the lower categories. For example, there were 152.3 questions with 3 alternatives crossed out, but in 36.8 of these questions the correct answer was one of the alternatives crossed out. One way to handle this problem is to allocate these 36.8 questions equally to the three lower categories (i.e., 2, 1, and 0 alternatives crossed out). When this procedure is followed, the adjusted scores became 115.5, 23.1, 19.8, and 41.6 questions. That is, these are the number of questions on which the subjects *correctly* eliminated 3, 2, 1, and 0 alternatives as wrong answers to the questions.

Given these adjusted scores, how can we test the hypothesis that a subject responds to a test item by eliminating anywhere from zero to $n - 1$ alternatives and then randomly selects the correct answer from the remaining alternatives? We can use the adjusted scores to predict performance on the ranking form. Specifically, on the ranking form one would expect 144.0 correct first choices $[(115.5) + .5(23.1) + .33(19.8) + .25(41.6)]$, 28.6 correct second choices $[.5(23.1) + .33(19.8) + .25(41.6)]$, 17.0 correct third choices $[.33(19.8) + .25(41.6)]$, and 10.4 correct fourth choices $[.25(41.6)]$. As shown below, the obtained values were quite close to the predicted values. The expected value for the

Choice	Predicted	Obtained
1st	144.0	142.4 ± 4.7
2nd	28.6	27.6 ± 2.2
3rd	17.0	17.1 ± 1.6
4th	10.4	12.7 ± 1.6

number of correct fourth choices lay outside the 95 per cent confidence interval (the last number in the third column), but even there the difference between obtained and predicted was not too large. Thus, it would appear that the X0 hypothesis can predict fairly accurately the results of the ranking form and, for the present data, is clearly the most nearly correct of the four hypotheses tested.

It is suggested, then, that on a recognition test the subjects eliminate a certain number of alternatives as incorrect and randomly select the correct answer from the remaining alternatives. Which alternatives and how many they cross out clearly would depend upon the subjects and upon the particular distractors used. It is not necessary that the subjects consciously adopt this strategy (although undoubtedly in some cases subjects do deliberately try first to cross out as many distractors as possible). All that is claimed is that the subject's performance on a recognition test can be described as if he had adopted this procedure.

If a test were relatively homogeneous in content and if the distractors in the items were of comparable attractiveness, then one would be justified in talking about the probability of a given subject rejecting any given distractor as incorrect. If this probability were known, then the number of items in which 0, 1, 2, . . . , $(n - 1)$ alternatives could be eliminated would be given by the binomial $(p + q)^{n-1}$. We can obtain an estimate of p from the X0 form; for the X0 form $n = 4$. We can (either for each subject individually or for the group as a whole) determine $\bar{X}$, the mean number of distractors eliminated per item, then use the standard formula for the mean of a binomial [in the present case $\bar{X} = (n - 1)p$] to obtain an estimate of p. Having found an estimate of p, this value can in turn be used in the binomial to predict the number of items in which 0, 1, 2, or 3 distractors will be eliminated.

This procedure was followed for the X0 form and the results were quite clear: the binomial did not apply. Specifically, there were far too few items with two alternatives crossed out and far too many items with no alternatives crossed out. This finding held both for individual subjects and for the group as a whole. However, it can be argued that the General Information test is a very heterogeneous test consisting, as it does, of various items from 20 different categories. Thus, it would be reasonable to expect some subjects to be quite ignorant in some areas and thus be unable to eliminate any distractors, yet be quite knowledgeable in others and so able to eliminate all distractors.

As a further test of the applicability of the binomial to the number of alternatives crossed out, we used an X0 form for a regular scheduled hour exam in the introductory psychology course. The exam covered approximately one-third of the semester's work and consisted of 70 multiple-choice four-alternative questions selected from the instructor's manual for the text (Morgan, 1956). As in the General Information test, the students were merely instructed that on each question they should cross out as many wrong alternatives as possible without crossing out the correct answer. It was felt that such a test would be more homogeneous than the General Information test.

Twenty-four students took the test, and the mean number of questions with 3, 2, 1, and 0 alternatives crossed out was 59.3, 7.6, 1.5, and 1.6 with standard deviations of 9.7, 7.8, 2.8, and 3.0, respectively. The mean number of *correct* answers crossed out was 21.5, 2.3, and 0.0 for 3, 2, and 1 alternatives, respectively. If you do not correct for guessing (i.e., increase the mean number of correct answers crossed out by $\frac{1}{3}$, $\frac{1}{2}$, and 1), and if you assign the errors (i.e., number of correct answers incorrectly crossed out) to the next lower category, then, using the group mean ($\bar{p} = .813$, $s = .065$) as an estimate of p, the binomial fits very well. The table below shows both the predicted number of questions with 3, 2, 1, and 0 alternatives correctly crossed out and the obtained means ± the 95

Alternatives	Predicted	Obtained
3	37.6	37.8 ± 3.20
2	26.0	26.9 ± 2.78
1	6.0	3.7 ± 1.75
0	0.5	1.7 ± 1.35

per cent confidence interval. However, if you do correct for guessing and/ or distribute the errors equally among all lower categories, then the binomial definitely does not fit the obtained distribution.

It would seem, then, that the evidence for the applicability of the binomial is rather equivocal. Nevertheless, because of the considerable advantages that accrue, let us proceed as if it were legitimate to talk about the probability of a subject rejecting any given distractor and so use the binomial $(p + q)^{n-1}$ to describe the distribution of questions with $0, 1, 2, \ldots, (n-1)$ distractors eliminated. According to the hypothesis under investigation, the subject will in effect select at random from the alternatives not crossed out. Thus, the probability of being correct on any given question is $1/(n - x)$, where x is the number of alternatives correctly crossed out and can assume the values $0, 1, 2, \ldots, (n-1)$.

Given the binomial distribution $(p + q)^{n-1}$ for $x = 0, 1, 2, \ldots, (n - 1)$ which describes the distribution of questions with the various number of distractors crossed out, and given $1/(n - x)$ as the probability of a correct answer to the question, it is a simple matter to obtain a statement for R, the proportion of correct answers on the entire test, as a function of p. When $n = 2$ we find:

$$R_2 = \frac{1 + p}{2}$$

When $n = 3$ $\qquad R_3 = \frac{1 + p + p^2}{3}$

When $n = 4$ $\qquad R_4 = \frac{1 + p + p^2 + p^3}{4}$

And in general $\qquad R_n = \frac{1 + p + p^2 + \cdots + p^{n-1}}{n}$

Thus, R_n is a polynomial in p of degree $n - 1$ and each term in the polynomial has as its coefficient n^{-1}.

We have then a statement giving the interrelationships among R, the proportion of correct responses on the test as a whole; p, the probability of eliminating a distractor as incorrect; and n, the number of alternatives in each question. Theoretical curves giving R as a function of p for several different values of n are shown in Figure 2–1. Except for the case where $n = 2$ all the curves are positively accelerated, and their slopes increase with p.

It is generally agreed that a test item makes the maximum number of discriminations when the proportion of correct responses R is .50. The dotted line in Figure 2–1 is drawn at this value to facilitate comparisons among the different curves. It is impossible for $R_2 = .50$ provided, of course, $p > 0$. For a three-alternative item $R_3 = .50$ when $p = .37$, for a four-alternative item $R_4 = .50$ when $p = .55$, and the necessary p value steadily increases with n. The four-alternative item is commonly used on many objective tests, and it would appear that, for the maximum number of discriminations, each distractor should have about a 50:50 chance of being eliminated as incorrect.

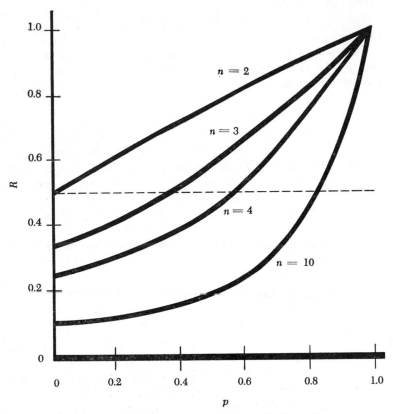

FIG. 2–1. R as a function of p for several values of n.

Perhaps the clearest implication of Figure 2–1 is that, for any given p value, R_n should decrease as n increases. That is, as the number of alternatives per item increases the test score should decrease. Since this would also be expected just on the basis of chance, it is necessary to introduce a correction for guessing. The standard correction for guessing can be represented as $R_c = R - W/(n-1)$, where R_c is the corrected score and R and W the proportion of right and wrong answers, respectively. Assume that on a given test the subject is required to answer all items. Since $R_n = (1 + p + p^2 + \cdots + p^{n-1})/n$, $W = 1 - R$, and $R_c = R - W/(n-1)$, it follows that

$$R_{c_n} = \frac{p + p^2 + p^3 + \cdots + p^{n-1}}{n-1}$$

Thus, the proportion of right responses corrected for guessing is also a polynomial in p of degree $n-1$, and each term (except p^0) has as its coefficient $(n-1)^{-1}$.

What happens to R_{c_n} as n increases? For $0 < p < 1.00$ and $n = 2$, 3, 4, . . . , as n increases, the numerator increases in steps of p^x where $x = 2, 3, 4, \ldots, (n-1)$ while the denominator increases in steps of 1. Since $p^x < 1$ it follows that R_{c_n} must decrease as n increases. Thus, even when the scores are corrected for guessing, the proportion of correct answers should decrease as the number of alternatives increases.

In studies of the role of the effect of number of alternatives on acquisition, Riley (1952) and Brogden and Schmidt (1954) report results which indicate that learning time increases with number of alternatives. More relevant, Teghtsoonian (1958) found (Experiment III) significantly better recognition of three-digit numbers presented once when 4 alternatives were used than when 16 alternatives were used in the recognition test; scores were corrected for guessing. Schwartz (1961) found that the recognition of a list of five digits decreased as the number of alternatives increased from 6 to 16; however, no effect was found for lists of five prefamiliarized two-letter words.

In order to obtain additional evidence, we undertook two further tests of the effect of number of alternatives on recognition. In the first test the subjects were given lists of 20 words to study for 30 seconds by means of the method of whole presentation. Then, they tried to identify as many of these 20 words as possible when shown a longer list of 40, 80, 120, or 160 words. One replication required four different lists, and there were four replications per subject. Order was counterbalanced by a Latin square design to control for practice effects. All lists were selected from the Thorndike-Lorge (1944) list of the 4,000 most common English words (G count of 20 and up), and the 20 test words were randomly selected from and randomly located in the longer lists. There were 11 subjects from an advanced psychology course, and they were tested individually.

When corrected for chance, the mean proportion of correct responses was .56, .54, .44, and .42 for lists of 40, 80, 120, and 160 alternatives, respectively. An analysis of variance gave an F ratio of 9.30 which, with $df = \frac{3}{30}$, was significant at beyond the .001 level. Thus, R_{c_n} decreased as n increased.

In the second test we again made use of the General Information test. Starting with 200 questions of four alternatives each we made 67 two-alternative questions, 67 three-alternative questions, and 66 four-alternative questions merely by deleting 2, 1, or 0 distractors, respectively. The questions in each category (i.e., two-, three-, or four-alternative questions) and the distractors deleted were both determined in a completely random method. We then administered the test to 97 subjects, students in the introductory sociology course at the University of Vermont who, in all probability, were very similar to the students in the general psychology course.

When corrected for guessing the mean proportion of correct responses was .723, .696, .646 for two-, three-, and four-alternative questions, respectively. An analysis of variance gave an F ratio of 35.61 which, with $df = \frac{2}{192}$, was significant at well beyond the .001 level. Also, t tests showed that the two adjacent differences were both significant at beyond the .01 level. Thus, the second test substantiated the first. It would seem then that there is considerable evidence to suggest that, as predicted, R_{c_n} does decrease as n increases.

The results of the variable-alternative form of the General Information test can be used to test another aspect of the proposed relationships. It has already been suggested that R_n is a polynomial in p of degree $n - 1$. Knowing R_n for $n = 2$, 3, and 4, we can then get three independent estimates of p. Since basically it is all the same test, these three estimates of p should agree closely. The values of R_2, R_3, and R_4 were .861, .797, and .735; the resulting estimates of p were .723, .781, and .797, respectively. The latter two estimates were almost identical, and the first does not seem far off. Thus, the estimated values of p for the three independent subtests seem to agree fairly well.

Finally, from the proposed relationships it is possible to make certain predictions about the rate at which performance changes with number of alternatives for different probability values. As one goes from $n = 2$ to $n = 3$ the slope of the curve $R_{c_n} = f(n)$ is $-pq/2$ (considering the slope as $\Delta R_{c_n}/\Delta n$). From $n = 3$ to $n = 4$ the slope is $p^3/3 - p^2/6 - p/6$, and from $n = 4$ to $n = 5$ the slope is $p^4/4 - p^3/12 - p^2/12 - p/12$. These three slopes are greatest for p values of .50, .61, and .68, respectively. In general, the slopes are small for very high and very low p values. This means, then, that changing the number of alternatives within the range of 2 to 5 will have the greatest effect on the corrected recognition score for p values at and slightly above average, but relatively inconsequential effects for extreme p values.

It is possible to get predicted slopes for the variable-alternative form of the General Information test. We used as a p value the average of the three parts (i.e., two-, three-, and four-alternative items); the mean p value was .767. Going from $n = 2$ to $n = 3$ the predicted slope was

—.089 and the obtained slope was —.027 ± .020; from $n = 3$ to $n = 4$ the predicted slope was —.076 and the obtained slope was —.050 ± .017. Thus, in both cases the predicted slopes were outside the 95 per cent confidence intervals. While it appears then that the obtained slopes were significantly lower than predicted, still the magnitude of the difference was not too large, and the predicted values were, in both cases, well within one standard deviation of the obtained means.

To summarize, we have tried to set up and test several hypotheses about how a subject identifies the correct alternative on a multiple-choice item. The most promising hypothesis appears to be that, on each item, the subject's performance could be described as if he had eliminated as many distractors as possible and then randomly selected from the remaining alternatives. It was suggested that one could postulate a p value, the probability that any given distractor could be eliminated as incorrect. Although the evidence for a fixed probability value was not overwhelming, this notion was retained as a useful concept. It was shown that, as predicted, performance on a recognition test deteriorated as the number of alternatives per item increased, even when scores were corrected for guessing. However, while the scores did go down, they did not decrease quite as rapidly as predicted.

It would appear then that the X0 hypothesis has some merit. At least to some extent subjects identify the correct response on a multiple-choice item by eliminating as many distractors as possible and then randomly selecting from the remaining alternatives. What implications does this hypothesis have for the measurement of retention by the method of recognition?

First, the X0 hypothesis emphasizes the critical role of the distractors in any recognition test. The particular distractors selected and the ease with which they can be eliminated will (to the extent to which this hypothesis is correct) completely determine performance. As an example of the importance of the distractors, Postman, Jenkins, and Postman (1948) found that significantly more similar distractors (i.e., distractors similar to the correct alternative) were incorrectly chosen as correct than would be expected by chance.

Second, the X0 hypothesis would predict that recognition and recall are not necessarily equivalent methods of measuring retention. That is, recall tests the ability of an individual to produce the correct response while recognition tests the ability of an individual to eliminate the incorrect responses; these are not necessarily the same. In their methodological study Postman and Rau (1957) conclude, "The shape of the retention curve varies with . . . the method of measurement" (p. 267). Specifically, they feel that recognition measures the extent to which the item or items learned have been differentiated from other members of the same population, while recall measures the "availability of the individual items for active reproduction without support from reexposure to the original learning materials" (p. 217).

Third, the X0 hypothesis could help explain why recognition is often much better than recall. To take a specific example, Hollingworth (1913) repeatedly presented a list of 50 adjectives with instructions to give the opposite adjective. Then, after 60 to 75 presentations, he tested for the retention of these pairs of adjectives, first by recall and then by recognition. The median recall was 27 out of 50, yet half the subjects were able to recognize all 50 when shown a total of 100 pairs of adjectives. Why was the difference so large? Simply because the subject would identify the pairs not on the list even though he could only produce slightly more than half the pairs himself.

For such an explanation to be correct it is necessary that knowledge of list membership develop at a more rapid rate than recall. Indirect evidence is provided by studies of free recall (Deese, 1959b; Murdock, 1960); the incidence of extra-list intrusions seems to be quite low even when recall is far from perfect. (Such intrusions apparently are a function of interitem associative strength; see Deese, 1959a). More direct evidence is provided in a study by Cofer (1961). In one variation of the experiment he read a list of 15 words once, had subjects match list length in free recall, then for each item recalled had the subject indicate whether he was sure the item had been on the list, was sure it had not been on the list, or was uncertain. Over-all, subjects were more than 80 per cent accurate in assessing list membership. For the lists of unrelated words the subjects were 97.5 per cent accurate when they checked a word recalled as having been on the list (personal communication). If subjects are this accurate with a list of 15 words presented once, it does not seem unreasonable to assume that they would have a fairly accurate idea of list membership of a list of 50 adjective pairs presented some 60 to 75 times.

In conclusion, it is readily admitted that the X0 hypothesis is a rather simple and unsophisticated hypothesis about recognition as a method of measuring retention. Also, it is not in perfect accordance with all the facts. However, it does show how performance on a recognition test should vary as a function of the number of alternatives and the probability of eliminating distractors. There are undoubtedly other implications of the X0 hypothesis beyond those suggested in this paper; the quantitative formulation should be of benefit both in finding these implications and in testing them empirically.

REFERENCES

Binder, A., & Feldman, S. E. (1960) The effects of experimentally controlled experience upon recognition responses. *Psychol. Monogr.*, **74**, No. 9, 1–43.

Brogden, W. J., & Schmidt, R. E. (1954) Effect of number of choices per unit of a verbal maze on learning and serial position errors. *J. Exp. Psychol.*, **47**, 235–240.

Cofer, C. N. (1961) Inter-item associative strength and immediate free and forced recall. Paper presented at East. Psychol. Ass., Philadelphia.

Coombs, C. H., Milholland, J. E., & Womer, F. B. (1956) The assessment of partial knowledge. *Educ. Psychol. Measmt*, **16**, 13–37.

Cronbach, L. J., & Merwin, J. C. (1955) A model for studying the validity of multiple-choice items. *Educ. Psychol. Measmt*, **15**, 337–352.

Deese, J. (1959a) On the prediction of occurrence of particular verbal intrusions in immediate recall. *J. Exp. Psychol.*, **58**, 17–22.

Deese, J. (1959b) Influence of inter-item associative strength upon immediate free recall. *Psychol. Rep.*, **5**, 305–312.

Hollingworth, H. L. (1913) Characteristic differences between recall and recognition. *Amer. J. Psychol.*, **24**, 533–544.

Kinney, L. B., & Eurich, A. C. (1932) A summary of investigations comparing different types of tests. *Sch. & Soc.*, **36**, 540–544.

Luh, C. W. (1922) The conditions of retention. *Psychol. Monogr.*, **31**, No. 142, 1–87.

Morgan, C. T. (1956) *Introduction to psychology*. New York: McGraw-Hill.

Murdock, B. B., Jr. (1960) The immediate retention of unrelated words. *J. Exp. Psychol.*, **60**, 222–234.

Postman, L., Jenkins, W. O., & Postman, D. L. (1948) An experimental comparison of active recall and recognition. *Amer. J. Psychol.*, **61**, 511–519.

Postman, L., & Rau, L. (1957) Retention as a function of the method of measurement. *Univer. Calif. Publ. Psychol.*, **8**, 217–270.

Riley, D. A. (1952) Rote learning as a function of distribution of practice and the complexity of the situation. *J. Exp. Psychol.*, **43**, 88–95.

Schwartz, F. (1961) Immediate memory and amount of information. Paper presented at East. Psychol. Ass., Philadelphia.

Seward, G. H. (1928) Recognition time as a measure of confidence. *Arch. Psychol.*, N. Y., **16**, No. 99, 1–54.

Teghtsoonian, R. (1958) The influence of amount of information on performance in a recognition test of verbal learning. Unpublished Ph.D. thesis, Harvard University.

Thorndike, E. L., & Lorge, I. (1944) *The teacher's word book of 30,000 words.* New York: Bureau of Publications, Teachers Coll., Columbia Univer.

COMMENTS ON PROFESSOR MURDOCK'S PAPER

James Deese

THE JOHNS HOPKINS UNIVERSITY

Murdock sees what are, I believe, the important problems in the study of recognition. These are (1) the size of the set of alternatives from which a subject must choose in making his recognition choice, and (2) the nature of the set of alternatives. The latter includes the absolute probability that any particular alternative will be eliminated for any given stem, but also the interaction of that alternative with other alternatives to a given stem. Murdock deals almost exclusively with the former problem.

The total problem of recognition is enormously difficult, since it seems almost certain that, in general, there are interactions between alternatives such that the probability of any given alternative being eliminated is altered by the presence of other alternatives. We have always assumed that the probability of a correct choice is dependent upon the incorrect alternatives which are presented. This belief, however, has generally taken the form of considering the independent probabilities of each of the distractors (to use Murdock's term) as correct. I suspect, however, that distractors are not always, and indeed most frequently may not be, independent. The chance of one or another of them being mistaken for the correct alternative is altered by the presence of the others in the set. Murdock does not deal with this problem, and I mention it here only to illustrate the magnitude of the problem of recognition.

Murdock deals chiefly with the problem of the choice of one alternative from among several. He points out that, in principle, the single-alternative true-false item is not different from the multiple-choice kind of item. He also implies that the multiple-correct-choice test is not different in principle, though I am less sure that this is so. In any event, he restricts his discussion to the single-correct-choice kind of item until the very end of his paper, where he discusses a particular experiment. For the purposes of this experiment, I suspect that the multiple- and single-correct-alternative kinds of tests are comparable.

Murdock begins by testing four hypotheses. It would be very easy to become involved in a discussion of these, though I don't believe that Murdock's chosen purpose would be served by such a discussion. The first three of Murdock's hypotheses are trivial; they are different ways of stating what I think we know well already. He states them in the null form, and by restating them in the form of their outcomes, one can say that it is possible to construct a set of questions which produces individual differences among subjects, another that even when subjects do not choose the correct item, they may have a greater than chance success of choosing it among the remaining alternatives, and that each alternative does not have the same probability of being chosen as correct.

Murdock's fourth hypothesis is more important, since it specifies a model of the recognition process. Murdock's hypothesis says that subjects eliminate anywhere from zero to $n - 1$ alternatives as incorrect and then randomly choose among the remaining. Rather than discuss how Murdock gets to this hypothesis, and whether or not he is justified in going ahead as if it were so, I shall discuss some of the implications of the hypothesis itself, and what Murdock does about these implications.

He does not intend the hypothesis as an explicit description of what individuals actually do (though evidence can be found on any multiple-choice test that some students actually do adopt the strategy of crossing out incorrect alternatives). He intends the hypothesis as a means of generating distributions which are approximations to actual distributions found in the results of multiple-choice tests of recognition.

The heart of Murdock's paper is found in the use of his model to generate R, the proportion of correct answers on a test, from an average probability of eliminating the incorrect alternatives. To arrive at this, he adopts the simplifying assumption that all alternatives are about equally likely to be eliminated as incorrect, and hence that their distribution can be specified by an average probability, irrespective of their number or composition.

The results, illustrated in Murdock's figure, are very interesting. Murdock does fail to mention one implication, perhaps because it is so obvious. The implication is that with a very large number of alternatives (ten or greater) and with an average probability of .5 or less of any alternative's being eliminated, the resulting number of correct responses does not seriously depart from $1/n$, the number of alternatives.

It seems to me that Murdock's assumptions apply more nearly to something like Riley's paired-associate experiment in which the correct responses were arbitrary nonsense syllables to be chosen from a set of variable size, than to the real test items that Murdock uses. More precisely, Murdock's model should fit almost exactly a multiple-choice test of nonsense syllables given, say, after one exposure in a paired-associate presentation. Such a test might be of genuine theoretical advantage, for one could control, by selection of the syllables themselves, some of the possible interactions between members of the set.

In working out the implications of his model, Murdock asserts that it is necessary to assume that knowledge of list membership develops at a more rapid rate than recall in verbal learning experiments. Rather, it seems to me essential, for certain kinds of material, that knowledge of list membership completely determines free recall. In other words, certain kinds of recall tests come close to meeting Murdock's condition of eliminating incorrect alternatives.

Murdock cites Cofer's experiments on the ability of subjects to assess list membership from their own recall protocols. With lists in which subjects can generate nearly all of the members of the lists by generating larger sets (as is the case in category clustering or in interword associative structure experiments), the main problem the subject faces is the elimination of incorrect alternatives.

All free recall in which individuals make use of redundancy may be of this kind, since the problem for the individual in such a situation is simply to eliminate the redundant items from the larger set of redundant items that do not belong on the particular list or subset that the individual is trying to recall. Thus, one way to look at the problem of free recall is to ask how subjects eliminate items from the set they can generate by grammatical rule, association, or what have you.

In theory, even a random list could be generated by having an individual produce all the words in his vocabulary. While intrusions, in general, increase in recall with the length of the list presented to a subject, they do so very slowly and constitute a small fraction of the total production in recall. Thus, subjects do discriminate between words they think are on the list and those they don't. In recognition the entire set is laid out before the subject, while in free recall he must generate his own set. Thus, recall is production plus some discrimination, while recognition is only discrimination.

Accept the proposition that a completely redundant set presented for free recall will produce no errors and, a little more obviously, that a completely redundant set presented for recognition with all alternatives correct will produce no errors. Then, a subset from a completely redundant set will produce errors of commission (intrusions) in recall, and that same subset presented for recognition in the larger set will produce errors of recognition. A partially redundant subset from a larger set will produce failures of recall as well as errors of commission, but in recognition, I believe, will produce fewer errors.

We now have some techniques for a theoretical comparison of recall and recognition, techniques to which Murdock has added. I think that the next step is to work out some of the implications of these techniques for more detailed comparisons, for which I take the above example to be a suggestion, not a possibility. In conclusion, I should remark that what I have said here is in contradiction to what I have said earlier about the free recall of clustered or associatively related words being free from editing. A revision of this view is forced by Cofer's data and by an acceptance of something like Murdock's cross-out hypothesis.

SUMMARY OF CONFERENCE DISCUSSION

A major concern of much of the discussion was to find ways to describe the recognition process in a fashion consonant with the empirical finding that correct recognition can occur under circumstances which are not associated with correct recall.

Underwood asked for a better description of the meaning of habit strength in recognition, but Deese thought that information theory, not

S-R theory with its emphasis on habit strength, might yield a more suitable analysis. There was much concern with the identification of the variables which differentiate recognition from recall. Deese stressed that a basic difference is that in recall the subject must produce a set of responses, whereas in recognition the set of responses is provided for him. Melton cited the experiment by Davis, Sutherland, and Judd (1961). They took a subset of 15 numbers between 10 and 99, and asked their subjects either to recall the subset or to recognize the 15 from a larger set. Recognition and recall did not differ under these circumstances, presumably because the sets, under these conditions, were more equally available and perhaps more comparable in recognition and recall than is the case usually.

Postman mentioned that in free recall there often must be response learning, and he asked: What training input is required for recognition? He felt that this is a more meaningful question to raise than the question of strategies a subject might use. In this comment he was apparently responding to remarks made by Mandler, who expressed concern that Murdock's treatment was applied to group data and thus might not fit the case of the individual with his particular mnemonic devices and strategies. Mandler asked: What if the model does not fit individual subjects, even though it fits the group?

Brown argued that Murdock's procedure could conceivably not test recognition at all. Consider the question, "What is the first book of the Bible?" The answer, "Genesis," might be chosen because it is associated with a beginning. The subject is not asked, "Do you recognize this?" or "Have you seen this recently?" and he may never have seen the wording of the stem and of the correct alternative as they appear on the test. Hence, coding procedures during learning (how do they relate to the question asked?) and the subject's verbal transformation procedures at the time of test are important.

Wickens wondered whether there are differences in the antecedents to recognition and recall. He commented also that R-S as well as S-R learning and priming may be influential in recognition, but not, or to a lesser degree, in recall. It was suggested that recall be investigated following familiarization procedures (Noble; cf. also Chapter 4).

Goss schematized two different conditions at the time of recognition: (1) that in which the subject recalls the correct responses either completely or incompletely, and (2) that in which the subject does not recall the correct response at all. He suggested that if complete recall takes place, the subject compares the recalled response with the alternatives on the test until he finds a "match" and then goes on to the next question. This procedure obviates eliminating any remaining incorrect alternatives and thus is, to this extent, at variance with Murdock's X0 hypothesis. If incomplete recall takes place, the subject makes as much use as possible of matching between recalled and presented responses. If there is no recall of specific responses occasioned by the stem, the subject may make a choice in terms of which alternative "looks the most familiar." When Goss was asked what "looks familiar" means (Mandler) in the no-recall condition, he indicated that generalization might take place in terms of past experience with textbooklike statements, specialized vocabularies, and so on; but stressed that it is only in the no-recall condition that the real difficulties begin, that the complete- and incomplete-recall conditions pose lesser problems and may account for much of correct recognition. He cited experiments by Vallance (1947) which found that students who prepared for an essay examination got higher scores on a multiple-choice examination than students who prepared for a true-false examination.

However, several participants felt that difficulties remained even in the condition where correct recall takes place. Deese pointed out that the subject may recall a large number of responses when confronted by the stem and will find it difficult to choose the correct one from the associated set. Goss felt this problem was more appropriate in free recall than in multiple-choice recognition. Mandler wanted to know what "matching" consists of when the subject recalls and then "matches" his recollection with the alternatives. How might a machine be programmed to do this? Staats said that it is possible to train an organism, such as a rat, to "match" with appropriate reinforcement schedules. Deese said that perhaps discrimination and matching hypotheses should lead us to discrimination theory. Postman pointed out that we can get recognition when there is no recall but that Goss's theory in two cases requires that some recall occur.

Mandler suggested that when a subject is given two lists of responses with instructions to give responses which are in both lists, he starts with responses of the first list all having comparable probabilities. He then scans the second list, and when he comes to a response which was in the first list, he selects this response because its probability increases, thus producing a criterial difference between its probability and the probabilities of the other responses. In recognition, seeing the correct response could raise its probability. Melton asked how this model would account for subjects who are trying to fake low scores on a test and hence must choose a wrong alternative rather than a right one, and Mandler agreed that this would pose difficulties. Melton suggested that a "set" factor could switch responses around.

The notion of a signal-to-noise ratio, as used in certain kinds of psychophysical studies, was suggested as a means of assessing the probability of the correct alternative, given particular sets of incorrect alternatives. Jenkins described signal detection curves reported by Egan (1958) which show a plot of the probability of correct signal detection when the signal is actually present against the probability of incorrect signal identification (signal not present). The points fall on a negatively accelerated function and represent judgments made under instructions (1) to respond only if sure the signal is there, (2) to respond without certainty of the signal's presence, and (3) to respond with an intermediate degree of certainty. Jenkins thought this model has relevance to recognition; the signal-to-noise ratio concept might be paralleled by adjusting the discriminability of the alternatives. An easy item would be, "The third book of the Bible is (a) ingratiating (b) Leviticus (c) Russell's hat"; it would be made much more difficult if the alternative, Deuteronomy, were added to the set or replaced one of the obviously wrong alternatives. Jenkins felt this model to have some promise because it avoids threshold variation from item to item and subject to subject. Egan (1958) has applied this system to recognition memory.

Questions were raised as to how the signal-to-noise ratio might be specified in the case of recognition situations. Jenkins said one could use the responses of subjects who think these responses are correct; one could devise a number of items, administer them, and obtain the curves for responses to the alternatives. To Noble's question whether this is the item difficulty curve of test construction, Jenkins said he would want a different distribution than that used in psychometrics. Wickens pointed out, and Jenkins agreed, that juggling the difficulty of the alternatives is analogous to varying the noise, not the signal. Underwood wondered how this would help. It seemed to him that it leads us to similarity among alternatives. Deese thought the number of alternatives an additional variable. Jenkins thought Mink's situation (Mink, 1957) a parallel; the signal was the correct stimulus (seen previously) to which the subject was to respond, and the noise was its associates to which the subject responded (incorrectly) as a function of their associative relation to the signal. Underwood thought the model similar to Rothkopf's (1957) work with Morse code in which he induced similarity from errors. Noble pointed out that Robinson's (1927) definition of similarity was in terms of common elements.

In another connection, Melton raised the point that in recognition studies we should perhaps get at a lower level, i.e., ask the subject whether he has ever experienced a stimulus before, rather than asking which of several alternatives is the correct one. This prompted Shepard to say that perhaps the use of verbal materials misleads us. We tend to think in terms of an implicit response when we deal with verbal materials, but with nonverbal materials the subject may function in a more passive manner. This led to the following question: If the later recognition of a stimulus is not to be explained by assuming that some response was associated with that stimulus during the earlier presentation, then how is it to be explained? Shepard answered that something like the trace notion might be considered a possible alternative. He mentioned that a model for recognition memory that he himself had recently proposed assumed that the presentation of a stimulus left behind a trace that subsequently diffused out into the surrounding "space" of similar stimuli. The probability that any particular stimulus would be recognized as having been presented before is, according to this model, simply proportional to the strength of this passive trace in the vicinity of that stimulus at that time (Shepard, 1961; Shepard and Teghtsoonian, 1961).

In a further discussion of what a response in recognition might be, Postman said it might be an emitted but not an overt response; Melton used the example of the PGR. But Shepard considered this analysis to be unsatisfactory in the case of the recognition of familiar pictures. Deese said pictures could be encoded verbally, but Shepard felt that pictures would be remembered better than any verbal descriptions of those pictures.

Shepard mentioned an unpublished experiment of his in which he presented about 600 pictures and then 68 test pairs to subjects. For each of the test pairs, just one of the two pictures had been presented in the earlier sequence of 600, and the subject was to try to indicate which one that was. His subjects were able to make the correct choice for 97 to 98 per cent of these pairs. (With a similar procedure for monosyllabic words—drawn from a smaller total population—the corresponding figure dropped to about 88 per cent.) He contrasted this recognition procedure with another possible procedure in which the subject would be told one of two verbal responses, e.g., A or B, which were to be associated with each of a large number of pictures. Then the subject would be confronted with test pairs in which one picture had been associated with A and the other with B. He predicted that subjects would have more difficulty with this latter task because it is easier to remember whether a picture has or has not been seen at all than to remember whether one that has been seen should be called A or B. For this reason, he considered the explanation of recognition memory in terms of S-R habit growth to be incomplete.

Comparability between pictures and words as stimuli was discussed from several angles. Deese pointed out that pictures contain many features which can be used for discrimination, and that, depending on the overlap of such items, it might be possible to code and group by subjects. He proposed simple dot patterns as better materials with which to study this point. Mandler reported that although CVCs elicit relatively few associations by the continuous, 30-second method, both adjectives and pictures of simple scenes elicit only about 20 per cent more. He pointed out that comparable ratings—for example, semantic differential profiles—are lacking for words and pictures. Subjects probably name or summarize a picture verbally and then associate to these responses.

Tests, sometimes included in introductory texts, which require the subject to view a group of pictures of faces and then select from a second group those which had appeared in the first were mentioned as giving evidence that recognition of pictures under these circumstances is not very good. Deese expressed the opinion that Shepard's experiment could be done with a suitable selection of words and pictures with the same results for each. To illustrate how pictures might be chosen to produce a group which would be very difficult to discriminate, Melton suggested, for use with Americans, pictures of the faces of a Chinese graduating class.

In response to Shepard's contention that the superior recognition of pictures cannot be due to the association of a verbal label, Russell pointed out that verbal responses are not the only ones which may be associated with the pictures. But Shepard thought that, if this is the case, then nonverbal responses carry most of the determination in his recognition task.

Deese was not convinced by Shepard's arguments that a different set of variables controls recognition, on the one hand, and response learning on the other. The same variables may have somewhat different effects on the two processes, but he felt our usual concepts are probably adequate to recognition. We are looking, he said, for a special process in recognition, with unique properties, such as the image. But in the past, the postulation of the image led to no differential consequences, and there is no point to the postulation of a special process unless there are differential consequences. Responding to this, Shepard stated the opinion that theories based upon notions of traces or images could be found to have consequences different from those of theories based upon notions of S-R habits. But in order to bring these differences into sharp relief, both kinds of notions will need to be made more precise and explicit. He saw some significance in the fact that people who are trying to construct actual machines that will be capable of recognizing stimuli are building processes into them that, according to him, are more analogous to images or schemata than to internalized verbal responses. He referred, here, to the machines proposed by Selfridge (1958) and by Rosenblatt (1960).

Underwood made the general point in relation to recognition that what may be associated with the correct alternative is an approach response, but that typically no avoidance response is trained to the incorrect alternatives. Postman could not see the objections to habit terms and habit growth in the analysis of recognition. Habit variables influence recognition, though their slopes are not as steep in relation to recognition as they are in recall. Recognition, however, is insensitive to many manipulations to which recall is sensitive, such as the variable of intentional-incidental learning. Mandler summarized Postman's suggestions as to variables influencing recognition: response learning, repetition of the list, and number of alternatives; Deese added another factor, the discriminability of the alternatives.

The discussion included the role of computer programs as an alternative to S-R theory. Shepard felt it would be appropriate to look at machines built to "match." Mandler discussed two ways to use computer analogues: (1) to build a machine that recognizes as efficiently as possible, and (2) to construct a program which would simulate human recognition behavior, including errors. As between these two, it was agreed by many but not all of the participants that the second was the better strategy for psychologists. However, some objection was voiced to both kinds of program on the grounds that neither was of help in deciding what variables should be included. Wickens pointed out that Newell, Shaw, and Simon (1958) introspected on their activities and put the characteristics their introspections yielded into a machine for the sentential calculus.

REFERENCES

Davis, R., Sutherland, N. S., & Judd, B. R. (1961) Information content in recognition and recall. *J. Exp. Psychol.*, **61**, 422–429.

Egan, J. P. (1958) Recognition memory and the operating characteristic. *Tech. Note*, Contract No. AF 19(604)-1962, June 15, 1958. Indiana University Hearing and Communications Laboratory, Bloomington.

Mink, W. D. (1957) Semantic generalization as related to word association. *Tech. Rep. No. 17*, Contract No. N8oNR-66216, Office of Naval Research and University of Minnesota.

Newell, A., Shaw, S. C., & Simon, H. A. (1958) Elements of a theory of human problem solving. *Psychol. Rev.*, **65**, 151–166.

Robinson, E. S. (1927) The "similarity" factor in retroaction. *Amer. J. Psychol.*, **39**, 297–312.

Rosenblatt, F. (1960) Perception simulation experiments. *Proc. IRE*, **48**, 301–309.

Rothkopf, E. Z. (1957) A measure of stimulus similarity and errors in some paired-associate learning tasks. *J. Exp. Psychol.*, **53**, 94–101.

Selfridge, O. G. (1958) Pandemonium: A paradigm for learning. *Symposium on the mechanization of thought processes.* London: H. M. Stationery Office. Pp. 511–535.

Shepard, R. N. (1961) Application of a trace model to the retention of information in a recognition task. *Psychometrika, 26,* 185–203.

Shepard, R. N., & Teghtsoonian, M. (1961) Retention of information under conditions approaching a steady state. *J. Exp. Psychol., 62,* 302–309.

Vallance, T. (1947) A comparison of essay and objective examinations as learning experiences. *J. Educ. Res., 41,* 279–288.

Chapter 3

STIMULUS SELECTION IN
VERBAL LEARNING

Benton J. Underwood

NORTHWESTERN UNIVERSITY

This paper deals with discrepancies between the apparent stimulus term and the actual stimulus in verbal learning experiments. The stimulus term presented to the subject will be called the *nominal* stimulus; the characteristic or characteristics of the stimulus which the subject actually "uses" to cue a response will be called the *functional* stimulus. Thus, this inquiry is concerned with potential discrepancies between the nominal and functional stimulus—between what the investigator commonly assumes to be the stimulus and what in fact serves functionally as the stimulus.

Theories, or other analytical devices, inevitably make assumptions about the functional stimulus; generally speaking, this assumption is that the functional stimulus and nominal stimulus are identical. That is to say, if the nominal stimulus is *qor*, it is usually assumed that all apparent characteristics of *qor* serve as the functional stimulus or, perhaps more accurately, serve as the stimulus compound. In so far as there are discrepancies between the functional and nominal stimulus, the investigator may be misled. Whatever the implications of such discrepancies (if they exist), the search for them could be pursued as an area of investigation in its own right. But if theories make isomorphic assumptions about the nominal and functional stimulus, it might be argued that the search for discrepancies is propaedeutic to theories. However that may be—and certainly theories cannot wait for all necessary data—there seems to have been little systematic empirical attention given in verbal learning to the potential discrepancies under discussion. Of necessity, therefore, the present discourse will be rather short on data and long on speculation.

The problem of discrepancies between nominal and functional stimuli is not a new one for other areas of learning, particularly animal learning. Certain critical theoretical issues in discrimination learning revolve around what aspect or what components of the stimulus situation *is* the functional stimulus. The study of nominal compound conditioned stimuli and the relative functionality of the components has been an active area of investigation in classical conditioning. These (and other) areas of research have sensitized investigators in animal learning to be wary of assuming the isomorphism between the nominal and functional stimulus. It is well realized that it is an empirical problem to determine just what aspect, if any, of the nominal stimulus cues the response which is being measured. And, of course, the whole problem of experimental control is built around the premise that the specified nominal stimulus must be the only consistent cue available for a response. So, while some attention has been paid the matter of the discrepancy between the nominal and functional stimulus when the entire area of learning is considered, little attention has been paid to it as a systematic problem in the area of verbal learning. The present paper, therefore, aims to point out that the consideration of such discrepancies in verbal learning may be more important than the handful of applicable studies would seem to indicate.

Two other prefatory remarks are in order. First, no implication is intended that the stimulus presented to the subject is the "true" stimulus; clearly, any effective stimulus presented to the subject must have sensory and subsequent neurological representation. Of course, the question could be raised as to whether or not an ineffective stimulus presented to the subject has any sensory and neurological representation, but the present paper will not get involved in this issue.

The second point is raised by the use of the term *selection* in the title. As will be seen, there is some evidence for selection of certain aspects of the stimulus compound usually presented to the subject. There is reason to believe that this is an active process in the sense that the adult human subject often deliberately chooses certain characteristics of the stimulus compound as the cue. But, even if this is true, there remains the question of whether or not the nonselected components will, as a consequence of being consistently present with the initial functional stimulus, become themselves functional. This, it would seem, is an empirical problem; some small amount of relevant data will be presented shortly.

The presentation will be divided into two sections. First, the paired-associate situation will be examined for discrepancies between nominal and functional stimuli, and secondly, the inquiry will be directed toward such discrepancies which are peculiar to serial learning.

PAIRED-ASSOCIATE LEARNING

The full importance of the implication of discrepancies between nominal and functional stimuli in paired-associate learning first came to the writer's attention in 1958. This is not to imply that there is not a longer history to the problem in existing literature, although if there is such a history in a systematic sense, it is not apparent to the writer. The observations which called attention to the problem were made by Mattocks under the author's direction and are reported in Underwood and Schulz (1960). Mattocks had subjects learn a paired-associate list consisting of eight pairs with trigrams as stimuli and common three-letter words as responses. By our conception of meaningfulness, the trigrams had very low meaningfulness, and they had no formal similarity since 24 different letters were used in constructing them. The subjects learned the list to one perfect recitation. Following learning, Mattocks systematically questioned the subjects as to how they had formed associations between each pair in the list. Out of the total of 280 associations (35 subjects with eight associations each), subjects could verbalize the method of association for 205. Of these 205, 62 per cent of the reports made it clear that the subject believed that he had used only the first letter of the trigram as the functional stimulus. The high frequency of occurrence of such reports made it likely that they were valid in some degree, but one does not always take subject reports at face value. However, assuming that the reports did represent some approximation to the true state of affairs, certain implications followed which, the more they were mulled over, the greater became their ramifications. One of these implications merely supported what most have long suspected, namely, that the college sophomore is a perfect confirmation of the law of least effort. Why fuss around with all three letters of the stimulus when a single one will do the trick? However, from among more systematic implications, I have chosen three by way of illustrating the importance of considering possible discrepancies between the nominal and functional stimulus.

Meaningfulness and Interstimulus Similarity. At the time Mattocks made his observations we were working on problems related to meaningfulness. The data of our experiments, in line with the work of most other investigators, had been showing that with low formal similarity the effect on learning of variations in response meaningfulness was much greater than comparable variations in stimulus meaningfulness. Of course, when trigrams are responses, the subject must acquire the full three letters so that they are recallable; logically, with the same items as stimuli he need not learn them in this thorough fashion, and, according to the reports of Mattocks's subjects, they were performing logically. An implication of these facts is that if we forced the subject to attend to all the elements in the stimuli—all the letters—the relationship between stimulus meaningfulness and learning would become considerably sharper than customarily found with trigram stimuli. One obvious way of "encouraging" attention to the entire stimulus term is to make the interstimulus similarity so high that in order to evolve a differential cue for each trigram, more than a single letter would have to be involved. That is, by increasing interstimulus similarity one might minimize the discrepancy between the nominal and functional stimulus. Differences in the strength of associative connections between the letters of the trigrams (differences in meaningfulness) might, under these circumstances, produce a sharper meaningfulness-learning function. This reasoning implies, of course, that there should be an interaction between stimulus meaningfulness and interstimulus similarity. More particularly, on the assumption that with high-meaningful stimuli, e.g., *cat*, the subject *does* attend to all letters as a unit, and that he doesn't with low-meaningful stimuli with low interstimulus similarity, then the effect of an increase in interstimulus similarity should be greater with low meaningfulness than with high meaningfulness.

Transfer Experiments. Another implication of possible discrepancies between nominal and functional stimuli may be illustrated by transfer experiments when formal interlist stimulus similarity is varied by repeating letters in the stimuli of the first and second lists. An illustration may make this clear. Suppose that the stimulus in the first list is *vof*, and the corresponding one in the second list is *gof*. If the interstimulus similarity of the first list is low so that only the first letter is used as the functional stimulus, then the so-called high similarity between the stimuli in the two lists may be nonfunctional. It seems highly probable, therefore, that some transfer studies in which formal interlist stimulus similarity has been varied have given us a misleading estimate concerning the true effects of the similarity because of the discrepancy between the nominal and functional stimulus.

In Yum's (1931) experiment on what now would be called stimulus generalization, nonsense syllables were used as stimuli and on tests one or more letters of the syllables were changed. His results showed that if the first letter was changed, generalization was less (performance was poorer) than if other letters were changed. This would be expected if subjects had used only the first letter as the functional stimulus. Of course, one could also argue that removal of the first letter denies to the subject the necessary cue to elicit the second and subsequently the third letter; hence, it denies the subject the entire stimulus compound. So, Yum's data do not *require* an interpretation in terms of stimulus selection.

Context Effects. Another area of research in which discrepancies between nominal and functional stimuli may be of considerable importance will be discussed at some length. This area of research is usually referred to as the study of context effects on retention. In these studies, two or more distinct components make up the nominal stimulus. On retention tests one of the components is removed to determine the effect of the removal on retention. In terms of the present orientation, such studies can be viewed as studying the discrepancy between the nominal and functional stimulus. It might be inferred that one could remove all components except the functional component without impairing retention. Such an interpretation would be opposed to one which asserts that all stimuli present consistently will in some way contribute to, or be a part of, the stimulus which evokes the response. Another way of expressing this is to say that a true compound conditioned stimulus is developed and that the removal of any part of the configuration will cause at least a partial decrement in response strength or response probabilities. These two alternative interpretations have enough systematic importance to justify examining data in some detail.

The classical context experiments may be exemplified by the method used by Weiss and Margolius (1954). The verbal stimuli were double nonsense syllables of 80 per cent association value, and the responses were common words. Each of the nine paired-associates was placed on a card of a different color, and consistently so, during all learning trials. Learning was carried to one perfect trial with retention taken after 24 hours. On the retention tests different stimulus conditions were imposed for different groups. For one group the stimuli were the same as during learning (control). For a second group the verbal units were present, but the cards were all homogeneous gray; the color cue was removed. For a third group only the color cards were presented at recall; the verbal stimuli were removed. The mean recall scores were 7.37, 3.25, and 5.37 for Groups 1, 2, and 3, respectively. Each mean differed significantly from any other mean, although there was no difference among the three groups in learning.

How does one interpret such data? The recall is clearly best when the original context—the entire stimulus configuration—is reinstated at recall. But does this mean that both verbal and color components were being associated independently with the response word? Or, does it mean that a configuration was being associated with the response word? These are certainly two possibilities. But there is at least a third one, with two versions, namely, that for a given subject one or the other of the two components is the functional stimulus for all responses, but that not all subjects "use" the same component; or that for a given subject one component may be the functional stimulus for some responses, and the other component for other responses. In terms of this interpretation, from the Weiss-Margolius data it could be inferred that the color was more frequently the functional stimulus than was the syllable, since a group not having color cards during learning took longer to learn than the three groups being considered, although the difference was not dramatic. Furthermore, the group having only color at recall gave more correct responses than the group having only syllables. Obviously, if the configuration is important, the syllables are a less important part of this configuration than the color. In any event, there are no facts in this study which *require* the interpretation that a response becomes attached to each component independently or that a configuration is involved as the functional stimulus. It is quite possible that the subject selects aspects of the stimulus compound as the functional cue, and when this cue is not present, no response occurs. Indeed, it seems quite possible that we may err if we conceive of the college sophomore as being a tabula rasa on which all nominal stimuli present at the time of learning become associated with a response, and that, therefore, most effective recall will occur if all nominal stimuli are present. While it is true that in these types of situations best recall *will* occur when all stimulus components are present, this may be because such procedures always allow the functional stimulus to be present; the parts of the nominal stimulus not involved as functional cues may be just excess baggage.

We have been seeking data appropriate for choosing among these alternative ways of viewing the situation where context changes are involved. Some initial data will be presented, not as a solution, but as an indication of the direction in which the solution may lie (Underwood, Ham, and Ekstrand, 1962).

On the belief that subjects *do* select the most effective functional stimulus from a compound stimulus, we asked ourselves how to vary effectiveness. One obvious notion was that given two components to a stimulus, one of low meaningfulness and one of high, the subject will select the component of highest meaningfulness. We made up a list of seven difficult trigrams for stimuli with considerable interstimulus similarity so that a single letter could not be used as a functional stimulus. Ideally, the other component should be another verbal unit but of high meaningfulness. However, we chose to make our experiment continuous with the Weiss-Margolius study and therefore used colored rectangles surrounding the verbal unit as the other component. The seven different colors were clearly differentiated from each other, and each would immediately elicit a distinctive name, e.g., *brown, red, blue*, etc. Our assumption was that these colors would have higher meaningfulness than the trigrams. Single-digit numbers were used as responses in the paired-associate lists.

During learning both the trigrams and the colors were consistently present, and the subjects were told before learning that this would be the case. Immediately after learning to one perfect trial, transfer tests were given, these being different for each of three subgroups of 20 subjects each. One group (control) was simply given continued trials on the first list. A second group was given only the color rectangles as stimuli for the second list, and the third group was given only the trigrams as stimuli for the second list. For the group having only colors on the second list, transfer was 100 per cent; the "acquisition" curve was indistinguishable from that of the control. This tells us that color alone was a complete and effective functional stimulus; the presence of the compound was not necessary. On the other hand, the third group, which was given only trigrams on the transfer list, did not show zero transfer; an average of 2.7 responses was correct on the first transfer trial although subsequent learning of this transfer list proceeded very slowly. Since color was 100 per cent effective as a stimulus and since the trigrams showed some degree of effectiveness as stimuli, it is clear that more than one of the two components was an effective stimulus for at least some of the subjects for at least some of the responses. Thus, we can rule out the configuration learning in this condition because the color stimulus alone was a completely effective stimulus. That we can rule out configuration learning for this condition, whereas such was not possible in the Weiss-Margolius study, is probably to be attributed to the lower meaningfulness of our verbal stimuli. The fact that some small amount of learning occurred with the trigram stimuli allows two possible alternative conclusions. First, each component may, in the cases where the trigram elicited a response on the transfer test, be independent stimuli; that is, either the color or the trigram will elicit the response. The second interpretation would be via mediation. An association may have developed between the trigram and the color stimulus so that when the trigram is presented, the mediation runs from trigram to color to response. We have no basis on which to choose between these two alternatives. The results of this experiment are taken as further evidence for selection of stimuli by subjects in paired-associate learning. A somewhat similar study has been performed by Sundland and Wickens (1962).

Having shown that discrepancies between the nominal and functional stimulus do occur in paired-associate learning under certain circumstances, we now turn to a more difficult analytical situation, serial learning.

SERIAL LEARNING

In paired-associate learning there is little question as to the nominal stimulus—the stimulus under experimental control. In paired-associate learning the problem of stimulus selection concerns the possible fractionalization of the nominal stimulus resulting in a discrepancy between the nominal and functional stimulus. In serial learning we normally think of each item (except the first and the last) as serving both a stimulus function and a response function. Thus, if the series is A-B-C-D-E, we think of B as being the response to A and also a stimulus for C. This conception is usually called serial association. To a certain extent the stimulus selection encountered in paired-associate learning is applicable to serial learning. However, certain unique problems arise in serial learning. As will be seen, there is a question as to whether or not the investigator can completely specify the nominal stimulus complex, and, therefore, it becomes difficult to determine the selection processes that the subject may impose on the situation when learning occurs. However, it is the major purpose of this section to raise questions about the adequacy of the classical serial-association notion. To raise the questions is one matter; to search for answers is quite another, and, as will be seen, research data which may be construed as bearing on the questions are sparse. Nevertheless, some tentative probes are available which may somewhat circumscribe the search. To set the background adequately requires an initial consideration of some facts in paired-associate learning.

Simultaneous Stimulus and Response Functioning in Paired-associates

In 1938 Primoff published a study which illustrates a fact leading to the first puzzle concerning the stimulus in serial learning. Primoff ran parallel conditions for both lists of nonsense syllables and lists of three-letter words. One list was constructed so that items in the list served double functions; they served as both stimulus terms and response terms. Thus, some of the word pairs were *use-eye, eye-hat, hat-jug,* and so on. Of course, the pairs were presented in different orders on each learning trial so that the subject never consistently had the same word as a stimulus term and as a response term in contiguous pairs. A second list was constructed in the conventional manner in that no item was used as both a stimulus term and a response term. Primoff presents data showing the difference in rate of learning these two types of lists; there were enormous differences. For the standard list of words, 8.5 trials were required, and for the double-function list, 21.3 trials were required. The same large difference was found for nonsense syllables, the values being 21.5 trials and 41.7 trials.

The facts of the Primoff study do not seem to be in question since Young (1961)[1] has recently found the same phenomena. In his tests with nonsense syllables of both high and low meaningfulness Young got differences in learning rate of the same order of magnitude as had Primoff.

For the present purposes, the above facts raise two questions. First,

[1] Dr. Young has generously made available to the writer the results of several unpublished studies dealing with the functional stimulus in serial learning and with related problems. In the reference list these must necessarily be cited as unpublished.

how does one explain such facts? Why should the double-function list be so much more difficult to learn than the standard list? Primoff felt that at least part of the greater difficulty was due to backward associations. That is, given A-B and B-C in the same list, there would be a strong tendency, when B was in the stimulus position, to evoke A because of the backward association between A and B. It is a fact that such errors occurred with a frequency of about 20 per cent of the frequency of correct responses. Young approached the issue in a somewhat different fashion. He conceptualized the problem by representing it as a continuum of stimulus-response similarity, the case of identity being merely the extreme of the similarity dimension. He ran a list which had partial identity of letters among stimulus and response terms; thus, this list had higher stimulus-response similarity than a standard list but lower stimulus-response similarity than the double-function list. As Young expected, the rate of learning this list fell in between the rates for the standard and the double-function lists. The Young and the Primoff notions can probably be reduced to essentially the same level. High stimulus-response similarity must have a way of producing its effect, and this would seem to mean that the stimulus term B may tend to elicit the stimulus term A because of the similarity of B to the correct response to A. The many recent studies on backward associations clearly make such explanations quite feasible. Nevertheless, we should not rule out the possibility that other factors may be contributing to this great effect. For example, is it possible that there is something difficult in using a verbal unit both as a stimulus and as a response term when new associations are being formed? Is there a habitual classification process or processes, well established, which sets some items aside to be responded to and others to be responded with? Does the double-function list, by preventing this initial coding, set habits in opposition which are not entirely associative habits developed in the learning of the particular list? The answers to these questions are not apparent; they may be irrelevant questions for it is possible that the great inhibitory effect observed by Primoff and Young can be handled by interference developed entirely by the process of forming associations in the list.

The second puzzle raised by the inhibitory effect of the double-function list carries the problem directly to serial learning. As noted earlier, the usual conception of serial learning is a chain association in which each item *does* serve the dual function of a stimulus and a response. How can this be if such a powerful inhibitory effect exists when the double function is required in paired-associate learning? Without citing data it seems fair to say that if one equates the number of associations to be formed in a serial and in a paired-associate list, serial learning occurs more rapidly than does paired-associate learning. Indeed, it appears that if the pairs of a standard paired-associate list are presented in the same order, trial after trial, the subject will quickly abandon paired-associate learning and will learn the response terms as a serial list. Thus, if an item is serving a dual function in a serial list, it does not seem to produce the inhibitory effect observed in paired-associate learning.

To the question of why the double function doesn't inhibit serial learning whereas it does inhibit paired-associate learning, there are at least two possible answers. There is, first, the obvious fact that in a serial list an item serves its two functions in immediate succession; the response function always precedes the stimulus function in a thoroughly consistent manner. In paired-associate learning, where the orders are changed from trial to trial, this consistency is not present. But, having said this, it is not an easy matter to provide a mechanism by which the differences in learning can be mediated. If backward associations are responsible for the inhibitory effect in paired-associate learning, why shouldn't this be also true in serial learning? An obvious answer is that the subject, in learning a serial list and having just seen B prior to the appearance of C, is not going to say B when C appears. The recency of B prevents the backward association from C to B from operating. It is a fact that such overt errors rarely occur, but this does not mean that the interference could not be present.

A second alternative as to why the double function of items doesn't inhibit serial learning whereas it does in paired-associate learning may lie in our misconceptions of the functional stimulus in serial learning. If the stimulus for C in a serial list is not B, the problem disappears since items will not be serving a double function. Much of the remainder of this section is concerned with an elaboration of this possibility, namely, that the conception of serial learning handed down through the years may not represent, in fact, the way in which serial lists are learned.

To suggest the possibility that B might not be the stimulus for C in a serial list immediately requires the naming of an alternative stimulus. First, there is the position an item holds in the list. Thus, the stimulus for that item might be thought of as the numerical position in the series. Second, the stimulus might be a position on a spatial dimension which is independent of a numerical position as such. One may even conceive of a point on a temporal dimension as distinct from a point on a spatial dimension. Since a given item always occurs at a given time after any other event in a serial list, a temporal point could be a stimulus. If one or more such events or points on a dimension do form the "true" stimulus in serial learning, the double-function enigma is resolved since under such circumstances the item has no double function. Some data in support of this notion are available; although, as will be seen, the final outcome does not offer a clear-cut resolution to alternative points of view.

Investigations which may be interpreted as getting at this problem make use of transfer paradigms. These studies may now be examined.

Transfer from Paired-associates to Serial List

Assume a situation in which common words are used as stimulus and response terms in a paired-associate list. Assume further that under such circumstances there is little discrepancy between the nominal and functional stimulus. Finally, let the list be a double-function list. After this list is learned, if the items are now formed into a serial list so that the associations developed in paired-associate learning are now appropriate for serial learning, will there be positive transfer? The answer is yes. Primoff (1938) had conditions relevant to this question; and, although his control condition was not ideal, it seems clear that there was positive transfer. After taking 21.3 trials to learn the double-function list, 5.9 trials were required to learn the appropriately derived serial list. In one published experiment Young's (1959) data also indicated considerable positive transfer in going from a double-function paired-associate list to a serial list. In a further study (Young, Milauckas, and Bryan, unpublished) conditions were arranged so that in one condition the double-function paired-associate pairings were consistent with the ordering in the serial list, while in another condition the items in the serial list were so arranged that associations developed in the paired-associate list were inconsistent with those required in the serial list. A control was used, this group having learned an irrelevant paired-associate list before being given the serial list. All three groups learned exactly the same serial list, the differences in the two experimental conditions being accomplished by differences in the pairs in the paired-associate list.

The results of the Young et al. study show positive transfer when the serial items are ordered appropriate to the associations acquired in the paired-associate list, but in fact the positive effect is quite small and is significant only with a very high degree of learning of the paired-associate list. However, negative transfer was quite marked when the serial list ordering was inconsistent with the associations learned in the paired-associate list.

These data would seem to indicate that when a double function is acquired for each item in a paired-associate list, there is a positive effect in learning the serial list. This implies, in turn, that under these circumstances the subject does master the serial list by using the items in a double-function manner. The fact that the positive transfer is not as great as one might expect, however, may suggest that learning these serial lists in that manner is not "natural" for the subject. Nevertheless, let us accept the fact that the subject can learn a serial list in the traditionally conceived manner in which each item serves successively its response and then stimulus function. We may now inquire what happens when the transfer is reversed; that is, the subject first learns a serial list and then transfers to a paired-associate list.

Transfer from Serial to Paired-associate List

If the learning of a serial list occurs in the manner in which it has been conceived traditionally, where A is the stimulus for B, B for C, and so on, then it would seem that there should be heavy positive transfer from the serial list to the double-function paired-associate list. Studies by Young and his students give very little support to this expectation. The essential facts may be listed as a series of points.

1. Transferring from a serial to a paired-associate list of the double-function type produces initial positive transfer on the first few trials, but in trials to learn to one perfect recitation, little facilitation is noted (Young, 1959; Young, unpublished). The positive effect appears to be produced in the learning of the pair formed from the first two items in the serial list and perhaps from the last pair. It will be noted that neither the first nor last pair in the serial list serves a dual function if serial association is the rule.

2. If the items from a learned serial list are placed in a random fashion in the paired-associate list, no transfer of any kind is observed (Young, unpublished). It was as if the serial learning was completely irrelevant to the paired-associate learning.

3. The failure to find positive effects in going from the serial to the paired-associate list might be attributed to the dual-function in-hibitory effect discussed earlier as occurring in the paired-associate list. This is not the source of the failure to demonstrate positive transfer. Young (1962) derived paired-associate lists in which each item served only as a stimulus or as a response in the paired-associate list, and still no heavy positive transfer was observed. Thus, if the serial list consisted of A-B-C-D-E-F, the paired-associate list consisted of A-B, C-D, E-F.

4. One could think of the stimulus in a serial list as consisting of two or more preceding stimuli. Young (1962), therefore, took two preceding items from the serial list and used them as the stimulus complex for a given response item in a paired-associate list. Thus, A and B were given as the stimulus for C in paired-associate learning. The facts listed earlier did not change.

These studies would seem basically to deny the assertion that in the serial list the typical stimulus for a given item is the item which precedes it. If the functional stimulus was of such a nature in these studies, why wasn't more marked transfer obtained in learning the paired-associate list? The answer may lie in the fact that the preceding item is not the stimulus; some other factor or factors may be functioning as the stimulus, at least for many of the items.

It is quite feasible to consider a spatial or numerical position in a series as an effective stimulus in serial learning. It has long been known that in retroactive inhibition studies intrusions occur which can only be attributed to the identity of serial position of items in two lists (Melton and Irwin, 1940). Indeed, the fact that retroactive inhibition can be produced with disparate serial lists, lists which have little similarity, may be due to the acquiring of two responses to the same serial position in the two lists. In short, the fact that position as such could function as a stimulus seems a reasonable possibility. But contrary evidence must now be admitted.

The Rehula Study. This study was done as a Ph.D. dissertation at Northwestern University. It was designed to provide specific tests of certain implications of the two alternative notions concerning the functional stimulus. These implications can be best understood by examining the lists and procedures Rehula used. He constructed two serial lists of bigrams (two-letter units). In one list each bigram consisted of two strongly associated letters so that response learning as such should be minimal. Thus, the responses should be readily available. A second list was also constructed of bigrams but in this case the association between the two letters was low while the association between the last letter of a bigram and the first letter of the next bigram was strong. Response learning under these circumstances should be slow, but since there was a strong association between the last letter of one bigram and the first letter of the next one, serial association (if such occurs) should be enhanced. However, it can be seen that if learning occurs by serial position, the list in which the association between the letters within a bigram is strong should be more rapid than in the list in which the association between the letters is weak. Strong versus weak associations between the letters of each bigram essentially constitute differences in meaningfulness. If the items are learned to serial position stimuli, the fact that the bigrams with low meaningfulness had strong associative connection between the last letter of one bigram and the first letter of the next should not result in a positive effect; indeed, it might even produce a negative effect. Therefore, it seems clear that if subjects learn with serial positions as functional stimuli, the list with the high-meaningful items should be learned more rapidly than the list with low-meaningful items.

But, suppose subjects *do* learn serially, with each item being the functional stimulus for the next. No clear prediction can be made in the learning because one list will be favored in acquiring the responses but not in associating serially; the other list will be favored in serial associations but not in acquiring responses. Rehula prepared for this contingency. After the lists were learned a transfer test was used. In this test, the same items which had occurred in original learning were employed, but the entire list was shifted so that the item previously in the eighth position became the first item in the list and the first became the eighth. Thus, except for the new location of the blank space used to distinguish trials, the order of the items remained the same in the shifted list. Rehula's reasoning was that if subjects had been learning by using serial position as a stimulus, this shift should cause considerable disruption. On the other hand, if subjects had learned serially, only very slight disruption (due to change in position of the pause between trials) would be anticipated.

Without considering minor variations, Rehula's results can be summarized as follows: (1) There was no difference in learning the initial lists; thus, there was no evidence that serial positions were serving as stimuli. (2) In learning the shifted lists, both groups performed about equally well and at a level indicating nearly perfect transfer (as compared with controls who continued learning the original list). These facts left Rehula no alternative but to conclude that on the basis of his data the hypothesis which says that position serves as a functional stimulus for serial learning was not supported. His inclination was to accept the traditional serial-association notion, or some elaboration of it, as best handling his data.

We have seen that a number of potential stimuli exist as the nominal stimulus complex for a response in serial learning, namely, (1) the preceding item, (2) two or more preceding items, (3) numerical position, (4) spatial position, (5) temporal position, and (6) others unidentified. The above experiments have attempted to determine a particular functional stimulus from this complex. Young's work seems to indicate that the preceding item (or items) is *not* the functional stimulus, but no data show clearly what the functional stimulus is. Rehula's work would seem to eliminate position as a stimulus. There is not much left to *be* the stimulus from among those that have been identified as potential stimuli. Of course, what may be happening is that one part of the nominal stimulus serves as the functional stimulus in one situation and another part in another situation. Therefore, the results of Young's work and Rehula's work need not necessarily be considered at odds. For example, in his studies Young always used meaningful words while the meaningfulness of the units used by Rehula would probably be said to be of lower meaningfulness. There is some evidence (Underwood and Postman, 1960) that the lower the meaningfulness of the items in the serial list, the greater the sequential dependencies of the items at recall. This could mean that serial association is more likely to occur with items of low meaningfulness than with items of high meaningfulness. Contrariwise, when items have high meaningfulness, the associations may be more likely formed to serial positions. The two alternative conceptions which have been the focus of discussion may much oversimplify the situation. Even Young's data indicate that some serial associations may be formed. So also, patterning and chaining and combinations of numerical position, spatial position, and temporal positions may be involved.

SUMMARY AND CONCLUSIONS

The available evidence indicates clearly that in paired-associate learning one may expect discrepancies between the nominal and functional stimulus. From among the elements of a compound nominal stimulus the subject may select an element which becomes the functional stimulus. Presumably a similar selection may take place in serial learning, but the data give no clear picture of the consistent selection of a single component. Until the ambiguity of the stimulus in serial learning is removed, it will be difficult to evaluate alternative stimulus-response theories of serial learning phenomena, e.g., the bowed serial position curve.

In presenting illustrations of stimulus selection in paired-associate learning it was apparent that assumptions were made about the nature of the situation in which stimulus selection occurs and why it occurs. These may now be summarized.

1. Generally speaking, the college sophomore will use the minimally necessary differentiating component for the functional stimulus. He apparently minimizes stimulus redundancy.

2. When verbal units of more than one letter are used as nominal stimuli, whether or not stimulus selection occurs depends upon the meaningfulness of the unit as a whole: the higher the meaningfulness, the less the selection.

3. When two or more distinct classes of units are used as a nominal stimulus (a compound), the initial and primary functional stimulus will be the one with the highest meaningfulness. Certain data have indicated that it is unlikely that a configuration becomes a functional stimulus when two or more classes of units are involved, but more than one component may have some functionality.

Finally, it may be noted that concept formation often requires stimulus selection: From among the elements of compound stimuli the subject is required to select or identify one or more elements which are consistently present when another event occurs. The evidence which has been presented indicates that a comparable selection occurs at a low level in rote paired-associate learning.

REFERENCES

Melton, A. W., & Irwin, J. McQ. (1940) The influence of degree of inter-polated learning on retroactive inhibition and the overt transfer of specific responses. *Amer. J. Psychol.*, **53**, 173–203.

Primoff, E. (1938) Backward and forward association as an organizing act in serial and in paired associate learning. *J. Psychol.*, **5**, 375–395.

Rehula, R. J. (1960) A test of two alternative hypotheses of the associations that develop in serial verbal learning. Ph.D. dissertation, Northwestern University.

Sundland, D. M., & Wickens, D. D. (1962) Context factors in paired-associate learning and recall. *J. Exp. Psychol.*, **63**, 302–306.

Underwood, B. J., Ham, M., & Ekstrand, B. (1962) Cue selection in paired-associate learning. *J. Exp. Psychol.*, **64**, 405–409.

Underwood, B. J., & Postman, L. (1960) Extraexperimental sources of inter-ference in forgetting. *Psychol. Rev.* **67**, 73–95.

Underwood, B. J., & Schulz, R. W. (1960) *Meaningfulness and verbal learning.* Chicago: Lippincott.

Weiss, W., & Margolius, G. (1954) The effect of context stimuli on learning and retention. *J. Exp. Psychol.*, **48**, 318–322.

Young, R. K. (1959) A comparison of two methods of learning serial associa-tions. *Amer. J. Psychol.*, **72**, 554–559.

Young, R. K. (1961) Paired-associate learning when the same items occur as stimuli and responses. *J. Exp. Psychol.*, **61**, 315–318.

Young, R. K. (unpublished) Some evidence on the nature of the stimulus in serial verbal learning.

Young, R. K. (1962) Tests of three hypotheses about the effective stimulus in serial learning. *J. Exp. Psychol.*, **63**, 307–313.

Young, R. K., Milauckas, E. W., & Bryan, J. D. (unpublished) Serial learning as a function of prior paired-associate training.

Yum, K. S. (1931) An experimental test of the law of assimilation. *J. Exp. Psychol.*, **14**, 68–82.

COMMENTS ON PROFESSOR UNDERWOOD'S PAPER

Roger N. Shepard

BELL TELEPHONE LABORATORIES, INCORPORATED

I found myself generally sympathetic with the views expressed in Underwood's paper. Indeed there is much there to support a recent change in the direction of my own thinking. However, the burden of my remarks will be that the existence of phenomena of the kind con-sidered by Underwood may raise problems for the prevailing stimulus-response, or S-R, treatment of verbal learning that are more serious than Underwood, himself, explicitly acknowledges. It may of course be that, during the preceding conference on verbal learning (see Cofer,

1961), the notions to which I am about to give voice may already have been espoused—or, worse, demolished. Nevertheless, in my present state of ignorance on this point, I have no choice but to ask your forbearance and plunge ahead.

Now the justification for the heavy concentration of the study of verbal learning on tasks of the so-called rote variety is not, presumably, that this variety is intrinsically the most interesting, or that serial or paired-associate paradigms are convincing models of the kind of learning that is of practical concern outside the laboratory. (Certainly the contribution of the now vast literature on rote learning to recent attempts to construct efficient programs for automated teaching could only be characterized as minuscule.) Rather, the usual justification begins, the study of a process as intricate as that of human learning presents formidable difficulties even under the most auspicious circumstances. Surely, then, we should at least permit ourselves the benefit of confining our early investigations to its most elementary manifestations. And this, the argument concludes, is clearly insured by selecting those tasks that are currently classified as rote.

Partly as a consequence of this concentration on rote tasks, perhaps, there has been a pervasive reliance on the S-R framework. This is reflected not only in the form of the explanatory models that have grown out of the empirical work but also in the very language used to talk about the work itself. Nevertheless, this framework has evinced an impressive serviceability—at least as gauged by the number of experiments and theoretical principles that have flowered under its aegis. Some of these principles have even shown promise of accounting for apparently more complex phenomena that are not customarily subsumed under the term "rote." As just one of many such instances, I refer to Baum's (1954) demonstration that some of Heidbreder's results on the learning of concepts can be explained on the basis of a principle of stimulus generalization alone.

Optimism as to the potential payoff of the attempt to understand verbal learning via the study of rote learning has been somewhat dampened, however, by recent intimations that it stems from an overzealous preoccupation with data obtained by averaging over subjects, stimuli, and/or trials. Indeed, some dark omens can already be discerned among recent findings of learning theorists who, having satisfied themselves with their accounts of mean curves of acquisition, generalization, and forgetting, are turning increasingly to a more detailed examination of the individual events as they unfold from one trial to the next. And here we may have to own that the stimulus-response-reinforcement paradigm (which has proved so effective in dealing with simple conditioning in animals) may be less than adequate as a model for what occurs during a single trial of a verbal learning experiment. I won't attempt anything like a complete coverage of the inadequacies of current S-R formulations of verbal learning here; particularly since many of these have already been spelled out with telling force in Chomsky's (1959) review of Skinner's monograph on verbal behavior and also in the recent book by Miller, Galanter, and Pribram (1960). Instead I shall confine myself to an examination of only those inadequacies to which we are more or less specifically led in following some of the ramifications of Underwood's distinction between the "nominal" and the "functional" stimulus.

We come to the crux of the matter as soon as we try to frame an explicit statement of the consequences of signaling to a subject that his response on a given trial was correct. Certainly the notion that feedback of this kind serves merely to reinforce the connection between the presented stimulus and its ensuing response will be useful only to the extent that these two events can be properly specified. A physical specification, however complete, will not generally suffice. For, as Underwood observes, a stimulus is typically compounded of several different parts, or aspects, and there is abundant evidence that the response is often based upon only a subset of these rather than upon the total configuration. At the very outset, then, we confront what might be called the problem of attention.

Of course the fact that there is only a partial sampling of the attributes of a stimulus does not itself render the phenomenon of attention refractory to S-R analysis. Indeed S-R machinery of considerable elegance and precision is already available for cases in which this sampling is independent and random on each trial (Estes, 1959). S-R analysis also remains feasible if the sampling is governed by demonstrable variations in what Underwood terms the psychological "effectiveness" of the separate aspects of the stimuli. Presumably this is partly the case in those experiments, cited by Underwood, in which subjects were found to respond primarily on the basis of only the first letter of nonsense trigrams or to respond more on the basis of the color of the card upon which the nonsense syllable was printed than on the basis of the nonsense syllable itself. Such effects do indeed require us to maintain a careful distinction between the functional and the nominal stimulus. However, to the extent that these effects are consistent across subjects and from one trial to the next, they can be handled, for example, by running preliminary experiments to calibrate the psychological effectiveness of each of the components of the stimuli.

Before turning to cases in which selective sampling appears in more perplexing guises, I should like to point out that the extent to which such sampling takes place at all can vary greatly depending upon the nature of the stimuli. At one extreme, there are stimuli that subjects almost inevitably analyze into separate components or dimensions. Nonsense trigrams undoubtedly fall in this class since subjects are as likely to react to the individual letters as to their combination as a whole. The geometrical figures of studies on concept learning are also examples since subjects easily classify these into separate groups on the basis of their size, color, or shape. At the opposite extreme are those stimuli that are almost invariably reacted to as unitary, unanalyzable wholes. Colors, olfactory stimuli, speech sounds, and perhaps faces or facial expressions, are representative of this class. This important factor—of the degree of analyzability of the stimuli—is probably highly correlated with the factor of meaningfulness specifically considered by Underwood. For, as he suggests, a familiar and meaningful three-letter word like *cat* tends to be reacted to in a more unitary manner than an arbitrary trigram like *xur*. (Indeed, the latter tends to be spelled whereas the former tends to be pronounced.)

In our own studies of the learning of classifications, we have found it desirable to maintain a distinction between pure stimulus generalization, on the one hand, and selective attention or abstraction, on the other. Because selective attention evidently intervenes only to the extent that the stimuli are of the analyzable or dimensionalized variety, our results strongly suggest that learning is more amenable to simple S-R analysis in the case of the more homogeneous or unitary stimuli. In particular, when we used stimuli of this latter type (namely, eight Munsell colors), we found that the difficulties of learning different classifications of the stimuli conformed rather well with quantitative predictions derived from a model for pure stimulus generalization (Shepard and Chang, in press). Thus we were able to sharpen and extend the more qualitative results of Baum to which reference has already been made.

In contrast to this success, the predictions of the same generalization model failed in a very striking way when classification experiments of a similar kind were performed using highly dimensionalized stimuli (Shepard, Hovland, and Jenkins, 1961). The predictive failure in this second case seemed quite clearly attributable to the fact that the subjects attended selectively to the separate dimensions of the stimuli.

We have more recently adduced additional support for this distinction between stimuli that are and those that are not analyzed into their component dimensions in some as yet unpublished experiments on identification (or paired-associate) learning. To go into the details of this work would take us too far afield. So I shall simply mention in passing that, whereas the pattern of stimulus generalization when the stimuli were Munsell colors was previously found to conform to a Euclidean metric (Shepard, 1958), the intervention of something like selective attention with more dimensionalized stimuli resulted in clear violations of the requirements of this metric. This may have rather wide implications for multidimensional scaling methods since these have universally been erected on the assumption that the underlying metric is Euclidean.

The central problem with which we are concerned in the present context, however, is one of furnishing a sufficiently exact characterization of the consequences of reinforcing a particular stimulus-response sequence. It will not do to say only that the function of such reinforcement is to strengthen the tendency of that particular response to follow that particular stimulus, if for no other reason, because the inevitable occurrence of stimulus and response generalization will insure that the connections between other stimuli and responses will be affected as well. But the phenomenon of pure stimulus generalization does not itself pose insurmountable difficulties provided that the stimuli are chosen to be of the unitary or relatively unanalyzable type. This is in part because in this simple case the set of stimuli to which the effects of reinforcement generalize to some prescribed degree forms a roughly spherical (or, more correctly, ellipsoidal) neighborhood in the "space" of similar stimuli surrounding the original conditioned stimulus. (Indeed this is the crucial condition for the applicability of the Euclidean metric mentioned above; see Shepard, 1960.) Moreover, treatment is particularly easy with this class of stimuli since this spherical region of generalization about any particular stimulus typically remains relatively invariant from one subject or occasion to the next.

With highly dimensionalized stimuli, however, the emergence of selective attention calls for more elaborate predictive machinery. For, if a subset of the properties of a stimulus has been prescinded from the total complex, the effects of reinforcement will no longer spread uniformly in all directions throughout the spherical region defined by pure stimulus generalization. Instead, these effects will be transmitted to only those stimuli that have the prescinded properties, and those stimuli do not define a spherical neighborhood but a narrow slice extending across the entire space. Here we encounter the two facts: That there are many alternative slices that a subject can choose on a given trial, and that his particular choice must depend upon the outcomes of the preceding trials. These facts are amply demonstrated by the finding that subjects can achieve perfect discrimination between stimuli that have many components in common as well as by recent results on the learning of classifications (e.g., see LaBerge and Smith, 1957; Binder and Feldman, 1960, pp. 15–22; Shepard, Hovland, and Jenkins, 1961, pp. 30–32). But, until we can predict (or at least infer) what component properties are in fact selected on a particular trial, attempts to specify the consequences of reinforcement are, it seems to me, destined for frustration.

The hope that even this kind of control over attention may prove tractable within the S-R framework evidently rests on the possibility that rules of the S-R type can be extended to cover the act of attending, itself. Some encouraging headway in this direction has already been achieved by recent models for observing responses (Atkinson, 1961; Holland, 1958; Wyckoff, 1952, 1954; Zeaman and House, 1962) and for the adaptation of cues (Restle, 1955; Bourne and Restle, 1959). Many of the formal models that have been explicitly proposed, however, seem to suffer from certain deficiencies that I shall not go into here since my views have already been expressed elsewhere (Shepard *et al.*, 1961).

What I would like to point out, here, is that the successful predictions of models of this kind have often been more in the area of concept learning than in the area of rote learning. The reason for this appears to be that in the former area, only, experiments are intentionally contrived just so that the solution requires the subject to narrow his attention to a certain subset of dimensions usually referred to as the "relevant dimensions." (Hence the solution of the problem is sometimes taken as prima-facie evidence for a mechanism of selective attention or abstraction.) In the case of the rote learning of paired-associates, on the other hand, no special attempt is made to force the subject to attend to just certain aspects of the stimuli. Since the act of attending is therefore less constrained by the contingencies of reinforcement in this case, its occurrence is very likely more difficult not only to predict but also to detect. Indeed, it is only as a result of more searching analyses, such as those undertaken by Underwood, that we begin to realize that this rather complicated mechanism may have been operating unnoticed in rote learning all along.

All of this leads me to agree with Underwood's statement, at the conclusion of his summary, to the effect that the usual paired-associate learning may not be as "rote" as we have been supposing. It also raises the possibility that, just as Baum proposed to understand concept learning on the basis of a principle of stimulus generalization derived from studies of rote learning, we may now find ourselves returning to illuminate this so-called rote learning on the basis of mechanisms (like selective attention) isolated in studies of concept learning.

One of our own paired-associate experiments resembled the one performed by Mattocks and described in Underwood's paper. In our experiment the three components of each stimulus were not letters of the alphabet, however, but pictures of familiar objects. In one condition no two of the eight stimuli had any component pictures in common. This corresponds to the condition imposed by Mattocks. We also included another condition, though, in which each picture was shared by four of the eight stimuli. Just as Underwood's argument requires, we found that the second condition (which could only be mastered by attending to all three components) was enormously more difficult than the first (Shepard, Hovland, and Jenkins, 1961, pp. 11–12). We did not go on to test whether the subjects in the first condition were in fact attending to the pictures in only one of the three positions, but such a test could presumably be made by determining whether there are two of the three positions for which the pictures could be altered without impairing performance. Certainly the statements made by some of the subjects during postexperimental interviews make this seem a not unlikely possibility.

The observation that I want to bring out here, however, is that during these interviews several subjects alleged that they proceeded systematically by attending to the pictures in one position at a time even in the more difficult condition. They claimed, in particular, that they began by learning a division of the eight responses into two subgroups of four each on the basis of the two alternative pictures appearing in just one of the three positions. Then, when they had mastered this division, they attempted a finer breakdown of the responses on the basis of the pictures in one of the other positions. These reports bore a striking resemblance to the subjects' descriptions of their procedure for learning classifications of these same stimuli. (Interestingly, it turns out that the assumption that subjects do in fact proceed in this manner predicts a gradient of generalization of just the shape that was actually observed in this experiment.)

Now behaviorists are often disposed to regard the subject's report about what he was doing as a sort of epiphenomenal concomitant of the underlying behavioral process and as something that should therefore not be taken seriously. However, it is not necessary to rely exclusively on the verbal accounts subsequently supplied by the subjects; there are suspicious signs in the behavioral data themselves. Figure 3–1, for example, shows the detailed performance during one learning session of one of the six subjects intensively studied by Shepard, Hovland, and Jenkins (1961). In this particular run, the alternative pictures were a screw or a nut in the top position, a candle or a light bulb in the lower left, and a violin or a trumpet in the lower right. On any given trial one of the eight possible stimuli constructed in this way was presented, and the subject made one of eight designated verbal responses (letters of the alphabet). Correction was supplied by the usual method of anticipation. The cumulative curves in Figure 3–1 were constructed by adding a unit increment to curve I, II, and/or III, for any given presentation (trial), depending upon whether the actually presented stimulus and the stimulus for which the subject's response would have been correct differed in the top, lower left, and/or lower right positions, respectively.

As can be seen, after about 25 presentations curve I rather abruptly leveled off, and for the succeeding 45 presentations this subject made no errors that could be attributed to pictures in the top position. Note that this is not a random fluctuation; the probability of responding correctly with respect to the top picture for 45 consecutive presentations

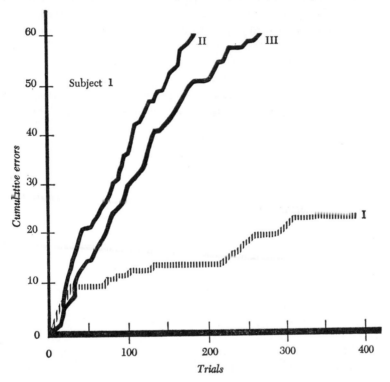

Fig. 3–1. Cumulative errors made by one subject in the experiment by Shepard, Hovland and Jenkins (1961).

by chance alone is the probability of getting a run of 45 consecutive heads while flipping a fair coin. At the same time, however, the other two curves are rising at very nearly the rate expected on the assumption of random guessing. It is, therefore, as if the subject were attending only to the top position and had, in effect, classified the eight responses into the four letters that go with the screw and the four letters that go with the nut. Note, too, that shortly after trial 200 (following a series of about 80 trials during which the subject again appears to be responding almost entirely on the basis of the top position) there is a pronounced burst of errors suggesting that the subject was no longer attending exclusively to this position.

For a more recent paired-associate experiment we selected a set of eight less complex stimuli. Indeed, each stimulus consisted simply of a circle with one radial line. These stimuli differed in only two dimensions: the size of the circle and the angle of the radius. In the analysis of this experiment the errors were subdivided into four classes depending upon whether the two stimuli that were confused on a given trial had a large difference in size (S), a small difference in size (s), a large difference in angle (A), or a small difference in angle (a). Subjects 15 and 20 from this experiment have been selected for illustration here because the symmetrical relation between their results emphasizes the difficulty of trying to predict the dimension that will claim a particular subject's attention. Note that, after about 35 presentations, Subject 15 ceased to confuse stimuli with large differences in size (curve S in Figure 3–2).

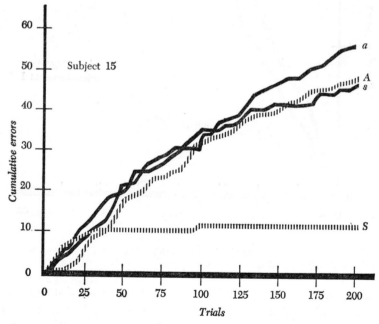

Fig. 3–2. Errors made by one subject in relation to dimensions of stimulus difference in paired-associate learning.

Errors involving stimuli differing only in angle, however, continued to be made as before (curves A and a). Subject 20, who was run under the same conditions, exhibited a complementary pattern. After about the same number of trials, this subject essentially stopped confusing stimuli

with large differences in angle (curve A in Figure 3–3) while continuing
to confuse those differing only in size (curves S and s).

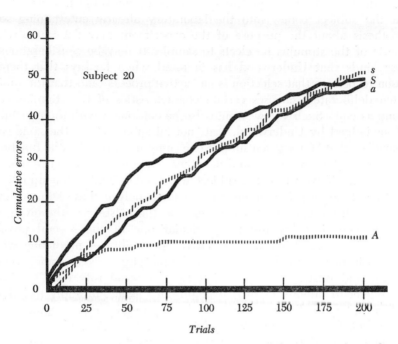

Fig. 3–3. Errors made by another subject in relation to dimensions of stimulus difference in paired-associate learning.

Now it is true that, of the many curves of this kind that we have
plotted for highly dimensionalized stimuli, many rise to their asymptotes
in the more or less smooth and predictable fashion that we should
expect on the basis of the usual S-R laws of habit growth. Just as often,
however, these curves are puzzlingly erratic. Moreover, sudden changes,
when they do occur, occur in different curves and at different times
for different subjects. Consequently, to average them all together
would be to obscure the true volatility of the underlying process. On the
other hand, to attempt to account for the individual zigs and zags of
curves like those in Figure 3–1—let alone the timing of their occurrences
—would seem to put a rather heavy strain on present predictive machinery. It appears that the subject's performance is in part governed by
processes that are not under direct experimental control.

Perhaps we should heed the neurophysiological theorists Hebb (1949)
and Lashley (1951) when they remind us that a stimulus does not im-
pinge on a passive system but interacts with a dynamic process in a
continual state of flux. Certainly, if the act of attention can be influenced

by the outcomes of previous trials, then it may also be subject to the control of this covert, ongoing process—a process, moreover, that has antecedents in the pre-experimental history of the subject. Thus the fact that the subject comes into the laboratory already entertaining some hypothesis about the purpose of the experiment may determine which aspects of the stimulus he elects to sample. It may be considerations of these kinds that Underwood has in mind when he says that there is reason to believe that selection is an "active process" and that the subject "often deliberately chooses certain characteristics of the stimulus compound as cue." Such a view would also be consonant with the possibility, acknowledged by Underwood, that "not all subjects 'use' the same component" or that "for a given subject one component may be the functional stimulus for some responses and the other component for other responses."

But, then, if we present a subject with highly analyzable stimuli, we should not be surprised if he does in fact analyze these stimuli—even though such an analysis is not essential to the mastery of the given rote task. Indeed, just because no particular one of the several possible analyses is required, we may forfeit the possibility of predicting which one will in fact be made. Thus it may be that, by the very choice of nonsensical and unstructured materials for the usual rote task, we invite the subject to impose his own structure and hence, to apply techniques that we intentionally study only in the supposedly more complex tasks of concept formation, problem solving, and invention. Conversely, the possibility should be considered that, by reverting to more meaningful materials, we can sometimes reduce the play of selective attention and hence promote, in the subject, a simpler and more predictable pattern of behavior.

Suppose, for example, that the stimuli in a paired-associate list are the eight highly meaningful three-letter words exhibited in Figure 3–4. Note that each of these words has one of just two alternative values (i.e., letters) for each of three different dimensions (i.e., positions within the word). The resulting "cubical" structure of this set of words is therefore formally identical to that for each of the sets of eight stimuli in the studies (already mentioned) by Shepard, Hovland, and Jenkins (1961, p. 4). On the other hand, the three values that were combined to make up each stimulus in those earlier experiments did not constitute a meaningful whole, and so those stimuli were more nearly analogous to nonsense trigrams than to three-letter words (but, again, with letters overlapping in the same way). Now subjects presumably would react to the three-letter words in a more uniform manner and, in particular, with less selective attention to the individual letters. If this is the case, then, according to our own earlier arguments, the introduction of the more meaningful stimuli should entail a reduction in the marked variation in difficulty determined previously for the different types of classifications (designated I through VI by Shepard, Hovland, and Jenkins, 1961). At the same time, the difficulties of learning these different classifications should conform more closely to the prediction from the pattern of inter-stimulus generalization as determined during identification learning. That is, when a stimulus acquires a high degree of meaning, it may lose some of its originally highly dimensionalized character and become, instead, a psychologically coherent unit. (Ambiguous words with two distinct meanings are of course another matter.)

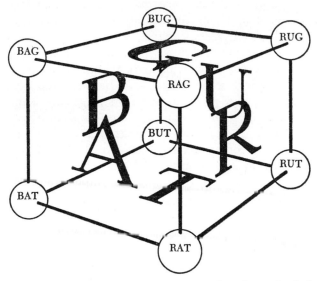

Fig. 3–4. Eight words, each with two alternative values for each of three different dimensions.

In any case it should prove instructive to make comparisons between identification and classification learning with such a set of eight mean-ingful words and, also, to relate the results to a similar comparison made both with nonsense trigrams having the same cubical structure and with sets of meaningful and meaningless trigrams for which there is no over-lap of letters. Certainly, as Underwood maintains for identification learn-ing, an appreciable interaction should be anticipated between the two factors of meaningfulness and formal intra-list similarity. Indeed, one of Underwood's students (McGehee, 1961) has already found that an increase in the extent to which letters are shared among the trigrams of a paired-associate list produced a marked rise in error for a low-meaning-ful list but no rise at all for a high-meaningful list. However McGehee did not investigate classification learning (nor did she arrange the over-lapping of letters to conform with our cubical structure).

So far I have concentrated on cases in which the discrepancy between the functional and the nominal stimulus can be attributed to a selection of some subset of the components within each nominal stimulus. My argument has turned around the idea that, if we aspire to a rigorous application of the S-R-reinforcement paradigm to such cases, then we must be prepared to face the problem of specifying which of the many possible subsets is (or will be) sampled on any given trial. This problem cannot be dismissed on the grounds that its ramifications are insufficiently general to warrant urgent attention at the present time. Note, for example, that the extreme case in which a choice is made as to whether or not to sample the stimulus at all may underlie such diverse phenomena as the Von Restorff effect, the serial position curve, and Rock's (1957) controversial results (e.g., see Feigenbaum, 1959). As if this problem were not difficult enough, though, I should now like to pass on to cases in which the discrepancy between the functional and the nominal stimulus may prove to be of a still greater complexity.

One kind of complication becomes manifest as soon as we turn from identification and classification tasks to tasks with a serial structure. For, as Underwood rightly contends, the selection of the cues to constitute the functional stimulus on a given trial in serial learning is not necessarily confined to the components of the nominal stimulus itself. That is, without looking at the current stimulus at all, a subject might still be able to respond correctly on the basis of the preceding stimulus, or on the basis of his position within the list, and so on. The inconclusiveness of the several experiments that have tried to establish just which of these potential cues is actually operative may well be due, as Underwood suggests, to the fact that different subjects may select different ones at different times.

Of course the paired-associate paradigm does not categorically exclude complications of this general kind either. In particular, when the stimuli and responses possess a clear linear ordering, a factor of "spatial" position may enter in identification learning that is somewhat analogous to the factor of temporal position in serial learning. This is illustrated by an experiment by McGuire (1961) in which the response numbers 1 through 9 were assigned either in order or at random to nine circles varying only in size. It appears that the large differences that McGuire found between the difficulties of the orderly and the random assignment cannot be accounted for on the basis of the interaction to be expected between the pattern of stimulus generalization and that of response generalization alone (see Shepard, 1961). Perhaps the functional stimuli in this case are not merely constructed from their corresponding individual nominal stimuli but, in addition, are organized into a latent linear array or "cognitive map." Complications of this kind are evidently of a different order from those usually ascribed to a mechanism of selective attention.

They might better be subsumed under the notion of recoding. Certainly the fact that recoding of stimuli can have an effect upon learning seems to have been amply demonstrated. Computer specialists, for example, have long known that their memory spans for binary digits could be substantially augmented by recoding these, in groups of three, as octal digits (e.g., see Miller, 1956). Miller, Galanter, and Pribram have indicated, further, how the pattern of errors can itself be qualitatively altered by the adoption of a recoding system (1960, pp. 126–127). A phenomenon of this kind was rather clearly revealed in the performance of one of the six subjects investigated (over a period of weeks) in the Shepard-Hovland-Jenkins study of the learning of classifications (1961, pp. 35–38). Both the shape of the gradient of stimulus generalization and the rank order of the difficulties of the different types of classification for this one subject departed in a very striking way from the corresponding results for all of the other subjects. In our report of these experiments we tried to show how an explanation for the otherwise perplexing (though highly reliable) performance of this subject could be found in the unique encoding system that she alone adopted (and described to us during the postexperimental interviews).

The problem, for S-R theories, raised by the existence of alternative encoding schemes for the same set of stimuli is, again, one of specifying what subset of stimuli has been affected by a particular reinforcement. Note, however, that there is also a somewhat analogous problem of delimiting the response. An interesting illustration of this is provided by an experiment on the formation of concepts under noncontingent reinforcement reported by H. M. Jenkins (at the 1960 meeting of the AAAS). He presented pairs of digits and instructed his subjects to produce a third number as a response. The responses were then said to be correct or incorrect according to a prearranged schedule, however, and so no "solution" was possible. Nevertheless the subjects almost invariably claimed to have discovered rules—typically rather complex ones—governing the supposed assignment between the "correct" responses and their stimuli.

Consider a particular trial in which the stimulus consists, say, of the digits 5 and 2. In such a case the subject might venture the response "7." The question then is: What would be the consequences if, in accordance with the prearranged schedule, this response were designated as correct? Analysis of subsequent responses tended to confirm the view that such feedback would not simply serve to reinforce the probability of the response "7" or even to reinforce the conditional probability of this response in the presence of the stimulus composed of 5 and 2.

Rather, its primary effect seemed to be to reinforce the particular rule or hypothesis that the subject was using to generate the response. In this instance the rule might be to add the two digits when the first is larger than the second.

That the subject takes particular account of the comparative sizes of the two digits may represent an attempt to accommodate a negative outcome on an earlier trial. That is, it may have happened that when addition (which had been adventitiously reinforced for several trials) was then non-reinforced, the subject searched for some special property of the new pair of digits that might account for its exclusion from the domain covered by the addition rule. Out of the large number of special properties that could have been abstracted from this new pair of digits, this subject hit upon the fact that the first digit was smaller than the second. He might then have framed the supplementary hypothesis that the digits should be multiplied (rather than added) in this case. This supplementary rule might then be reinforced on an ensuing trial or, if not, the subject could try some other operation (e.g., subtraction). Thus, by subdividing the class of stimuli to which a given rule is presumed to apply, the subject can always protect his fortuitously validated theories from subsequent disconfirmation. Such attention to the special features of the stimuli is, again, a kind of selectivity governed, in part, by the hypothesis currently being maintained.

In fine, then, as I have pursued some of the threads in the tangle of problems connected with the notion of the functional stimulus, I have come to feel that talk about the gradual strengthening and weakening of S-R bonds may have to be supplemented (if not, indeed, supplanted) by talk about "hypotheses," "heuristics," "strategies," "plans," or "schemata." In this feeling, moreover, I am evidently not entirely alone (e.g., see Attneave, 1957; Bruner, Goodnow, and Austin, 1956; Chomsky, 1957, 1959; DeSoto, 1960, 1961; Krechevsky, 1932; Lashley, 1951; Miller, Galanter, and Pribram, 1960; Newell, Shaw, and Simon, 1958; Oldfield, 1954; Piaget, 1952, 1957; Restle, 1960, 1961, in press; Taylor, 1960; Wertheimer, 1945). Some have even gone so far as to suggest that we shall need a theory of thinking before we can have a complete theory of the fine-grain behavior in "rote learning."

Others, of course, have contended that we already have too many theories of thinking and that what we need, instead, are more data. But it seems to me that we do not yet have a *single* theory of thinking in the sense that I intend here. For, to have a theory in this sense would be to have a statement of the rules of operation of the constituent mechanisms that is so explicit and so precise that it could be converted directly into a program for a digital computer. It is not that it must be so converted, but only that it must be that explicit and precise. Only then can we be truly sure of its susceptibility to empirical test. And we *can* then be sure for, even if no more direct method of test is available, we can at least resort to the method of computer simulation. From this standpoint, to have a satisfactory theory of thinking is to have, in essence, the design for a machine that will, in fact, think.

Now attempts have of course been made to subsume thinking under the rubric of the S-R scheme. Typically this is done by generalizing the notions of stimulus and response to include unobservable mediational events that are presumed to be governed by the same simple laws already inferred from the study of their overt analogues. Still, to anyone who has programmed a digital computer, it will be eminently clear how far short such "theories" fall from the requisite degree of explicit detail. True, upper- and lowercase S's and R's are arranged into elaborate diagrams, replete with connecting arrows. But, while there is no doubt as to the heuristic value of such schematic constructions, there has been a signal lack of demonstration that such constructions will actually generate, in detail, the behavior they purport to explain.

There has, I think, been an implicit and uncritical acceptance, as entirely sufficient in itself, of the one dominant methodology in this area, i.e., a methodology which might loosely be classified as "the experimental analysis of behavior." According to this, one strives, by means of increasingly refined experimental manipulations, to isolate the gross factors (such as number and distribution of repetitions, similarity and meaningfulness of stimuli, etc.) that affect over-all performance. No matter how many such factors have been isolated, however, the question is seldom raised as to whether it is possible to proceed in the reverse direction and show that the factors isolated in this way are sufficient to provide a complete and detailed account of the trial-by-trial performance of any one subject.

Thus, after Underwood has raised a number of interesting questions about the performance of subjects under certain experimental conditions, we find him concluding that "they may be irrelevant questions for it is possible that the great inhibitory effect observed by Primoff and Young can be handled by interference developed entirely by the process of forming associations in the list." This, it seems to me, is the point at which we might profitably pause in our proliferation of explanatory mechanisms and frame at least some of these in a sufficiently precise manner so that we can determine just what phenomena they can in fact handle.

Now the models of some of the more mathematically oriented S-R theorists are, of course, capable of reconstructing the behavior observed in certain relatively simple learning situations in considerable detail (e.g., see Bower, 1961; Bush and Mosteller, 1955; Estes, 1959). But the tests of these models have generally been confined to a comparison, with the observed behavior, of consequences derived from the models by strictly mathematico-deductive methods. For this reason, attempts to extend these models to some of the more interesting and complicated phenomena arising in verbal learning experiments have often foundered in a quagmire of intractable mathematics.

With the advent of high-speed digital computers, however, the possibility of computer simulation has now emerged as a viable alternative to the mathematico-deductive method of testing theories. Thus, as a promising adjunct to the experimental analysis of behavior, we now have the complementary methodology, viz., the experimental *synthesis* of behavior. The basic idea is this: If the assumptions that we tentatively propose to explain the behavior observed under certain prescribed conditions are formulated with sufficient precision, then we can program the computer to operate in accordance with those assumptions. Thereupon, whenever we supply the appropriate initial conditions, we can simply observe the behavior of the computer, empirically, to see whether it actually does match the behavior of our human subjects under the corresponding conditions. The only reason for using the computer is, of course, that—however simple each one of our assumptions may appear in isolation—the way in which they will interact together under the prescribed boundary conditions cannot possibly be determined simply by inspection. Precisely because this is so, we must be prepared to find, in the behavior of the computer, a significant departure from that of our human subjects. Then begins the protracted process in which we alternate between tinkering with the assumptions and retesting the adequacy of the resulting simulation. The hope is that this process will converge on an acceptable theory.

Although simulation methods have already proved valuable in the physical sciences, their potential usefulness in the behavioral sciences is just beginning to be realized—largely as a result of the pioneering work of Newell, Shaw, and Simon (1957, 1958). Already a number of efforts are under way to ply these methods in the study of verbal learning (e.g., see Feigenbaum, 1961; Feldman, 1961; Hovland and Hunt, 1960; Hunt and Hovland, 1961; Newell, Shaw, and Simon, 1958, 1960a, 1960b). Feigenbaum, in particular, has set himself the task of simulating human performances in both paired-associate and serial learning experiments. However, in order to give one concrete illustration of this approach, I am going to confine my remarks to the attempt by Feldman to simulate the behavior of human subjects in what might be regarded as one of the simplest of the verbal learning situations, namely, the two-choice guessing experiment (Feldman, 1959, 1961). On each trial of this experiment a given subject is presented with one of two alternative events. The event to be presented on each trial is selected at random; but the subject is nevertheless instructed to guess, before each new trial, which of the two events will occur on that trial. This situation is, of course, different from the usual paired-associate or serial-learning situation. Still Feldman's novel approach to it does suggest a way of dealing with the central problems with which I have been concerned here, viz., the problem of the fluctuation of attention and the problem of individual differences in strategies and recoding schemes.

Now just because this two-response situation is apparently so simple, it has seemed particularly amenable to mathematical treatment by the S-R learning models. Indeed, such models have been shown to account for certain gross features of subjects' performance, such as the asymptotic probabilities of the two responses (Bush and Mosteller, 1955, p. 280; Estes and Straughan, 1954; Feldman and Newell, 1961). However there is a serious question whether these models actually furnish even an approximate representation of what is really going on in this binary-choice experiment. First of all, it seems obvious that, if the two events are no longer drawn entirely at random but, rather, are chosen in accordance with some prearranged pattern (such as the pattern of double alternation), the subject will soon pick up this new regularity and, thereafter, will respond with perfect accuracy. Moreover, the results reported by Galanter and Smith (1958) indicate that the point at which this pattern is detected is marked by a striking discontinuity in the performance of the subject. But there is nothing in the S-R learning models to suggest the capability of such a transition to errorless performance in the two choice experiment. Of course in the usual two-choice experiment there is no pattern, but the fact that subjects do detect a pattern when it is there is strong presumptive evidence for the notion that they are in some sense looking for patterns even when there are none. Certainly that is the kind of thing that is suggested by Jenkins's study, already cited, on noncontingent reinforcement. Now it may be that if the subject "knows for sure" that the sequence is not prestructured in any way, then he will no longer look for (and, hence, be able to find) patterns (cf. Miller, 1958). But this is exactly the condition under which the probability-matching behavior predicted by the S-R learning models appears to break down (e.g., see Morse and Rundquist, 1960).

Feldman's approach is entirely different. He was not content to account merely for the mean asymptotic probability of response but sought, in addition, to account for the exact choice made on each trial by each subject. He supposed that, in order to attempt a prediction of the next event, the subject invokes one hypothesis out of a certain repertory of hypotheses characteristic of that particular subject. Thus one subject's repertory might include these hypotheses: (a) that the event presented last will be repeated in the ensuing sequence (e.g., 000 . . . or 111 . . .), (b) that the sequence will exhibit single alternations (010101 . . .), (c) that the sequence will exhibit double alternations (00110011 . . .), and (d) that the experimenter will try to "throw me off" (i.e., he will change the event on the next trial from what it would otherwise have been but, except for this one trial, my previous hypothesis will remain in effect). The way in which the subject switches between the individual hypotheses in his repertory is then considered to be governed by deterministic rules together with their parameters (which must be estimated from the data). Thus one unique feature of Feldman's approach is that he ends up by constructing a different model for each individual subject. In particular, not only do the parameters governing the selection of hypotheses differ from one subject to the next, but the hypotheses, themselves, differ too.

Actually Feldman's subjects were instructed not only to make their prediction on each trial but also to state their reason for making that particular prediction. The set of hypotheses used by any one subject was then inferred, in part, on the basis of his resulting verbal protocol. Moreover, Feldman attempted to predict these stated reasons as well as the predictions for which they were offered as justifications. In order to avoid circularity in this enterprise, Feldman constructed the model for each separate subject and estimated the parameters for that model on the basis of the first 100 trials only. The test of the model then consisted in letting the program run autonomously for another 100 trials and comparing its resulting output with the record of the actual performance, during the second 100 trials, of the corresponding subject. Both Feldman and his mentor, Newell, have reported that at some point in the perfection of the model for a given subject the simulation seems to "lock in" with the subject's behavior. Newell, in particular, has argued that, when the internal process is finally reduced to the correct units, the appearance of fundamental unpredictability of the fine-grain behavior of human subjects seems to evaporate.

Unfortunately, an enormous amount of work is required in order to achieve this kind of tight account of human behavior. For this reason progress is likely to be quite slow by these methods. Furthermore the objection might be raised that these methods do not lead to general knowledge, that when N models have been fitted to N subjects, this gives us no more leverage in dealing with subject $N + 1$. This objection may, however, prove premature. Although there may always be a residuum of unique processes in each subject, certain general features or mechanisms common to many subjects may begin to emerge. Certainly a very substantial fraction of Feldman's computer program is retained when he proceeds from one subject to the next. In any case, if our objective really is to understand in detail what is behind the particular pattern of behavior observed for each individual subject in a verbal learning experiment, what other alternative do we have? I can think of none.

I should like to conclude with this final comment: My insistence that a theoretical formulation be rendered in such a manner that it could be converted into a computer program does not in itself predispose us toward any particular type of theory. Any of the general-purpose digital computers now in use is (if supplied with enough magnetic tape) equivalent to a universal Turing machine and can, therefore, simulate any other machine—including man. The model resides wholly in the program supplied to the computer and not at all in the hardware of the computer itself. For this reason any model can be programmed— provided only that it is sufficiently explicit. Now the models that are being developed by Newell, Simon, and Shaw and their students are not strictly S-R models. That is, although they are necessarily tested by comparing predictions with observed responses emitted in the presence of manipulable stimuli, the specific machinery that is assumed to intervene between the stimuli and the responses is not conveniently described by the traditional rules of S-R habit growth. If the S-R theorists are confident that they, too, can account for verbal behavior in this kind of detail, then I think these new methods pose for them a considerable challenge—to show that they can.

REFERENCES

Atkinson, R. C. (1961) The observing response in discrimination learning. *J. Exp. Psychol.*, **62**, 253–262.

Attneave, F. (1957) Transfer of experience with a class-schema to identification-learning of patterns and shapes. *J. Exp. Psychol.*, **54**, 81–88.

Baum, M. (1954) Simple concept learning as a function of intralist generalization. *J. Exp. Psychol.*, **47**, 89–94.

Binder, A., & Feldman, S. E. (1960) The effects of experimentally controlled experience upon recognition responses. *Psychol. Monogr.*, **74**, No. 9 (Whole No. 496).

Bourne, L. E., Jr., & Restle, F. (1959) Mathematical theory of concept identification. *Psychol. Rev.*, **66**, 278–296.

Bower, G. (1961) Application of a model to paired-associate learning. *Psychometrika*, **26**, 255–280.

Bruner, J. S., Goodnow, J. J., & Austin, G. A. (1956) *A study of thinking.* New York: Wiley.

Bush, R. R., & Mosteller, F. (1955) *Stochastic models for learning.* New York: Wiley.

Chomsky, N. (1957) *Syntactic structures.* The Hague: Mouton.

Chomsky, N. (1959) Verbal behavior (a review of Skinner's book). *Language,* **35**, 26–58.

Cofer, C. N. (Ed.) (1961) *Verbal learning and verbal behavior.* New York: McGraw-Hill.

DeSoto, C. B. (1960) Learning a social structure. *J. Abnorm. Soc. Psychol.,* 60, 417–421.

DeSoto, C. B. (1961) The predilection for single orderings. *J. Abnorm. Soc. Psychol.,* 62, 16–23.

Estes, W. K. (1959) The statistical approach to learning theory. In S. Koch (Ed.), *Psychology: A study of a science.* Vol. II. New York: McGraw-Hill. Pp. 383–491.

Estes, W. K., & Straughan, J. H. (1954) Analysis of a verbal conditioning situation in terms of statistical learning theory. *J. Exp. Psychol.,* 47, 225–234.

Feigenbaum, E. A. (1959) An information processing theory of verbal learning. *RAND Report P-1817.* Santa Monica, Calif.: RAND Corporation.

Feigenbaum, E. A. (1961) The simulation of verbal learning behavior. *Proc. West. Joint Computer Conf.* Pp. 121–132.

Feldman, J. (1959) An analysis of behavior in two choice situations. Unpublished doctoral dissertation, Carnegie Institute of Technology.

Feldman, J. (1961) Simulation of behavior in the binary choice experiment. *Proc. West Joint Computer Conf.* Pp. 133–144.

Feldman, J., & Newell, A. (1961) A note on a class of probability matching models. *Psychometrika,* 26, 333–337.

Galanter, E. H., & Smith, W. A. S. (1958) Some experiments on a simple thought problem. *Amer. J. Psychol.,* 71, 359–366.

Hebb, D. O. (1949) *The organization of behavior.* New York: Wiley.

Holland, J. G. (1958) Human vigilance. *Science,* 128, 61–67.

Hovland, C. I., & Hunt, E. B. (1960) The computer simulation of concept attainment. *Behav. Sci.,* 5, 265–267.

Hunt, E. B., & Hovland, C. I. (1961) Programming a model of human concept formation. *Proc. West. Joint Computer Conf.,* Pp. 145–155.

Jenkins, H. M. (1960) Formation of concepts under noncontingent reinforcement. Paper presented at annual meeting of AAAS, New York.

Krechevsky, I. (1932) "Hypotheses" in rats. *Psychol. Rev.,* 39, 516–532.

LaBerge, D. L., & Smith, A. (1957) Selective sampling in discrimination learning. *J. Exp. Psychol.,* 54, 423–430.

Lashley, K. S. (1951) The problem of serial order in behavior. In L. A. Jeffress (Ed.), *Cerebral mechanisms in behavior.* New York: Wiley. Pp. 112–146.

McGehee, N. (1961) Stimulus meaningfulness, interstimulus similarity and associative learning. Unpublished doctoral dissertation, Northwestern University.

McGuire, W. J. (1961) A multiprocess model for paired-associate learning. *J. Exp. Psychol.,* 62, 335–347.

Miller, G. A. (1956) The magical number seven, plus or minus two: Some limits on our capacity for processing information. *Psychol. Rev.,* 63, 81–97.

Miller, G. A. (1958) Free recall of redundant strings of letters. *J. Exp. Psychol.*, **56**, 485–491.

Miller, G. A., Galanter, E., & Pribram, K. H. (1960) *Plans and the structure of behavior*. New York: Holt, Rinehart & Winston.

Morse, E. B., & Rundquist, W. N. (1960) Probability-matching with an unscheduled random sequence. *Amer. J. Psychol.*, **73**, 603–607.

Newell, A., Shaw, J. C., & Simon, H. A. (1957) Empirical explorations of the logic theory machine. *Proc. West. Joint Computer Conf.* Pp. 218–230.

Newell, A., Shaw, J. C., & Simon, H. A. (1958) Elements of a theory of human problem solving. *Psychol. Rev.*, **65**, 151–166.

Newell, A., Shaw, J. C., & Simon, H. A. (1960a) A variety of intelligent learning in a general problem solver. In M. C. Yovits & S. Cameron (Eds.), *Self-organizing systems*. New York: Pergamon.

Newell, A., Shaw, J. C., & Simon, H. A. (1960b) Report on a general problem-solving program. In *Information processing, proceedings of the international conference*. Paris: UNESCO. Pp. 256–264.

Oldfield, R. C. (1954) Memory mechanisms and the theory of schemata. *Brit. J. Psychol.*, **45**, 14–23.

Piaget, J. (1952) *The origins of intelligence in children*. New York: International Universities Press.

Piaget, J. (1957) *Logic and psychology*. New York: Basic Books.

Restle, F. (1955) A theory of discrimination learning. *Psychol. Rev.*, **62**, 11–19.

Restle, F. (1960) Note on the "hypothesis" theory of discrimination learning. *Psychol. Rep.*, **8**, 194.

Restle, F. (1961) *Psychology of judgment and choice: A theoretical essay*. New York: Wiley.

Restle, F. (in press) The selection of strategies in cue learning. *Psychol. Rev.*

Rock, I. (1957) The role of repetition in associative learning. *Amer. J. Psychol.*, **70**, 186–193.

Shepard, R. N. (1958) Stimulus and response generalization: Tests of a model relating generalization to distance in psychological space. *J. Exp. Psychol.*, **55**, 509–523.

Shepard, R. N. (1960) Similarity of stimuli and metric properties of behavioral data. In H. Gulliksen & S. Messick (Eds.), *Psychological scaling: Theory and applications*. New York: Wiley. Pp. 33–43.

Shepard, R. N. (1961) Role of generalization in stimulus-response compatibility. *Percept. Mot. Skills,* **13**, 56–62.

Shepard, R. N., & Chang, J. J. (in press) Stimulus generalization in the learning of classifications. *J. Exp. Psychol.*

Shepard, R. N., Hovland, C. I., & Jenkins, H. M. (1961) Learning and memorization of classifications. *Psychol. Monogr.*, **75**, No. 13 (Whole No. 517).

Taylor, D. W. (1960) Toward an information processing theory of motivation. In M. R. Jones (Ed.), *Nebraska symposium on motivation*. Lincoln, Nebr.: University of Nebraska Press. Pp. 51–79.

Wertheimer, M. (1945) *Productive thinking*. New York: Harper.

Wyckoff, L. B., Jr. (1952) The role of observing responses in discrimination learning. *Psychol. Rev.*, **59**, 431–442.

Wyckoff, L. B., Jr. (1954) A mathematical and an electronic model for learning. *Psychol. Rev.* **61**, 89–97.

Zeaman, D., & House, B. (1962) An attention theory of retardate discrimination learning. In N. R. Ellis (Ed.), *Handbook in mental deficiency: Psychological theory and research*. New York: McGraw-Hill.

SUMMARY OF CONFERENCE DISCUSSION

In conjunction with Shepard's discussion of the general problem arising when the subject recodes the stimuli, Deese referred to unpublished studies on concept formation by Sonia F. Osler and associates in which parital reinforcement was used. Young children were able to solve the tasks, but logicians, mathematicians, and other highly trained people often failed, apparently because of the strategies they use.[1]

To Shepard's suggestion that in conjunction with rote learning we need an explicit theory of thinking which could be programmed into a machine there were several reactions. Deese said the evidence shows that we do not have stimulus control in rote learning. Noble questioned whether a machine is necessary, and Shepard agreed that it is not necessary for simple theories. For complex theories, however, construction is easy, Shepard said, but it is difficult to test their consequences without a machine. Noble maintained that machines are not necessary to such an enterprise.

Mandler made the point that Shepard's emphasis on programming does not actually differ from the advocacy of hypothetico-deductive models but that models of the latter kind, such as those proposed in the 1930s, were often loose and indeterminate. The theorist cannot "cheat" when he works with a computer as he could with the earlier models.

Noble felt that Shepard's description of programming was not different from the way in which the hypothetico-deductive method is used, and Mandler added that one could possibly program the mathematico-deductive theory of rote learning in a machine.

[1] Perhaps relevant to this point is a finding in one published experiment (Osler and Trautman, 1961). It was found that highly intelligent children had more difficulty with complex stimuli than with simpler stimuli, a difference not present for children of normal intelligence. Osler and Trautman suggest that children of high intelligence make and test hypotheses during concept formation and attribute the difficulty with the complex stimuli to the fact that such stimuli yield many more hypotheses than the simple stimuli. Osler and Trautman suggest that the children of normal intelligence acquired the concepts by means of associative learning; thus, complexity of stimuli made no difference to their performances (Ed.).

Postman could not see how notions like strategies and schemata are more helpful than the concepts of nominal and functional stimuli. Why, he asked, are the latter concepts taken as evidence that rote learning theory has failed?

Deese answered that the problem of nominal and functional stimuli had been ignored until Underwood's analysis. Rote learning theory has emphasized the wrong things, as any undergraduate student knows before he starts to read (and be influenced by) rote learning theory. Postman said, however, that some of the inconsistencies in analysis had been uncovered by rote learning theory; he felt these inconsistencies do not suggest a failure of S-R theory.

Shepard's discussion of the flaws in the formulation of the binary-choice situation by Estes and by Bush and Mosteller led Mandler to observe that a subject will often ignore evidence which might permit him to be correct rather than behave in accordance with probability matching only. In one experiment he has used six pairs of nonsense syllables, some of which are accompanied by check marks and some of which are not. The subject is to learn where the check marks are. For example, the pairs symbolized by A-B, B-A, B-C, and C-A are accompanied by check marks; those symbolized by A-C and C-B are not. During early trials the subjects show probability matching rather than accurate responding to the stimulus information.

Among the various comments occasioned by this experiment was one by Deese who argued that, as in studies of rote learning, the data in the probability-matching situation have been examined only partially. This is because too much emphasis is placed on averaging of data so that learning curves and serial position curves can be plotted. The advantage of an approach like Shepard's is that one must look at the data in new and different ways. Shepard suggested that apparent probability matching may mask the fact that the subject is trying various hypotheses which lead to reinforcement.

Mandler suggested that we need methods and theories to predict what the subject's strategy will be. He told his subjects to look for stimulus information; despite this they matched probabilities. Wickens said this discussion returns us to the old continuity-noncontinuity problem in discrimination learning (cf. Hilgard, 1956, pp. 434–445). In that work the experimenters set up their studies so that the stimulus could be identified; then S-R laws were sought. S-R theory has often postponed this task of identifying the stimulus, but Underwood has now undertaken it. Wickens said he was reminded by Feldman's situation of the problem, in the rat studies of discrimination learning, of designating the rat's "hypothesis" in an insoluble discrimination problem. Noble emphasized that the hypotheses were identified in the subject's behavior. Staats pointed out that Feldman's procedure (of building a model for each subject on the basis of the first 100 trials in a two-choice situation and then testing it on the next 100 trials) involves an R-R law and that from these results we have no notion of what the antecedent conditions are. There was considerable discussion of this point, with several participants unwilling to discount R-R laws, especially in the absence of likely S-R alternatives.

Underwood said he finds it hard to see why Shepard's discussion prevents an S-R analysis. He dislikes too narrow an identification of the Bush-Mosteller formulation with S-R theory since the category is much broader than any one formulation. Underwood said that he, himself, is not a theorist but uses S-R theory as a tool for analysis. This really does not imply a theory. Most analyses in verbal learning are of this kind implying only that the situation is broken down into its components.

Deese asserted, however, that while S-R does not designate a theory, it is certainly a tradition. The variables involved, such as frequency, all go back to Thomas Brown. There is a real continuity between Brown and the present. Shepard's formulation is different and would not necessarily lead to concern with the variables, such as frequency, with which S-R work has traditionally been concerned.

Underwood, speaking in further explanation of his point of view, described an experiment which he did because of his interest in the relation of rote learning to concept formation. Concept learning is involved in some rote learning situations, and to study this problem an exaggerated situation was set up. Four high-frequency responses to each of eight category names were selected from the Connecticut norms (Cohen, Bousfield, and Whitmarsh, 1957). In one condition a 16-unit paired-associate list was constructed in which pairings were consistent; e.g., four animal names used as stimulus terms were paired with four countries used as responses. In another condition, the pairings were erratic. While the initial performance on the systematic list was better than that for the erratic list, performance of the latter ultimately became better. In our analyses of the effects of intra-list similarity, we have used five subphenomena—phenomena which are empirical. These subphenomena, while they can be shown to be operating also in the above experiment, cannot alone account for the obtained results. Obviously, either the combination laws for the subphenomena are complex, or other unidentified processes are operating. However, the failure of the analysis to account for these particular results (through the use of the five factors) does not deny the usefulness of the approach.

Underwood went on to describe a mediational analysis of this experiment which had been suggested to him by Howard Kendler. Perhaps, in an inconsistent list, the mediator extinguishes. A test of this was made by using the concept name as one of the four responses. This made no difference in the results, however.

Jenkins indicated that the subject must select the aspect of the stimulus to which he is to respond in the context of the response to be associated to the stimulus. In Underwood's situation this is difficult because some of the concepts (e.g., animals and birds) are linked, and the common parts will mesh with the stimuli in the same way. In the erratic lists, there is a chance to find the nonoverlapping parts whereas in the consistent list the common mediators each strengthened four terms. Deese said the subject must find a unique mediator for each pair. He suggested the construction of lists with associative mediators which would not be categorically related.

Jenkins described an experiment in which formal similarity was compared to associative similarity. The results show an interaction between these factors and the side of the pair on which they were used.

Further discussion emerged concerning theoretical formulation. Shepard repeated his plea for rigorous models, apparently responding to the immediately preceding suggestions and findings. He felt that what Underwood had said did not constitute a complete account. Underwood replied that he can specify whether an effect will be positive or negative but not how much the effect will be.

Mandler expressed the opinion that the variables suggested by Underwood could be conceptualized as strategies. Mediation is one possible strategy; the physical similarity in S and R is another. Subjects vary in the strategies they use, and maybe all variables do not work the same way for all subjects. S-R psychologists have tended to assume uniformity in this respect.

Postman equated research on strategies with the study of individual differences. Mandler accepted this equation and said that for different subjects different stimuli might be operating. The term "different strategies" may mean that there is a different concatenation of variables for different subjects. Shepard, Mandler said, wants to know what these variables are and thinks Underwood's variables are not powerful enough.

Miller asked if by instructions the differences among subjects could be eliminated. Underwood said instructions are not potent in these situations. Deese suggested the use of low-frequency associates to the category names. Staats argued for experiments in which the classes are built in rather than taken from norms. Wickens thought the use of recognition tests during the course of learning these pairs would have value, and Murdock, that lists with varying amounts of intra-list response similarity might be used; tests could be run with other arrangements of the pairs.

Staats reemphasized his suggestion that interword relations be built in, and Noble agreed that this suggestion is in the direction that research should take. However, Miller pointed out that control, even in this case, is not complete, and Deese, that the learning process in such an experiment and the one on the basis of which the norms are acquired may not be the same. Miller and Melton said Staats is looking for a meaning-free environment.

Mandler said that we must be able to specify how subjects select their hypotheses and how the hypotheses operate. Jenkins pointed to the experiments on the water-jar problem (Luchins, 1942) as an attempt to prime the subject to proceed in one way rather than another. With animals we can force behavior to occur to the stimulus as we see it. He went on to say that each subject brings to the experiment a style or a "Tom Sawyer" variable. Shepard said H. M. Jenkin's experiment confirms this. The fact that even those subjects who were reinforced 100 per cent of the time did not settle upon the simplest possible rule suggests that they entered the situation with the assumption that the rules would be complex.

Postman asked if what is meant is that operations are to be found which will reduce individual differences. Mandler said that we have not attended enough to the variables which control hypothesis formation. The demonstration of strategies, by itself, is not exciting. Postman offered two alternatives. One is to make certain that the subject will use the stimulus that the experimenter has designated as the stimulus. The other is to concentrate on the study of individual differences, themselves. Deese appeared to reject the second alternative; he thought, instead, that we need to vary stimulation in such a way as to obtain control over the strategies being used. Postman said that Underwood's methods permit us to tease out what is common.

Mandler argued that attention is an important variable, and Deese, that one can find a strategy in the subject's responses and then concentrate on studying it.

Postman felt this approach was one which might improve control in an experiment, but Deese said it is a way to study a variable which is of interest in its own right.

Mandler suggested that research on individual differences is not incompatible with the study of antecedent variables, though investigators who stress individual differences should pay more attention to antecedent variables than they do. Miller advocated the collection of elaborate material on individual subjects in order to develop assumptions as to the ways in which, over a period of time, they construct hypotheses. One would try to interrelate these assumptions so as to account for the hypothesis formation. With such data on a number of subjects a typology might emerge, or there might be consistencies among them, or each might be unique. Miller wondered at what point, on what subject matter, this kind of research would be most valuable. To Goss's objection that all that such research would yield is a collection of case histories, Miller replied that he knows of no better way to get at the variables of concern.

Brown asked if theory shifts in simulation studies as computers improve. Shepard answered negatively, saying that present computers can do anything that any computer can do, although speed may increase in the future. Brown also asked whether a program must be tried out in actuality. Shepard replied that the final test is to do so. Brown asked if it is impossible to program an S-R theory. Shepard said they could be programmed if sufficiently explicit. He went on to say that Hull's theory is not at a state of development where it can be programmed. Russell reminded the group that Hull had always pleaded for explicitness in theory construction.

Peterson pointed out that Underwood could explain his experiment by the use of three principles already mentioned: (1) When there is a small class of alternatives, response learning is favored; (2) a distinctive set of alternatives favors cue learning; (3) response learning tends to come early, cue learning later.

Deese reported an experiment showing, also, a change in a phenomenon as a function of stage of learning. Horowitz (1961) compared the free recalls of two lists of trigrams, one of which was high in intra-list similarity and the other low. Early in learning, free recall was facilitated by high intra-list similarity, but this facilitation disappeared later. Ordering, which required the subjects to reconstruct the serial order in which the items were presented, was uniformly facilitated by low intra-list similarity.

REFERENCES

Cohen, B. H., Bousfield, W. A., & Whitmarsh, G. A. (1957) Cultural norms for verbal items in 43 categories. *Tech Rep. No. 22*, Contract No. Nonr-631(00), Office of Naval Research and University of Connecticut.

Hilgard, E. R. (1956) *Theories of learning.* (2nd ed.) New York: Appleton-Century-Crofts.

Horowitz, L. M. (1961) Free recall and ordering of trigrams. *J. Exp. Psychol.,* **62,** 51–57.

Luchins, A. S. (1942) Mechanization in problem solving. The effect of Einstellung. *Psychol. Monogr.,* **54,** No. 248.

Osler, Sonia F., & Trautman, Grace E. (1961) Concept attainment: II. Effect of stimulus complexity upon concept attainment at two levels of intelligence. *J. Exp. Psychol.,* **62,** 9–13.

Chapter 4

MEANINGFULNESS AND FAMILIARITY

Clyde E. Noble

MONTANA STATE UNIVERSITY

During the past ten years psychologists have discovered more about meaningfulness and familiarity than in the preceding sixty-five. Although scientific recognition of the existence of these attributes dates from Ebbinghaus (1885), whose classic monograph on the learning and retention of verbal materials has been the prototype of most subsequent research on human associative processes, present knowledge is largely an achievement of modern laboratory methods. That research in this field is also virtually a United States monopoly should be comforting to those who view space races and missile gaps with alarm. The germinal ideas of multiple associations (James, 1890), association value (Glaze, 1928), frequency (Thorndike, 1932), acquaintance (Robinson, 1932), and transfer (McGeoch, 1942) have been elaborated by our younger generation of Functionalists into an impressive body of fact and hypothesis. Elegant theory may not be yet, but systematic empiricism is definitely out of the programmatic stage. Basic concepts of verbal learning and performance are here now, laws of their interaction are emerging, and my guess is that prediction with understanding is not far off.

The publication of *Meaningfulness and Verbal Learning* by Underwood and Schulz (1960) represents the apogee of current development in this area. Their book provides a rich source of new hypotheses for research workers, and careful analysis of it will generate heady reinforcement schedules for professional and novice alike. Assuming that the reader possesses this timely map of the terrain, we may proceed rather selectively toward certain landmarks which seem to have strategic as well as tactical value. In this essay, therefore, I shall examine some of the salient features of meaningfulness and familiarity as *concepts*, with emphasis upon the roles they play in verbal behavior. The analytic technique will be a combination of the logical and empirical. My aim, in brief, is not a review but a critique—a critique of the manner in which these two operationally defined variables are employed in contemporary research.

MEANINGFULNESS

Introduction

One of the best-established generalizations about verbal behavior is that speed of acquisition and performance level, other things constant, depend on the characteristics of the stimulus material to be memorized. Not only meaningfulness but also familiarity, affectivity, number of units, alliteration, color, similarity, assonance, size, rhythm, modality stimulated, and statistical organization are relevant variables (McGeoch and Irion, 1952; Woodworth and Schlosberg, 1954; Deese, 1958). We shall consider only the first two factors in this chapter, but it is well to be reminded of the broad territory covered by the term *stimulus material.* Recent interest in such topics as mediation and item selection in verbal learning serves to reemphasize the importance of conducting thorough assessments of the nature of the materials which human subjects are required to learn.

Although his successors are sometimes given all the credit, Ebbinghaus was well aware of the importance of differential associations. Not for aesthetic reasons alone did he memorize six stanzas of Byron's *Don Juan* in English. Ebbinghaus invented the nonsense syllable in an attempt to solve the problem of controlling the number and nature of previously learned connections, and he foresaw some of the complexities which result from sequential combinations. The latter problem was attacked vigorously by Müller and his colleagues (1900) around the turn of the century, then later more comprehensively by Melton (1936) in this country. But consonant-vowel-consonant (CVC) combinations happened to evoke even more associations in English than in German, so the research strategy of the post-Müllerian era (1928 to 1935) shifted from attempts to neutralize prior experience to studies designed to measure the nature and amount of its effect. Another phase supervened in the 1950s, when association value was joined by meaningfulness. As I have indicated elsewhere for dissyllabic and CVC material, the heterogeneity of meaningfulness can be quantified by at least two parameters: central tendency and variance. For dissyllables (e.g., ARGON to ZUMAP) the covariation is positive and monotonic (Noble, 1952a); for CVCs (e.g., BAC to ZUY) the function resembles an inverted U, with variance maximal for central tendencies in the middle range (Noble, 1961c). The difference should not unsettle us. Different scaling procedures often have this effect.

There is no doubt that the psychometric approach to the control problem begun by Glaze has contributed materially to the search for *correlational* laws of what I shall term the $R_1 = f(S \to R_2)$ type. Examples (Melton, 1929; Noble, 1952b) are the functions relating response measures of difficulty (R_1) to either the association value or the meaningfulness of stimulus material (S) which has been scaled according to independent response criteria (R_2). The well-known inductive limitations of such laws, however, have motivated us more recently to devise procedures for training specified degrees of meaningfulness into our subjects (Parker and Noble, 1960). By manipulating certain antecedent conditions we can assert that the facilitation observable in learning different materials is, in principle at least, an effect of specific causes and not due to artifacts or to the confounding influences of other variables. I shall symbolize this second, more *experimental* kind of law as $R_1 = f(S \dashrightarrow R_2)$, denoting by the broken arrow a laboratory-induced connection to distinguish it from the nonexperimental data characterized by the solid arrow in the first case above. Although new, and still technologically somewhat awkward, I believe the latter approach has greater theoretical potential than does the former. Its main advantage will be to help in the identification and explanation of interaction laws of the type $R_1 = f[S_1(S_2 \to R_2)]$, represented by plotting proficiency (R_1) as a joint function of practice (S_1) and meaningfulness ($S_2 \to R_2$) defined as before (Noble, 1961b). Because predictability and rationalizability are the chief pragmatic criteria one looks for, experimental laws firmly supplement (though they need not supplant) correlational laws.

Thus we now have two methodologies—the normative and the manipulative. And fortunately we derive from them similar kinds of empirical law connecting frequency measures of response proficiency as the primary class of dependent variables to stimulus meaningfulness as the independent variable. But what exactly is *meaningfulness?* We must now come to grips with this term. Have psychologists reached concordance on its definition? Some writers (Woodworth and Schlosberg, 1954; Underwood and Schulz, 1960) say or imply that it is an old notion, basically the same as association value—yet neither concept is defined in standard psychological dictionaries (Warren, 1934; English and English, 1958). When exact definitions are employed, functional peculiarities turn up (Noble, Stockwell, and Pryer, 1957; Noble, 1961d) which incline me to the conclusion that association value scales are inferior on four counts to scales of meaningfulness (Noble, 1961c). Other writers have related or equated meaningfulness to such notions as perceptual organization (Koffka, 1935; Katona, 1940), pre-differentiation (Gibson, 1942), familiarity (Underwood, 1949), statistical dependency (Miller and Selfridge, 1950), and pronounceability (Underwood and Schulz, 1960). These expressions are not all independent. Several are either synonyms at the formal level or correlates at the empirical level; but whatever we decide to call it, the concept of associativity must be defined by explicit operations. The histories of *instinct* and *insight* warn us to be careful not to mistake definitions for theories, concepts for laws. Have we fared better with meaningfulness? In one sense, yes. In another, no.

About a decade ago, I proposed a solution (Noble, 1952a) to the problem of how best to introduce meaning and meaningfulness into systematic psychology. Although many psychologists seem to be favorable, a few have taken issue with this program. It goes without saying that mine is only one of several possible approaches, but unfortunately the published criticisms reveal misunderstandings of the purpose and methodology of the associationistic view of meaning I suggested. More serious, however, is the evidence that certain writers are confused about the logic of defining behavioral attributes in general. In order to clarify my own conception of meaningfulness (m) for the reader, as well as to correct others' misconceptions of it, I would like to present now a reexamination of the basic rationale together with an evaluation of recent experimental developments. This analysis will be followed by brief rejoinders to the critics, in the course of which a few comments on concept formation in science may not be untimely.

Background

Let me begin by indicating the origin of my interest in meaningfulness. About 1948, while conducting research on the variables affecting reminiscence and distributional phenomena in verbal learning, I recognized the need for a more rational, objective, and reliable concept of meaningfulness than was available. Specifically, the work of Melton (1929), Hull et al. (1940), McGeoch (1942), and Buxton (1943) had suggested to me that meaningfulness might act as a performance factor offsetting the development of habit interference (Noble, 1950). The general dependency of difficulty upon association value had of course been known for years, but methodological inadequacies in the independent variable precluded exact determinations of the functional relationship. Aside from unknown reliability and a rather primitive set of defining operations, the chief defect in the Glaze type of norms was the absence of any underlying theoretical frame of reference. Even Hull (1933) did not attempt to rationalize the term "meaningfulness" when he selected 320 CVCs for special measurement purposes in a verbal learning context. Nor was "meaningfulness" mentioned as a possible variable in his theory of rote learning (Hull et al., 1940).

It seemed to me that the discovery of quantitative laws and the formulation of precise deductions concerning verbal behavior would be accelerated by introducing a meaning index having not only high reliability and a more objective verification basis but also an explicit linkage with the theory of habit formation. There had been anticipations of this before, but nothing very tangible. McGeoch believed that the place to look for an explanation of the facilitative effect of meaningfulness was among the laws of learning and transfer (1942, pp. 159–160). Similar views, traceable to the British associationists, appear in such doctrines as Titchener's (1909) context "theory" of meaning and James's (1890) association "theory" of memory. Yet all these thinkers appeared reluctant to proceed beyond a verbal level of analysis. At the risk of sounding heretical, I must confess to being impressed by one remark of Titchener's: "If the translation out of common sense into science is to be made at all," he wrote, "psychology is the science in which the equivalent of meaning will be found" (1915, p. 118). The great Structuralist's own notion was that core experiences (sensations and images) acquire meaning via contextual associations. As Boring later interpreted his master:

It was not really a new theory; Berkeley had practically said it; but Titchener gave it explicit formulation and importance. In simple form it was this: it takes two mental processes to make a meaning. When a sensation or image is added ("accrues") to a sensation or image, one has a meaning in the form of a perception or an idea. It is no new thought to a logician that a meaning is a relation. Here we have Titchener saying that a conscious meaning is a conscious relation, and specifying the nature of the relation (1938, p. 93).

More explicit, but equally subjectivistic, was James's principle of multiple associations:[1]

. . . the more other facts a fact is associated with in the mind, the better possession of it our memory retains. Each of its associates becomes a hook to which it hangs, a means to fish it up by when sunk beneath the surface. Together they form a network of attachments by which it is woven into the entire tissue of our thought. "The secret of a good memory" is thus the secret of forming diverse and multiple associations with every fact we care to retain (1890, Vol. I, p. 662).

Historically, especially in the philosophical literature, meaning has been construed in a number of other ways (cf. Ogden and Richards, 1923; Allport, 1955; Osgood, Suci, and Tannenbaum, 1957), but at least one influential writer (Watson, 1925) thought we did not need such a concept in psychology. Here are Watson's reasons:

[1] Modern echoes of the Jamesian view are found in the various mnemotechnic systems available to the lay public. That of Furst (1949), for instance, is actually called the *hook method* (p. 65). Practical mnemonics have been panned by academicians since the 1900s, but we rarely get around to conducting impartial tests of the validity of such claims.

One of the chief criticisms directed against the behaviorist's position is that it is absolutely inadequate in its account of meaning . . . may I point out that the logic of the critic is poor here? The theory must be judged on these premises. The premises of the behaviorist contain no propositions about meaning. It is an historical word borrowed from philosophy and introspective psychology. It has no scientific connotation. . . . Here is the story as I see it, since the behaviorist in order to protect himself must give some kind of account of it. . . .

If you are willing to agree that "meaning" is just a way of saying that out of all the ways the individual has of reacting to this object, at any one time he reacts in only one of these ways, then I find no quarrel with meaning. . . . In other words, when we understand the genesis of all forms of an individual's behavior, know the varieties of his organization, can arrange or manipulate the various situations that will call out one or another form of his organization, then we no longer need such a term as meaning. Meaning is just one way of telling what the individual is doing. So the behaviorist can turn the tables upon his critics. They cannot give any explanation of meaning. He can, but he does not believe the word is needed or that it is useful except as a literary expression (pp. 200–201).

Elsewhere, Watson (1924) promulgated Behaviorism's vigorous position on meaning as a defined concept in the following lucid passage:

From the behaviorist's point of view the problem of "meaning" is a pure abstraction. It never arises in the scientific observation of behavior. We watch what the animal or human being is doing. He "means" what he does. It serves no scientific or practical purpose to interrupt and ask him while he is in action what he is meaning. His action shows his meaning. Hence, exhaust the conception of action—*i.e., experimentally determine all of the organized responses a given object can call forth in a given individual, and you have exhausted all possible "meanings" of that object for that individual.* To answer what the church means to men it is necessary to look upon the church as a stimulus and to find out what reactions are called out by this stimulus in a given race, in a given group or in any given individual. Parallel with this query we can carry out another as to why the church calls out such and such responses. . . . In other words, it becomes like all others in psychology, a problem for systematic observation and experimentation. We have emphasized these general statements about meaning in this connection because it is often said that thinking somehow peculiarly reveals meaning. If we look upon thinking as a form of action comparable in all its essential respects to manual action, such speculations concerning meaning in thinking lose their mystery and hence their charm (pp. 354–355).

Noting the analogue of Pavlovian conditioning (i.e., bell *means* food), the Functionalist Carr (1925) forecast the wedding of meaning and association and adopted a similar empirical attitude to Watson's:

Meaning is not an observable process, an independent item of experience. It has no separate existence apart from that which means and that which is meant. Meaning is an abstract and conceptual term . . . An observable meaning process no more exists than does a "dog in general" (p. 124).

Watson was a remarkably courageous and incisive writer, but he had his share of philosophical shortcomings. I think Carr, being more flexible, appreciated the relational strategy. To avoid some of the methodological pitfalls of Behaviorism's brittle nothing-but doctrine of meaning requires a little tolerance of both Structuralism and Functionalism—plus a shade more sophistication about the use of empirical concepts in science. The interpretation which follows is a behavioristic account of meaning and meaningfulness which attempts to maintain consistency between the logical and empirical approaches. No claim is made for originality—let alone comprehensiveness—but I do think that, experimentally at least, we have gone beyond Titchener and his contextualistic predecessors. As for Carr and Watson, they were confident all along that should the future indicate the need, an acceptable objective analysis could be worked out.

Rationale

My central theme is that a systematic approach to quantifying meaningfulness should begin with the proposition that the noun *meaning* refers linguistically to a dyadic relation between terms. Using the terminology of symbolic logic, this meaning relation may be described as transitive, symmetrical, and reflexive. That is, when we say that one word *means* another, we use the transitive verb to represent a syntactical connection exhibiting these three cardinal properties. To illustrate with a few current research items: (1) S-R mediation phenomena exemplify transitivity, (2) paired-associate R-S learning reflects symmetry, and (3) most identifying responses (e.g., pronouncing a verbal stimulus) are instances of reflexivity.

The emphasis here is on the so-called connotative rather than the denotative properties of meaning, so it will make sense presently to describe a word having many connotations as being more meaningful than one having few. Connotation, lexicographers seem to agree (though not a few of them dislike the distinction), is the linguistic equivalent of association. For the reader who is not excessively anticlassical, the passage below will make the point:

A word *connotes* all of the attributes which are not denoted but which are associated with it. Thus the word *pig* denotes a young swine of either sex. It connotes filth and gluttony and high-pitched squealing, the little pig that went to market, the one that built his house of bricks, various characters in literature that have gone by that nickname, and whatever else, in addition to its basic denotation, the word may conjure up in the mind of one who hears or reads it (Evans and Evans, 1957, p. 114).

One of the most meaningful concepts in our language, from the connotative point of view, ought to be *Christmas*. Indeed, a search for the "meaning" of Christmas did not go unrewarded. I found exactly two dozen different referents in the following delightful extract from a popular magazine article entitled "Christmas Is Many Things":

. . . the wonder of a child at the first snowflake, the tenderness of a mother rocking her baby to sleep, the quiet strength of a father reading a story to his children . . . the imagination that makes a small boy hear the prancing of reindeer hoofs . . . the hush of twilight, the magic of midnight, the promise of dawn . . . the love that knits together a family across distance and time . . . the shining hope of peace . . . the faith that has endured . . . the remembrance of the Child of Bethlehem . . . the music of bells, the tinkling of tree ornaments, the voices of the church choir . . . the music of the carolers . . . the tree . . . giving . . . welcome . . . the fun of dashing through the snow in a one-horse open sleigh . . . the finger-licking joy of decorating cookies . . . the fun of dragging in the yule log and dressing up a sleigh . . . the festive board . . . the party buffet (*Anonymous*, 1959, pp. 15–27).

Since I chose to model my technical term upon contemporary usage, it was evident that the logical relation of signification could be coordinated with the psychological process of association by defining *meaning* as a hypothetical connection between a stimulus and a response. So far so good, but there was another matter to contend with. Two alternatives face the scientist who must name an empirical operation: He may either adapt an already familiar term, or coin a new one. Both procedures have advantages and disadvantages. The first option is useful in communicating with laymen who typically react unfavorably to technical jargon, but equivocal and sometimes contradictory referents of the terms must be learned. Examples are *force* in physics, *information* in mathematics. Both derive from ordinary speech. The second option benefits from univocality of definition, but the initial unfamiliarity of a coined term is often a source of prejudice and may delay its acceptance. Examples are *hypothalamus* in anatomy, *chronaxie* in physiology. Either way, research workers who form concepts are bound to draw fire from some sector, for "One man's overtechnicality is another's exact and economical statement" (English and English, 1958, p. vii). The terminologies of most sciences contain a mixture of the two kinds of terms, and psychology is no exception.

If I may use the language of Thorndike's or Hull's system, meanings are being regarded here as habit bonds with no consideration taken of their magnitudes. Of course the habit or excitatory strength of a given stimulus may turn out empirically to be a relevant variable in accounting for some behavioral effects due to meaningfulness, but I did not include any "intensity" factor as a necessary part of the initial definition of meaning. That S *sometimes* evokes R is the fundamental condition for the assertion S *means* R. Should the need ever arise to consider "meaning strength" a simple redefinition will be sufficient to extend the concept's usefulness, but it would be unwise to prejudge the issue. Redefinition is best accomplished in the light of accumulating empirical data where theoretical considerations also warrant it. At the moment, I know of no compelling evidence for altering the basic conception.

Still, there is another problem. Meaning, despite its transitivity, is not a serial relation because it fails to manifest asymmetry and irreflexivity. At first sight this appears to preclude any attempts at measurement. But one does not measure relations. Consider physics: The dimension measured by manipulating a yardstick is *length*, not "longer than." Like similarity (Noble, 1957; Noble 1961a), therefore, the meaning relation is intrinsically nonmeasurable. Happily, though, we have a potential behavioral variable (attribute) in the number of associations aroused by different words. All that is needed is a class of operations (e.g., counting) to quantify the multiple-response evocation powers of verbal stimuli. Why not call this property *meaningfulness?*

The number of learned and generalized responses (overt associations) which a stimulus elicits must be proportional to the number of individual connections, so for every newly acquired response there is at least one added meaning (connection). An appropriate behavioristic index of meaningfulness is therefore given statistically by the average (mean or median) number of continued[2] written associations made by a representative sample of subjects during a standard time interval (60 seconds). To denote this purely empirical, response-defined variable I suggested the mnemonic symbol *m* (for meaning*fulness*, not meaning). Operationally, the arithmetic mean number of associative responses to a given verbal stimulus is

$$\bar{m} = \frac{\Sigma R}{N} \tag{1}$$

where R is the number of responses and N is the number of subjects.

Reliability

Pursuing the foregoing rationale, a frequency scale of 96 two-syllable words and paralogs was developed in 1950 on a sample of 119 military personnel at Lackland Air Force Base (Noble, 1952a). The stimulus

[2] *Continued* associations are those which are successively elicited by the same stimulus and are not to be confused with either *free* or *controlled* associations. The number of different responses emitted in continued association typically exceeds that found in the free or Kent-Rosanoff technique, but the two methods are roughly comparable as far as the identification of high-frequency associates goes (Cofer, 1958).

material ranged from paralogs like GOJEY ($\bar{m} = .99$) to actual words like KITCHEN ($\bar{m} = 9.61$). Or, taking medians ($\dot{m}$) instead of means in equation 1 to secure more appropriate measures of central tendency for certain purposes (Noble, 1953), the range of $\dot{m}$ was from .00 to 9.13 (Noble, 1958).

By these criteria, meaningfulness is an objective psychological attribute whose scale (m) has a nonarbitrary zero origin and a specifiable unit of measurement; furthermore, the numerals have cardinal as well as ordinal properties. But is the quantitative concept of m reliable; i.e., Can different investigators obtain about the same scale values consistently? Employing the method of intergroup correlation (Noble, 1955a), calculations of the (corrected) reliability of the Lackland $\bar{m}$ scale yield a coefficient of .993 (Noble and McNeely, 1957). This high consistency has been confirmed in the Pittsburgh laboratory (Rocklyn, Hessert, and Braun, 1957) with an average (uncorrected) reliability of .96 for subjects from 20 to 66 years of age and of wide educational differences. Recently we reported college norms for 100 cases on the Montana population (Noble and Parker, 1960) which have a (corrected) reliability of .994 and which correlate .965 with the original military norms. As expected, our college students produced a significantly higher over-all association frequency, but only by about two words on the average. Analyses of the scoring rules indicated that even if one fails to follow my original criteria of response acceptability (Noble, 1952a) there will be little effect on the scale's precision, although unrestricted (unedited) associations will raise the values computed from equation 1 by approximately half a unit.

The m scale thus constitutes an important advance over earlier association-value scales whose logic was unspecified, which were less objective, and whose reliabilities were unknown. Let us turn next to the question of the validity of the concept defined by equation 1.

Validity

By validity I refer to the ultimate scientific utility of a concept, i.e., the extent to which it enters into lawful relationships with other empirically defined variables. Whether such correlations exist, of course, is entirely a matter of fact transcending the arbitrary character of definition (Bergmann, 1957). It may be tempting to regard variables with high communality as independent, alternative measures of the "same" concept, but this view, like the notions of face and construct validity, has weaknesses (Bechtoldt, 1959). One is the tendency of those holding this doctrine to confuse reliability and validity; another drawback is that operationally distinct concepts sometimes get slurred together; a third problem is that scale and regression factors may be disregarded. Since any of these consequences may interfere with the orderly development of laws and theories, it will be desirable to keep separate the various correlates of m until more is understood of their natures.

To date there is evidence that m is related to at least ten other response-defined variables. Brief descriptions of these intercorrelations follow in simple functional notation denoted by the symbol ϕ:

1. $m' = \phi(m)$. Scaled ratings of the meaningfulness (m') of dissyllabic nouns, in which standard-score transformations of five-point ratings indicate the relative number of associations evoked by a verbal stimulus, have a product-moment correlation of .918 with $\bar{m}$. This statement is based on unpublished m' data taken from 140 college subjects at Louisiana State in 1955, compared with $\bar{m}$ values from our Montana norms (Noble and Parker, 1960). The Louisiana subjects were asked to rate the 96 items of the original list for *degree or amount of meaningfulness,* unspecified further. Typed cards bearing the words were presented to each subject in a random order. Frequencies in the five categories (labeled Very Low, Low, Average, High, and Very High) were converted to x/σ scores by the Edwards-Attneave method of successive intervals. Test-retest reliability, computed on the means of two sessions two minutes apart, was .985. The average error estimated from the test of internal consistency was 2.2 per cent.

A similar definition of scaled meaningfulness (m'), developed more recently for CVC material, calls specifically for comparative judgments of *number of associations* (Noble, Stockwell, and Pryer, 1957; Noble, 1961c). Again a five-point rating schedule was used (labeled None, Below Average, Average, Above Average, Very Many), from which m' values were computed as medians on a psychological scale of x/σ units. For 200 subjects from the Montana population, the m' scale for all 2,100 CVCs ranges from .00 (xoj) to 4.78 (MAN). The estimated average error is only 1.9 per cent. When measurements of m' are placed in correlation with $\bar{m}$ values established upon CVCs by *variants* of the 60-second production method (Noble, 1952a), the r's are positive and significant as predicted by the Noble-Stockwell-Pryer (1957) hypothesis. I found, for example, that a hundred 30-second $\bar{m}$ values from Mandler's (1955) 34 Harvard subjects have a product-moment coefficient of .72 with the Montana m' norms, while the r between our m' norms and twenty-three 40-second $\bar{m}$ values taken by Underwood and Schulz (1960) on 54 California subjects is .71.

Since the Harvard and California studies used different association periods and did not sample the full range of CVCs, the question of the exact regression of m' on m cannot be settled this way. To obtain the needed data, I recently recruited 200 additional subjects and had them respond by the standard 60-second method of written association to a

representative set of 21 CVCs. The (corrected) reliability coefficients are
.999 for edited values and .996 for unedited values, based on a random
split of the sample into 100 cases each. After the overall edited $\bar{m}$ values
were calculated according to equation 1, they were grouped into seven
categories of three stimuli each along the abscissa. When the means of
their corresponding m' values were plotted on the ordinate, the CVC
curve appearing in Figure 4–1 resulted with $r = .911$. For comparative
purposes I have added the curve for dissyllabic material to the same
graph, arranged in eight groups of 12 items each. It is evident that m'
is some positive, curvilinear function of m for both types of material.
With correlation ratios (eta) of .946 for the 96 dissyllables and .963
for the 21 CVCs, analysis of variance tests indicate significant depar-
tures from linear regression ($P < .05$). Now that the range of scaled
meaningfulness values for trigrams has been extended by the addition of
real words and the task and population factors equalized, the hypothesis
of proportionality between m' and m for CVC material can no longer be
retained. According to Figure 4–1, the alternative hypothesis that $\phi(m)$

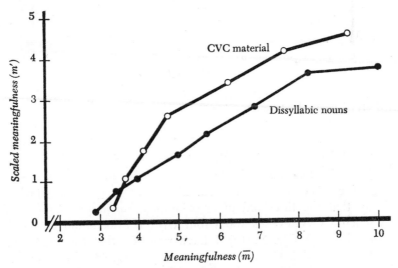

Fig. 4–1. Curvilinear relationship between scaled meaningfulness (m') and written
meaningfulness ($\bar{m}$) for two types of verbal material based on grouped data.

is curvilinear may also be applied to dissyllabic material. In general,
therefore, we must treat m and m' as distinct but related concepts
(Noble, 1962).

  2. $a = \phi(m, m')$. Association values (a) of CVCs, defined in the
Glaze-Krueger tradition by the relative frequency of subjects reporting
one or more associations, have an r of only .65 with Mandler's (1955)

analogue of $\bar{m}$, due partly to nonlinear regression and population differences. When both sets of scores are taken from the same population and $\bar{m}$ is computed in the standard manner, association value is found to be a nonlinear, probability function of meaningfulness. Figure 4–2

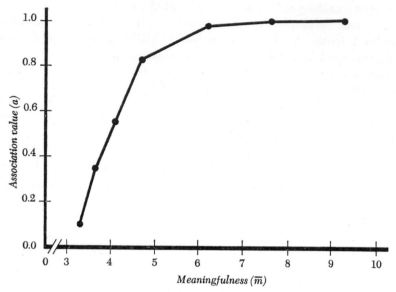

Fɪɢ. 4–2. Regression of association value (a) upon meaningfulness ($\bar{m}$) for 21 selected CVCs grouped into seven categories.

shows the same 21 CVCs mentioned above, grouped again into seven categories along the $\bar{m}$ scale, with their corresponding a values averaged along the ordinate. The rank-difference (rho) correlation is 1.00, and no test of curvilinearity is needed. For what it may be worth, one could say that the threshold of association-value judgments ($a = .50$) occurs when a CVC evokes about four written associations on the average. Elsewhere (Noble, 1961c) I have reported that the regression of a on m' is sigmoidal. Consequently, as we have pointed out on several occasions before (Noble, Stockwell, and Pryer, 1957; Noble, 1961d), the fact that a is a very insensitive measure of m' at the upper end of the scale seriously restricts its usefulness for quantitative purposes. Figure 4–2 justifies the application of the same restriction to a as a measure of m. To recent comments on the method of measuring CVC trigrams for a, m, and m', there is a reply (Noble, 1962) which goes into greater detail than is necessary here. Also, to forestall any uncertainty about the $a = \phi(m')$ function, let me call the reader's attention to an erratum in the first printing of my chapter 6 in Cofer (Noble, 1961d): instead of Figure 6–2 (p. 142), the plot should have been the same as the upper (a) curve in Figure 5 of my monograph (Noble, 1961c, p. 510). Both text and figure caption correctly stated that a is a sigmoidal function of m'. Since Archer's (1960) scale exhibits a similar regression on m', I would classify it as a measure of association value rather than of meaningfulness (Noble, 1961c; Noble, 1962).

3. $f = \phi(m)$. Scaled ratings of the familiarity (f) values of dissyllables, employing standard-score transformations indicating the relative number of times (n) the subject has experienced (received and articulated) the stimulus, show an index of correlation of .92 with $\bar{m}$ (Noble, 1953). There is also a rank-difference correlation of .83 between frequency of use in the language (Thorndike and Lorge, 1944) and the $\bar{m}$ values of 60 words from the Lackland m scale. We know from other research (Noble, 1954; Noble 1960) that f is a hyperbolic function of experimentally induced n, so it appears likely that f and m are related via the frequency factor. I shall return to this issue later.

4. $e = \phi(m)$. Mean ratings of the emotionality (e) of dissyllables, defined by conventional affectivity categories (Woodworth and Schlosberg, 1954), correlate .57 with $\bar{m}$ (Noble, 1958). Whether this relationship is another case of covarying n or evidence of something more complex like the Carr-Peters judgmental theory of feeling (McGeoch and Irion, 1952) remains to be determined by future research.

5. $d = \phi(m)$. Deviation scores (d) of judgments of dissyllables on Osgood's (1952) semantic differential, computed as the mean departure from neutral ratings, have a correlation of .71 with $\bar{m}$ (Jenkins and Russell, 1956). This fact is consistent with the positive relationship noted earlier between central tendency and variance (cf. p. 77). Further discussion of the semantic differential will also be deferred to a later section.

6. $p = \phi(m')$. Underwood and Schulz (1960) have reported mean estimates of the difficulty of pronouncing CVCs. Their values are based on 181 subjects and defined by a nine-point rating schedule of pronounceability, which I shall call p. The categories (labeled Easy through Average to Hard) produced mean p values which correlate $-.78$ with 100 items from our Louisiana norms (Noble, Stockwell, and Pryer, 1957). As shown in Figure 4–3, the regression of 145 Northwestern p values on their corresponding Montana m' values is curvilinear. In order to show a positive relationship, I have taken the liberty here of reversing the direction of the ordinate in keeping with the concept of pronounceability. Eliminating one point, the data can be categorized into nine groups of 16 cases each. The product-moment coefficient (r) is .80, whereas the correlation ratio (eta) is .85. An analysis of variance gives an F ratio of 5.74, which indicates a significant departure from linearity ($df = \frac{7}{135}$;

$P < .001$) in the direction of a parabola. The log-log inset to Figure 4–3 represents a rough test of this hypothesis. When p is plotted against $\bar{m}$ (as one can deduce from Figure 4–1) the curvature is even more pronounced, being essentially flat beyond $\bar{m} = 6$ for 14 CVCs common to the two studies.

7. $w = \phi(m')$. Several investigators (DiMascio, 1959; Archer, 1960; Underwood and Schulz, 1960) have noted that CVCs of high association value (a) occur with greater frequency in the natural language than do CVCs of low a value. This was, of course, part of the *raison d'être* for

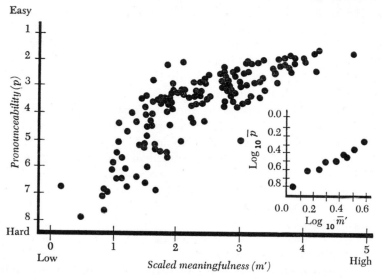

Fig. 4–3. Pronounceability (p) as a function of scaled meaningfulness (m'). The log-log inset is a test of the parabolic hypothesis for nine categories of the data.

association-value norms in the first place. Increasing meaningfulness should also raise the likelihood of a CVC being a word. Letting the symbol w denote the proportion of CVCs appearing as real words (parts of speech) in a 1960 abridged dictionary, Figure 4–4 shows the relationship between w and m' for all 2,100 items in the Montana norms (Noble, 1961c). The data have been grouped into nine categories by half-unit steps along the abscissa. It is clear that the relative frequency of words increases as a complex function of scaled meaningfulness. The $w = \phi(m')$ correlation, employing the rank-difference method, is .996.

8. $s = \phi(m)$. Mean ratings of 116 subjects' self-predicted learning speed (s) have been found (Underwood and Schulz, 1960) to correlate .90 with the $\bar{m}$ values of 86 dissyllables from the Lackland norms (Noble, 1952a). The Northwestern nine-point rating schedule (labeled Difficult

through Average to Easy) was also applied by 58 subjects to 90 CVCs from our Louisiana sample (Noble, Stockwell, and Pryer, 1957) with similar results: $r =$ .86. Significantly, Underwood and Schulz point out that number of associations, familiarity, and pronounceability were the judgmental criteria most commonly mentioned by their raters in assigning s values. There was a correlation of .92 between p and s for the 86 dissyllables.

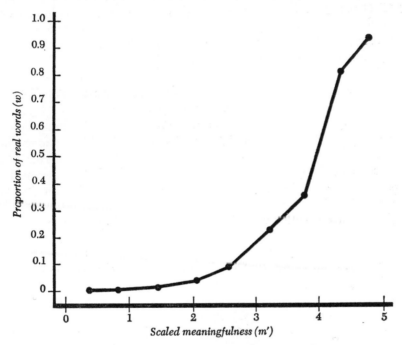

F_IG. 4-4. Proportion of CVCs which are actual words (w) found in various categories of scaled meaningfulness (m').

9. $l = \phi(m, m')$. Proficiency in serial as well as paired-associate learning (l) varies directly but nonlinearly with $\bar{m}$ (Noble, 1952b; Noble and McNeely, 1957; Dowling and Braun, 1957; Braun and Heymann, 1958; Noble, 1961c) and m' (Noble, Stockwell, and Pryer, 1957). In addition, meaningfulness interacts with amount of practice (Noble, 1961b; Noble, 1962), the facilitative effects of m and m' are greater on the R term than on the S term (Cieutat, Stockwell, and Noble, 1958; Cieutat, 1959; Hunt, 1959), and retention scores covary with m up to seven days (Dowling and Braun, 1957).

10. $i = \phi(m, m')$. Individual differences in ability (i) interact with $\bar{m}$ (Noble, 1952b; Noble and McNeely, 1957) and m' (Cieutat, Stockwell,

and Noble, 1958; Cieutat, 1959), suggesting a correlation between associative fluency and verbal ability. I tested this hypothesis on data from the Lackland population (Noble, 1952a) by correlating each subject's total number of associations with his raw score on the Word Knowledge Test (BI602A) of the USAF Airman Classification Test Battery. The r was .32, which is significant. Further evidence has been reported by Mandler and Huttenlocher (1956); they got similar correlations between associative fluency (i) and paired-associate learning scores (l) employing CVC material. On the other hand, Underwood and Schulz (1960, p. 48) describe an unpublished association-value study by Scheible which fails to support the hypothesis. This might be done more extensively, and with m rather than a. I would predict positive results under these conditions; i.e., subjects with higher fluency scores (in terms of average m values) should perform at higher levels on a standard verbal learning task than those with lower scores.

Because of nonlinear regressions and certain quantitative limitations on some of the variables, the exact functional relationships among these ten different concepts cannot be determined at the present time. But there is no doubt on simple correlational grounds that meaningfulness plays a central role in verbal behavior. Underwood and Schulz (1960) concur in this judgment, although they prefer to subsume most of the variables I have mentioned under a single rubric (M) and to regard frequency of experience—not without some ambivalence—as the fundamental (necessary and sufficient) causative factor. As we shall see again in the section on familiarity, my own hunch is that frequency (n) is necessary but not sufficient to the meaning-performance contingency. The other necessary condition, which I believe makes them jointly sufficient, is number of associations.

The close agreement between subjects' ratings of meaningfulness (m') and the actual number of associations they produce (m) provides commonsense support for the rationale underlying equation 1. Yet we need not stop here. Laws of the $R_1 = f(S \rightarrow R_2)$ type, as I said earlier, have their shortcomings. Consider an *experimental* test of the hypothesis that the facilitating effect of meaningfulness is due to the number of associations evoked by the stimulus material. If it could be demonstrated that systematic variations in m appear in the recall operations after subjects have learned different numbers of arbitrary responses to stimulus words of the same original m value, would it not constitute a partial confirmation of our associationistic view of meaningfulness? The validation would be complete if, when such words are placed in the *response* position of a paired-associate list, rate of acquisition were faster for those S-R pairs containing higher induced m value. For then we would have a law of the type $R_1 = f(S \rightarrow R_2)$. The performance measures ought to be a positive, curvilinear function of *m*, resembling the curves of earlier experiments where *m* was a response-defined task parameter rather than a stimulus-produced manipulated variable. Preliminary evidence that the hypothesis under discussion is fundamentally correct was reported at the 1960 meeting of the American Psychological Association in Chicago (Parker and Noble, 1960). Twenty subjects were taught 0, 3, 6, or 9 arbitrary associations to dissyllables of low *m* value which were later put in the response positions of paired-associate lists. After 20 practice trials on these pretrained lists we found that proficiency (*l*) was significantly greater for the items of higher experimentally induced *m* value. The function relating *l* to *m*, as predicted for that amount of training, was negatively accelerated. It is shown in Figure 4–5.

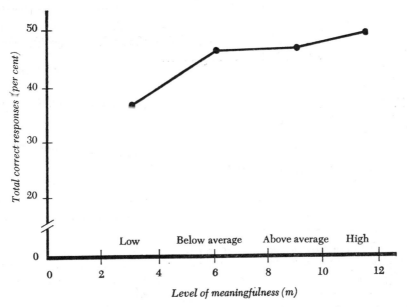

FIG. 4–5. Paired-associate learning proficiency as a function of experimentally produced meaningfulness in the response term.

A more extensive investigation ($N = 144$), designed to assess the influence of differential familiarization (*n*), was recently completed with similar results (Parker and Noble, 1963). There were four training conditions, followed by a recall test and 20 paired-associate transfer trials. An experimental group served in a replication of the above study; an experimental-familiarized group was treated the same, in addition receiving 32 familiarization trials on the R-term items having no associations; a control group practiced only on the paired-associate task but had items of the same normative m value substituted for items with experimentally acquired m; finally, a control-familiarized group was treated like the control group except for 32 familiarization trials on the low m items. The outcome of this experiment was also consistent with our hypothesis that number of associations is critical to the effect of meaningfulness on performance. Familiarization (n) could no more be invoked to explain the R-term facilitation due to m than could changes in association value (a) be used to account for the familiarization effects reported by Riley and Phillips (1959). A word of caution, however. Parker and I observed that m and n seemed to interact; in one analysis the experimental-familiarized group was nearly independent of m. Whether this was a case of real interaction or some artifact of group differences, we could not ascertain within the limits of our experimental design. Certainly there are many problems concerning meaning-frequency relationships yet to be solved. Before turning to a detailed consideration of familiarity and frequency, let us consider some criticisms of my approach to meaningfulness.

Criticisms

F. H. Allport. In reviewing various "theories" of meaning and discussing their implications for perception, Allport made the claim that "Noble defines meaning as identical with Hull's habit strength" (Allport, 1955, p. 571). This is not correct. "The present analysis," I wrote, "does not assert meaning and habit strength to be identical concepts, although they have some common properties" (Noble, 1952a, p. 423). Following this I added a paragraph explicating some of the many differences. The emphasis throughout my paper was on *number* not *strength* of associations. Allport also stated that my method of measuring m "would seem to depend upon the meaning of the associated words" (Allport, 1955, p. 571). This is also incorrect; the operations defined by equation 1 take no account of the nature of the overt associations other than rejecting illegible responses, perseverations, or failures of set (Noble, 1952a, p. 425). I was not concerned with the relevance, prepotency, or connotations of the (continued) associations—only their frequency.

Allport seems to be philosophically hostile to all S-R interpretations in behavior science. He doubts, for instance, that "theories" of this kind are flexible enough to deal with what he regards as the "nuances" of "subtle" matters like meaning and meaningfulness (Allport, 1955, p. 465). Another objection stems from his espousal (p. xix) of two kinds of natural law: quantitative and nonquantitative ("structural"). But there is no real dichotomy here. This is the old quality-quantity issue of classical philosophy. The key to the puzzle (Bergmann, 1957) runs as follows: Every defined concept of the descriptive variety includes in its referents one or more undefined (qualitative) symbols which are always in principle identified by observation. When numerical (quantitative) terms also appear in the defining expression, we have a mere variation on the fundamental theme of scientific concept formation. Equation 1 specifies a quantitative S-R concept; hence, for Allport it is inadequate. Yet how can one know whether a method is or is not adequate except by making an attempt to apply it?

C. E. Osgood. In his significant article on meaning (Osgood, 1952) and subsequently in book form (Osgood, 1953; Osgood, Suci, and Tannenbaum, 1957), Osgood has proposed a quite different approach from the one outlined in this chapter. He construes "meaning" as a hypothetical, fractional, unconditioned, mediating reaction (r_m) which becomes conditioned to a stimulus word (sign) regularly accompanying some other stimulus event (significate). Such molecular (implicit) representational, anticipatory responses (Hull's "pure stimulus acts") are clearly not identical with molar (explicit) word association; hence it is not surprising to find Osgood resorting to a different measurement procedure in order to quantify his r_m concept. The result is the semantic differential, which assigns to any word (e.g., KITCHEN) multiple-scale values along 20 adjectival bipolar attributes based on seven-point graphic rating schedules. Factor analyses of the judgmental data attempt to reduce the word to a point in hyperspace describable by a minimum number of attributes (e.g., *evaluative, potency, activity* factors).

Osgood's work purports to rationalize and measure a conception of "meaning" which corresponds to technical usage in philosophy and descriptive semantics, but linguists and lexicographers have expressed doubts whether the semantic differential taps the meaning of signs in this sense (Brown, 1958; Weinreich, 1958; Carroll, 1959; Saporta, 1959). According to Brown, "the [semantic] differential solves none of the problems of meaning posed by philosophers and does not even observe the distinctions of which they feel most confident" (Brown, 1958, p. 114). In Carroll's opinion, it "completely fails to index the referential meaning of the most ordinary nominal concepts. Much less can it express the denotative content of the term MEANING" (Carroll, 1959, p. 76). Weinreich suggests that "what the 'semantic differential' measures is not the 'meaning,' but chiefly the affect, or the 'emotive influence,' of words" (Weinreich, 1958, p. 347). By now Osgood and his colleagues are willing to concede this point, and they regard "'attitude' as one of the major dimensions of meaning-in-general" (Osgood, Suci, and Tannenbaum, 1957, p. 189); no longer do they claim that their index is purely semantical. "Perhaps we should admit that the word 'meaning' is used in several senses," they conclude; "whether or not it is *meaning* that we are measuring, then, would seem to be merely a matter of choice of terms" (p. 325).

Given Osgood's commitment to an amplitude-affect view together with his evident intent to capture broad terrain in the psycholinguistic field, an attack upon my rather modest frequency-association notion was hardly unexpected. The attack came (Osgood, Suci, and Tannenbaum, 1957) with these two charges:

1. "[Noble] has seriously proposed that the meaning of a sign is nothing more than the number of different associations between it as a stimulus and other signs as responses" (p. 16). . . . "JELLY, JEWEL, and HEAVEN have approximately the same m-scores and hence, presumably, nearly the same meaning" (Osgood et al., p. 17). Charge No. 1 is simply untrue. I did not say that meaning *is* the number of associations. This is what Watson (1924, 1925) or Carr (1925) might have said a quarter-century earlier. What I did say, illustrating with a diagram (Noble, 1952a, fig. 1), was this:

Since . . . *meaning* is a relation between terms, let us define the meaning-fulness of this *situation* as the number of Hs subsisting between S and the several Rs taken together. More specifically, the *particular* meanings of S_x are: $H_1, H_2, H_3, \ldots H_n$, and different conceptual combinations of these Hs yield different *numbers* of meanings (p. 422). . . . A neutral S, by the present definitions, is meaning*less;* an S conditioned to twenty Rs is more meaning*ful* (i.e., has more meanings) than is one conditioned to ten, and so on (p. 429).

Some confusion may have arisen from the generic term "meaning" used in the titles of my early papers, such that the aforementioned explicit distinction between *meaning* and *meaningfulness* was overlooked or forgotten by hasty readers. I certainly regret any difficulties my poorly phrased titles may have caused, for it is evident that the ghost of Watsonian meaning (*vide supra*, p. 81) was casting a longer shadow in 1952 than I realized. As for the Osgoodian interpretation in charge No. 1 of different words having the same m value, this is unadulterated nonsense. Indeed, it fits neither my m nor Osgood's r_m. Carroll (1959) believes that in this criticism Osgood et al. "seem to protest too much. . . . One might with equal justice . . . remark that because MOTHER, MUSIC, and HOME have highly similar profiles [on the semantic differential] they must have the same 'meaning'" (1959, p. 77).

2. "It is his basic notion—that meaning and association can be equated—which is wrong. Does BLACK mean *white* because this is the most common associate? Does NEEDLE mean *sew*, BREAD mean *butter*, MAN mean *woman?*" (Osgood et al., p. 17). I do not know what to make of charge No. 2. Osgood et al. seem to be concerned that m does not have "good" conceptual properties. If their reference is to the concept

defined by equation 1, in what sense is a concept "right" or "wrong"? And if they are *not* referring to equation 1, they must have been inferring laws which were not even available at mid-century. Perhaps all they intended to say was that unpleasant emotional responses were evoked by some of the associations they had to equation 1 or to my title word, "meaning." But one does not have to tolerate an objectionable symbol like *m*. Another will do. Any other, in fact. All concepts, qua symbols, are eliminable in principle; only the operations count. As a rule, the conceptual properties of a term are judged "good" or "right" if it turns out to play a significant role in theory. The outcome cannot be armchaired, unfortunately; observational data are also required. As I warned earlier in the chapter, defined terms (concepts) in the empirical sciences should not be mistaken for the factual propositions (laws) into which they may enter. Next, we come to the meaning versus association argument of charge No 2. Quite properly, Osgood *et al.* say that "a basic distinction must be drawn between the meaning of a sign and its associations" (1957, p. 16); that I concur should be clear from the passages quoted above (p. 96). It is regrettable that these gentlemen achieved so complete a misunderstanding of the association-frequency viewpoint. Most other psychologists have accepted the relational meaning of *meaning* and the associational meaning of *meaningfulness*. Among those who have not been blinded by the Osgood-Suci Tannenbaum smoke screen is Bugelski (1960). As he sums it up:

According to Osgood, [Noble's *m*] measures nothing but associations and throws no light on the nature of meaning. For example, Osgood argues, a common association to Mary as a stimulus might be Sally. . . . Does Sally *mean* Mary? . . . There is nothing especially damaging about the argument that Sally cannot *mean* Mary. If Mary is what occurs to you when Sally is presented as a stimulus in verbal form, then Sally may be an occasional "meaning" of Mary at least on a verbal level. It is one of the potential discriminated responses one might make in a given context. To deny that Sally means Mary implies that one has a different appreciation of what "meaning" means (pp. 313–314).

Of course (I hasten to reply to Osgood *et al.*) BLACK means *white* in the Kent-Rosanoff word-association procedure! But not because the responses which subjects give are the *most common* associates. It is because they are *associates*. Osgood repeated this slip at our first ONR-NYU conference (Osgood, 1961, p. 105) in commenting on research data reported by Bousfield showing that a word-association rationale "adequately accounts for the process of making ratings on the semantic differential scales" (Bousfield, 1961, p. 84).

Comparing our work with Osgood's, A. W. and C. K. Staats (1959) have correctly discerned that *m* is probably correlated with such "intensity" variables as d and e^3 (Jenkins and Russell, 1956; Noble, 1958) due to the fact that "the same operation strengthens both: the more often a word is paired with its word associates, the stronger the connections between them. In addition, the [Osgoodian] meaning of the associates is conditioned to the word" (1959, p. 143). Since I would not wish to restrict the applicability of the m technique to *verbal* behavior, I believe there is considerable merit in their following statement:

A more complete conception of meaning than the theory of word associates must include reference to the systematic pairings of verbal stimuli and various aspects of the environment, and to the properties acquired by the verbal stimuli as a result of this process (Staats and Staats, 1959, p. 143).

Following up this point, they and their coworkers (A. W. Staats, C. K. Staats, Finley, and Heard, 1961) have recently demonstrated that it is possible to make semantic differential indices of meaning (r_m) experimentally independent of association-frequency indices of meaningfulness (m). That one can untie variables in the laboratory which are normally tied in nature, as we have done for m and f (Noble, 1953; Parker and Noble, 1963), is an important tour de force which contributes more to an understanding of the basic processes involved than captious polemics about "good" versus "bad" properties of concepts. As with Osgood's writings, however—but to a lesser degree—I sense a misinterpretation on the part of the Staatses (1959) that my 1952 paper was intended to be "something more" than "*an* analysis of meaning." I have tried to show again in this essay that my original purpose was not to construct a *theory* of word association. What m and its network of correlates may grow into is another matter, and I hope it will continue to be viable, but the record should be clear that I began with little more than a rationalized operational definition. Viewed from this angle, and recalling once again that only laws (empirical statements)—not concepts (defined terms)—can be true or false, the conclusion is inescapable that most of the critics have gone astray by reading too much into the present approach.

A final set of remarks relating to a basic difference between Osgood's approach and mine will conclude this section. It is fairly obvious that he wants his notion of *meaning* (r_m) to be multidimensional whereas I prefer my *meaningfulness* (m) unidimensional. More than this, Osgood is after a supertheory of meaning; by contrast, m is (or began as) merely an associational addendum to Hull's system. Part of Osgood's predilection

---

[3] They might have added familiarity (f), which I think would be a good "intensity" candidate for the semantic differential (cf. Noble, 1953; Noble, 1954; Noble, 1960).

for complexity undoubtedly stems from his stated desire to communicate equally with psychologists and linguists, but I suspect a deeper motive. I think he may have fallen for the *mystique* of meaning.

FAMILIARITY

Introduction

The meaningful is always familiar, but the familiar is not always meaningful. In capsule form, this is the problem we must deal with in this section. Permit me to introduce it with a personal anecdote.

Back in student days, armed with my trusty *Webster*, I used to experience a common browsing phenomenon. Whenever I stalked through that dictionary hunting for the "meaning" (definition) of some word, my eyes would often fall upon a heading (like *hagiolatry*) which marked the first and last vocabulary entries on a page. Suppose I were after *hafnium* (p. 447) or *halide* (p. 449) on a chemistry assignment. Chances are I became incidentally familiarized with *hagiolatry* because it was right there in boldface type (at the top right of p. 447). But I did not learn the "meaning" (synonym) of *hagiolatry*. In fact, it still isn't very meaningful to this day, although I did eventually manage to subvocalize the phrase "worship of saints" as a paired associate. Encyclopedias, musical scores, and mathematics textbooks provide other sources of these *déjà vu* experiences. We have all had them. Indeed, it is surprising that psychologists have been so tardy in discovering that the correlation between familiarity (f) and meaningfulness (m) is non linear and imperfect (Noble, 1953). One would think that a few years' observation of the discrepancies between recognition and reproduction tests in college classrooms would have led to some research before 1953.

Rationale and Reliability

By contrast with meaning and meaningfulness, the concept of familiarity has provoked little or no philosophical argument among psychologists. A mere glance at our technical dictionaries (Warren, 1934; English and English, 1958) supports this contention, for familiar stimuli are defined as those which the organism has received via direct experience. The adjective *familiar*, Webster says, had its roots in the Latin *familia* meaning *family*, hence "closely acquainted or intimate." Another interesting synonym, now archaic, is "accessible." More recent ones are "well known" and "frequent." *Familiarity*, the noun, refers of course to the state of being familiar. Now these formal definitions are only helpful up to a point—if we wish to go beyond them we must decide on a set of repeatable procedures, observations, or manipulations to realize the concept of familiarity empirically.

About thirty years ago Thorndike observed casually that "the repetition of a situation does, of course, cause increased familiarity with it" (1932, p. 63), but at various times other psychologists have wondered whether a distinct concept of familiarity is necessary. Underwood, for example, once said that "meaningfulness . . . is the same characteristic as implied by the term *familiarity*" (1949, p. 411). More recently (Underwood and Schulz, 1960) he seems to have accepted the view presented in this chapter. My own position in 1953 ran as follows:

Theoretically, the familiarity of a stimulus (or response) may be regarded as some function of its frequency of occurrence in an organism's history. Humans may experience familiarity with a verbal stimulus in a number of ways: through the special senses of vision or audition, by means of speech (spoken or implicit), or by writing. By these means familiarity may become a learned stimulus attribute. The learning process is at least descriptively clear. Frequency of stimulation—including that which is response-produced, or proprioceptive—is a necessary condition of learning. That it is not also a sufficient condition is attested to by the research reviewed by McGeoch. . . . For verbal learning, as in many other types, some kind of reinforcement or knowledge of results seems jointly necessary.

Stimulus frequency is a variable to which a judge may be motivated and set to respond differentially. The empirical procedure of eliciting such differential responses might be by requiring S to point to a list of stimuli singly to indicate their degrees of *familiarity* to him. . . . In brief, a consideration of the attribute of familiarity (f) reveals that it is a concept definable by the operations involved in a psychological (or psychometric) scaling method (Noble, 1953, p. 89).

Invoking the law of comparative judgment and employing the method of successive intervals, I defined f in terms of subjects' estimated frequency of contact with a set of 96 dissyllabic verbal stimuli. Their responses were recorded on a five-point graphic rating schedule (labeled Never, Rarely, Sometimes, Often, Very Often). Sampling 200 subjects from the original Lackland population, I first transformed the rating distributions of the words and paralogs into normalized standard scores, then measured the median f values by a formula identical to that used for m' above. The values ranged from .00 to 5.66, and the test of internal consistency showed an average error of only 1.9 per cent. An earlier sample of 100 subjects produced f values for the same stimulus material which correlated $r = .99$ (Noble, 1953), indicating very high reliability for this interval scale of familiarity.

Validity

Part of the scientific utility of the familiarity concept (f) has already been specified in the section above on meaningfulness (*vide supra*, p. 89), where it was noted that an index of (curvilinear) correlation of .92

was found between f and m (Noble, 1953). In that study I also attempted to determine the mathematical function relating familiarity and written meaningfulness (m). To a first approximation, the best-fitting equation was exponential in form:

$$f = A(1 - 10^{-Bm}) + C \qquad (2)$$

where A, B, and C are empirical constants having the values 6.04, $-.067$, and .28, respectively. Now the reader may begin to wonder (especially as he recalls the operational similarity of f and m' and the curvilinear regression of m' upon m in Figure 4–1) whether f really differs from m'. The most direct way to answer this question would be to analyze graphically the relationship between f values (based on the 1953 Lackland data) and m' values (based on the 1955 Louisiana data) to see whether f is a linear function of m'. This is done in Figure 4–6, where the 96

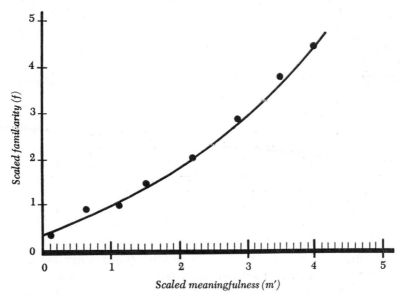

FIG. 4–6. Exponential curve relating scaled familiarity (f) to scaled meaningfulness (m') for 96 dissyllables grouped into eight categories. The equation was fitted by the method of successive approximations.

dissyllables have been categorized into 8 groups of 12 each. The graph suggests that scaled familiarity is not proportional to scaled meaningfulness but instead increases in a positively accelerated manner. I conclude that f is therefore not the same function of m that m' is of m. The equation relating familiarity to scaled meaningfulness (m'), determined by successive approximations, appears to be of the power type:

$$f = A(2.718)^{Bm'} + C \qquad (3)$$

where *A, B, C* are empirical constants having the values 2.02, .276, and — 1.67 respectively, and where 2.718 is the base of the natural system of logarithms. By means of a goodness-of-fit index computed directly from the eight residuals of the paired empirical (f) and theoretical $(\tilde{f})$ ordinate values,[4] a predictability of 99.60 per cent is obtained. The corresponding squared product-moment coefficient (linear assumption) accounts for 98.08 per cent of the variance in f. On mathematical as well as logical grounds, therefore, I think my original hypothesis that familiarity and meaningfulness are independent concepts is still tenable.

This doctrine is not new, although its quantitative rationale may be. In his celebrated chapter on memory in the *Principles of Psychology*, James (1890) considered the question of an introspective difference between meaningfulness and familiarity:

If a phenomenon is met with . . . too often, and with too great a variety of contexts, although its image is retained and reproduced with correspondingly great facility, it fails to come up with any one particular setting, and the projection of it backwards to a particular past date consequently does not come about. We *recognize* but do not remember it—its associates form too confused a cloud. . . . These are cases where too many paths, leading to too diverse associates, block each other's way, and all that the mind gets along with its object is a fringe of felt familiarity or sense that there *are* associates. A similar result comes about when a definite setting is only nascently aroused. We then feel that we have seen the object already, but when or where we cannot say, though we may seem to ourselves to be on the brink of saying it. That nascent cerebral excitations can effect [*sic*] consciousness with a sort of sense of the imminence of that which stronger excitations would make us definitely feel, is obvious from what happens when we seek to remember a name. It tingles, it trembles on the verge, but does not come. Just such a tingling and trembling of unrecovered associates is the penumbra of recognition that may surround any experience and make it seem familiar, though we know not why (Vol. I, pp. 673–674).

Jamesian familiarity, then, can be a residue of meaningfulness. As the opening aphorism of this section indicated, I would agree—although I would still insist that the (logical) relation connecting f to m is asymmetrical; in other words, f can occur independently of m.

Evidence of an experimental nature, in which f values were produced by laboratory-controlled exposures (n), has been presented in detail elsewhere (Noble, 1954; Arnoult, 1956; Noble, 1960). The law appears to be of the hyperbolic form:

$$f = \frac{n}{B(n) + C} \qquad (4)$$

[4] The index is simply 100 multiplied by the expression $1 - (\sigma^2_{res}/\sigma_f^2)$, where σ^2_{res} = variance of the residuals = $\Sigma(f - \tilde{f})^2/N$.

where B and C are empirical constants.[5] Equation 4 applies equally well to the stimulus class of random shapes and to that of dissyllabic paralogs, the goodness-of-fit indices exceeding 99 per cent. Figure 4–7 summarizes these findings and reinforces my original belief (Noble, 1953) that familiarity is a learnable attribute of stimuli.

Learning Experiments. As in the case of meaningfulness, there had been intimations of familiarity's role in verbal behavior long before my work (e.g., Winzen, 1921; Robinson, 1932). It was nearly 1950, however, before the quantitative influence of n on recognition and familiarity behavior was determined (cf. studies reviewed by Underwood and

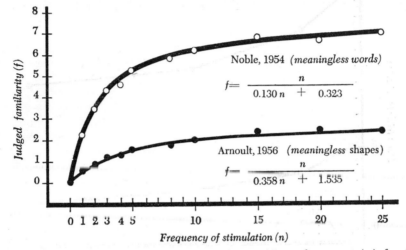

Fig. 4–7. Hyperbolic functions relating familiarity (f) to frequency (n) for two different classes of stimuli.

Schulz, 1960). A major deterrent to rapid advance in this area had been the lack of an operational criterion for specifying degrees of "acquaintance." But once the physical and psychological components of the premature Robinsonian law were experimentally isolated (Noble, 1954), one could hardly miss the probable inference (from studies relating l to m, m to f, and f to n) that proficiency in serial and paired-associate learning might also be dependent upon amount of familiarization; i.e., $l = \phi(n)$.

Employing dissyllabic material of low m and f value in a six-item serial learning task, significant facilitation was indeed found (Noble, 1955b). Furthermore, it increased in amount as n was varied between the values of 0 and 20 exposure articulations. Figure 4–8 presents a re-

[5] There is no reason to expect the parameters common to equations 2, 3, and 4 to be interchangeable.

analysis of trials-to-criterion data from that experiment. Difficulty in *serial* learning is thus a decreasing, negatively accelerated function of n. Whether n is a learning or a performance variable is not strictly determinable from the experiments done up to now, although my guess is that n like m (Noble, 1961b) is a performance factor which will not produce differential transfer effects. It is, of course, a learning or habit factor in the limited context of the strictly familiarization experiments (e.g., Figure 4–7).

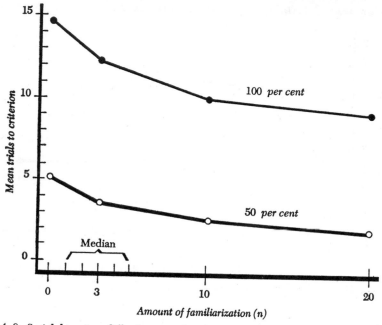

Fig. 4–8. Serial learning difficulty as a function of frequency (n) for two levels of mastery.

The *paired-associate* learning task, while more analytical, has opened a veritable Pandora's box of complexities. Winzen (1921), one of Müller's students, reported forty years ago that 20 prelearning exposures to pronounceable syllables which were then placed in either the S or the R position facilitated performance in an S_{20}-R_0 condition but not in an S_0-R_{20} condition. A dozen other experiments reviewed elsewhere by Underwood and Schulz (1960) and by Gannon and Noble (1961) have gotten conflicting results, but anyone who examines their manifold differences will not be surprised. As Gannon and I concluded recently:

The use of confounded and incomplete designs, unrelated or inadequate control procedures, Ss of heterogeneous experience, diverse types or amounts of familiarization, different learning materials, and varied methods of testing for transfer renders impossible any comparative evaluation of the present findings in the same context with the above studies. About all that can be done from a constructive point of view is to urge that the reader be cautious in trying to resolve these conflicting reports, and to judge each set of experimental data in the light of its own methodology (Gannon and Noble, 1961, p. 20).

Our own experiment—which adhered to the procedural standards of the present series (e.g., double articulation and use of dissyllables)— employed 120 subjects in a five-group constant-trials design. Four combinations of amount (0 versus 20 exposures) and locus (S versus R) of n were included plus an unfamiliarized control group. Winzen's data were definitely confirmed and the following new observations made: (1) Relevant S-term familiarization led to higher proficiency than R-term familiarization; (2) there was an early increase in error scores after irrelevant S-term familiarization; (3) rates of acquisition of corrects and elimination of errors were essentially parallel following the first reinforcement, leaving no interaction between S or R and practice; (4) relevant R-term familiarization had no influence as compared with the controls; and (5) there was no sign of a nonspecific (learning-to-learn) familiarization effect. The obvious conclusion—referring to stimulus-frequency hypotheses suggested by the Cieutat-Stockwell-Noble (1958) and Underwood-Schulz (1960) studies—is that operations giving rise to variations in m and n have different behavioral results. These concepts may not therefore be considered identical.

When I mentioned this experiment at the 1959 ONR-NYU conference (Noble, 1961a), there were several raised eyebrows along the Northwestern-Berkeley front (due perhaps to advance information on experiments I and IV of the Underwood-Schulz book), but Dr. James J. Jenkins kindly offered to have the Gannon-Noble study replicated in the Minnesota laboratory. This project has since been completed by his colleague, Dr. David T. Hakes (1961), with confirmatory results. Using four groups of 20 subjects each (omitting the control condition) but retaining the same method and materials, Hakes got borderline S-term facilitation ($F = 3.77$; $df = \frac{1}{76}$) and a significant practice effect ($F = 92.06$; $df = \frac{15}{1140}$; $P < .001$) but no other main effects or interactions. By pooling the $R+$ scores of his S_{20} groups ($797 + 721$) and S_0 groups ($683 + 584$) over the 17 trials, I calculate mean $R+$ totals of 37.95 and 31.68, respectively. Interpreting Hakes's obtained F ratio now as a t of 1.94, the probability is less than .03 that the directional outcome $S_{20} > S_0$ is due to chance (single-tailed hypothesis). But what of the other experiments which, granting that they employed different procedures, gave either null or opposite results? At least two factors seem to be critical: (1) whether the S term is articulated or not, and (2) whether the stimulus material consists of pronounceable dissyllables or CVCs. Let us take up the problems of pronunciation and stimulus material in that order.

Pronunciation. Dr. Rudolph W. Schulz (personal communication) is conducting an extension of the Gannon-Noble (1961) experiment with Mr. Irving F. Tucker in the Iowa laboratory, which promises to clarify the first factor. The Schulz-Tucker study replicates our S_0 and S_{20} familiarization conditions, but adds an S_{60} condition together with three other analogous groups of subjects who are not required to pronounce the S terms. Preliminary results on 6 groups of 24 cases each are shown in Table 4–1. The interaction between amount of familiarization and S-

Table 4–1

Mean Total Correct Responses during Trials 2–17 in the Schulz-Tucker Experiment

Instructions about S term	Amount of S-term familiarization (n)		
	0	20	60
Pronounce	31.04	36.21	37.21
Do not pronounce	39.25	35.42	30.62

term instructions is significant ($F = 3.78$; $df = 2/138$; $P < .05$). It is apparent that the *decremental* (satiation?) effects of stimulus familiarization reported by Underwood and Schulz (1960) are associated with the nonpronunciation method whereas the *facilitative* (predifferentiation?) effects reported by Gannon and Noble (1961) and by Hakes (1961) are linked with the two-term articulation method. Schulz believes that the latter phenomenon is due to a longer S-R (anticipation) interval, but only a specifically designed distributed practice experiment would settle the question of n interacting with the duration of the S-R interval.[6] No

[6] A few months after this second ONR-NYU conference, Schulz and Tucker (1961) reported the above experiment (experiment I) together with a sequel (experiment II), in which the two-second anticipation interval for each of the five pairs was increased to four seconds in a 2 by 2 design replicating the first and third columns of Table 4–1. Mean $R+$ totals for $n = 0$ versus 60 were 47.30 versus 49.77 for the pronunciation condition and 53.33 versus 54.60 for the nonpronunciation condition. None of the F ratios was significant, leading Schulz and Tucker to suggest that "the effective length of the anticipation interval may covary with number of familiarization trials" (p. 7) and that "stimulus familiarity, per se, (i.e., when the effective length of the anticipation interval is equated) does not influence the associative process in the learning of verbal paired associates" (p. 9). Although this new hypothesis runs counter to the Gannon-Noble and Hakes conclusions, I am not convinced that the Schulz-Tucker data (experiment II) are free of confounding factors. Not

convincing explanation is available yet for the decremental influence of nonpronunciation. Recall scores, as we shall see, are not affected this way.

Material. There is a study in progress[7] in the Montana laboratory bearing on the second factor mentioned above. We have run 60 subjects under eight conditions to date. All were first given articulation-familiarization training (spelling) on seven CVCs of low-scaled meaningfulness ($m' = 1.52$) from our current norms (Noble, 1961c) for either 1, 2, 4, 8, 16, 32, or 64 exposures (n). The average n is about 18, which will be a convenient number to cite. Second, a free-recall test evaluated their ability to reproduce (print) the CVCs experienced during the first phase. Instructions were carefully worded to avoid biasing any ordered emission behavior. Finally, the subjects received 50 trials of paired-associate learning in which the seven familiarized items occurred either as S terms or as R terms, joined by two other new pairs ($n = 0$) for matching purposes (no F ratios were significant). Both S and R were articulated according to standard operating procedure in this laboratory. Half the subjects received the S_{18}-R_0 condition, while the other half received the S_0-R_{18} condition. There were also two different sets of CVCs and two distributional modes of presentation, but we may limit the present discussion to the over-all results shown in Figure 4–9. Group S_0-R_{18} is slightly superior to Group S_{18}-R_0 ($t = 1.54$; $df = 38$; $P < .10$), but their average (pooled) performance is significantly superior to the S_0-R_0 control conditions ($t = 2.83$; $df = 39$; $P < .001$). The first result (a between-groups double-tailed test) is consistent with some of the Undor-

---

only did they lengthen the interstimulus interval by two seconds, but they also increased the intertrial interval by two seconds—a total of 12 seconds extra per trial in experiment II. What do we usually find with distributed practice? Higher proficiency. Examination of the two Schulz-Tucker studies reveals exactly that. What is needed is an uncontaminated test of the anticipation interval hypothesis. Perhaps special shutter or illumination techniques will have to be developed in order to break the natural tendency for longer stimulus durations to be correlated with more spaced responding when today's primitive memory drums are employed. In the meantime, a better design would be simply to alternate blanks between S_1 and R_1, S_2 and R_2, etc., for the *long* anticipation interval versus inserting blanks between R_1 and S_2, R_2 and S_3, etc., for the *short* interval. At least this procedure would equate stimulus durations, interstimulus, and intertrial periods, although the postfeedback or R-S intervals would vary. One final remark: While I cannot discount the possibility of an intrinsic interaction between amount of familiarization (n) and temporal factors (t), this has yet to be unambiguously demonstrated. Even so, it would not necessarily invalidate the relevancy of n as a performance variable; n and t may turn out to be joint determiners of the phenomenon all of us are trying to understand.

[7] Assisting in this experiment are Blaine L. Baker, Charles H. Koski, and Richard K. Smith, under contract with the Office of Naval Research.

wood-Schulz (1960) experiments, and if replicable, will illuminate another puzzling difference between the findings of the Northwestern and Montana laboratories. The second result (a within-groups single-tailed test) indicates that *some* CVC familiarization, either of S or R, is facilitative as compared with *none* when using our methods. I believe this experiment, when fully executed, will provide us with a more adequate picture of the major variables and their interrelationships.

Recall. While we are on the subject of frequency-learning research, it might be timely to report that our recall data agree completely with

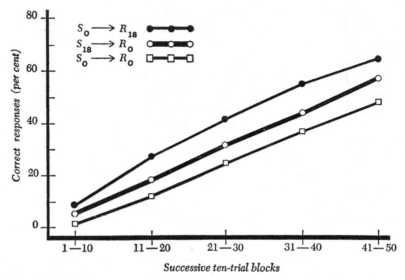

FIG. 4–9. Paired-associate learning proficiency as a function of amount of practice for three different conditions of CVC familiarization (n).

the Underwood-Schulz ("spew") hypothesis (1960, chap. 6) that the order of emission of verbal responses is determined by past frequency of experience (n). This statement does not imply, however, that their two-stage analysis of the verbal learning process is completely acceptable. In their experiment I (Schulz's dissertation), 2 per cent of the first three CVCs the subjects gave during free recall had an n value of 1, 22 per cent had $n = 10$, 33 per cent had $n = 20$, and 43 per cent had $n = 40$. Our current data are quite similar, generating a rank-difference coefficient (rho) for 40 cases of .94 between the percentage measure and n for a comparable analysis of order effects. From an experimental point of view, there is no reason to doubt this dependency of emission order on familiarization. Indeed I would like to christen it the "Underwood-Schulz law." We also measured per cent correct free recall as a function of n for 60 cases. This rho was 1.00, yielding a function curving upward in a positive, negatively accelerated manner like Schulz's data. The two curves are shown in Figure 4–10. Similar findings have been reported by Bush and Mosteller (1955) and Waugh (1962).

Printed vs. Emitted Frequency. Referring to the earlier section on meaningfulness (p. 91, Figure 4–4), we noted that $w = \phi(m')$. This type of analysis is related to those performed by Underwood and Schulz by which they hoped to translate the m and m' variables into frequency values based on monogram (single-letter), bigram (double-letter), and

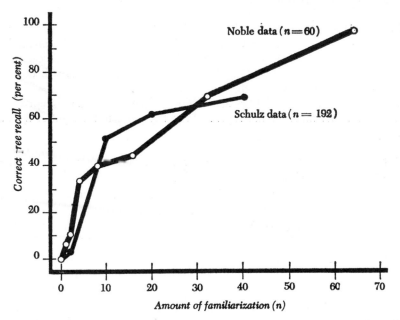

Fig. 4–10. Accuracy of free recall as a function of frequency (n) in two independent experiments.

trigram (triple-letter) counts. Their conclusion was that monogram frequency of use predicted well but that bigram and trigram counts failed. A few comments are appropriate here on the relevance of their conclusion that "printed frequency of letter sequences is not related to speed of learning" (p. 284), and is therefore not "a good predictor of degree of initial integration of a multi-letter unit" (p. 289). To begin with, our serial and paired-associate experiments (Noble, 1955b; Gannon and Noble, 1961) suggest only that n facilitates *performance;* we have no evidence on direct *habit-strength* effects. This may be splitting hairs at the present state of knowledge, but I think the point is worth mentioning in view of so many recent statements in the literature about "speed" and "rate" of *learning* or *association* being dependent on m and n. At any rate, because of what they judged to be a breakdown of the frequency theory, Underwood and Schulz suggested obtaining data on *emitted* frequency.

I have done just this in order to compare subjects' written CVC sequences with the frequency-of-use counts of Underwood and others. I recruited a total of 219 naïve subjects from our introductory psychology population and had them simply write down any consonant, then any vowel, then another (different) consonant on 3- by 5-inch cards. The instructions were as follows:

Think of the letters of the alphabet. Now think of the consonants only—that is, all letters except the vowels (A, E, I, O, U). Any consonant letter will do. Write it down on the card. Do not look at your neighbor's card.

Next, think of the vowel letters (U, O, I, E, A). Any vowel will do. Write this letter down to the right of the other one.

Think of the consonant letters again. Any consonant will do, except the one you gave the first time. Do not repeat. Write this letter to the right of the other two.

After 19 cases were eliminated at random to give a convenient sample size of 200, the relative frequencies presented in Table 4–2 resulted. The r between the monogram U count (Underwood and Schulz, 1960, p. 69) and the 21 consonants of column C_1 in Table 4–2 is .01, which is not significant, but the V and C_2 columns correlate .80 and .60, respectively, with U. Responses to C_2 (given C_1 and V) correlate only .24 with the U count for 120 selected CVCs, whereas my own C_1 and C_2 columns have an r of .28. To answer the inevitable question whether the C_1 values are occurring at chance frequencies (9.52 out of 200 for each consonant), I performed a chi-square test; for $df = 20$, the obtained value of 232.51 is significant ($P < .001$). Apparently, then, college subjects emit their first consonants in a very systematic way, but one which is statistically independent of printed text frequencies.

This was what I had expected. My next step was to compare the relationships between m' and emitted CVC sums on the one hand and printed U-count sums on the other. This pair of curves is shown in Figure 4–11, where the m' values have been grouped for clarity into nine class intervals. Considering the low correlations mentioned above, the agreement between the two curves is surprisingly close; the product-moment correlations are .960 and .958 for mean m' values versus the mean CVC and U counts, respectively. Perhaps Underwood and Schulz will wish to revise their pessimistic verdict on generated frequency values as predictors of meaningfulness. These results should be compared later with trigram counts and with other monogram-combination rules.

Predicting Learning Scores. A horse of a different color is the prediction of proficiency in learning experiments. Underwood and Schulz (1960) report in chapter 10 that their pronounceability (p) ratings of paired-associate R terms are more highly correlated with learning scores (l) than are m or m' scores. For 21 trigrams, with the p factor held constant by a partial correlation technique, they reduce the $l = \phi(m)$

Table 4–2

Relative Frequency of Emitted Letters
($N = 200$)

Letter	C_1	V	C_2
A		.290	
B	.240		.070
C	.120		.035
D	.045		.070
E		.245	
F	.040		.065
G	.045		.025
H	.035		.030
I		.185	
J	.045		.015
K	.050		.035
L	.055		.085
M	.080		.060
N	.005		.050
O		.175	
P	.030		.045
Q	.020		.000
R	.050		.060
S	.045		.070
T	.050		.120
U		.105	
V	.000		.005
W	.015		.045
X	.005		.050
Y	.015		.005
Z	.010		.060
Σ	1.000	1.000	1.000

correlation from .84 to .04. As noted above (p. 86), however, the $\bar{m}$ values collected by Underwood at Berkeley on CVCs correlate only .71 with our new Montana m' norms (Noble, 1961c). Employing their own learning and pronounceability scores but our m' values for the 10 CVCs presented in their table 52 (Underwood and Schulz, 1960, p. 267), I find the following r's: .96 between l and m', .74 between l and p, and .61 between m' and p. If p is partialed out, the $l = \phi(m')$ correlation of .96 is unaffected. On the other hand, if m' is held constant, the $l = \phi(p)$ correlation drops to .68. For these limited data, then, and for what such a demonstration may be worth in view of the nonlinearity revealed in Figure 4–3 above, it appears that rated pronounceability has no effect on the law relating paired-associate proficiency to the rated meaningfulness of the R terms. Meaningfulness, in other words, is still the best predictor of CVC learning scores we have except when CVCs of low m' value are available with known frequency histories.

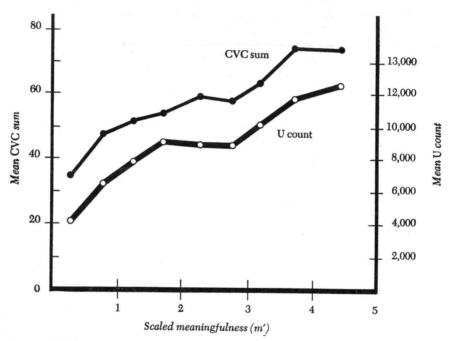

Fig. 4–11. Emitted vs. printed CVC letter counts as a function of scaled meaningfulness (m').

Defining trigram frequency in terms of the occurrences of speech sounds (syllables) instead of mere letter contiguities, as Underwood and Schulz prefer, Johnson (1962) has reported pronounceability to be less important to learning than either frequency or the number of words subjects produce which contain these syllables. By the way, some verbal learning experiments have been erroneously interpreted as showing that f is a more powerful variable than a or m'. Lindley's (1960) data appear to constitute such a case, but if learning scores (l) from his table 2 (p. 368) are plotted against modern a or m' values (Archer, 1960; Noble, 1961c) instead of Glaze or Krueger values, a perfect monotonic relationship is found between l and either a or m'. A similar reevaluation was reported by Archer (1961) for his scale. Analysis of variance tests on the m' values for the critical groups (1 vs. 2, 2 vs. 3) in Lindley's experiment yields significant differences $(t > 2.78;\ df \geqq 25;\ P < .01)$. His results, therefore, are just as easily attributed to variations in meaningfulness or association value as to familiarity.

As a closing commentary on the role of familiarization in experimental attempts to increase the predictability of verbal learning performance, I would like to recall a suggestion I made at our first ONR-NYU conference (Noble, 1961d). On the hypothesis that verbal learning of CVCs can be considered an instance of selective learning in general, I proposed that familiarization operations be employed "to build in a repertoire of equiprobable yet independent response tendencies" to find out whether the "memory drum task would then constitute a verbal analogue of the nonverbal selective learning situation" (1961d, p. 135). The primary objective of such pretraining was to produce determinate probabilities of reaction at the beginning of learning, thereby permitting an unequivocal test of the general acquisition formula

$$R_p = a(i)^{r^N} \tag{5}$$

where R_p is probability of a correct response, a is asymptotic level of performance, i is initial probability, r is rate of acquisition, and N is number of practice trials.[8]

Mr. Gordon F. Gerrish (1961) has just completed a master's thesis in the Montana laboratory which supports this hypothesis. He familiarized 160 subjects by our standard exposure-articulation method with eight CVCs (mean $m' = 2.4$) until free recall was perfect. Their average "guessing" probability on trial 0, therefore, had a theoretical[9] initial R_p value of $\frac{1}{8} = .125 = i$. If pretraining with n had not been administered, as one could deduce from Figure 4–10, the i parameter would have been indeterminate, thus failing to satisfy the boundary conditions of equation 5. After guessing the eight-item order on trial 0, all subjects were given 50 practice trials on a random permutation of the same list by the serial-anticipation procedure at a three-second rate. When R_p scores were plotted as a function of N for five homogeneous ability groups of 10 cases each (stratification based on total $R+$ scores), the family of curves shown in Figure 4–12 resulted. The equation

$$R_p = 1.00(.125)^{r^N}$$

---

[8] The symbols a, i, r, N have special meanings here which differ from previous usages in this chapter.

[9] The mean empirical R_p value was .119, which is not significantly different from .125 $(z = .059)$.

agreed closely with the data, yielding goodness-of-fit indices ranging from 97.4 per cent to 99.0 per cent. Analysis of variance tests
revealed significant effects of practice, ability, and their interaction
($P < .001$).

Overview

In addition to furthering the theoretical coordination of verbal and
nonverbal selective learning phenomena, Gerrish's investigation nicely
illustrates the practical uses to which familiarization may be put in the
functional analysis of human behavior. More important, perhaps, is the

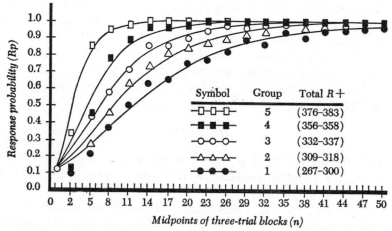

FIG. 4–12. Serial learning proficiency (R_p) as functions of amount of practice (N)
for five ability groups. The general equation is rational.

growing inductive conviction that parameters like initial proficiency,
rate of change, and asymptotic level are complex resultants of the *interaction* of practice, individual differences, and the nature of the stimulus
material (Noble, 1961d). Research workers must realize, therefore,
that organismic (human-factor) variables together with stimulus and
response variables are joint determinants of action—that the muting of
any one will produce incomplete laws and attenuate our efforts to
fully understand man as a verbal animal responding to stimuli.

Thus we come full circle back to meaningfulness, with increased
understanding of its intimate relationship to familiarity. Frequency, beyond reasonable doubt, is a necessary yet insufficient condition to the
development of meaningfulness. Acting alone—without multiple associations—it produces only familiarity. Notwithstanding the old saw that
familiarity may breed contempt, we can agree that f has certainly
generated a lot of research on verbal learning and verbal behavior. The

same is true of *m*. Considered from the logico-empirical viewpoint as operationally defined concepts, it is my judgment that *m* and *f* survive analysis with adequate rationale, high reliability, and widespread validity.

SUMMARY

In this chapter I have reexamined some of the conceptual properties of meaningfulness (*m*) and familiarity (*f*) from a logical as well as an empirical point of view. Analyses of the rationale, reliability, and validity of *m* and *f* indicate that they are sound, stable, and significant concepts. As dependent or response-defined variables, familiarity is generated by frequency alone while meaningfulness is produced by frequency plus multiple associations. This hypothesis explains why the meaningful is always familiar but the familiar is not always meaningful. Both factors have powerful effects on verbal behavior, the manipulable or causal operations apparently producing nontransferable performance changes in man which are specific to the material being learned.

REFERENCES

Allport, F. H. (1955) *Theories of perception and the concept of structure.* New York: Wiley.

Anonymous (1959) Christmas is many things. *Amer. Home*, 62, 15–27.

Archer, E. J. (1960) A re-evaluation of the meaningfulness of all possible CVC trigrams. *Psychol. Monogr.*, 74, No. 10 (Whole No. 497).

Archer, E. J. (1961) Supplementary report: Familiarity or low validity? *J. Exp. Psychol.*, 62, 207–208.

Arnoult, M. D. (1956) Familiarity and recognition of nonsense shapes. *J. Exp. Psychol.*, 51, 269–276.

Bechtoldt, H. P. (1959) Construct validity: A critique. *Amer. Psychologist*, 14, 619–629.

Bergmann, G. (1957) *Philosophy of science.* Madison, Wis.: University of Wisconsin Press.

Boring, E. G. (1938) Titchener on meaning. *Psychol. Rev.*, 45, 92–95.

Bousfield, W. A. (1961) The problem of meaning in verbal learning. In C. N. Cofer (Ed.), *Verbal learning and verbal behavior.* New York: McGraw-Hill. Pp. 81–91.

Braun, H. W., & Heymann, S. P. (1958) Meaningfulness of material, distribution of practice, and serial-position curves. *J. Exp. Psychol.*, 56, 146–150.

Brown, R. W. (1958) Is a boulder sweet or sour? *Contemp. Psychol.*, 3, 113–115.

Bugelski, B. R. (1960) *An introduction to the principles of psychology.* New York: Holt, Rinehart & Winston.

Bush, R. R., & Mosteller, F. (1955) *Stochastic models for learning.* New York: Wiley.

Buxton, C. E. (1943) The status of research in reminiscence. *Psychol. Bull.*, **40**, 313–340.

Carr, H. A. (1925) *Psychology*. New York: Longmans.

Carroll, J. B. (1959) Review of Osgood *et al.*, *The measurement of meaning*. *Language*, **35**, 58–77.

Cieutat, V. J. (1959) Supplementary report: Stimulus and response meaningfulness (m') in paired-associate learning by hospitalized mental patients. *J. Exp. Psychol.*, **58**, 490.

Cieutat, V. J., Stockwell, F. E., & Noble, C. E. (1958) The interaction of ability and amount of practice with stimulus and response meaningfulness (m, m') in paired-associate learning. *J. Exp. Psychol.*, **56**, 193–202.

Cofer, C. N. (1958) Comparison of word associations obtained by the methods of discrete single word and continued association. *Psychol. Rep.*, **4**, 507–510.

Deese, J. (1958) *The psychology of learning*. (2nd ed.) New York: McGraw-Hill.

DiMascio, A. (1959) Learning characteristics of nonsense syllables: A function of letter frequency. *Psychol. Rep.*, **5**, 585–591.

Dowling, R. M., & Braun, H. W. (1957) Retention and meaningfulness of material. *J. Exp. Psychol.*, **54**, 213–217.

Ebbinghaus, H. (1885) *Über das Gedächtnis*. Leipzig: Duncker & Humblot. (1913) H. Ruger & C. Bussenius (Trans.) New York: Teachers College.

English, H. B., & English, A. C. (1958) *A comprehensive dictionary of psychological and psychoanalytical terms*. New York: Longmans.

Evans, B., & Evans, C. (1957) *A dictionary of contemporary American usage*. New York: Random House.

Furst, B. (1949) *Stop forgetting*. New York: Greenberg.

Gannon, D. R., & Noble, C. E. (1961) Familiarization (n) as a stimulus factor in paired-associate verbal learning. *J. Exp. Psychol.*, **62**, 14–23.

Gerrish, G. F. (1961) Serial verbal learning as a joint function of amount of practice and individual differences. Unpublished M.A. thesis, Montana State University.

Gibson, E. J. (1942) A systematic application of the concepts of generalization and differentiation to verbal learning. *Psychol. Rev.*, **47**, 196–229.

Glaze, J. A. (1928) The association value of non-sense syllables. *J. Genet. Psychol.*, **35**, 255–267.

Hakes, D. T. (1961) Familiarization (n) as a stimulus factor in paired associate verbal learning. Paper reported to Midwest. Psychol. Ass., Chicago.

Hull, C. L. (1933) The meaningfulness of 320 selected nonsense syllables. *Amer. J. Psychol.*, **45**, 730–734.

Hull, C. L., Hovland, C. I., Ross, R. T., Hall, M., Perkins, D. T., & Fitch, F. B. (1940) *Mathematico-deductive theory of rote learning*. New Haven, Conn.: Yale University Press.

Hunt, R. G. (1959) Meaningfulness and articulation of stimulus and response in paired-associate learning and stimulus recall. *J. Exp. Psychol.*, **57**, 262–267.

James, W. (1890) *Principles of psychology.* New York: Holt, Rinehart & Winston.

Jenkins, J. J., & Russell, W. A. (1956) Basic studies on individual and group behavior. *Annu. Tech. Rep.,* Contract No. N8onr-66216, Office of Naval Research and University of Minnesota.

Johnson, R. C. (1962) Reanalysis of *Meaningfulness and verbal learning. Psychol. Rev.,* **69**, 233-238.

Katona, G. (1940) *Organizing and memorizing.* New York: Columbia University Press.

Koffka, K. (1935) *Principles of Gestalt psychology.* New York: Harcourt, Brace.

Lindley, R. H. (1960) Association value and familiarity in serial verbal learning. *J. exp. Psychol.,* **59**, 366-370.

McGeoch, J. A. (1942) *The psychology of human learning.* New York: Longmans.

McGeoch, J. A., & Irion, A. L. (1952) *The psychology of human learning.* (2nd ed.) New York: Longmans.

Mandler, G. (1955) Associative frequency and associative prepotency as measures of response to nonsense syllables. *Amer. J. Psychol.,* **68**, 662–665.

Mandler, C., & Huttenlocher, J. (1956) The relationship between associative frequency, associative ability, and paired-associate learning. *Amer. J. Psychol.,* **69**, 424–428.

Melton, A. W. (1929) A comparative study of the materials employed in experimental investigations of memory. Unpublished M.A. thesis, Yale University.

Melton, A. W. (1936) The methodology of experimental studies of human learning and retention. *Psychol. Bull.,* **33**, 305–394.

Miller, G. A., & Selfridge, J. (1950) Verbal context and the recall of meaningful material. *Amer. J. Psychol.,* **63**, 176–185.

Müller, G. E., & Pilzecker, A. (1900) Experimentelle Beiträge zur Lehre vom Gedächtnis. *Z. Psychol.,* Ergbd. 1.

Noble, C. E. (1950) Absence of reminiscence in the serial rote learning of adjectives. *J. Exp. Psychol.,* **40**, 622–631.

Noble, C. E. (1952a) An analysis of meaning. *Psychol. Rev.,* **59**, 421–430.

Noble, C. E. (1952b) The role of stimulus meaning (m) in serial verbal learning. *J. Exp. Psychol.,* **43**, 437–446; **44**, 465.

Noble, C. E. (1953) The meaning-familiarity relationship. *Psychol. Rev.,* **60**, 89–98.

Noble, C. E. (1954) The familiarity-frequency relationship. *J. Exp. Psychol.,* **47**, 13–16.

Noble, C. E. (1955a) Scale reliability and the Spearman-Brown equation. *Educ. Psychol. Measmt,* **15**, 195–205.

Noble, C. E. (1955b) The effect of familiarization upon serial verbal learning. *J. Exp. Psychol.,* **49**, 333–338.

Noble, C. E. (1957) Psychology and the logic of similarity. *J. Gen. Psychol.,* **57**, 23–43.

Noble, C. E. (1958) Emotionality (e) and meaningfulness (m). *Psychol. Rep.*, **4**, 16.

Noble, C. E. (1960) Supplementary report: Familiarity and frequency. *J. Exp. Psychol.*, **59**, 432–433; **60**, 418.

Noble, C. E. (1961a) Comments on Professor Underwood's paper. In C. N. Cofer (Ed.), *Verbal learning and verbal behavior*. New York: McGraw-Hill. Pp. 217–223.

Noble, C. E. (1961b) Meaningfulness (m) and transfer phenomena in serial verbal learning. *J. Psychol.*, **52**, 201–210.

Noble, C. E. (1961c) Measurements of association value (a), rated associations (a'), and scaled meaningfulness (m') for the 2100 CVC combinations of the English alphabet. *Psychol. Rep.*, **8**, 487–521 (Monogr. Suppl. 3-V8).

Noble, C. E. (1961d) Verbal learning and individual differences. In C. N. Cofer (Ed.), *Verbal learning and verbal behavior*. New York: McGraw-Hill. Pp. 132–146.

Noble, C. E. (1962) Reply to comments on the measurement of CVC trigrams. *Psychol. Rep.*, **10**, 547–550.

Noble, C. E., & McNeely, D. A. (1957) The role of meaningfulness (m) in paired-associate verbal learning. *J. Exp. Psychol.*, **53**, 16–22.

Noble, C. E., & Parker, G. V. C. (1960) The Montana scale of meaningfulness (m). *Psychol. Rep.*, **7**, 325–331.

Noble, C. E., Stockwell, F. E., & Pryer, M. W. (1957) Meaningfulness (m') and association value (a) in paired-associate syllable learning. *Psychol. Rep.*, **3**, 441–452.

Ogden, C. K., & Richards, I. A. (1923) *The meaning of meaning*. London: Kegan Paul.

Osgood, C. E. (1952) The nature and measurement of meaning. *Psychol. Bull.*, **49**, 197–237.

Osgood, C. E. (1953) *Method and theory in experimental psychology*. New York: Oxford.

Osgood, C. E. (1961) Comments on Professor Bousfield's paper. In C. N. Cofer (Ed.), *Verbal learning and verbal behavior*. New York: McGraw-Hill. Pp. 91–106.

Osgood, C. E., Suci, G. J., & Tannenbaum, P. H. (1957) *The measurement of meaning*. Urbana, Ill.: University of Illinois Press.

Parker, G. V. C., & Noble, C. E. (1960) Effects of experimentally-produced meaningfulness (m) on paired-associate learning. *Amer. Psychologist*, **15**, 451. (Abstract)

Parker, G. V. C., & Nobel, C. E. (1963) Experimentally-produced meaningfulness (m) in paired-associate learning. *Amer. J. Psychol.*, in press.

Riley, D. A., & Phillips, L. W. (1959) The effects of syllable familiarization on rote learning, association value, and reminiscence. *J. Exp. Psychol.*, **57**, 372–379.

Robinson, E. S. (1932) *Association theory today: An essay in systematic psychology*. New York: Century.

Rocklyn, E. H., Hessert, R. B., & Braun, H. W. (1957) Calibrated materials for verbal learning with middle- and old-aged subjects. *Amer. J. Psychol.*, **70**, 628–630.

Saporta, S. (1959) Review of Osgood *et al., The measurement of meaning. Amer. Anthropologist,* **61**, 159–160.

Schulz, R. W., & Tucker, I. F. (1961) Stimulus familiarization in paired-associate learning. Paper reported to Psychonomic Soc., New York.

Staats, A. W., & Staats, C. K. (1959) Meaning and *m*: Correlated but separate. *Psychol. Rev.,* **66**, 136–144.

Staats, A. W., Staats, C. K., Finley, J. R., & Heard, W. G. (1961) Independent manipulation of meaning and *m. Tech. Rep. No. 15,* Contract No. Nonr-2794(02), Office of Naval Research and Arizona State University.

Titchener, E. B. (1909) *Lectures on the experimental psychology of the thought processes.* New York: Macmillan.

Titchener, E. B. (1915) *A beginner's psychology.* New York: Macmillan.

Thorndike, E. L., *et al.* (1932) *The fundamentals of learning.* New York: Teachers College.

Thorndike, E. L., & Lorge, I. (1944) *The teacher's word book of 30,000 words.* New York: Bureau of Publications, Teachers Coll., Columbia University.

Underwood, B. J. (1949) *Experimental psychology.* New York: Appleton-Century-Crofts.

Underwood, B. J., & Schulz, R. W. (1960) *Meaningfulness and verbal learning.* Chicago: Lippincott.

Warren, H. C. (1934) *Dictionary of psychology.* New York: Houghton-Mifflin.

Watson, J. B. (1924) *Psychology from the standpoint of a behaviorist.* (2nd ed.) Philadelphia: Lippincott.

Watson, J. B. (1925) *Behaviorism.* New York: Norton.

Waugh, N. C. (1962) The effect of intralist repetition on free recall. *J. verbal Learn. verbal Behav.,* **1**, 95–99.

Weinreich, U. (1958) Travels through semantic space. *Word,* **14**, 346–366.

Winzen, K. (1921) Die Abhängigkeit der paarweisen Assoziation von der Stellung des besser haftenden Gliedes. *Z. Psychol.,* **86**, 236–252.

Woodworth, R. S., & Schlosberg, H. (1954) *Experimental psychology.* (Rev. ed.) New York: Holt, Rinehart & Winston.

COMMENTS ON PROFESSOR NOBLE'S PAPER

Albert E. Goss[1]

UNIVERSITY OF MASSACHUSETTS

For those interested in the role in verbal learning of association values and meaningfulness of discrete stimuli—more broadly, of their meaning-

[1] My indebtedness to various colleagues and students is expressed on pages 125–126. General support for this article and much of my recent research has been provided by the Personnel and Training Branch, Office of Naval Research, through Contract Nonr–2691(00) with the University of Massachusetts.

fulness with a capital M—the past 12 months have been exciting. First, Underwood and Schulz published their *Meaningfulness and Verbal Learning* (1960), whose merits Professor Noble has already recognized in the superlative; I wholly concur. Second, the recent quickening of normative and experimental work noted by Professor Noble has been, perhaps, even more obvious than before. Illustrative are Archer's (1960) and now Noble's (1961) revised and extended norms for CVC trigrams and Epstein, Rock, and Zuckerman's (1960) extensive, though for me puzzling, series of experiments. Third, Professor Noble has thoughtfully provided us with both an exposition of the historical and theoretical rationale for his work on meaningfulness—lowercase meaningfulness, m, to preserve his distinction—and a useful summary of the diverse relationships of m to other classes of variables for whose discovery he and his coworkers are so importantly responsible. Also, F. H. Allport's and Osgood's criticisms of Noble's conception of m were, I think, answered convincingly. In essence, Professor Noble has brought us to and even partly over the threshold of the next step in the theoretical and experimental analysis of the role of meaningfulness of discrete stimuli in human learning.

The next step is going beyond the intercorrelations involving m and other response-defined variables which Professor Noble has summarized to assimilation of data on m and its correlates within a framework of more general stimulus-response concepts and principles so that, using such concepts and principles, it is possible to deduce those intercorrelations, those additional relationships described by Underwood and Schulz, and those as-yet-uninvestigated relationships of concern in other and in future experiments. Both to return us to and initiate this next step is the general purpose of my discussion. I say "return" because I shall first describe a number of previous attempts to go beyond intercorrelations, one of which, that of Sheffield, is the most important antecedent of the analysis which I shall propose. This analysis has three parts. The first is a relatively detailed consideration of observed and inferred stimulus-response elements and relationships of those situations which are the source of most of the normative information about M and related attributes of discrete stimuli, namely, meaningfulness scaling and word-association situations. The concern of the second part is classes of antecedents to those elements and relationships, their properties, and their possible general consequences. The third part focuses on the role of those elements and relationships in verbal paired-associate and serial-anticipation learning. The focus is limited to these two learning situations because they are the only ones for which a reasonable amount of experimental data is available. Within these situations (also because of limited data) only acquisition is considered.

ANTECEDENTS, PARTICULARLY SHEFFIELD

Among the antecedents to current notions about the nature and consequences of meaning and meaningfulness, as Noble notes, are, remotely, the British associationists and, in the same mentalistic tradition, such more recent theorists as James and Titchener. As Professor Noble has noted, Watson was suspicious of the concept of meaning. But as I have shown elsewhere (1961, p. 289), Watson (1924, p. 355) did present an "objective analysis" of meaning which, except for the absence of $_sH_R$'s, was essentially the same as Noble's (1952a). And another early behaviorist, Dashiell (1928, p. 503), presented a stimulus-response, associationistic analysis of meaning. It is a simple step from these analyses of meaning to meaningfulness. Neither Watson nor Dashiell, however, regarded meaning—or would have regarded meaningfulness—as basic concepts or principles; meaning and meaningfulness, like many terms, were or would have been considered only labels—convenient but dispensable in a systematic sense—for certain stimulus-response relationships. Watson's and Dashiell's suggestions, however, contained at most only hints as to the "mechanisms" or, better, of the general concepts and principles involved in effects of meaning and meaningfulness on phenomena of human learning. And in these and other analyses often only one of at least three broad classes of mechanisms has been proposed. These are (a) stimulus pre-differentiation or, more narrowly, response-mediated dissimilarity or distinctiveness; (b) response patterning and availability; and (c) indirect mediation by perceptual or verbal responses.

The first of these classes of mechanisms, stimulus pre-differentiation, has been stressed, for example, by Gibson (1940, pp. 223–225). The greater the meaningfulness of stimuli, the greater their differentiation and, therefore, the more rapid the acquisition of tasks requiring discriminative responses. Unfortunately, Gibson was unclear regarding the bases of such differentiation in general and of meaningfulness in particular, with consequent obscurity as to what to observe and what to manipulate. Hovland and Kurtz (1952) recognized the possible relevance of this mechanism as a basis for the direct relationship between ease of serial-anticipation learning and syllable familiarization.

A variant of stimulus differentiation is stability of stimuli produced by responses to stimuli of the task. Thus, to explain the direct relationship between rate of acquisition of serial anticipations and amount of prior familiarization with the task stimuli, Noble (1955) hypothesized:

Prior practice in verbalization might also serve to attenuate response variability during the initial presentation of the list. Let us postulate with Hull (1943) that verbal responses produce characteristic internal cues (s). In the anticipation learning situation, such cues may interact with the stimulus traces left by the intralist items to form compound conditioned stimuli ($\check{s}$). Assume further that the proprioceptive components of these stimulus patterns grow increasingly stable with training in pronounciation, but at a decreasing rate. Now, from Hull's postulate of the generalization of habit strength ($_sH_r$), it follows that the effective habit strengths ($_s\bar{H}_r$) during the learning phase will be maximally controlled by those stimulus compounds having the least variability, and minimally conversely. Expressed in more simple terms, strength of conditioning is dependent upon stimulus constancy. From the foregoing, it can be deduced that initial proficiency in the present task should be a positive curvilinear function of n. One could also invoke this principle to explain the writer's (1952b) demonstration of the facilitative role of meaning (m) in serial verbal learning. The fundamental fact seems to be that words of higher m value are more uniformly pronounced. It also happens that the difficulty-meaning relationship, to a first approximation, is a decreasing curvilinear function (p. 336).

Underwood and Schulz (1960, pp. 293–295) considered but, for various reasons, rejected essentially the same interpretation of the mechanism underlying M of stimulus members. They called this interpretation stimulus integration.

Some theorists have emphasized response patterning and availability. For example, dividing paired-associate learning into two stages, the response-learning stage and the associative stage, Underwood and Schulz concluded that "M (defined as number of associates elicited or number of subjects getting an association within a limited period of time) was not a relevant attribute for the response-learning phase of verbal units" (p. 284). Instead, "the easier the unit is to pronounce and the higher the generated values, the greater is the degree of initial integration of the letters, hence, the less the proportion of the formal learning process which must be devoted to integration of the letters" (p. 290). In turn, pronounceability and generated values are conceived as directly related to emitted spoken frequency; "spoken" subsumes both vocal and writing responses. Though less exclusively concerned with M, Mandler (1954) had earlier called attention to the role of response integration in diverse verbal learning phenomena. Response integration also involves learning that responses are in a list. Such increased response availability, as Hovland and Kurtz (1952) and Underwood and Schulz have suggested, may be another consequence of familiarization.

With respect to indirect mediation by perceptual or verbal responses, though Reed (1918a, 1918b, 1918c) was not explicitly concerned with the role of M as currently defined in paired-associate learning, his analysis of the role of "associative aids" in the formation, transfer, and retention of associations between stimulus and response members is a precursor of mediation accounts of the effectiveness of M. Pertinent as precursors also are theory and data on incdiate association revived by Peters (1935), related to semantic generalization by Cofer and Foley (1942), and developed further in the past several years by Jenkins, Russell and their students (e.g., Russell and Storms, 1955; Jenkins, 1959b), and by Cofer and his students (e.g., Cramer and Cofer, 1960). *M* is related to mediating associations in Underwood and Schulz's *associative probability* hypothesis for the associative stage of learning: "The greater the number of associates elicited by a stimulus, the greater is the probability that one of these will link up with another item" (p. 296).

Underwood and Schulz, of the theorists mentioned, recognized all three possible bases of the effects of *M*: stimulus differentiation or, more restrictedly, stimulus integration or, more narrowly still, integration of stimuli produced by responses to task stimuli; response patterning and availability; and mediating responses. Response patterning and availability, however, were their primary concern; the other mechanisms received relatively brief attention and only in the last chapter. Therefore, the most complete analysis of the role of *M* in verbal learning is still that outlined by Sheffield (1946) fifteen years ago. Morikawa has recently reaffirmed a capsule version of Sheffield's notions, and my associates and I have combined Sheffield's notions with those embodied in analyses of response-mediated dissimilarity and discrimination and of response-mediated similarity and generalization (Goss, Nodine, Gregory, Taub, and Kennedy, 1962; Levitt and Goss, 1961).

Sheffield's analysis began with five definitions, three of which are pertinent here:

The meaning of a stimulus pattern is defined as the complex of perceptual responses that is aroused by the stimulus pattern because of past learning. . . .

The intrinsic meaning of a stimulus pattern is the part of the meaning that is based on stimulations provided by the stimulus-object which is the source of the stimulus pattern. . . .

The extrinsic meaning of a stimulus pattern is defined as that part of the meaning that is not part of the intrinsic meaning (pp. 11–12).

Sheffield then proceeded to consider "factors in the learning of material with unrelated meaningful items"; response patterning, stimulus differentiation, and perceptual mediation of verbal responses (pp. 14–30).

Response patterning "refers to the coordination of successive response elements into a sequence that behaves as a single unit of response" (p. 15). Such patterning, it is presumed, increases the distinctiveness of response-produced stimulation at any point in a particular sequence, lessens interference due to response similarity and stimulus similarity, and reduces the number of connections which must be learned. Though considered a correlate of extrinsic meaning or essentially M, response patterning is regarded as definitionally independent of M; nor is it a consequence of M.

Greater differentiation of stimuli is presumably based on different intrinsic meanings, on different extrinsic meanings, and on orienting responses which expose more discriminable features of stimuli. Miller and Dollard's (1941) analysis of the role of response-produced cues in mediating associations, generalization and discrimination was the source of Sheffield's suggestion of the latter two sources of stimulus differentiation. Subsequently, Goss (1955) elaborated Miller and Dollard's (Dollard and Miller, 1950; Miller and Dollard, 1941) analyses of response-mediated similarity and generalization and, particularly, of response-mediated dissimilarity and discrimination. (It was planned, in a subsequent paper, to extend these mechanisms to an analysis of meaningfulness, familiarity, and rehearsal in verbal and motor learning. That paper never reached final form.)

Returning to Sheffield's analysis, he notes that differentiation based on extrinsic meanings might have contradictory implications for the relationship between acquisition rate and degree of extrinsic meaning of stimuli. One implication is that the greater the number of responses evoked by a stimulus, the greater the trial-to-trial variability of response-produced stimulation with consequent reduction in acquisition rate (p. 25). Sheffield then states an alternative and preferred implication: "The more specific and invariant the meaning of a word the more effective it would be as a stimulus for an associative connection" (p. 25). The intrinsic meaning of words, however, is regarded as providing potentially more constant acquired distinctiveness.

Sheffield assumes the formation of associations both between verbal stimuli and perceptual responses and between perceptual stimuli produced by those responses and verbal responses. Mediation of verbal responses is then treated as a consequence of four properties of the perceptual responses involved in the extrinsic meaning of stimuli. First, the stimuli produced by the perceptual responses are regarded as constituting a more sizable proportion of the "total stimulus field at any moment" than the visual stimulus. Assuming trial-to-trial constancy of those stimuli, their presence should facilitate acquisition. On the surface at least, this implication is contrary to that stemming from the possible direct relationship between extent of extrinsic meaning and trial-to-trial variability in response-produced stimulation. Second, Sheffield suggests that perceptual responses may produce stimuli more distinctive than the verbal stimuli which evoke them: This seems essentially a restatement of the notion of stimulus differentiation based on extrinsic meaning. Third, he assumes that compatibility among perceptual responses and of perceptual responses with verbal responses is greater than compatibility among verbal responses. Therefore, "mediated stimulus-response connections can be based on more precise contiguity of stimulus and response during learning" (p. 28). Fourth, in addition to these preceding "formal properties of perceptual responses and perceptual response-produced stimulation . . ." another major aspect of mediated connections "is the greater opportunity to draw on prior learning, especially when the verbal material consists of unrelated meaningful items that have been combined in an unfamiliar sequence" (p. 29). The greater the meaningfulness of ostensibly unrelated items, the greater the likelihood of such indirect mediation through perceptual responses.

Morikawa (1959) postulated that paired-associate learning by the anticipation method usually involves three concurrent types of learning: *stimulus discrimination,* which he related to Gibson's concept of stimulus differentiation (1940) and possibly to the Gibsons' (1955) notion of perceptual learning; R-*item acquisition,* conceived as indicated by *M* and strengthened by familiarization, which he related to Mandler's (1954) concept of response integration; and *reinforcement of* S → R *paired-association,* for which the requisite correct anticipations are contingent on R-*item acquisition* and *discrimination of* S. This third type of learning he regarded as indispensable, but S-*item acquisition* is regarded as dispensable. Mediating associations are not mentioned.

In summary, Sheffield's analysis involved three classes of concepts and principles: response patterning and availability, stimulus differentiation, and perceptual mediation of verbal responses. In general, the greater the *M*, the more likely the presence of these presumably facilitative factors and hence the easier the learning. Underwood and Schulz stressed the first of these factors, ignored or perhaps rejected the second, and introduced the third seemingly as implicit verbal mediating responses without the additional or alternative label "perceptual." Morikawa also stressed the first class, recognized the second, but did not mention the third. The thesis of my proposed analysis is that, for the present, all three classes of concepts and principles should be retained, though not necessarily in the exact form in which they have been used.

PROPOSED ANALYSIS

Already noted are the diverse antecedents to the analysis proposed here, most importantly the more general analyses of Miller and Dollard and of Goss and Sheffield's more specific analysis. In addition, I have drawn extensively on an unpublished paper by Harvey Lifton, written at the University of Massachusetts in 1957–1958, in which he reviewed then-available normative, experimental, and theoretical materials on the scaling of M of discrete stimuli and on relationships between M and both serial-anticipation and paired-associate learning. Furthermore, I have benefited from the interchanges among the participants in a seminar at the University of Massachusetts in the fall of 1960 largely devoted to the role of M, familiarization, and similarity in paired-associate learning. Participants were Jean Carl Cohen, Barbara S. Musgrave, Barbara F. Nodine, Calvin F. Nodine, Sally Perry, and Daniel Rosen. Barbara S. Musgrave has done her best to keep me informed about current work on word-association phenomena; and Herbert Levitt, Harvey Lifton, and

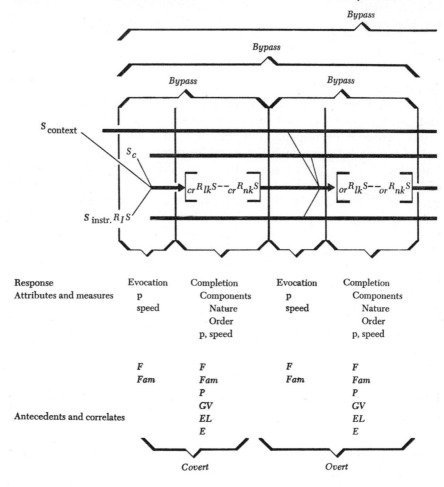

FIG. 4–13. Analysis of observed and inferred stimulus-response elements and relationships involved in single- and multiple-association methods of obtaining relationships between criterion stimuli (S_c) and overt associations for meaningfulness scaling and word-association norms. Also indicated are those aspects of the stimulus-response relationships which, presumably, are directly or indirectly determined by, or indi-

particularly Calvin F. Nodine have collaborated in attempts to organize previous work on the role of stimulus characteristics in paired-associate learning and to extend such work through a number of experiments on such learning as functions of stimulus characteristics, drive, and percentage of occurrence of response members. That these experiments would not have been possible without support from the Training and Personnel Branch of the Office of Naval Research is quite evident.

The present analysis, it will be recalled, is developed in three parts: stimulus-response elements and relationships of meaningfulness scaling

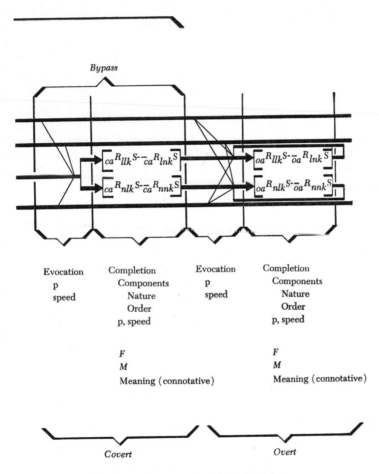

cated by, antecedents and correlates, such as *F, Fam, P, GV, EL, E, M,* and connotative meaning. (Denotative meaning, which involves a relationship between instances of some class of things, properties, or relations and the same repetition or naming response, is not shown.)

and word-association situations; classes of antecedents to those elements and relationships, their properties, and their possible general consequences; and theory and data on the role of those elements and relationships in verbal paired-associate and serial-anticipation learning.

Elements and Relationships of Meaningfulness Scaling and Word-association Situations

Figure 4–13 presents an analysis of observed and inferred stimulus-response elements and relationships involved in single-association and multiple-association methods of obtaining relationships between criterion stimuli and overt associations for word-association norms and for scaling M. As they become pertinent, specific aspects of this scheme are described, elaborated, and justified. The general order is single- and multiple-association methods; elements and relationships of the scheme; and aspects of those stimulus-response elements and relationships which, presumably, are directly or indirectly determined by or indicated by various experimental antecedents and correlated attributes, respectively. The latter includes antecedents such as frequency of opportunity for response to a stimulus or emitted frequency of response to a stimulus (F). Among the attributes are ratings of familiarity of or frequency of prior exposure to stimuli (Fam), ratings of pronounceability (P), ratings of ease of learning (EL), ratings of emotionality (E), number of subjects responding to a stimulus with a single overt association response or mean number of overt association responses in some set time interval (M), actual responses of association hierarchies and their probability profiles as obtained for groups or individual subjects (connotative meaning), and coefficients reflecting frequencies of single-letter responses to successively longer letter sequences (generated values or GV).

Single- and Multiple-association Methods. Professor Noble distinguishes between association value of a stimulus, a, obtained by limiting subjects to indicating whether or not they have any association to each stimulus (the single-association method) and meaningfulness of that stimulus, m, obtained by instructing subjects to produce as many different associations as possible in some fixed time interval (the multiple-association or production method). As Noble (1961) recognized, however, data obtained by the latter method can be converted to essentially the same form as data obtained by the former method by simply dichotomizing each subject's multiple responses to each stimulus as "none" or "one or more."

The conventional word-association situation resembles that of the single-association method. In both, a single association or response other than repetition of the stimulus is desired. One difference is that subjects are allowed more time to produce word associations than has been the practice in scalings by the single-association method. Another difference is that, in scaling association values, response content has been disregarded, while the objective of investigations of word associations has been to obtain profiles of frequencies of members of narrow to broad classes of responses. But associations obtained for scaling association values could be scored for content, and failure to respond in two or three seconds in word-association situations could be considered "no association" and the content of any associations obtained during or after that interval ignored.

The first associations obtained by the multiple-association method might be treated in the same fashion as word associations (e.g., Cofer, 1958; Barbara S. Musgrave, personal communication). Or instructions for word associations might be altered to require subjects to respond with as many different associations as possible in some fixed time interval. Profiles of the frequency of first, second, third, etc., associations to each stimulus might be determined out to the point of too few available responses. Thus, contingent on instructions and time allowed for responding and on whether or not content of responses is considered, meaningfulness scaling and word-association situations can be classified in the manner shown in Table 4-3. Clearly, as Cofer (1958) earlier

Table 4-3

Classification of Meaningfulness Scaling and Word-association Situations in Terms of Method and Consideration of Response Content

Response content considered	Method (instructions and time allowed)	
	Single association	Multiple association
Yes	Conventional word-association situation	Continuous association to specific stimuli
No	Noble's a	Noble's m
	Underwood and Schulz's M	

recognized, these two situations are but special combinations, and though not shown, the transitions from one to the other with respect to method and content of responses are graded rather than qualitative. The relationships of Table 4-3, as they stand, constitute a partial rationale for the observed correlations between a and m and suggest that this correlation should vary with instruction and time-interval variables. Also, the relationships of Table 4-3 partially justify placing both meaningfulness scaling and word-association situations within the same analytical scheme as well as Underwood and Schulz's subsuming a and m under M.

Elements and Relationships of the Scheme. Presentation of each criterion stimulus (S_c) is, given sufficient time, presumed to elicit two types of responses. One type is responses of covertly ($_{cr}R_{1k}S$, ... ,

$_{cr}R_{nk}S$) or overtly ($_{or}R_{1k}S, \ldots, {}_{or}R_{nk}S$) repeating verbal stimuli or, with form stimuli, covert or overt responses which constitute a unique name or identification of each different stimulus. This type, henceforth labeled repetition and naming or, for brevity, recognition responses, approximates what Sheffield considered the intrinsic meaning of a stimulus pattern. The other type, responses of the association hierarchy, includes all other covert or overt responses including what are, grammatically, synonyms for a criterion recognition response. This type approximates what Sheffield considered the extrinsic meaning of a stimulus pattern. But neither type has been restricted to perceptual responses. Nor is it certain, presently at least, that the "perceptual" is necessary or desirable, even tautologically.

Both covertly and overtly, each recognition response—in brackets and indicated by the r subscript—is conceived as usually made up of a series of more elementary components—individual sounds or syllables. Each of these is designated $_{cr}R_{ik}S$ or $_{or}R_{ik}S$. The c and o subscripts before the r subscript of each component indicate that response occurrence is covert or overt, respectively; and the first of the number subscripts indicates an arbitrary "correct" order of component responses and stimuli they produce. The k subscript indicates order of occurrence of components during each presentation of S_c. Not included is a subscript to indicate occurrence of a component during a particular ordinal presentation of S_c.

Each response of the association hierarchy has an a subscript preceded by c or an o for, respectively, covert or overt occurrence of that response. The first number subscript designates the rank of that response in a hierarchy proceeding from the strongest or most probable response with a rank of 1 to the weakest or least probable response with probability still above zero. The second number subscript indicates an arbitrary correct order of the component responses and the stimuli they produce; and the k designates actual order of occurrence of responses of an association hierarchy during each presentation of S_c. Because most association responses are presumably well integrated, it is assumed that the order of occurrence of components is essentially invariant from trial to trial. Not included is a subscript to indicate the occurrence of components during a particular ordinal presentation of S_c.

Several strands of evidence justify the inference of occurrence of covert recognition responses. Froeberg (1918, p. 158), for example, reports that at first his subjects were unable to inhibit articulation of the nonsense syllable stimuli; such articulation persisted under the condition of simultaneous presentation. Guthrie's (1933) subjects reported holding "the first item in mind until the second appeared" (p. 365). Repetition responses are the inferred basis of most intermodal transfer (Lifton and

Goss, in press). Also, Liberman and associates (Liberman, Harris, Hoffman, and Griffith, 1957) have hypothesized implicit pronunciations of synthetic consonants as the basis of apparent acquired distinctiveness in discriminations among those consonants. To predict the apparent superiority of prompting to confirmation conditions of learning paired-associates, Cook and Kendler (1956; Cook, 1961) postulated occurrences of covert responses of repeating both stimulus and response members. Finally, Bousfield and collaborators (e.g., Bousfield, Whitmarsh, and Danick, 1958) have found it desirable to assume the occurrence of recognition responses—they label them verbal representation responses —in their analysis of the basis of semantic generalization. Described elsewhere (Goss, 1956) are some more general grounds for inferences of mediating responses in general, of which covert repetition and naming and also covert responses of the association hierarchy are special cases.

Each S_c of meaningfulness scaling and word-association situations can occur in varying contexts under different instructions. For the present analysis, it suffices to note that contextual stimuli are presumably present during the sequence of stimulus-response events set off by presentation of S_c. Often contextual stimuli may not be important determinants of recognition responses. But Cofer and associates (e.g., Cofer, 1960), Howes and Osgood (1954), Musgrave (1960), and others have shown that contextual words modify hierarchies of associations to criterion stimuli.

Instructions are conceived as evoking responses which persist and which, through the stimuli they produce, influence recognition responses and also responses of association hierarchies. Whether or not covert recognition responses continue to occur, either in complete or shortened form, is probably in part determined by instructions. Certainly the probability and form of occurrence of overt recognition responses are substantially influenced by instructions.

Stimuli produced by responses to instructions probably function most importantly as determinants of the particular covert and overt responses of association hierarchies. Whether or not those responses occur overtly, how many occur, and their nature and relative strengths are presumably determined by instructions to respond overtly, to make only one response or as many different responses as possible, and to respond with any idea, only with words referring to sensory properties, etc. (e.g., Jenkins, 1959a; Woodworth and Schlosberg, 1954). As Russell has suggested in his paper, the stimulus-response relationships involved in giving and responding to instructions and their effects on recognition responses and on responses of association hierarchies are, at present, conjectural. But as Russell has also suggested, their origin, properties, and consequences have been and can be investigated systematically and experimentally.

In general, recognition responses are presumed to occur before responses of association hierarchies and, unless subjects are instructed otherwise, covertly. Stimuli produced by the recognition responses along with the S_c, contextual stimuli, and stimuli produced by responses to instructions constitute the stimulus pattern evoking the first association response. Time permitting, the stimuli produced by each association response, in patterns with the S_c, contextual stimuli, and stimuli produced by responses to instructions, determine each successive, further association response. The occurrence of each successive response from onset of the S_c on involves probabilities of occurrence of each successive particular component of a response unit, speed of evocation of the first component, and speed of completion of the entire sequence of components. Strictly, speed of completion is summed speeds of evocation and speeds of completion of successive components of a unit.

Instructions, training to respond rapidly, or both may lead to bypassing covert recognition responses, overt recognition responses, or covert association responses either singly or in combinations of the first and second, of the first and third, or of all three. Such bypassing may involve elimination of some but not all components of these units.

Shown below the measures for evocation and completion are the more important of the presumed antecedents to and correlates of M. Frequency of opportunity to respond to a stimulus or emitted frequency of response to a stimulus (F) should be directly related to probability of evocation and completion and to speed of covert and overt recognition responses.

F is also shown as an antecedent to the probability and speed of covert and overt association responses. The direct relationship between frequency of the primary and speed of evocation of an overt association observed in word-association experiments is indirect support for this suggestion (Woodworth and Schlosberg, 1954). Not shown are the variables of frequency and other conditions of prior pairings of the S_c and covert and overt recognition responses and stimuli on the one hand with, on the other hand, the stimulus originally eliciting each association response.

Generated values (GV) presumably estimate probability and speed of particular components of a response in a particular order. Such values are regarded as directly related to frequency of opportunity to experience letter sequences or of their emission. In addition, Underwood and Schulz (1960) suggest that responses to two-letter stimuli may be in part determined by and hence reflect alphabetical-sequence habits, continuation habits, initial habits, context habits, selection habits (pp. 221–225), and the sound associated with a single-letter or two-letter stimulus (p. 291).

Ratings of familiarity of or frequency of prior exposure to stimuli (Fam) and also ratings of pronounceability (P), estimated ease of learning (*EL*) and emotionality (*E*) are regarded as reflecting probability and speed of evocation and completion of covert and overt repetition responses.

M is shown as primarily reflecting the number of responses in an association hierarchy for a particular discrete stimulus. The connotative meaning of a discrete S_c is conceived as the actual probability profile of responses to that stimulus or, alternatively, the hierarchy of association responses. Such profiles have usually been based on responses for groups of subjects; therefore they only approximate those for individual subjects. Also, such profiles are presumably influenced by context and instruction factors. Consequently, a given S_c might be conceived as having a core of responses which are relatively invariant through different contexts and instructions (similar to Sheffield's intrinsic meaning) along with additional responses specific to each different combination of contexts and instructions (similar to Sheffield's extrinsic meaning).

That these antecedents and correlates are interrelated follows from a consideration of prior conditions of learning and such principles as contiguity, frequency, and recency. However, as Underwood and Schulz have shown so well, variables like frequency may operate in devious fashion. The association of increasing numbers of responses to an S_c, for example, requires more frequent presentation of the S_c. *F* and *M*, therefore, should be directly related, though the correlation would not be perfect since some S_c's might be paired many times with only a few association responses. To the degree that *GV* and *P* are partly functions of frequency, they too should be directly, though not perfectly, related to *M*. Ratings of *Fam*, *EL*, and *E* may actually be rating of *P*, *M*, or *F*. Because of the relationships of the latter measures to *M*, direct relationships between *M* and the former rating measures would be expected.

Antecedents, and Properties and General Consequences

Antecedents. Table 4–4 summarizes some broad classes of variables presumably antecedent to the stimulus-response relationships depicted in Figure 4–13. Many of the variables of these classes may be relatively immediate determinants of recognition responses and of responses of association hierarchies. Here, however, the emphasis is their significance in subjects' more remote experiential histories.

Repetition and naming responses (${}_rR$) are seen as influenced by attributes of the S_c and the nature of the response, the S_c-${}_rR$ variables. Focusing on the S_c, both type and modality of presentation are likely to be important factors. Broadly, two types are conveniently and usefully distinguished; physical things, objects, and relations and isomorphic representations thereof; and letter sequences, some of which are words. Both types may range from the simple to the complex, and they may

Table 4-4

Remote and More Immediate Experiential Antecedents to Stimulus-response Elements and Relationships of Repetition and Naming Responses and to Responses of Association Hierarchies, and General Properties and Consequences of Those Responses

Antecedents	Properties	Consequences
Repetition and naming responses		

Antecedents

S→R:
Focus on S_e
  Types (simple to complex) — Things, properties, relations } Alone / Combination
    Letter sequences, words
  Modality — Auditory } Alone
    Visual / Other } Combination
    { Same components, order, modality / Units per se / Components of units / Units as components }

Focus on $_rR$
  Form — Pronouncing / Spelling
  Modality — Vocal / Graphic
  { Components, order, modality differ singly or in various combinations }

Context
  Relatively specific — Things, properties, relations / Letter sequences, words   (Some are basis for association hierarchies)
  Audience and locale
Instructions
Stimuli
Responses and response-produced stimuli

Properties

Evocation speed
  Mean
  Variability
Completion speed
  Stability of components
  Number nature
  Order
Speed components run off
  Mean
  Variability

Consequences

Similarity of $_rR$ response generalization
Stability of stimulation produced by $_rR$:
  Qualitative } Similarity of stimuli,
  Quantitative } stimulus generalization
Rehearsal of repetition responses
Opportunity for responses of association hierarchy with respect to:
  Occurrence } Stability of those that
  Rehearsal } occur and of stimuli they produce

Antecedents	Properties	Consequences
Responses of association hierarchy		

Antecedents

Classes of variables influencing responses of repeating and naming (because, in turn, such responses influence responses of association hierarchies)
Responses of association hierarchy considered subclass of relatively specific "contextual" stimuli and responses to those stimuli preceding or following a particular S→$_rR$. Such accompanying responses become association responses as a function of
  Contiguity, frequency, recency, differential reinforcement, etc.
  Specific cues emphasizing an association, e.g., A is B

Properties

Stability
  Between units } Number nature
  Within units } Order
Speed of
  Evocation
  Completion

Consequences

Similarity of association responses, response generalization
Stability of stimulation produced by association responses
  Qualitative
  Quantitative
Rehearsal of associations
Probability of occurrence of association responses
  With preestablished association with $_rR$
  Which include $_rR$ and response to be conditioned to S_e

be presented alone or in combination. And letter sequences and words may be presented or occur in auditory, visual, or proprioceptive modalities singly or in combination. Successive experiences may involve the same components of an S_c, in the same order or arrangement, and in the same modality. With respect to the components of a complex S_c, they may be incomplete or complete. S_c may appear in complete form alone or as a component of some larger unit. But successive experiences are more likely to involve differences in components, in their order, and in their modality either singly or in various combinations. Should the differences be small, there should be some transfer through successive experiences.

Focusing on $_rR$, recognition responses may take two forms, pronouncing or spelling; and they may occur in two modalities, vocal or graphic. As for the S_c, the $_rR$ may be essentially the same from trial to trial or the components, their order, and the modality may differ to some degree, either singly or in various combinations. And the form may be the same or different.

Contextual factors have been divided into relatively specific stimuli— things, properties and relations or letter sequences and words—or characteristics of audiences and locales. As with the S_c-$_rR$, the focus may be on the stimulus or the response, and the further distinctions with respect to S_c and $_rR$ apply to these contextual stimuli and the responses they evoke. Some of the contextual stimuli are the basis of the responses of the association hierarchy of a particular S_c. Regarded as audience characteristics are the number and sex of individuals present. Locale characteristics include the nature and size of rooms and other features of physical sites. That audience and locale characteristics function as cues is suggested by a variety of findings (Musgrave, 1960).

The instructions variables have not been elaborated except to note that the focus may be on instructions as stimuli or on the responses they arouse and their response-produced stimuli.

The responses of the association hierarchy of an S_c are, in part, a function of the S_c-$_rR$ variables. Stimuli produced by covert or overt occurrence of the $_rR$ are elements of the stimulus pattern evoking at least the first association response. The responses of the association hierarchy are essentially the responses to a subclass of the relatively specific contextual stimuli. The responses of repeating those relatively specific contextual stimuli which have been frequently and recently in close temporal contiguity with an S_c become, it is assumed, the responses of the association hierarchy of that S_c. Other conditions, such as differential reinforcement, may be relevant; and S_c and these contextual stimuli may be paired with additional cues, such as an "is," between them, which may serve as cues to focus subjects' acquisition of a particular association response to an S_c. Pertinent here are experiments concerned with establishing response hierarchies experimentially (e.g., Peterson, 1956; Peterson and Peterson, 1957; Osgood and Anderson, 1957; Goss and Sugerman, 1961) and experiments concerned with the conditioning of meaning (e.g., Staats, 1961) and attitudes (e.g., Rhine and Silun, 1958; Solley and Messick, 1957).

Properties and General Consequences. The properties of the stimulus-response relationships have, for the most part, already been described. Not emphasized, however, are trial-to-trial stability in the number nature and in the order of the components of covert and overt recognition responses and trial-to-trial stability of the responses of association hierarchies. Such stability can be within each component response or between such responses. In general, frequent and recent prior experiences should lead to occurrence of particular components in a particular order with higher probability and faster speed.

The lines from properties to consequences depict the presumed primary consequences of those properties. The first two related consequences of recognition responses are similarity among such responses and both qualitative and quantitative stability of response-produced stimuli. The greater the speed and stability of naming responses, the less their similarity to other responses and also the less the similarity of their response-produced stimuli to those produced by other responses. Consequently, both response generalization based on similarity among responses and stimulus generalization based on similarity among response-produced stimuli should be reduced.

The faster the evocation and completion of recognition responses, the longer the time available for rehearsing them and for occurrence and rehearsal of responses of the association hierarchy. Also, the association responses that do occur should be more stable. Stability of association responses should decrease both response similarity and similarity among response-produced stimuli.

Faster evocation and completion of association responses increases opportunity for their rehearsal. Stability both within responses and between responses and faster speeds should also, through greater frequency, increase the probability of association both with recognition responses to accompanying stimuli and with association responses to accompanying stimuli. A further consequence is that more association responses could occur to increase the likelihood of indirect or mediating associations based on previously established associations between association responses and recognition or association responses to other S_c's.

M of Discrete Stimuli in Paired-associate and Serial-anticipation Learning

Paired-associate learning, in contrast to conventional serial-anticipation learning, permits manipulative separation of stimulus and response functions of discrete stimuli. For this reason, data on the role of M of discrete stimuli in stimulus and response positions in paired-associate learning have been of greater interest to experimenters and are here emphasized relative to data on the role of M in serial-anticipation learning.

Table 4–5

Observed and Inferred Consequences of M-related Properties of Stimulus Members, Response Members, and Relationships between Stimulus Members and Responses to Response Members of Paired-associate Learning

Stimulus members	Response members	Between stimulus and response members
Dissimilarity of $_rR$ Response-mediated dissimilarity of stimulus members based on 1. Stability of stimuli produced by $_rR$ 2. Dissimilar $_rR$-produced stimuli 3. Orienting responses to more distinctive features of stimuli and on distinctive stimuli produced by $_rR$ to those features Time for occurrence and rehearsal of 1. $_rR$ to stimulus members 2. Association responses to stimulus members 3. Anticipations of $_rR$ to response member 4. Association responses to response members Division of stimuli into 1. Intra-list or extra-list 2. Stimulus members or response members	Dissimilarity of $_rR$ Same as for stimulus members but probably less important Same as for stimulus members but less important than occurrence and rehearsal of $_rR$ to response members Same as for stimulus members	Direct relationships Transitional probabilities Last letter or syllable to first letter or syllable Unit-unit Similarity of stimulus and response members and of $_rR$ thereto Indirect relationships Responses of association hierarchy of stimulus member, response member, or both serving as mediating response or associative aid Principle

Paired-associate Learning. M and related attributes of both stimulus members and response members of paired-associates have usually been directly related to acquisition rate with variations in M and related attributes of response members more potent than the same variations in stimulus members (e.g., Goss, Nodine, and Levitt, 1961; Goss, Nodine, Gregory, Taub, and Kennedy, 1962; Morikawa, 1959; Noble, 1962). Table 4–5 summarizes possible consequences of observed and inferred relationships involved in responding to discrete stimuli both as stimulus members and as response members which may underlie these direct relationships between acquisition rate and M and other attributes of stimulus and response members.[2] Also noted are possible relationships between and among stimulus and response members of paired-associate units which may contribute to the observed direct relationships.

The observed direct relationships, with few exceptions, have been with sets of paired-associate units with stimulus members which were relatively dissimilar to each other and to their paired and other response members and with response members which were relatively dissimilar to each other. More specifically, the stimuli, whether serving as stimulus members or response members, have had no or few common elements so that both as seen and in terms of recognition responses they were of low formal similarity. Also, the stimuli have had different connotative and denotative meanings so that they were dissimilar with respect to meaning or overlap of responses of their association hierarchies. But formal similarity and similarity in terms of meaning among stimulus members, among response members, and between stimulus and response members are variables which also influence acquisition rate (Goss, Nodine, and Levitt, 1961; Goss, Nodine, Gregory, Taub, and Kennedy, 1962; Levitt, 1959; Levitt and Goss, 1961; Morikawa, 1959). Moreover, these variables might be expected to combine in some fashion with M and related attributes of stimulus and response members. A relatively comprehensive analysis, therefore, must be in terms of M and related attributes of stimulus and response members of varying similarity—both formal and with respect to meaning—among stimulus members, among response members, and between stimulus and response members. The analysis is developed here in terms of: (a) M of stimulus members of low and then of increasing similarity, (b) M and similarity of response members, and (c) relationships between stimulus and response members.

A. *Stimulus members.* Considering first possible consequences of elements and relationships involved in responding to stimulus members, high M of stimulus members would presumably indicate that responses of repeating a verbal stimulus or of naming a form stimulus are evoked and completed rapidly with relatively little trial-to-trial variability in speed of evocation, speed of completion, and form of response. The stimuli produced by such responses should be stable. With stimulus members of low formal similarity, to which subjects respond with dissimilar recognition responses, the important potentially facilitative attri-

[2] Both Saltz and Newman, at the 1960 meeting of the Psychonomic Society, proposed relatively complete "revised and extended" conceptions of the processes and principles of paired-associate learning. Their conceptions overlap both Sheffield's and the present analysis though there are differences in both content and emphasis.

butes of the recognition responses would seem to be marked trial-to-trial stability of the patterns of external-initiating stimuli and response-produced stimuli, more time for occurrence and rehearsal of subsequent responses of the association hierarchy of a stimulus, and more time available for the occurrence of anticipation or recall of the to-be-associated recognition responses to paired response members.

Because of trial-to-trial stability and more time for rehearsal of recognition responses, identification of stimulus members as belonging to a particular list should be rapid. Also, rapid learning of stimulus members as whole units and as belonging to a particular list would give subjects more time to find parts which, for a particular list, are more distinctive than the whole stimulus and to make more distinctive recognition responses to those parts. Both should further reduce formal similarity. Finally, more time would be available for subjects to abbreviate recognition responses to whole stimuli or to their distinctive parts. Thus more time would be available for anticipation or recall of responses to response members. M presumably reflects amount of prior exposure to a stimulus in a variety of contexts. Therefore, the greater the M, the greater subjects' prior experience in seeking out more distinctive parts, in making more distinctive recognition responses, and also in abbreviating recognition responses to whole stimuli or to their parts. A further consequence would be more rapid division of stimuli of a list into stimulus members or response members.

The important, facilitative attributes of responses of the association hierarchy of stimulus members are less clear. In fact, with respect to these responses Sheffield introduced what might be called the paradox of the M of stimulus members: M is directly related to acquisition rate, but greater M might indicate greater trial-to-trial variability in association responses and response-produced stimuli with consequent retardation of learning. Sheffield, it will be recalled, then stressed what he regarded as an alternative implication: "The more specific and invariant the meaning of a word the more effective it would be as a stimulus for an associative connection" (p. 25). By "the more specific and invariant the meaning of a word," he may have meant degree of similarity among stimulus members with respect to meaning or overlap of responses of the association hierarchy. The less such overlap—"the more specific the meaning of the word"—the less the response-mediated similarity and generalization, and hence the more rapid the acquisition of a different response to each different stimulus member. Thus, while greater M might lead to greater trial-to-trial variability with respect to the stimulus pattern involving each stimulus member, there would be compensating response-mediated dissimilarity among those stimulus patterns.

M merely indicates that subjects under given instructions and in a certain interval make a given number of different responses to a stimulus. Conceivably, the greater the M, the more stable such a sequence of responses through successive trials. This may be Sheffield's, "the more . . . invariant the meaning of the word." Thus, while more responses might occur to increase stimulus variability, they might occur in more stable chains to reduce such variability. Also, since the conventional 2:2-second rate probably permits occurrence of only one or two association responses on a given trial, any increased stability of the chain might reduce the potentially inhibitory aspect of M to negligible importance.

Only one or two responses of the association hierarchy of a stimulus member may occur on each presentation of that member. Consequently, the faster speeds of evocation and completion, presumably indicated by high M, would provide more time for rehearsing those responses, should such rehearsal be desirable. Also, the faster speeds would increase the time available for anticipation or recall of the recognition responses to paired response members. As noted above, under the usual 2:2-second rate of presentation of stimulus and response members of a pair, with an essentially zero interval between successive pairs, it is doubtful that more than one or two association responses to a stimulus can occur on each trial. Unless, of course, the conditions are such that subjects concentrate on the stimuli of just one or two pairs on each trial. The intertrial interval, however, may be long enough for the occurrence and rehearsal of more extensive chains of associations.

Increasing the formal similarity of stimulus members should increase the similarity of repetition responses. Also, subjects are more likely to make the same naming response to increasingly similar form stimuli unless, through instructions or acquired distinctiveness training, they are able to make different naming responses to similar form stimuli (Arnoult, 1957; Goss, 1955; Spiker, 1956). Increasing the similarity of stimulus members with respect to meaning—overlap of responses of association hierarchies—might increase the similarity of patterns consisting of initiating stimuli and stimuli produced by association responses. Such increasing response-mediated similarity and generalization might be counteracted by instructions or prior training which results in subjects making different association responses to stimulus members with overlapping association hierarchies. Increasing the similarity of stimulus members might also increase the tendency for subjects to respond to a stimulus member with recognition responses to other stimulus members rather than with the recognition response to its paired response member.

Regardless of M, similarity of stimulus members and acquisition rate should be inversely related. But M of stimulus members and their similarity might combine in relatively complicated fashion. Increasing

M presumably indicates increasing stability of recognition responses and response-produced stimuli. Up to some point, therefore, the greater their stability, the less any generalization among recognition responses and, more importantly, the greater any possible distinctiveness of patterns made up of external stimuli and stimuli produced by those responses. Such response-mediated dissimilarity should facilitate acquisition of different responses to each different stimulus member. Beyond some presently undeterminate point, however, similarity of recognition responses and response-produced stimuli should retard acquisition of different responses to each different stimulus member. Then, conceivably, the greater stability of responses and response-produced stimuli might result in more response-mediated similarity and generalization and hence slow the acquisition of discriminative responses to stimulus members.

Increasing M may also indicate greater stability of responses of association hierarchies. If so, essentially the same considerations apply with respect to the relationship between stimulus similarity and response-mediated dissimilarity and similarity based on association responses to stimulus members as were suggested for recognition responses to stimulus members.

Regardless of similarity among stimulus members or between stimulus members and response members, however, M should be a direct indicant of subjects' prior experiences in seeking out more distinctive parts and in making more distinctive recognition responses. M should also be a direct indicant of their prior experiences in abbreviating recognition responses to whole stimuli or to their parts. In fact, with greater similarity among stimulus members such prior experience would become increasingly important and might partially counterbalance inhibitory effects of greater similarity. Also, the greater the M, the more likely it is that subjects have had experience in making more distinctive association responses to particular stimuli in particular contexts.

Satisfactory data on the pertinence and relative weights of these possible bases of the direct relationship between acquisition rate and M of stimulus members are virtually nonexistent. The three important approaches have been prior familiarization, pre-differentiation or acquired distinctiveness training, and experimental induction of meaning or meaningfulness. Prior familiarization with stimulus members has subsequently been inhibitory (Sheffield, 1946; Underwood and Schulz, 1960), ineffectual (Goss, Nodine, and Levitt, 1961; Hakes, 1961b; Morikawa, 1959), and facilitative (Cieutat, 1960; Gannon and Noble, 1961; Hakes, 1961a; Noble's paper).[3] Weiss (1958) found response familiarization to be

[3] Sheffield's familiarization procedure is better classified as a condition for establishing response-mediated similarity or acquired equivalence of cues; it is later described in greater detail.

superior to stimulus familiarization, but the design did not permit determination of whether the former was facilitative or the latter inhibitory. The apparent inconsistencies of these functions presumably reflect differences in familiarization conditions and in conditions of subsequent paired-associate learning. For example, the Schulz and Tucker data indicate that whether or not subjects pronounce stimulus members overtly during paired-associate learning under a 2:2 rate determines whether familiarization training which involved overt verbalization of stimulus members is facilitative or inhibitory, respectively.

Whatever the resolution of other differences in results, only some familiarization conditions may prove facilitative and then only under some subsequent conditions of paired-associate learning. Determination of facilitative combinations and the bases of their effects, and also of inhibitory combinations and the bases of their effects, requires extensive further experimentation.

The considerable literature on pre-differentiation and acquired distinctiveness training is, at present, essentially irrelevant to an understanding of the bases of the direct relationship between M and acquisition rate. First, most of the experiments explicitly concerned with the effects of pre-differentiation and acquired distinctiveness training have been with nonverbal stimuli. Second, with one exception (Vanderplas and Garvin, 1959), relationships of M to acquisition rate have been investigated only with verbal stimuli. Third, acquired distinctiveness training has been with stimuli of high similarity, while the stimulus members of lists used to establish relationships between acquisition rate and M have been of low or indeterminate relative similarity.

Sheffield's symbolic training condition might be considered acquired distinctiveness training as were some of the conditions of experiments by Crawford and Vanderplas (1959), by Bailey and Jeffrey (1958), and by Saltz and his students. Under Sheffield's symbolic training, subjects learned a different motor response to each trigram stimulus. The effect of such training, however, was inhibitory rather than facilitative. As suggested below, this may have been due to competition between the responses acquired in symbolic training and responses of the criterion task.

Controls in mediate-association studies in which subjects learn one response to a particular stimulus in the first stage and a different response to that stimulus in a later, test stage could be viewed as approximating the acquired distinctiveness paradigm. However, the stimuli to which these responses are learned have been relatively dissimilar so that it is questionable that stimuli produced by any responses acquired during the first stage would have increased their dissimilarity. Also, the usual time intervals of such training have been short so that interference was as likely or more likely than chaining. Finally, only in the Crawford and Vanderplas experiment and in Bailey and Jeffrey's first experiment were there adequate additional controls to assess any acquired distinctiveness.

The pertinent conditions of Crawford and Vanderplas's experiment are, in their notation for the stimulus-response relationship among the two or three stages of their conditions, D-E, A-B, and A-C (C-2) versus D-E, F-G, A-C (C-3) and —, A-B, A-C (C-5) versus D-E, —, A-C (C-6). The A-B training of C-2 and C-5 might lead to some acquired distinctiveness. The F-G list of the former pair of conditions controlled for nonspecific transfer from A-B to A-C but not for familiarization of A. The means of trials to criterion for C-2 and C-3 were 33.3 and 28.1, respectively, which might reflect slight inhibition due to B-mediated acquired distinctiveness of A. The D-E list of C-6 controlled for nonspecific transfer from A-B to A-C for C-5 but not for familiarization of A. The mean for learning A-C under condition C-5 was 26.6 while that for learning under condition C-6 was 31.6, which suggests that the A-B training of the former condition produced some slight facilitative acquired distinctiveness. Neither difference was statistically significant, but the 2:2-second rate might have produced enough counterbalancing negative transfer from A-B to A-C to prevent or reduce any facilitation due to acquired distinctiveness. Also, the stimulus members designated by A were probably not very similiar to each other. Consequently any training designed to produce acquired distinctiveness could only have had a small effect.

The "single S-R pair" condition of Bailey and Jeffrey's first experiment involved A-B pretraining and an A-C test (they labeled the test A-E). The three-second anticipation interval employed may have provided a relatively more favorable circumstance for chaining to occur rather than negative transfer, but this may have been more than counterbalanced by the requirement that subjects pronounce stimulus members. In terms of errors to criterion, the single S-R pair condition led to slightly better performance than did prior familiarization with the stimulus members. While in the predicted direction, the difference was small and not significant; but the stimulus members were of intermediate rather than high similarity, which might have precluded marked facilitation based on acquired distinctiveness. Unfortunately, in their third experiment, which was with stimulus members of high similarity, there was no control for nonspecific sources of transfer or for transfer based on selecting the discriminable pair of letters. The latter factor might even have been more pronounced in the three-response condition. At most, therefore, the results of experiments involving possible acquired distinctiveness of verbal stimuli have been, in some instances, in the predicted direction. When they were not, the conditions were such that inhibition due to other factors was as likely or more likely than facilitation based on acquired distinctiveness.

Saltz, Metzen, and Ernstein (1961) describe an unpublished study by Yelen, Whitman, and Frazier in which the presence of pre-differentiated nonsense syllables as stimulus members facilitated acquisition of difficult pairs and inhibited acquisition of easy pairs.

Sheffield's and Bailey and Jeffrey's are apparently the only attempts to induce differences in meaning and meaningfulness of stimulus members experimentally. Sheffield, who labeled his procedure "symbolic training," investigated the relationship between amount of such training and subsequent acquisition of anticipatory responses to those stimuli as stimulus members of paired-associate units. Unexpectedly, 10 trials of symbolic training had inhibitory effects which 20 trials did not entirely overcome. One reason may be Sheffield's inadvertent introduction of a possible condition for negative transfer. His procedures for symbolic training and familiarization training required overt motor rather than verbal responses. Indeed he seems to have conceived the responses actually being acquired as nonefferent "perceptual" events. However, it seems likely that during such training subjects verbalized the directions for the required motor responses covertly before making the motor responses. Thus the response chains being conditioned may have included covert verbal responses. Moreover, the single response to all familiarized stimuli of familiarization training is the condition for establishing acquired equivalence of stimulus members. Such acquired equivalence would be expected to have inhibitory rather than facilitative effects on subsequent acquisition of discriminative responses to those stimuli.

Should subjects have tended to make any verbal responses acquired during familiarization or symbolic training during subsequent learning of new verbal responses to those stimuli, some negative transfer stemming from conflict of responses in the same modality might have occurred. That amount of negative transfer to what could be considered subsequent A-C learning decreased with more of what could be considered prior A-B learning is consistent with indications that overlearning of A-B in an A-B, A-C paradigm may decrease the amount of negative transfer and sometimes might even produce positive transfer (Mandler, 1954).

Sheffield's requirement that subjects say the stimulus members overtly may have accentuated the negative transfer condition: There would be less time for the B response to occur before the C response, thus forming an interference rather than a chaining situation. Conceivably, 20 training trials were less inhibitory because subjects could make both the repetition response and the B response more rapidly before anticipating C. Arguing against this interpretation, however, is the fact that familiarization training which, under such circumstances, should have produced some response-mediated similarity was slightly less rather than more inhibitory than symbolic training.

As noted, Sheffield, like Gannon and Noble (1961) and Hakes (1961a), required subjects to say stimulus members overtly before anticipating. Under this condition of paired-associate learning, Gannon and Noble, Hakes, and Schulz and Tucker found familiarization to be facilitative. Sheffield obtained inhibitory effects. Differences in the condition of prior training may account for this discrepancy in findings: The former investigators strengthened only repetition responses while Sheffield's procedure involved familiarization of those responses plus the establishing of new association responses to the stimulus members.

Bailey and Jeffrey also had a condition in which subjects were expected to learn three different responses to the same stimulus. However, their procedure of three successive lists in an A-B, A-C, A-D relationship to each other might have involved successive negative transfer from each to the next. It is questionable, therefore, that subjects came into the test situation with stimulus members to each of which there were three different association responses of high, essentially equal strengths.

In sum, neither attempts to facilitate by including meaning and meaningfulness, nor experiments on effects of familiarization and acquired distinctiveness yet provide satisfactory data on the relevance and relative contributions of the mechanisms presumed to explain the direct relationship between acquisition rate and M of stimulus members.

B. Response members. Recognition responses to response members of high M, like such responses to stimulus members of high M, should be evoked and completed rapidly with high intertrial stability in speeds of evocation and completion and in form. More importantly, perhaps, such responses could occur and be completed earlier in the conventional rather short time intervals for anticipation or recall. Also, more opportunity for rehearsal should be available both alone and before or after occurrences of recognition responses and possibly of association responses to stimulus members. In turn, more frequent rehearsal should facilitate identification of the response members as members of a particular list and as response members rather than stimulus members.

Under the usual conditions of paired-associate learning it seems doubtful that stability of stimuli produced by recognition responses is an important factor. Nor is it likely that great weight would be attached to learning to seek out parts which are more distinctive than the whole stimulus and to making more distinctive recognition responses to those stimuli.

Consideration of the role of association responses to response members introduces what might be labeled the paradox of the M of response members. M is directly related to rate of acquisition of recognition responses to response members as anticipation or recall responses to stimulus members. But M indicates the number of association responses to a stimulus and it is not these responses which are learned, or more precisely, it is not these responses whose learning is required and observed. In fact, were these the responses which subjects are required to learn, it seems possible that the greater the number of different association responses evoked by a response member, the slower the acquisition of any one of these responses as the correct response to a paired stimulus member. Responses of the association hierarchies of response members of paired-associate units, therefore, probably have significant facilitative or inhibitory effects only as associative aids or mediating responses. This function is considered below as one aspect of relationships between stimulus and response members. Otherwise, the importance of M of response members is probably as a correlate or indicant of speed and stability of recognition responses.

Regardless of M of response members, rate of acquisition should be inversely related to their similarity as stimuli and to the similarity of the recognition responses and possibly of the responses of association hierarchies that those stimuli evoke. Formal similarity of response members as stimuli, which is usually confounded with formal similarity of recognition responses to those stimuli, often has a strong inverse relationship to acquisition rate (e.g., Goss, Nodine, Gregory, Taub, and Kennedy, 1962; Goss, Nodine, and Levitt, 1961; Levitt, 1959; Levitt and Goss, 1961). However, Underwood (1953a) reports an inverse relationship for errors but no effect on trials to criterion. When response members and their confounded recognition responses have little formal similarity but responses of association hierarchies overlap, such common-meaning similarity of response members has had from negligible effects (Underwood, 1953b) to significant inverse effects (Saltz, 1960; Underwood, Runquist, and Schulz, 1959). The latter finding suggests that association responses to response members may influence acquisition, presumably by increasing response-mediated generalization among response members.

Increasing confounded formal similarity of response members and their recognition responses should result in greater response generalization. But M is also presumably a direct indicant of speeds of evocation and completion of recognition responses and their stability. The latter of these, in particular, should result in less response similarity and hence less response generalization. For response members of increasing but equal formal similarity, therefore, M of response members should be directly related to acquisition rate. An exception to this prediction might be the relationship of M and acquisition rate with response members of very great formal similarity. With such response members, greater stability of recognition responses might increase response similarity and resultant response generalization.

Data on the pertinence and weights of these possible bases of the direct relationship between acquisition rate and M of response members are scarcely more adequate than the data for stimulus members. One approach has been familiarization training which, on the whole, has produced only slightly more compelling findings of a direct relationship between various kinds and amount of such training and subsequent acquisition with those stimuli as response members of paired-associates (Noble's paper; Morikawa, 1959; Saltz, 1960; Sheffield, 1946; Underwood, Runquist, and Schulz, 1959; Underwood and Schulz, 1960, pp. 101–110, 119–126).[4] But such facilitation has not always been obtained (Cieutat, 1960; Gannon and Noble, 1961; Goss, Nodine, and Levitt, 1961; Goss, Nodine, Gregory, Taub, and Kennedy, 1962; Hakes, 1961b). Again, these discrepancies may reflect differences in condition of familiarization or conditions of subsequent paired-associate learning.

Sheffield, and later Parker and Noble (1960; Noble's paper) in their two experiments, set up conditions designed to increase the meaning and meaningfulness of response members. Sheffield's subjects learned a single, different, relatively complex, overt motor response to each different stimulus while Parker and Noble's subjects learned, 3, 6, or 9 different verbal responses to each different stimulus. Sheffield's familiarization was that each subject learned the same common motor response to all response members. Because there was no difference in the extent of facilitation due to symbolic training or familiarization training, he concluded that response integration rather than meaning was the basis for the observed relationship between acquisition rate and M. Under Sheffield's symbolic training, however, subjects made only one different overt motor response to each different stimulus.[5] Therefore, whether the meaningfulness and range of meaning of each of those stimuli were varied is questionable.

The response members of Bailey and Jeffrey's test list had previously been stimuli to which one response or three successive, different responses were learned, or response members for three successive, different stimuli. Differences among pairs with these members and control pairs were not

[4] Sheffield's familiarization procedure could also be considered training to establish a common meaning among response members. Underwood, Runquist, and Schulz's response members were adjectives whose M is unknown but probably high. It is doubtful, therefore, that five familiarization trials with these stimuli would have increased response integration. Instead, the data suggested that such familiarization merely accelerates their availability for association with stimulus members. Crawford and Vanderplas's B-C, —, A-C (C-4) condition was better on A-C learning than their D-E, —, A-C condition, which, though the difference was not significant, is consistent with the notion that response familiarization aids later learning. But their B-C, D-E, A-C (C-1) condition led to slower A-C learning than did their D-E, F-G, A-C (C-3) condition, which suggests that response facilitation was inhibitory.

[5] As noted earlier, Sheffield's symbolic training and familiarization training may have involved the strengthening of covert verbal responses.

significant. However, because the three responses had been learned successively, the first two sets of pairs may not have been markedly different.

When Parker and Noble conditioned 3, 6, or 9 different verbal responses to each stimulus, they found a direct relationship between number of such responses and facilitation of subsequent paired-associate learning with those stimuli as response members. However, Parker and Noble's results are equivocal in that learning 3, 6, or 9 different responses to a stimulus involved approximately 60, 120, or 180 experiences in repeating the stimulus overtly. Thus, different amounts of strengthening of recognition responses were confounded with the different numbers of responses of meaningfulness training.

Noble uses findings of Gannon and Noble (1961) and of Hakes (1961a) that 20 familiarization trials with response members had no effect on subsequent paired-associate learning to justify his interpretation of the Parker and Noble results as due to the number of different responses to the response member rather than to the strengthening of recognition responses. Two comments are pertinent. First, Gannon and Noble and also Hakes gave only 20 familiarization trials, which is markedly less than the 60 trials with stimuli to which the three different responses were conditioned. Moreover, Parker and Noble's (Noble's paper) familiarization control was only 32 trials. Second, the requirement that subjects learn different responses may be a condition which occasions greater strengthening of recognition responses than Gannon and Noble's and Parker and Noble's familiarization procedure. At present, therefore, the relationship between acquisition rate and M seems best interpreted as primarily due to speed and stability of recognition responses to response members, to their greater availability, and possibly to various of the suggested further consequences of speed and stability of those responses.

C. *Relationships between stimulus and response members.* Stimulus members and the recognition responses they evoke and response members and recognition responses they evoke can be related directly or indirectly. M of stimulus members, of response members, or of both might reflect transitional probabilities from all or part of a stimulus member or from the last letters or syllables of recognition response to that stimulus member to the first letters or syllables of recognition responses to response members. To the degree that M of discrete stimuli is a direct indicant of transitional probabilities, M and rate of acquisition should also be directly related. Richardson and Erlebacher's (1958) table of ratings of common meaning and ease of learning of pairs of stimuli suggest that these attributes may be positively correlated with M of discrete stimuli. Battig's (1959) scalings, however, indicate that, under some circumstances, this relationship may be negligible. Nonetheless it seems reasonable that ratings of the similarity of meaning of pairs of stimuli or of strength of associations of one to the other might be at least slightly related in positive fashion to transitional probabilities between letters or syllables and to transitional probabilities from one response as a unit to another as a unit.

In one experiment, Goss, Nodine, and Levitt (1961) constructed paired-associate units in which M values of stimulus and response members were orthogonal to each other and somewhat independent of rated common meaning or rated ease of learning of the pairs of which they were members. M of stimulus members had no effect but both M of response members and ratings of their common meaning or of ease of learning were directly related to acquisition rate. Thus, acquisition rate may have been influenced both by integration of recognition responses, as indicated by M of response members alone, and by possible direct or indirect relationships between them, as indicated by ratings of common meaning and ease of learning of the pairs. Common meaning of pairs of stimuli may be due either to formal similarity of members of pairs and of recognition responses to those members or to overlap of association responses to those members. The former might be considered a direct relationship between stimulus and response members and the latter an indirect relationship.

With respect to formal similarity of stimulus and response members and of the recognition responses they evoke, up to the point of identical recognition responses, it seems likely that greater similarity slows learning. To make one response as a covert recognition response and another increasingly similar but still different response as an overt anticipation or recall would seem to be increasingly difficult. But this can be determined. Overlap of association hierarchies is a special case of indirect relationship between stimulus and response members. More generally, a stimulus member may evoke an association response which, in turn, is already associated with the recognition response to the response member or to another association response which evokes the recognition response to the response member. If so, time for anticipation or recall permitting, acquisition of the relationship between stimulus members and the recognition response to the response member should be facilitated by these mediating responses. Such mediating responses might ultimately be directly or indirectly evoked by letter-sequence components of stimulus and response members or by stimulus and response members as units.

Association responses to stimulus members and association responses to response members are the presumed primary bases of mediating associations. The larger the number of such responses—as indicated particularly, perhaps, by M of stimulus members—the greater the probability of facilitative indirect associations between stimulus members or stimuli produced by the recognition response they evoke and recognition responses to paired response members. The dilemma here, however, is that, in conventional lists in which stimuli are paired to avoid direct and indirect association between members of a pair, a stimulus member should have more of such indirect associations with recognition responses to response members of other units than with the recognition response to its paired response member. Therefore, the more such indirect association involved in increasing M of a stimulus, the greater the interference, with the possible consequence of slower rather than more rapid learning. To counteract this possibility, subjects may select indirect associations which minimize response competition. But the conditions for and the process of any such selection are obscure. Reed (1918a, 1918b) earlier concluded that "associative aids" which included mediating responses facilitated acquisition of correct responses, and Underwood and Schulz (1960, pp. 296–305) present analyses of subject's accounts of their learning which led them to the same conclusion. However, until data on mediating associations are available for stimulus and response members representing various combinations of M of discrete stimuli and representing various levels of common meaning of pairs of stimuli, these findings cannot be considered definitive. Present data on experimentally induced mediate associations (e.g., Crawford and Vanderplas, 1959; Russell and Storms, 1955; Cramer and Cofer, 1960; and Jenkins' paper) are not directly pertinent.

Another indirect relationship is the "deduction" of the response to a particular stimulus member by means of a mediating principle. In one experiment, for example, Goss, Nodine, and Levitt (1961) paired two stimulus members, one of which was the reverse of the other, with two response members, one of which was the reverse of the other. Formal similarity of the two stimulus members was high as was formal similarity of the two response members. But this combination was learned less slowly than had been expected. The suggested reason was that subjects could learn the response to one stimulus member and "deduce" the response to the other similar stimulus member by the principle: "The response to one stimulus member is the reverse of the response to the other."

Serial-anticipation Learning. Each item of serial-anticipation lists is a response member for the just preceding item and, perhaps, more remote preceding and succeeding items. Each item is also a stimulus member for the just succeeding and, perhaps, more remote stimuli. Accordingly, no new bases of the facilitative effects of M and familiarization are seemingly required.

M of stimuli of serial-anticipation lists (e.g., Noble's paper) and amount of familiarization with those stimuli (e.g., Hovland and Kurtz, 1952; Noble, 1955; Riley and Phillips, 1959; Underwood and Schulz, 1960, pp. 113–119) are both directly related to rate of acquisition. These data on facilitative effects of familiarization are more consistent than data from paired-associate learning on effects of familiarization with stimulus members, response members, or both. The parsimonious explanation is Noble's (1955) notion of reduced variability of stimuli produced by recognition responses supplemented by the notions that faster and more stable recognition responses to an item in both its stimulus and response aspects provide more time for rehearsal and greater likelihood of evocation and completion in the anticipation interval. Also, familiarization should increase response availability.

Responses of the association hierarchy may have some indirect effect, but both instructions and the conventional two-second rate probably minimize their importance. However this does not rule out possible direct effects through transitional probabilities or formal similarity of recognition responses. At present, there apparently are no directly pertinent data.

SUMMARY

The primary concern of this discussion of Professor Noble's paper, "Meaningfulness and Familiarity," was further development of the more general concepts and principles which presumably account for the relationships of M of discrete stimuli to other normative measures and of M to acquisition of paired-associate and serial-anticipation tasks which Noble had summarized. Pertinent antecedent analyses of the role of M in verbal learning, particularly Sheffield's analysis, were described. The proposed theoretical analysis was then developed in three parts. The first was a relatively detailed consideration of observed and inferred stimulus-response elements and relationships of meaningfulness scaling and word-association situations. The second focused on antecedents to those elements and relationships and on their properties and possible general consequences. The primary concern of the third part was the immediate and further consequences for acquisition rate of the presumed elements and relationships involved in responding to stimulus members, response members, or both, during paired-associate learning. The role of those elements and relationships in serial-anticipation learning was examined briefly.

REFERENCES

Archer, E. J. (1960) A re-evaluation of the meaningfulness of all possible CVC trigrams. Psychol. Monogr., 74 (Whole No. 497).
Arnoult, M. D. (1957) Stimulus predifferentiation: Some generalizations and hypotheses. Psychol. Bull., 54, 339–352.

Bailey, J. H., & Jeffrey, W. E. (1958) Response strength and association value in stimulus predifferentiation. *Psychol. Rep.*, **4**, 715–721.

Battig, W. F. (1959) Scaled difficulty of nonsense-syllable pairs consisting of syllables of equal association value. *Psychol. Rep.*, **5**, 126.

Bousfield, W. A., Whitmarsh, G. A., & Danick, J. J. (1958) Partial response identities in verbal generalization. *Psychol. Rep.*, **4**, 703–713.

Cieutat, V. J. (1960) Differential familiarity with stimulus and response in paired-associate learning. *Percept. Mot. Skills*, **11**, 269–275.

Cofer, C. N. (1958) Comparison of word associations obtained by the methods of discrete single words and continued association. *Psychol. Rep.*, **4**, 507–510.

Cofer, C. N. (1960) An experimental analysis of the role of context in verbal behavior. *Trans. N. Y. Acad. Sci.*, ser. II, **22**, 341–347.

Cofer, C. N., & Foley, J. P. (1942) Mediated generalization and the interpretation of verbal behavior: I. Prolegomena. *Psychol. Rev.*, **49**, 513–540.

Cook, J. O. (1961) Some principles underlying the programming of paired associate materials. Paper presented at First Conf. of Language Programmers for Automated & Self-Instructional Teaching Devices. University of Michigan, Ann Arbor, Mich.

Cook, J. O., & Kendler, T. S. (1956) A theoretical model to explain some paired-associate learning data. In G. Finch & F. Cameron (Eds.), *Symposium on air force human engineering, personnel, and training research*. Washington, D. C.: Nat'l Acad. Sci-Nat'l Res. Coun. Publ., **455**, 90–98.

Cramer, P., & Cofer, C. N. (1960) The role of forward and reverse association in transfer of training. *Amer. Psychologist*, **16**, 463. (Abstract)

Crawford, J. L., & Vanderplas, J. M. (1959) An experiment on the mediation of transfer in paired-associate learning. *J. Psychol.*, **47**, 87–98.

Dashiell, J. F. (1928) *Fundamentals of objective psychology*. Boston: Houghton-Mifflin.

Dollard, J., & Miller, N. E. (1950) *Personality and psychotherapy*. New York: McGraw-Hill.

Epstein, W., Rock, I., Zuckerman, C. B. (1960) Meaning and familiarity in verbal learning. *Psychol. Monogr.*, **74** (Whole No. 491).

Froeberg, S. (1918) Simultaneous versus successive association. *Psychol. Rev.*, **25**, 156–163.

Gannon, D. R., & Noble, C. E. (1961) Familiarization (*n*) as a stimulus factor in paired-associate verbal learning. *J. Exp. Psychol.*, **62**, 14–23.

Gibson, E. J. (1940) A systematic application of the concepts of generalization and differentiation to verbal learning. *Psychol. Rev.*, **47**, 196–229.

Gibson, J. J., & Gibson, E. J. (1955) Perceptual learning: Differentiation or enrichment? *Psychol. Rev.*, **62**, 32–41.

Goss, A. E. (1955) A stimulus-response analysis of the interaction of cue-producing and mediating responses. *Psychol. Rev.*, **62**, 20–31.

Goss, A. E. (1956) *Report on the University of Massachusetts conference on problem solving*. Amherst, Mass.

Goss, A. E. (1961) Early behaviorism and verbal mediating responses. *Amer. Psychologist*, **16**, 285–298.

Goss, A. E., Nodine, C. F., & Levitt, H. (1961) Stimulus characteristics and percentage of occurrence of response members in paired-associates learning under group administration. Paper presented at Psychonomic Soc., New York.

Goss, A. E., Nodine, C. F., Gregory, B. N., Taub, H. A., & Kennedy, K. E. (1962) Stimulus characteristics and percentages of occurrence of response members in paired-associates learning. *Psychol. Monogr.*, **76**.

Goss, A. E., & Sugerman, M. (1961) Paired-associates learning with varying relative percentages of occurrence of alternative response members. *J. Exp. Psychol.*, **62**, 24–34.

Guthrie, E. R. (1933) Association as a function of time interval. *Psychol. Rev.*, **40**, 355–367.

Hakes, D. T. (1961a) Familiarization (n) as a stimulus factor in paired-associate verbal learning: A replication. Paper presented at Midwest Psychol. Ass., Chicago.

Hakes, D. T. (1961b) The role of stimulus and response familiarization in paired-associate learning. Unpublished Ph.D. dissertation, University of Minnesota.

Hovland, C. I., & Kurtz, K. H. (1952) Experimental studies in rote learning theory. X. Pre-learning syllable familiarization and the length-difficulty relationship. *J. Exp. Psychol.*, **44**, 31–39.

Howes, D., & Osgood, C. E. (1954) On the combination of associative probabilities in linguistic contexts. *Amer. J. Psychol.*, **67**, 241–253.

Hull, C. L. (1943) *Principles of behavior.* New York: Appleton-Century-Crofts.

Jenkins, J. J. (1959a) Effects on word-association of the set to give popular responses. *Psychol. Rep.*, **5**, 94.

Jenkins, J. J. (1959b) A study of mediated association. *Studies in verbal behavior.* Rep. No. 2, University of Minnesota.

Levitt, H. (1959) The effects of sound intensity (drive) on paired-associates learning. Unpublished Ph.D. dissertation, University of Massachusetts.

Levitt, H., & Goss, A. E. (1961) Stimulus attributes and drive in paired-associates learning. *J. Exp. Psychol.*, **62**, 243–252.

Liberman, A. M., Harris, K. S., Hoffman, H. S., & Griffith, B. C. (1957) The discrimination of speech sounds within and across phoneme boundaries. *J. Exp. Psychol.*, **54**, 358–368.

Lifton, H., & Goss, A. E. (in press) Aural-visual transfer of paired-associates learning. *J. Gen. Psychol.*

Mandler, G. (1954) Response factors in human learning. *Psychol. Rev.*, **61**, 235–244.

Miller, N. E., & Dollard, J. (1941) *Social learning and imitation.* New Haven, Conn.: Yale University Press.

Morikawa, Y. (1959) Functions of stimulus and response in paired-associate verbal learning. *Psychologia*, **2**, 41–56.

Musgrave, B. S. (1960) The effect of verbal context factors on cloze and commonality scores. Unpublished M.A. thesis, University of Minnesota.

Newman, S. E. (1960) A selective mediation model of paired associate learning. Paper presented at Psychonomic Soc., Chicago.

Noble, C. E. (1952a) An analysis of meaning. *Psychol. Rev.*, 59, 421–430.

Noble, C. E. (1952b) The role of stimulus meaning (*m*) in serial verbal learning. *J. Exp. Psychol.*, 43, 437–446.

Noble, C. E. (1955) The effect of familiarization upon serial verbal learning. *J. Exp. Psychol.*, 49, 333–338.

Noble, C. E. (1961) Measurements of association value (*a*), rated associations (*a'*), and scaled meaningfulness (*m'*) for the 2100 CVC combinations of the English alphabet. *Psychol. Rep.*, 8, 487–521.

Osgood, C. E., & Anderson, L. (1957) Certain relations among experienced contingencies, associative structure, and contingencies in encoded messages. *Amer. J. Psychol.*, 20, 411–420.

Parker, G. V. C., & Noble, C. E. (1960) Effects of experimentally-produced meaningfulness (*m*) on paired-associate learning. *Amer. Psychologist*, 15, 451. (Abstract)

Peters, H. N. (1935) Mediate association. *J. Exp. Psychol.*, 18, 20–48.

Peterson, L. R. (1956) Prediction of response in verbal habit hierarchies. *J. Exp. Psychol.*, 51, 249–252.

Peterson, L. R., & Peterson, M. J. (1957) The role of context stimuli in verbal learning. *J. Exp. Psychol.*, 53, 100–105.

Reed, H. B. (1918a) Associative aids: I. Their relation to learning, retention and other associations. *Psychol. Rev.*, 25, 128–155.

Reed, H. B. (1918b) Associative aids: II. Their relation to practice and the transfer of training. *Psychol. Rev.*, 25, 257–285.

Reed, H. B. (1918c) Associative aids: III. Their relation to the theory of thought and to methodology in psychology. *Psychol. Rev.*, 25, 378–401.

Rhine, R. J., & Silun, B. A. (1958) Acquisition and change of a concept attitude as a function of consistency of reinforcement. *J. Exp. Psychol.*, 55, 524–529.

Richardson, J., & Erlebacher, A. (1958) Associative connection between paired verbal items. *J. Exp. Psychol.*, 56, 62–69.

Riley, D. A., & Phillips, L. W. (1959) The effects of syllable familiarization on rote learning, association value, and reminiscence. *J. Exp. Psychol.*, 57, 372–379.

Russell, W. A., & Storms, L. H. (1955) Implicit verbal chaining in paired-associate learning. *J. Exp. Psychol.*, 49, 287–293.

Saltz, E. (1960) Similarity and differentiation in verbal learning. Paper presented at Psychonomic Soc., Chicago.

Saltz, E., Metzen, J. D., & Ernstein, E. (1961) Predifferentiation of verbal stimuli in children. *Psychol. Rep.*, 9, 127–132.

Sheffield, F. D. (1946) The rôle of meaningfulness of stimulus and response in verbal learning. Unpublished Ph.D. dissertation, Yale University.

Solley, C. M., & Messick, S. J. (1957) Probability learning, the statistical structure of concepts, and the measurement of meaning. *Amer. J. Psychol.*, 70, 161–173.

Spiker, C. C. (1956) Experiments with children on the hypothesis of acquired distinctiveness and equivalence of cues. *Child Develpm.*, **27**, 253-263.

Staats, A. W. (1961) Verbal habit-families, concepts, and the operant conditioning of word classes. *Psychol. Rev.* **68**, 190–204.

Underwood, B. J. (1953a) Studies of distributed practice: VIII. Learning and retention of paired nonsense syllables as a function of intra-list similarity. *J. Exp. Psychol.*, **45**, 133–142.

Underwood, B. J. (1953b) Studies of distributed practice: IX. Learning and retention of paired adjectives as a function of intra-list similarity. *J. Exp. Psychol.*, **45**, 143–149.

Underwood, B. J., & Schulz, R. W. (1960) *Meaningfulness and verbal learning.* Philadelphia: Lippincott.

Underwood, B. J., Runquist, W. N., & Schulz, R. W. (1959) Response learning in paired-associate lists as a function of intralist similarity. *J. Exp. Psychol.*, **58**, 70–78.

Vanderplas, J. M., & Garvin, E. A. (1959) Complexity, association value, and practice as factors in shape recognition following paired-associate training. *J. Exp. Psychol.*, **57**, 155–163.

Watson, J. B. (1924) *Psychology from the standpoint of a behaviorist.* (2nd ed.) Philadelphia: Lippincott.

Weiss, R. L. (1958) The role of association value and experimentally produced familiarity in paired associate learning. Unpublished Ph.D. dissertation, University of Buffalo.

Woodworth, R. S., & Schlosberg, H. (1954) *Experimental psychology.* (Rev. ed.) New York: Holt, Rinehart & Winston.

SUMMARY OF CONFERENCE DISCUSSION

Much of the extensive discussion in this session was directed to clarification of points made by Goss in his comments, points which are adequately treated in the present written form of his paper and which, therefore, need not be repeated here.

Underwood asked Goss how he knew that all of the factors listed in Table 4–4 under antecedents are important. Goss indicated that further experimentation is necessary to verify this judgment in the case of several of the factors. Underwood thought that evidence concerning intra-sensory transfer suggests that some of the factors are not important. To this, Jenkins observed that subjects can discriminate between *lic* and *lik* on the basis of orthography but not pronunciation, suggesting intra-sensory differentiation. Deese indicated concern that oral and written responses to association test stimuli might differ but felt this difficulty could be overcome by discarding items in which commonality between response modes is low. Goss emphasized that his concern was not so much with contemporaneous variables as with antecedent ones, such as frequency. Melton asked whether frequency, as an antecedent variable to an association test response, is frequency of hearing or of reading items together.

Jenkins referred to Hake's experiment (1961) and others of its kind and expressed concern over the accuracy of the experimenter's judgment as to whether the subject has said the response correctly. In his laboratory, the responses of several subjects were recorded on tape and carefully analyzed. Some, but not very many, responses were seen to have been misscored. He suggested that perhaps the subject should write his responses, rather than say them, in order to overcome this source of error. Lengthening of the response period might, of course, be necessary if this were done to permit time for the subject to write his response, and Noble pointed out that such a change in method would limit continuity with other studies of paired-associate learning. He also asked if such a method could still be called verbal learning, since writing involves motor skills.

Deese pointed out that most of the norms with which Noble and Goss were dealing are derived from written responses which preserve orthography, whereas in the paired-associate situation the response is oral and is scored phonemically. Noble suggested that comparison of oral and written norms, when made, shows agreement. Deese said, however, that he had found many intrusions (errors) in written recalls whereas in oral recalls they are infrequent. He suggested that many errors may enter because the scoring is less rigid for oral recall. (We more easily accept "silent" as correct when "silence" is in fact correct.) There is not a perfect correlation between scoring (and other factors) in oral and written responding.

Jenkins pointed out that this problem is not involved in the familiarization effect. He said that Hakes has gone on to use paralogs, trigrams, numbers, and letters to separate the stimulus class from the response class. When these classes are distinctive, there is a response-familiarization effect in paired-associate learning, but stimulus familiarization is not helpful. In the case of the pair comprised of two paralogs (one as stimulus, one as response) it is not clear that familiarization has much effect. Irrelevant familiarization appears to be an important variable. Noble said that neither Schulz in his thesis nor Hakes used control groups; Jenkins pointed out, however, that Schultz obtained functions for numbers of familiarization trials, and Underwood that one trial is essentially a zero-trial control.

Mandler described an experiment by Fletcher and Tulving (unpublished) who used a list of 10 paired adjectives. For one group response items were omitted 50 per cent of the time (ORM), for another group the stimulus items were omitted 50 per cent of the time (OSM). The ORM (stimulus-familiarization) group learned significantly faster than the OSM (response-familiarization) group. Goss referred to this as a sort of partial-reinforcement experiment on both sides. Musgrave pointed out that backward as well as forward association goes on all through learning. Melton said that the interval allows for rehearsal of the prior pair.

In reference to Goss's point that m seems to be unimportant in serial learning whereas familiarization is important, Noble said that this is ironical because serial learning is supposed to be more complex than paired-associate learning.

Melton directed a question to Noble concerning his statement (p. 106) that only a distributed practice experiment could settle the question whether n interacts with the S-R interval. He asked how such an experiment could settle the question. Noble said the S-R interval should be varied, but Melton maintained that prolonging it would allow increased time in which the stimulus could be said and this would wipe out the differences which have arisen in experiments on stimulus familiarization (p. 105). Underwood said that Schultz has lengthened the stimulus interval and that the difference is eliminated. Noble said he meant the S-R interval, but Underwood and Melton pointed out that it had to be the stimulus interval because as the stimulus ceases, the response term appears. (This would depend on the particular technique used.)

Goss pointed out that the best performance of any group in the Schulz-Tucker experiment (Table 4–1) is made by the do-not-pronounce group with zero familiarization. Melton said this might be due to interference in do-not-pronounce conditions, where familiarization trials have been run. Probably the subjects tend to pronounce the stimuli after familiarization and will continue to do so or else have to suppress the response when told not to pronounce the stimuli. Noble said Schulz tells his subjects not to pronounce the stimuli, calling attention to the necessity of suppression of this response. Melton felt this might be a hypothesis to explain the inhibitory effects of familiarization and said this factor could be avoided by using other techniques.

REFERENCES

Fletcher, N. E., & Tulving, E. (1961; unpublished) The role of stimulus and response members in paired associate learning. University of Toronto.

Hakes, D. T. (1961) The role of stimulus and response familiarization in paired-associate learning. *Studies in verbal behavior.* Rep. No. 4, University of Minnesota.

Chapter 5

THE ACQUISITION OF SYNTAX[1]

Roger Brown and Colin Fraser

HARVARD UNIVERSITY

What is done in a developmental study of behavior depends upon the investigators' conception of the terminal state, the outcome of the development. Normal adults speaking their native language seem to us to possess a set of rules of word construction and sentence construction which enables them to go beyond the speech they have actually heard and practiced to the creation of lawful novelties. If new monosyllables are created, speakers of English will agree that *stug* is "better English" than *ftug*. Probably this is because they have shared implicit knowledge of the initial consonant clusters that are acceptable in English. If this new word is to be pluralized, they will agree that *stug*/-z/ is better than *stug*/-s/. Probably this is because they have shared knowledge of a rule of regular English inflection. If the new word is first heard in the sentence, "Here is some stug," they will agree that a second sentence, "The stug is there," is more likely to be grammatical than a second sentence, "A stug is there." Probably this is because they have shared knowledge of the syntactic rules for the employment of mass nouns.

The construction rules of which speakers have implicit knowledge are, in their explicit form, the grammar of a language. As these rules have been written down in traditional grammars, they constitute a collection of largely unrelated statements about such matters as the parts of speech, paradigms of conjugation and declension, the marking of gender, and the agreement of adjectives and nouns. Chomsky (1957) has shown that it may be possible to systematize traditional grammar into a mechanism for the generation of all the sentences of a language that are grammatical and none that are ungrammatical. Grammar becomes a theory for a range of phenomena—the sentences of a language—and also a program for generating sentences—a program that might be followed by an electronic

[1] The work described in this paper was supported by the National Science Foundation by a grant administered through the Center for Communication Sciences, M.I.T.

device (Yngve, 1961). It is the development in children of this kind of sentence-generating grammar that we are trying to study.

The child growing up hears, from his family, his friends, and the television, a large sample of the sentences of a language; and we think that he induces from the regularities in this sample an implicit grammar. First-language learning, so conceived, reminds us of two other operations with language: that of the linguist in the field and that of the adult learning a second language. The descriptive linguist trying to work out the structure of an unfamiliar tongue begins by collecting a large set of utterances—his "corpus." From regularities in the corpus and from inquiries of a native informant he induces rules that predict beyond what he has observed. One check on the adequacy of his rules is their ability to anticipate new utterances correctly. Another check is the ability of the rules to duplicate the distinctions made by a native informant who has been asked to judge whether each of a collection of utterances is or is not a well-formed sentence. It may be that the linguistic procedures for discovering syntax in distributional facts are a good model for the child's learning of his native language—with the difference that the linguist works deliberately and aims at explicit formulation whereas the child works unwittingly and arrives at implicit formulations. The child's syntax is made explicit for him in "grammar" school, but we suggest that he operates with syntax long before he is of school age.

In learning a second or foreign language it does not seem possible to memorize a list of sentences that is long enough to provide the right one when you need it. Somehow the situation is never exactly right for any of the sayings one has rehearsed. To be effective in a second language, the student must be able to "construct" sentences; and there are two techniques for giving him this ability. The traditional method is explicit instruction in the rules of grammar. With these rules and a stock of words one puts together the sentence to suit the occasion. A difficulty is that deliberate construction is a slow business, and the boat will have sunk before you can properly call for help. Some modern instruction treats the second-language learner like a child and has him practice again and again the same set of sentences. The sentences may be delivered to an entire group by film strip, or the student may pace himself with one of the Richards and Gibson pocketbooks. Eventually the student finds himself the creator of a new sentence—one not practiced, but somehow implied by what has been practiced. Second-language learning by sentence rehearsal relies on this step into automatic construction though nothing much seems to be known about how to contrive sets of examples that will facilitate its occurrence.

It has seemed to us, then, that first-language learning must have much in common with second-language learning and also with scientific techniques for the discovery of linguistic structure. The shared characteristic that is the ground of the analogy is the necessity in all three cases of inducing general construction rules from sets of sentences. Of course the analogy suppresses those features of first-language learning that are not to be found in the other two processes, and it has taken considerable pressure from reality to bring them to our attention.

This paper is divided into three sections. The first reviews some studies with invented linguistic materials which show that children do indeed have rules of word and sentence construction. The second discusses techniques by which an investigator might induce a child's generative grammar from a large collection of the child's utterances and the, possibly parallel, techniques by which the child could have induced that grammar from a large set of parental utterances. Most of the discussion in this section makes use of materials from a record of four hours of speech from one child of 25½ months. The third section discusses some substantive results from the records of 13 children between two and three years of age; these are the results that forced us to recognize that there are differences between children and either linguistic scientists or adult students of a second language.

EVIDENCE THAT CHILDREN HAVE CONSTRUCTION RULES

In the natural situation of the child with his family the best evidence that he possesses construction rules is the occurrence of systematic errors. So long as a child speaks correctly, it is possible that he says only what he has heard. In general we cannot know what the total input has been and so cannot eliminate the possibility of an exact model for each sentence that is put out. However, when a small boy says "I digged in the yard" or "I saw some sheeps" or "Johnny hurt hisself," it is unlikely that he is imitating. Furthermore, his mistake is not a random one. We can see how he might have made it by overgeneralizing certain existent regularities. Many verbs ending in voiced consonants form the simple past with /-d/ and many nouns ending in voiceless consonants form the plural with /-s/. The set of forms, *me, my, myself and you, your, yourself*, strongly suggests *he, his, hisself*. As it happens, actual English usage breaks with these simple regularities and prefers *dug, sheep*, and *himself*. By smoothing the language into a simpler system than it is, the child reveals his tendency to induce rules. Guillaume made this point in 1927, and illustrated it with a rich collection of French children's systematic errors.

A Study of Morphological Rules

Although Smith (1933) attempted to study the development of grammar by observing spontaneously occurring errors, it is more economical to invent materials such as nonsense syllables and try to elicit relevant information. This is what Jean Berko did for English inflections in her doctoral research (1958).

A child is shown the small animal of Figure 5–1 and told: "This is a *wug*. Now there are two of them. There are two _____." The experimenter holds her voice up to signal the child that he is to complete the sentence; he will usually supply *wug*/-z/. For a different animal the word is *bik* and the correct plural *bik*/-s/. For a third animal it is *niss* and the plural *niss*/-əz/. Printed English uses the letter s for all of these endings; but as the phonemic notation shows, and as attention to your own pronunciation will reveal, the endings are distinct. The rule in English is: A word ending in a voiceless consonant forms its plural with the voiceless sibilant /-s/ as in *cats*, *cakes*, and *lips*; a word ending in

This is a wug.

Now there is another one.
There are two of them.
There are two_____.

Fig. 5–1. Illustration of Jean Berko's method for eliciting inflections.

either a vowel or a voiced consonant forms its plural with the voiced sibilant /-z/ as in *dogs*, *crows*, and *ribs*; a word ending in the singular with either /s/ or /z/ forms its plural with /-z/ plus an interpolated neutral vowel as in *classes* and *poses*. We all follow these rules and know at once that a new word like *bazooka* will have, as its plural, *bazooka*/-z/, even though most speakers of English will never know the rule in explicit form.

Berko invented a set of materials that provides a complete inventory of the English inflectional system: the plural and possessive endings on nouns; the simple past, the third person present indicative, and the progressive on verbs; and the comparative and superlative on adjectives. She presented these materials as a picture-book game to children of preschool and first-, second-, and third-grade age levels and worked out the development of the rules with age.

The productivity of the regular inflections for children seems to be greater than it is for adults. Both kinds of subject were shown a picture of a man swinging something about his head and were told: "This is a man who knows how to gling. He glings every day. Today he glings. Yesterday he _____." Adults hang suspended between *gling, glang, glung,* and even *glought,* but children promptly say *glinged.* Dr. Berko also tested to see whether children who generalize the regular inflection would correctly imitate irregular forms or would assimilate them to the rules. She showed a picture and said, for instance, "Here is a goose and here are two geese. There are two _____." Most of her subjects said *gooses* and performed similarly with other irregular forms. These observations suggest that rules of great generality may survive and override a number of counter instances.

Knowledge of the paradigms of inflection could take a child beyond his corpus to the correct construction of new forms. It is not necessary to hear each new noun in its plural and possessive forms; these can be anticipated from the regular paradigm, and, except for an occasional *sheep* and *alumni,* the anticipation will be correct. The rules of inflection are rules of morphology, i.e., rules of word construction rather than rules of syntax or sentence construction. In English, though not in Russian and many other languages, inflection is a rather trivial grammatical system, and knowledge of inflection cannot take a child very far beyond his corpus. There is much greater power in syntax.

A Study of Syntactic Rules

The fundamental notion in linguistic syntax is that the words of any natural language can be grouped into classes which are defined by the fact that the members of a class have similar "privileges of occurrence" in sentences. Certain very large and rough syntactic classes are traditionally called the parts of speech. In English, count nouns like *house, barn, table,* and *fence* are words that can be plugged into such sentence contexts as: "See the _____," "I own a _____," "The _____ is new," and "This _____ is mine." If a child has learned to organize words into such classes, to enter them on mental lists of syntactic equivalents, he will have a very powerful means of getting beyond his corpus.

Hearing *car* as a new word in the sentence: "See the *car,*" a child could use this context as a basis for listing *car* with count nouns and so be prepared to hear and say such additional sentences as: "I own a *car,*" "The *car* is new," and "This *car* is mine." And a multitude of others. Of course the particular sentence uttered on a given occasion would depend on semantic and motivational factors, but the population of sentences from which the particular could be drawn would be established by the syntactic kinship linking *car* with *house, barn, table,* and *fence.*

What evidence do we have that a child acquires, with increasing experience of his native language, implicit rules of syntax? Brown and Berko (1960) invented a game for children that utilizes nonsense syl-

lables but not, as in the inflection game, for the purpose of eliciting endings. For one problem the child was asked: "Do you know what a wug
is?" He was then shown a picture of a little girl and told: "This is a little
girl thinking about a wug. Can you make up what that might mean?"
The picture was included only to engage the child's attention—it did not
portray the referent of the new word but only someone thinking about it.
The new word, *wug*, had been introduced in two sentences. In both
cases it was preceded by the indefinite article; it functioned once as a
noun complement and once as the object of a preposition. The positions
of *wug* in these two contexts serve to identify it as a singular count
noun. An adult speaker of English would have expected such additional
sentences as: "Wugs are good" and "That wug is new" to be grammatical.
Brown and Berko were interested in seeing whether young children
would answer the question: "Can you make up what that might mean?"
with a flow of sentences employing *wug* as a count noun.

In the complete study 12 nonsense syllables were used, and they were
placed in sentences identifying them as belonging to one of six parts of
speech. Where *wug* was to be identified as a transitive verb, the investigator said: "This is a little girl who wants to wug something." As an intransitive verb the same sentence was used with the omission of *something*. With *wug* as a mass noun the little girl would be "thinking about
some wug." *Wug* became an adjective by having the girl think of "something wuggy" and an adverb by having her think of "doing something
wuggily."

Children in the first, second, and third grades all went on to make up
sentences using their new words, but they did not always use them correctly. They did better as they got older and better at all ages with the
count noun, adjective, transitive and intransitive verbs, than with the
mass nouns and adverbs. For the purposes of the present argument[2]
the important result is that children showed an ability, increasing with
age, to construct grammatically correct sentences using new words.

The eliciting of speech with standard invented materials brings some
very desirable control to the study of grammar acquisition. It left us,
however, with the suspicion that we had only been chipping at the problem. The things we thought of doing were largely suggested by frag-
mentary facts about adult grammar and guesses as to what children

[2] The same children were given a word-association test employing familiar English
words belonging to the same six parts of speech involved in the nonsense-syllable
task. The principal finding was that the frequency of paradigmatic word associations (i.e., a response word that belongs to the same part of speech as the stimulus
word: *house-barn*, *run-walk*, and *milk-water*) was related, across the various parts
of speech and age groups, to the tendency to make correct syntactic use of the
nonsense syllables. This result was taken to mean that paradigmatic word associations
reflect the developing organization of vocabulary into syntactic classes.

would have to learn. If we were to collect a large number of utterances from an individual child, would it be possible to subject this collection to the kind of distributional analysis that a linguist applies to an unfamiliar language and thereby to discover the child's total generative grammar? Could one write grammar programs for children at different ages and describe language development as a sequence of progressively complicating programs?

INDUCING A GRAMMAR FROM A CORPUS

Before collecting any data we studied English grammar in its more traditional forms (Jespersen, 1905; Smart, 1925) and also in the recent works of Francis (1958), Hockett (1958), Chomsky (1957), and Lees (1960). The traditional works supply most of the substantive knowledge about word classes—knowledge which has been reinterpreted and systematized in recent works. The substance is often more effectively taught by the earlier grammars since this is knowledge that contemporary theorists often take for granted. The generative grammar, using constituent analysis and transformation rules, has been worked out for a part of English; but there is not yet a complete grammar of this kind for any language.

Rules of grammar are cultural norms; like other norms they are descriptive of certain regularities of behavior within a community, and they also are prescriptive in recommending this behavior to new members of the community. In general, the student of culture can discover norms either by observing behavior and inducing regularities or by asking participants in the culture (informants) to tell him what kinds of behavior are "right" (proper, correct) and what kinds are "wrong" (improper, incorrect). For example, if we were interested in the rules of etiquette of the American middle class, we might ask informants what a seated gentleman should do when a lady enters a room and what a hatted gentleman should do when a lady enters an elevator. In addition, we might observe the behavior of seated and hatted gentlemen in the two situations. When the cultural rules to be discovered are linguistic, the possible approaches are the same: direct inquiry of informants as to what it is proper to say and what it is not proper to say; direct study of what is, in fact, said. Students of grammar have varied in the degree to which they have relied on one procedure rather than another.

The partial generative grammars for adult speech that have thus far been written have been written to meet the test of the grammar-writer's own delicate sense of what is and what is not a well-formed sentence in his native language. This is a special case of the technique of direct inquiry of a native informant concerning right and wrong behavior; in the present case the investigator is his own informant. Of course the linguist working out a generative grammar believes his personal judgments of the "grammaticality" of utterances represent a community consensus. The evidence so far reported for judgments made by informants who are not linguists (Hill, 1961; Maclay and Sleator, 1960) suggests that there is some consensus on grammaticality in English but that the consensus is not perfect.

While we have adopted the generative model for grammar, we have not been able to use the method of the linguists who have written generative grammars. Clearly we ought not to rely on our own sense of grammaticality in writing the grammars of very young children. In addition, however, we have not found a way to make direct inquiries of native informants between 24 and 36 months of age as to what they regard as well-formed sentences. With older children judgments of grammaticality may possibly be elicited in terms of what it is "right" and "wrong" to say. With the younger children we have so far worked entirely from obtained behavior: a sample or corpus of what has actually been said.

It is by no means certain that the direct study of obtained speech is an alternative and equivalent approach to the eliciting of judgments of grammaticality. Chomsky (1957) certainly does not suggest that the notion of the "well-formed" or "possible" sentence can be operationally translated into the "obtained" sentence. Common observation shows that adult speakers of English often produce verbal sequences that are not well-formed sentences. In the case of such another set of norms as the rules of etiquette behavioral practice might depart rather radically from ideal recommendations. The truth is that the relation between grammatical norms and verbal behavior is quite unexplored both theoretically and empirically. Without waiting for clarification of this relation for adult speakers, we have proceeded to explore the possibility of writing rules for the actual verbal behavior of children. Chomsky (1957) has argued that there are no really adequate mechanical procedures for discovering an adequate grammar, and our experience causes us to agree with him. Still there are some helpful tips, and Harris (1951) is the best source of these. In addition to reading about grammars, we practiced working them out from a speech corpus long before we collected data of our own. As practice materials we used the records collected by Barker and Wright (1954) for their Midwest studies. If anyone has a taste for word games, the grammar discovery game is an engrossing one, and not surprisingly, it yields more understanding than can be obtained from the reading of theoretical works.

We decided to begin work in the age range from 24 to 36 months. The younger age is the approximate time at which most children begin producing two-word utterances (McCarthy, 1954). Some preliminary work showed us that by three years many children had about as complex a grammar as we were able to describe. We located 13 children in this age range whose parents were willing to have us spend a large part of one day at their homes recording the child's speech. For the first seven cases our procedures varied from one to another but for the last six they have been reasonably uniform.

The families were of the professional college-educated class, and it is likely that the linguistic behavior of these children was "advanced" in terms of age norms for the American population. Only 2 of the 13 children were acquainted with one another, and so, with the exception of these two, the speech of any one child in the sample could not have been directly affecting the speech of any other. Many of the families had first arrived in Boston just seven months earlier, and the speech of these parents had been learned in several different parts of the country.

We hoped to get as much speech as possible in as little time as possible and to have examples of the full variety of sentence types the child could produce. There were those who warned that the child would be shy and speechless in our presence; this was not the case. Mothers told their children that visitors were coming; and in general, we were eagerly welcomed, shown a parade of toys and games, and talked to rather steadily. It became clear that the child expected a guest to put in some time as a playmate; and so the recording was a two-man job with one of us taking data and the other prepared to play cowboy, horsie, blocks, coloring, trains, and the mule in "Kick the Mule." Several of the early records were made by Fraser alone, but for the last six cases both of us were always there. We found that by about noon we needed a rest and so went away for lunch, returning about two o'clock; the child took his nap in the interval. About half of each record was made before lunch and about half after lunch.

Much of the time the child was occupied with his normal routine of play, talking with his mother, washing, and eating. So long as these activities involved a reasonable amount of speech, we took no active part beyond delivering signals of attention and approval. When the operant level was very low, we sometimes tried to raise it. In the first days we did the sort of verbal prompting that is anyone's first notion of a technique for eliciting speech from children. You ask what something is called and this brings out vocabulary items—which are not useful for a study of grammar. Or you ask a "yes-no" question, such as: "Is that your horsie?" to which the answer is either "yes" or "no." We eventually learned that it is easier to "inspire" speech by doing something interesting than to elicit it with questions. If the adult "playmate" starts a game that is simple, repetitious, and destructive, the child will usually join him and start talking. A universal favorite is to build (painstakingly) an unsteady tower of blocks and register chagrin when the child sends it crashing down. A simple game involving implicit rules—such as the green blocks belong to me and the red ones to you—creates a situation in which negative sentences can be elicited. If the adult playmate breaks the established rule and moves one of the child's blocks, he is usually told that he is *not* to do that.

How were the child's utterances recorded? After trying several different things, we found that it was not restrictive to ask the mother to limit activities to one floor of the house and a small number of adjoining rooms. Then with two Wollensak tape recorders and long extension cords we were able, in the last six cases, to get almost everything on tape. The machines were handled by the "playmate," and the other member of the team made a continuous transcript of the child's utterances. This on-the-spot transcript was later checked against the tape and corrected into a final best version. Going over the tape takes about four hours to each hour of recording time.

What is the level of detail in the transcription? It is neither phonetic nor phonemic but only morphemic. It is, in short, as if we were to write down in conventional English spelling what an adult seemed to be saying in an interview. Of course the intelligibility of speech in the youngest children was not very good. We found it helpful to do no writing for the first half hour and to have the mother interpret for us everything her child said in that period. In this time we learned to allow for the child's phonetic peculiarities and sometimes found an initial near complete unintelligibility giving way to about 75 per cent intelligibility. At grammatically crucial points our general rule was to credit the child with the regular adult contrast if he made any sort of appropriate phonetic distinction. For instance, the emergence of the modal auxiliary *will* in a sentence like *I will get my book* is not at first marked with a well articulated /wil/ but probably only with a shift of the vowel formants in the word *I* toward a back vowel like /u/. If we could hear a difference between this *I* and the way *I* sounded in *I got my book*, the child was credited with *will*. For the last six cases we were ultimately able to transcribe fully an average of 78 per cent of the total utterances on the tapes; this is a degree of success quite similar to that reported in previous studies (McCarthy, 1954). Where we were uncertain about the accuracy of transcription, the material was placed in brackets. Utterances were also marked with the following symbols: I for a functional imperative, ? for an interrogative, M for an utterance that mimics an immediately preceding utterance from another person, and R for an utterance that is a response to a question.

One difficulty we had anticipated did not materialize—only one. We had thought that division of the flow of speech into utterances might be an uncertain business. In fact, however, the usual criteria of either a prolonged pause or a shift of speakers worked very well. There were few instances of uncertain utterance division.

For the last six cases we aimed at and obtained a minimum of 500 different utterances from each child. Since the utterance rate of the younger children is lower than that of the older children, we spent more time with the younger ones.

Methods for Discovering a Provisional Grammar

The process of grammar discovery has two facets. It is, most immediately, the technique of the investigator who is trying to describe the grammatical apparatus of a particular child. The investigator induces from obtained utterances a probable generative mechanism. Since, however, the child is also presumed to have built this internal mechanism by processing obtained utterances, it follows that the investigator's procedure may be a good model of the child's learning. Of course the child has not induced his grammar from his own sentences but rather from the somewhat more varied and complex sentences heard from adult speakers. A comparison of the recorded speech of mother to child with the speech of child to mother shows that the grammars induced by children from adult speech are not identical with the adult grammars that produced the sentences. The investigator of a child's speech, on the other hand, hopes to find the very grammar that produced the original utterances. Even so the similarity in the tasks of investigator and child is very great—to get from sentences to a grammar—and so while acting as investigators, we shall want to consider whether the child may have carried out operations similar to our own.

For the kind of grammar we are trying to write the fundamental problem is to discover the syntactic classes.[3] Members of a common class are supposed to have similar privileges of occurrence, and these privileges are supposed to be different from one class to another. In addition to syntactic classes our grammars will involve rules of combination describing the ways in which members of the various classes may be put in sequence. Generally the rules of combination will get simpler as the syntactic classes get larger and fewer. If *a* and *an* in English were words

[3] The generative grammar as Chomsky (1957) has described it is more than a set of sequence rules for syntactic classes; it also provides several levels of appropriate constituent analysis. We have so far not accomplished this result for the speech of children because we have not been able to invent appropriate behavioral tests of the child's sense of constituent structure. The requirement that a grammar make appropriate structural analyses does of course help greatly in the evaluation of adult grammars, and it is desirable to meet this requirement wherever it is possible to do so.

having identical privileges of occurrence, our grammar would be simpler than it is. As it stands, however, the two forms must be separated and a rule of combination written that requires *an* before count nouns with an initial vowel and *a* before count nouns with an initial consonant.

As a basic technique for the discovery of syntactic classes we might undertake to record for each different word in the corpus all of the utterance contexts in which that word occurs; in short we might make a concordance. The contexts of each word could then be compared with the contexts of each other word and tentative syntactic classes set up so as to put together words having many contexts in common and so as to separate words having few or no contexts in common.

To illustrate the method of shared contexts, we have taken from the record of Adam[4] (28½ months) the words: *here, there, Mum,* and *Dad.* In adult English *here* and *there* are locative adverbials while *Mum* and *Dad* are animate nouns. Will the pattern of shared contexts taken from Adam's record suggest the assignment of *here* and *there* to one class and *Mum* and *Dad* to a different class? In Table 5–1 all of the utterances containing these four words are listed and the shared contexts under-lined. The upper limit to the number of contexts that two words can share in a given record is set by the number of contexts obtained for the less frequent of the two. *Here* occurs in 48 different contexts, and *there* in 19. It would be possible for the two words to share 19 different contexts; in fact they share 8 or 42 per cent of the possible contexts. *Mum* occurs in 49 different contexts and *Dad* in 8; they share 38 per cent of the possible contexts. *Here* shares no contexts with *Mum* and none with *Dad,* and the same is true for *there.* The pattern of shared contexts suggests the class break that operates in adult English.

If one has read about the notion of syntactic equivalence but never actually lined up the contexts for sets of words, it is startling to find such small numbers of identical contexts—especially startling since *here-there* and *Mum-Dad* must be as near to perfect syntactic equivalence as any pairs of words in the language, and in addition, the short sentences and small vocabulary of a child maximize the probability of repetition. Is a 38 per cent overlap enough for us to assume that the members of a pair are interchangeable? It may be.

We have taken the word *here* alone and set down all its different contexts in the first half of Adam's record and also all of its different contexts in the second half of the record (Table 5–2). A context that has already appeared in the first half is listed again on its first appearance in the second half. *Here* in the first half is the same word as *here* in the second half, and so we know that these two *heres* are syntactic equiva-

---

[4] The names used in this report for identifying child subjects are not the actual names of the children who were studied.

Table 5–1
Total Contexts of Four Words in the Record of Adam

MUM

Here it is, Mum.
Here, Mum.
Here (the) coffee pot
    broken, Mum.
More sugar, Mum.
There it is, Mum.
What's that, Mum.
Mum, (where is the cards)?
Mum, (where's the rags)?
WANT COFFEE, MUM.
Want apple, Mum.
Want blanket, Mum.
Want more juice, Mum.
I want blanket, Mum.
I want (it), Mum.
I want paper away, Mum.
(The) pan, Mum.
I want apple, Mum.
I want blanket, Mum.
I want blanket now, Mum.
I want juice, Mum.
Mum, I want some, Mum.
Popeye, Mum?
I wanta do, Mum.
I wanta help, Mum.

I found, Mum.
I do, Mum.
I don't, Mum.
I get it, Mum.
(Gonna) dump, Mum.
Fall down, Mum.
Fall, Mum.
An apple, Mum.
Apple, Mum.
Again, Mum?
Out, Mum?
Salad, Mum?
SEE, MUM?
Coffee, Mum?
Turn, Mum?
No, you see, Mum?
No help, Mum.
Won't help, Mum.
Coffee, Mum.
HI, MUM.
Ok, Mum.
Here, Mum.
Mum, over here.
Enough, Mum.
Silver spoons, Mum.

DAD

See paper, Dad.
WANT COFFEE, DAD.
I want cream, Dad.
SEE, DAD?
Dad, want coffee?
Some more, Dad?
Work, Dad?
HI, DAD.

HERE

Here (a car).
Here all gone.
Here (block).
Here brick.
Here chairs.
Here coffee is.
Here comes Daddy.
Here flowers.
Here goes.
Here is.
Here it goes.
Here it is.
Here it is, Mum.
Here's it here.
Here light.
Here (mail) more paper.
Here more.
Here more bricks.
Here more blocks.
Here more firetruck.
Here more toys.
Here more truck.
Here Mum.
Here Mummy.
Here my bricks.

Here not a house.
Here stars.
Here (the) coffee pot
    broken, Mum.
Here the card.
Here the cards.
Here the cheese.
Here (the) flowers.
Here the paper.
Here (we go).
See the bolt here, see?
That block here.
That one here.
That one right here.
I put bucket here.
Come here.
Do here.
Leave that block here.
Put it here.
Here not a house.
Right here.
Over here.
Mum, over here.
Now here.

THERE

There goes.
There (he) goes.
There is.
There it goes.
There it is.
There it is, Mum.
There kitty.
There more block.
There more truck.
There more nails.
There Mum.
There my house.
There my nails.
There Noah.
I wanta put (it) right there
    . . . (under) the couch.
Me see (in there).
Blanket in there.
In there.
Right there.

SMALL CAPS identify contexts common to *Mum* and *Dad*.
Italics identify contexts common to *here* and *there*.

lents. In the first half the word occurs in 33 different contexts, in the second half in 19. There are four or 21 per cent of the possible shared contexts—a lower value than the value obtained for *here-there* and *Mum-Dad*.

Perhaps it would be possible to set an exact percentage-of-shared-contexts criterion for the assignment of two words to the same class, the criterion to be empirically determined from percentages of shared contexts of identical words at various levels of absolute and relative

Table 5–2

Contexts of the Word *Here* in the First and Second Halves of the Record of Adam

First Half		Second Half
Here all gone.	Here my bricks.	Here (a car).
Here (block).	Here not a house.	Here flowers.
Here brick.	Here (the) coffee pot	Here goes.
Here chairs.	broken, Mum.	*Here is.*
Here coffee is.	Here the card.	*Here it goes.*
Here comes Daddy.	Here the cards.	Here it is.
Here is.	Here the cheese.	Here's it here.
Here it goes.	Here the paper.	*Here more.*
Here it is, Mum.	That block here.	Here more blocks.
Here light.	That one here.	Here Mummy.
Here (mail) more paper.	That one right here.	Here stars.
Here more.	Come here.	Here (the) flowers.
Here more bricks.	Leave that block here.	Here (we go).
Here more firetruck.	(Put it) here.	See the bolt here, see.
Here more toys.	Here not a house.	In here?
Here more truck.	*Over here.*	(Over here)?
Here Mum.	Right here.	Mum, over here.
		Over here.
		Now here.

Italics identify contexts common to first and second halves.

frequency in two time periods. Clearly, the obtained percentages will be very unstable for small numbers of occurrences. For less frequent words only a mammoth speech sample would serve and the whole thing becomes a job for a machine. The basic problem of setting a criterion for that machine to use or of writing the program for working out a criterion may also be a problem in the child's learning of syntax.

Once the classes have been established by some shared-contexts criterion, some contexts will turn out to be more "diagnostic" or distinctive for a given class than will others. After *the* in English one can have count nouns in the singular, count nouns in the plural, and mass nouns (which are used in the singular only). After *a* one can have only count nouns in the singular and so this context is, for singular count nouns, the more diagnostic of the two. The introduction of new words to a child in highly

Table 5-3
Two-word Utterances with Recurrent Initial Words from Eve

A	Daddy	Mummy	's	See	That	The	There	Two
	bear	bear						
block			bird		bird	bird	bird	
					boat		boat	
								Bobby
book	book				book	book	book	
					bowl			
				boy	boy		boy	
					broken			
candle								
					car			
							carriage	
cricket							chair	chair
					cookie			
					cow			
			daddy		daddy		daddy	
		dimple						
					dirty			
		do						
dog								
					doggie			
							doll	
							dollie	
							Eve	
				eye				
fall								
					fuzzy			
								Gale
						girl		
		go					go	
							goes	
					going			
	honey							
					horsie	horsie		
							is	
kitty					kitty	kitty	kitty	
							man	
meatball								
								men
						mike		
				mummy	mummy		mummy	
nurse								
							pea	
						peas		
					Peter			
			picture					
pillow								
							potty	
					pretty			
		puff			puff			
						puppy		
				radio			radio	
					Rayma			
reel						reel	reel	reel
				rocker	rocker			
						rug		
					sun			
				that				
							'tis	
						whistle		
					wire			

Second words (left margin label)

diagnostic "tracer" contexts (like "Hi_____" for personal names) should be the best guarantee of subsequent correct usage.

A corpus of 500 utterances is not large enough to take us very far with a mechanical shared-contexts procedure. However, a generally adequate mechanical procedure for the discovery of grammers has not been worked out in any case. Grammar writing is for the present like theory writing in science, an undertaking for which there are some guides, clues, and models but not a set of guaranteed procedures. Let us therefore take one record, the utterances of Eve (25½ months) and, allowing ourselves a very free use of inductive reasoning, see what we can make of it.

It is a useful first step to restrict ourselves to the simplest utterances in the record, those of just two words, and among these, the utterances in which the initial word occurs at least twice. In Table 5–3 the recurrent initial words are listed at the heads of columns, and each row represents a second word that occurs in at least one utterance after one of the recurrent first words. The second word is listed in a column if it occurs after the word that heads the column, and so a filled square represents an obtained two-word utterance defined by the column and row headings.

Table 5–3 is simply a technique for making a first inquiry into shared contexts, an inquiry limited to the most frequently repeated and so most informative contexts. By comparing the filled slots for any two rows one can determine the number of shared contexts for two second words. By comparing the filled slots for any two columns one can determine the number of shared contexts for two initial words.

Table 5–3 is itself a descriptive grammar for an obtained set of two-word sentences. The table is a description that is only very slightly more economical than an actual listing of the sentences; the single slight economy is accomplished by writing the recurrent first words just once instead of repeating them on each appearance. The descriptive grammar of Table 5–3 can easily be turned into a generative grammar. Figure 5–2 presents the generative version. It reads, "In order to form an utterance: Select first one of the initial words; select, secondly, one from the class of words that are permitted to follow the initial you have chosen." A machine that can go through this program would produce all and only the obtained set of utterances.

Table 5–3 constitutes a list of different utterances; each is listed just once. In the original record the utterances varied in their frequency of repetition. One could write a generative grammar that would do a better job of mimicking the original record by setting probabilities at the various choice points: the route "That broken," for instance, ought to be taken more often than the route "That Rayma." A printed record turned out by this machine would be indistinguishable from actual obtained records, indistinguishable as a list of sentences but perfectly distinguishable in the life situation for the reason that the machine described takes no account of semantics. It is quite capable of greeting the appearance of Daddy with "That doggie" or "That cookie." We have a grammar machine, not a machine that is a complete model for human sentence production.

Now we want to go beyond the obtained sentences to the syntactic classes they suggest. Is there any ground for considering all of the initial

{ } means a choice of one of the contained sequences

$$\text{Utterance} \rightarrow \begin{cases} A & +C_1 \\ Daddy & +C_2 \\ Mummy & +C_3 \\ 'S & +C_4 \\ See & +C_5 \\ That & +C_6 \\ The & +C_7 \\ There & +C_8 \\ Two & +C_9 \end{cases}$$

$C_1 \rightarrow$ *block, book, candle, cricket, dog, fall, kitty, meatball, nurse, pillow, reel*

$C_2 \rightarrow$ *bear, book, honey*

$C_3 \rightarrow$ *bear, dimple, do, go, puff*

$C_4 \rightarrow$ *bird, Daddy, picture*

$C_5 \rightarrow$ *boy, eye, Mummy, radio, rocker, that*

$C_6 \rightarrow$ *bird, boat, book, bowl, boy, broken, car, cookie, cow, Daddy, dirty, doggie, fuzzy, going, horsie, kitty, Mummy, Peter, pretty, puff, Rayma, rocker, sun, wire*

$C_7 \rightarrow$ *bird, book, girl, horsie, kitty, Mike, peas, puppy, reel, rug, whistle*

$C_8 \rightarrow$ *bird, boat, book, boy, carriage, chair, Daddy, doll, dollie, Eve, go, goes, is, kitty, man, Mummy, pea, potty, radio, reel, 'tis*

$C_9 \rightarrow$ *Bobby, chair, Gale, men, reel*

FIG. 5–2. A grammar describing all and only the 89 utterances obtained.

words to be members of a single class? Consider first the possibility of a shared-contexts criterion, of the type dicussed, with reference to *here-there* and *Mum-Dad*.

The previous discussion was greatly simplified by restricting the problem to single pairs of words. However, the number of candidates for membership in a common syntactic class is generally greater than two, and that is the case with the initial words of Table 5–3. Each single word that is a candidate for inclusion can be compared for shared contexts with each other word in the presumptive class. The criteria for class identification must then prescribe minimal levels of overlap for the full set. This is a complicated problem for which many different solutions can be imagined.

In the present case the words *that* and *there* are the most frequent in the set. They share seven second words (*bird, boat, book, boy, Daddy, kitty,* and *Mummy*), which is 33 per cent of the number of contexts that could be shared. Of the other words in the set *'s, see, the, a, Mummy,* and *Daddy* all share at least one context with both *that* and *there* while *two* shares with *there* but not *that*. One might use the syntactically close pair *that* and *there* as touchstones and count as members any words that share at least one context with either critical word. That rule would put all of the initial words into the same syntactic class (Class 1).

What evidence is there that the entries in the rows of Table 5–3 constitute a second syntactic class? The words *bird, book, kitty,* and *reel* are most frequent. Since the contexts are the words of Class 1, and so are few, these frequent words have a high degree of mutual overlap. Using the four as touchstones, most of the words entered in rows could be entered in Class 2 on the criterion of having at least one context in common with one of the touchstones. A few, such as *dimple* and *do,* would be left out. Most of the words in Class 2 are count nouns, and if we had a larger corpus, we should probably find that *dimple* belongs here for Eve while *do* does not. Our criterion is probably not good enough to separate out just the few words that do not fit.

The members of a syntactic class are credited with identical privileges of occurrence. In Table 5–3 the initial words are far from having identical patterns of actual occurrence, and the second words are also far from this pattern. If the actual occurrences were identical in either set, then the assignment to a common class might be confidently made, but the assignment would not take us beyond what we have obtained. If we do go beyond what has been obtained in our description of privileges of occurrence, then of course, we will not have "proved" our description. This is the familiar problem of the impossibility of proving a generalization that goes beyond what has been examined—the very sort of generalization that is most valuable and which the human mind is most bent on making. We are, in the setting up of syntactic classes, trying to move from a partial similarity of actual occurrence to an identity of potential occurrence. This is the process of induction—uncertain but powerful.

To hold that the members of each of our present classes have identical privileges of occurrence is to hold that all the empty positions in Table 5–3 may properly be filled—they are utterances we should expect to hear from Eve. The generative grammar changes to the form of Figure 5–3. This grammar will turn out more sentences than Figure 5–2, and it ought to be very much easier to remember since the sequential contingencies are greatly simplified.

The utterances of Figures 5–2 and 5–3, since they are two-word utterances, can very well be thought of as a set of paired-associates. It is usually the case in paired-associate learning that initial words and second words occur always and only in their pair relation. In the present case some initial words and some second words occur in a variety of combinations. If these utterences were to be made up as experimental

Utterance $\rightarrow C_1 + C_2$

$C_1 \rightarrow$ *a, Daddy, Mummy, 's, see, that, the, there, two*

$C_2 \rightarrow$ *bear, bird, block, boat, Bobby, book, bowl, boy, broken, candle, car, carriage, chair, cricket, cookie, cow, Daddy, dimple, dirty, do, dog, doggie, doll, dollie, Eve, eye, fall, fuzzy, Gale, girl, go, goes, going, honey, horsie, is, kitty, man, meatball, men, Mike, Mummy, nurse, pea, peas, Peter, picture, pillow, potty, pretty, puff, puppy, radio, Rayma, reel, rocker, rug, sun, that, 'tis, whistle, wire*

FIG. 5–3. A grammar that results from filling in the blanks in Table 5–3. It predicts the 89 obtained utterances plus 469 others.

materials, what task could we set the subject? If he were simply asked to respond to each initial word with some one of the acceptable second words, then he could meet the requirements by learning single associates. Suppose, however, he is required to do what the grammar does—respond to each initial word with all acceptable second words. There could be two sets of materials: One made up on the model of Figure 5–2 with only the obtained secondaries occurring, and one on the model of Figure 5–3 with any member of Class 2 likely to occur after any initial word. I think we can foresee that for the first set of materials it would take a long time to learn the exact set of words that can go after each initial word. With the second set it should not take very long to learn the principle that any second word can follow any initial word, but it would take some time to memorize all of the second words. But after how many pairs, of what kinds, will subjects move to the generalization of

Figure 5–3? We think it would be interesting to try paired-associate learning of this kind.

Refinements on the Provisional Grammar. Turning to utterances of three or more words, we find evidence to indicate that not all of the members of Class 1 have identical privileges. Consider first the words *the* and *a*. Table 5–4a presents a set of utterances in which *the* or *a* occur after members of Class 1 and before members of Class 2. However, *the* and *a* do not occur after all members of Class 1; they do not occur after *the, a, Mummy,* or *Daddy*. There are no utterances like "The the doggie" or "The a horsie." These facts suggest that *the* and *a* should be withdrawn from Class 1 and set up as a new Class 3. The grammar would then be rewritten as in Figure 5–4a.

Table 5–4

Three-word Utterances That Refine the Original Grammar

a. Utterances with "the" or "a" in middle position

'S a man.	See the horsie.	That the bowl.	There the kitty.
'S a house.	See the radio.	That the cup.	
'S a Daddy.	See the reel.	That a horsie.	
	See a boat.		

b. Utterances with human terms in middle position

See Evie car.	That Mummy book.	There Evie car.
See baby eyebrow.	That Mummy hair.	There man coat.
	That Mummy paper.	
	That Mummy spoon.	
	That Daddy car.	
	That Daddy honey.	
	That man car.	
	That baby bed.	
	That Evie book.	
	That Evie dish.	
	That Evie pillow.	
	That Evie spoon.	

The optional markings in Figure 5–4a indicate that a class can be completely bypassed. It is necessary to make Class 3 optional so as to get sentences like "That bird" and "There boat." Making Class 1 optional makes it possible to obtain "The boat," "A book," and the like. If neither optional class is bypassed, we get such utterances as "That the cup" and "See the reel." If both optional classes are bypassed, we get such one-word utterances as "Dolly," "Book," "Reel"; and utterances of this kind were very numerous in Eve's record. We cannot get from this grammar such utterances as "The the horsie," "The that bird," "A see that," and other radically un-English sequences.

The grammar of Figure 5–4a does turn out some kinds of utterance for which Eve's record provides no models. It is possible, for instance, to obtain "Two the bear" or "Two a bird." Eve produced nothing like these, and for adults they are definitely ungrammatical. It is quite likely that *two* should go with *the* and *a* in Class 3 so as to yield: "That two bear" and "See two bird." However, Eve's record gives us no utterances like these, and indeed no three-word utterances including *two;* and so we may as well leave *two* in Class 1. We have identified a point at which more evidence is needed in order to choose between formulations.

( ) means that selection of the enclosed is optional

Utterance → (C₁) + (C₃) + C₂

$C_1 \rightarrow$ *Daddy, Mummy, 's, see, that, there, two*

$C_2 \rightarrow$ *bear, bird, block, boat,* etc.

$C_3 \rightarrow$ *a, the*

(*a*) Eve's grammar with the articles separated out.

Utterance → (C₁) + (C₃) + C₂

$C_1 \rightarrow$ *'s, see, that, there, two*

$C_2 \rightarrow$ *bear, bird, block, boat,* etc.

$C_3 \rightarrow$ *a, the,* plus human terms

(*b*) Eve's grammar allowing for possessives.

Fig. 5–4. Grammars suggested by three-word utterances.

There is another sort of utterance that the grammar of Figure 5–4*a* will produce for which Eve's record provides no model: "Mummy the bird" or "Daddy a book." These sentences do not use *Mummy* and *Daddy* in the vocative; the vocative would involve a distinctive juncture (pause) and intonation which is suggested in print by a comma (e.g., "Mummy, the bird"). An adult might form the vocative version as a kind of ellipsis of "Mummy, see the bird," but he would not form the nonvocative utterance that the grammar of Figure 5–4*a* produces.

Thus far, *Mummy* and *Daddy* are in the same limbo as *two;* there is reason for withdrawing them from Class 1, but we do not yet know where to put them. Eve's record provides no three-word utterances with *two;* but it does provide such utterances with *Mummy* and *Daddy,* and these are listed as Table 5–4*b.* We find *Mummy* and *Daddy* in middle position between *that* (a Class 1 word) and the Class 2 words: *book, hair, paper, spoon, car,* and *honey.* Furthermore, we find in this same position the words: *Evie, man,* and *baby.* All of these middle-position words are names of human beings, and so we may hypothesize that such terms constitute a syntactic class.

The difficulty now is that the middle position between Class 1 and Class 2 already belongs to Class 3, which is composed of *the* and *a.* This means that there are three clear options: (1) to include the human terms with *the* and *a* in Class 3, (2) to set up the human terms as a separate Class 4 and put this class in the selection sequence ahead of Class 3, and (3) to put the independent Class 4 in sequence after Class 3. Here now are examples of utterances that are predicted by the three versions of the grammar: (1) "That Mummy book," (2) "That Mummy the book," and (3) "That the Mummy book." Our interim decision is fairly clear. Since the record provides instances of (1) but not of either (2) or (3), we will put the human terms in Class 3 with *the* and *a* as indicated in Figure 5–4*b.* However, if a larger corpus were drawn, we would have to be on the alert to correct this decision.

It may be worthwhile to consider the very complicated rules required for adult English at an analogous grammatical point. Utterances like "Mummy book" and "Man car" and "Evie dish" are, we know from the situational contexts, Eve's version of the possessive; she omits the inflection. In forming possessives with human terms, the adult speaker will use an article before such generic human terms as *man* ("the man's car"), and so these terms cannot be classified as alternatives to *the* and *a.* With personal names like *Evie* the adult will form possessives; but with personal names, articles are never used, and so we will say "Evie's dish" but neither "The Evie's dish" nor "Evie's the dish." This means that personal names cannot be classified as alternatives to either the articles or the generic human terms. A final exasperating fillip is provided by the fact that some morphemes, like *Mummy* and *Daddy,* can serve either as personal names ("Mother's purse") or as generic terms ("the Mother's role") and so would have to be listed in two syntactic classes.

Even the simple grammar we have now produced for Eve involves double syntactic listing for some forms—the human terms. They must be in Class 3 because of such utterances as "That Mummy book," but they must also remain in Class 2 because of such utterances as "That Mummy." The combinational formula predicts "That Mummy Mummy" (Grandmummy?) which is reasonably probable but also "That Evie Evie," which would not be produced by an adult. As to whether Eve would say it, we cannot tell from the present materials.

Expansion of Eve's Grammar. Recurrence of a context is always what is needed for the identification of a syntactic class. We started with recurrence of initial members, but recurrence at the end of an utterance can be equally useful. In Eve's record there is a set of terminal recurrences (*all gone, broken, fall down, tired*) which appears in Table 5–5. The

Table 5-5
Utterances with Recurrent Second Members

		Initial Word										
Baby	Bird*	Carriage*	Chair*	Doggy*	Dolly*	Eyebrow	Kitty*	Micro-phone	Mummy*	Reel*	Rocker*	Some-thing
	all gone					all gone	all gone	all gone		all gone		
		broken	broken		broken						broken	broken
			fall down		fall down		fall down					
									tired			
tired				tired								

Second Member

180

* A word already identified as a member of C_2.

first thing to note is that most of the initial members of these utterances have already been identified as members of Class 2. Their appearance here with overlapping privileges of occurrence before *all gone, broken, fall down,* and *tired* is a valuable confirmation of the preliminary analysis.

Since the initial terms are already regarded as one class, we are inclined to assume that they have identical privileges of occurrence, which means that the empty cells could be filled. This makes a new Class 4 of *all gone, broken, fall down,* and *tired;* and we now have a second type of sentence. The full grammar (Figure 5–5a) involves two major routes corresponding to the two kinds of sentence.

$$\text{Utterance} \rightarrow \begin{Bmatrix} (C_1) + (C_3) + C_2 \\ C_2 + C_4 \end{Bmatrix}$$

$$C_1 \rightarrow \text{'}s,\ see,\ that,\ the,\ two$$

$$C_2 \rightarrow bear,\ bird,\ block,\ boat,\ \text{etc.}$$

$$C_3 \rightarrow a,\ the,\ \text{plus human terms}$$

$$C_4 \rightarrow all\ gone,\ broken,\ fall\ down,\ tired$$

(*a*) Eve's grammar with two basic sentence-types.

$$\text{Utterance} \rightarrow \begin{Bmatrix} (C_1) + (C_3) + C_2 \\ (C_3) + (C_2) + C_4 \end{Bmatrix}$$

$$C_1 \rightarrow \text{'}s,\ see,\ that,\ there,\ two$$

$$C_2 \rightarrow bear,\ bird,\ block,\ boat,\ \text{etc.}$$

$$C_3 \rightarrow a,\ the,\ \text{plus human terms}$$

$$C_4 \rightarrow all\ gone,\ broken,\ fall\ down,\ tired$$

(*b*) Eve's grammar with articles added to the new sentence-type.

FIG. 5–5. Grammars suggested by the terminal recurrence of Table 5–5.

There is a slight addition to be made to the grammar of Figure 5–5a. The addition is suggested by three sentences: "The chair broken," "The baby tired," and "The book fall down." The initial word *the* has already been placed in Class 3; and so it is a good guess that any word from Class 3 can appear in first position in this new sentence type; Figure 5–5b presents this version. Class 3 must be entered as optional in the grammar since most of the obtained sentences omit it.

It is not certain that our analysis of the limited materials in Table 5–5 is correct. The word *tired,* for example, does not actually overlap in the obtained distribution with any of the other second members. Our analysis, relying on the prior identification of the first members as Class 2, assumes that the overlap would occur if more sentences were gathered. However, it should be noted that *tired* occurs only after names of animate beings—*baby, doggy, Mummy*—whereas the other second members are not restricted in this way. This is a fragment of evidence pointing to the eventual separation of animate nouns from the general syntactic class of nominal expressions. This separation is a necessity for adult grammar; certain verbs can only take animate nouns as objects. We can say "It surprised John" or "It surprised the dog," but not "It surprised the chair." In our discussion of the possessive we considered the possibility of separating out a class of generic human terms. The distributional facts of adult English will show that this class has to be broadened into animate nouns (we can have "the dog's house" as well as "the man's car") and is the same class hinted at by the restrictions on *tired*. However, Eve's utterances are so few that we cannot be sure these restrictions would be maintained.

The reciprocal of *tired* in Table 5–5 is *broken,* for *broken* only occurs after inanimate nouns—*carriage, chair, dolly, rocker, something.* In adult English *broken* would be restricted in this way, but we cannot be sure that it will continue so for Eve. *All gone* is interesting because Eve uses this form where an adult speaker would not—after count nouns. We would not say "The microphone is all gone" or "A kitty is all gone." For us *all gone* goes after plural count nouns ("The microphones are all gone") or mass nouns ("The sand is all gone"). Eve does not give us any plural count nouns in this record and does not make a syntactic distinction between mass and count nouns, and she uses *all gone* without any discoverable restrictions.

The grammar of Figure 5–5b does not represent the distributional distinctions among the Class 4 members for the reason that we have so very little evidence on this point. Still, as we shall see in the next section, there are reasons for preferring to represent the distinctions rather than to assume identical privileges. If we were forced to freeze the grammar on the present evidence, it would probably be better to write the more differentiated version.

The sentences we have been discussing all begin with a Class 2 word (*bird, book,* etc.) with a prior Class 3 (*the, a,* etc.) being optional. There are many other sentences answering this description in Eve's record, but they do not have the recurrence of second members that made the sentences in Table 5–5 useful. These additional sentences are all unique and they vary in length: "Daddy fix it," "Eve listen to tick-tock," "The reel go round and round," etc. The best thing to do with these sentences, at present, is to make a cut after the Class 2 words (*Daddy, Eve, reel*) and call all of the remainder second members. These second members are, from the point of view of adult English, complex predicates. With our present inadequate materials we can only add them to *all gone, broken, fall down,* and *tired* as additional members of Class 4. There is not enough material for a finer breakdown. The fact that some of these complex predicates contain Class 2 words and some do not hints at an eventual distinction between transitive and intransitive verbs.

There remains a collection of utterances belonging to types already identified but modified by the addition of a rising interrogative intonation (?), and these appear in Table 5–6. Since instances of both kinds of

Table 5–6
Utterances of Previously Identified Types with "?" Added

Daddy fix this?*	'S a Daddy?*	See baby eyebrow?*	That block?*	Book?†
Daddy work?*	'S cow?*	See baby horsie?*	That Daddy?†	Daddy?*
	'S Daddy?†	See cow?*	That Evie	Doggie?†
	'S Mummy?*		spoon?*	

* An utterance that has occurred in its declarative form, i.e., without "?".

† An utterance that has been predicted in its declarative form but has not occurred.

utterance allowed by our grammar occur with the interrogative intonation, it seems reasonable to suppose that any sentence allowed by that grammar can be so modified. The result is the revised formula of Figure 5–6, which at one swoop doubles the number of sentences the grammar

$$\text{Utterance} \rightarrow \begin{Bmatrix} (C_1) + (C_3) + C_2 \\ (C_3) + (C_2) + C_4 \end{Bmatrix} (?)$$

$C_1 \rightarrow$ *'s, see, that, there, two*

$C_2 \rightarrow$ *bear, bird, block, boat,* etc.

$C_3 \rightarrow$ *a, the,* plus human terms

$C_4 \rightarrow$ *all gone, broken, fall down, tired, fix it, listen to tick-tock,* etc.

FIG. 5–6. Complete provisional grammar for Eve.

can generate. Figure 5–6 is the complete version of our provisional grammar.

There are several things worth noting about the grammar of Figure 5–6. It will produce most of the 500 utterances actually obtained from

Eve and will produce many thousands beyond the obtained. The only classes that are not optional in the grammar are the reference-making words of Class 2 (*bear, bird,* etc.) and Class 3 (*all gone, broken,* etc.). These are, by our observation, the forms that are used as single-word "mands" and "tacts" (Skinner, 1957) for some time before the two-word utterance begins.

The generative grammar written out as a formula suggests a distinction between lexical meanings and structural or syntactic meanings. The class listings are the lexicon and an utterance involves a shift of lexical meaning whenever there is a change in the selection within a class (e.g., from "That bird" to "That bear"). Structural meanings may perhaps be defined as those that shift whenever there is a change in the selections within the formula. Thus if we shift from the first major sentence route to the second, there seems to be a shift from demonstrative naming ("There bird" or "See boat") to prediction ("Bird all gone" or "Bear fall down"). If we shift from not selecting ? to selecting it, we shift from a declaration to an interrogation. It is more difficult to say what the changes of meaning could be that go with selecting or not selecting the various optional classes.

Testing the Adequacy of a Grammar

In our discussion of techniques for the discovery of a grammar we have repeatedly pointed to the existence of equally reasonable alternative decisions. The arbitrariness of choice could be somewhat reduced by taking a larger corpus. However, we are sure that the best-founded grammar will not be uniquely determined but will only be a good provisional try. The same thing is surely true for the rules a child induces from adult speech; they will be hypotheses about the form of future speech events. Is there any way to check such hypotheses?

Very roughly the test of a grammar must be the same as the test of any theory of empirical events—the ability to make correct predictions. In the present case this means the ability to anticipate sentences that have not entered into the construction of the grammar. One might, for example, have tested our grammar for Eve by taking a second large collection of utterances on the following day or days and seeing how many of those that occurred were predicted.

Three different kinds of successful prediction may be distinguished. There is, in the first place, the occurrence of an utterance already in the corpus from which the grammar was induced. This does not help to validate the grammar as a set of generalizations that go beyond the data; the occurrence of a familiar sentence could have been predicted from a simple list of sentences in the original corpus. There is, in the second place, the occurrence of an utterance not included in the original corpus but allowed for by the generalized rules. For example, Eve's record did not include the sentence "There horsie" though it did include "That horsie" and "The horsie." By adopting the general rule that any Class 2 word can follow any Class 1 word, the utterance "There horsie" is predicted. If it occurs, that fact would increase our confidence in the generalization.

Suppose that, in a second corpus collected from Eve, we obtained the utterance "That lion." The word *lion* did not occur in the original corpus, and so the utterance was not predicted. It is not to be expected that a speech sample of only 500 utterances would exhaust a lexicon, and it would be unreasonable to permit the incompleteness of a lexicon to discredit a grammar. It would be better to say that an utterance does not come within the province of a grammar unless all of its words are included in the lexicon of the grammar—the lexicon being the lists of forms belonging to each syntactic class. Therefore, the sentence "That lion" counts neither for nor against the grammar. However, the occurrence of this sentence enables us to add *lion* to the Class 2 list since the criterion for inclusion is occurrence after a Class 1 word, and *that* is such a word. Subsequent utterances such as "There lion" and "The lion" could be counted as evidence for the grammar since they are predicted once *lion* has been added to the lexicon.

We cannot think of any way to set a definite criterion as to the number of sentences, out of a collection of obtained sentences, that must be predicted for a grammar to be judged acceptable. It is clear, however, that the number of successful predictions can be increased by simply writing the grammar in the most general terms possible. We found, you recall, that the forms *all gone, broken, fall down,* and *tired* all occurred after Class 2 words (Table 5–5). Looking more closely at Table 5–5, we found that the word *broken* occurred only after the names of inanimate things and *tired* only after the names of animate things. This fraction of the grammar could have been written in either of the two forms presented in Figure 5–7. The less general form predicts 39 utterances, and the more general predicts these 39 plus 13 others. The more general form will make all the successful predictions made by the less general one and can possibly formulate some that the less general cannot. The way to write a "successful" grammar, if "success" is simply measured by the prediction of obtained events, is to write a grammar that predicts every conceivable sequence of obtained forms.

The job of a grammar, however, is to predict sentences that are possible while *not predicting sentences that are impossible.* This second part of the job gives an additional criterion of evaluation that will prevent us from always preferring the most general grammar. That grammar is preferred which predicts what does occur while predicting as little as possible what does not occur. Therefore, the less general grammar will be better than the more general one if it is equally successful in predicting what happens. A grammar should stay as close to the obtained materials as is consistent with generalizing beyond the obtained materials so as to predict future events. Only by invoking both criteria can we hope to obtain distinct grammars representing a developmental sequence.

$$\text{Utterance} \rightarrow C_2 + C_4$$

$C_2 \rightarrow$ *baby, bird, carriage, chair, doggie, dollie, eyebrow, kitty, microphone, Mummy, reel, rocker, something*

$C_4 \rightarrow$ *all gone, broken, fall down, tired*

(a) The more general form.

$$\text{Utterance} \rightarrow \begin{cases} C_2 + C_5 \\ C_{2\,an.} + tired \\ C_{2\,inan.} + broken \end{cases}$$

$C_2 \rightarrow$ *baby, bird, carriage, chair, doggie, dollie, eyebrow, kitty, microphone, Mummy, reel, rocker, something*

$C_{2\,an.} \rightarrow$ *baby, bird, doggie, dollie, kitty, Mummy*

$C_{2\,inan.} \rightarrow$ *carriage, chair, eyebrow, microphone, reel, rocker, something*

$C_5 \rightarrow$ *all gone, fall down*

(b) The more restrictive form.

FIG. 5–7. Alternative forms for a fragment of Eve's grammar.

Our next step in this research program will be an empirical and logical study of techniques for evaluating grammars in terms of their predictive powers.

In sum, the most that we are now able to conceive by way of grammar-evaluating techniques is a set of rough criteria for preferring one version to another. This problem of evaluation probably exists in implicit form for the child learning to speak. How does he judge of the adequacy of his inductions? He can see how well they anticipate what others say. He can construct new utterances and see whether others appear to find them acceptable and comprehensible. He can ask direct metalinguistic questions: "Mother, can one say 'The carriage is tired'?"

CHILD GRAMMAR AS A REDUCTION OF ADULT GRAMMAR

The provisional grammar we have written for Eve is not a grammar of adult English. Most of the utterances it generates are not, for us, grammatical sentences. We cannot accept "That horsie" or "Kitty all gone" or "There Mummy hair" or "Two chair." Words that seem to be syntactically equivalent for Eve are not so for us. For example, the words *see* and *that* are members of Class 1 for Eve and equivalent in that they can precede Class 2 words such as *doggie, dollie,* etc. For the adult who might say "That is a doggie" and "I see a doggie" *that* and *see* are syntactically unlike. For Eve the word *two* is roughly equivalent to *the* and *a*, but that is because she does not pluralize count nouns. It is clear that Eve does not speak adult English, and so we cannot use an adult English grammar to describe her speech. It would be quite misleading to list Eve's *that* as a demonstrative pronoun and her *see* as a transitive verb though that is a correct classification of these words in adult English.

Since the speech of the younger children in our set of 13 is clearly not English, it is necessary to "discover" the grammar that is implied by their utterances. We have not in this first try collected large enough corpora to write convincing grammars. However, for the younger children it does look as if we might manage with about 1,500 different utterances to get a good provisional grammar. The prospect of "discovering" grammars for the older children is not nearly so good. Since the older children have larger vocabularies and longer utterances, there is less of the recurrence that is the basis of a structural analysis. The anthropological linguist who wants to describe adult usage in an unfamiliar language is likely to try for 1,000 hours of speech, and there are times when we fear that not very much less than this would suffice for children of about three years.

The speech of the children in our collection, who are nearly three years old, is mostly English. They produce acceptable simple sentences. Furthermore, these simple sentences correspond very well with the set of English sentences for which a satisfactory generative grammar has been written by Chomsky (1957) and Lees (1960). For these records, then, it does not seem necessary to "discover" the grammar; it is quite reasonable to analyze them in terms of the syntactic categories of the adult grammar. We have done this job, classifying utterances under headings: copular sentences, transitive verb sentences, intransitive verb sentences, sentences with modal auxiliaries, sentences with progressives, sentences with preliminary verbs, imperatives, negatives, Wh-interrogatives, yes-no interrogatives, and unclassifiable fragments.

When this analysis in terms of an adult grammar had been done for the most advanced records, we realized that it could, with some additional assumptions, be extended to the records of all the other children. For the striking fact about the utterances of the younger children, when they are approached from the vantage point of adult grammar, is that they are almost all classifiable as grammatical sentences from which certain morphemes have been omitted. You may have noticed that while Eve's sentences are not grammatically "complete," they are somehow intelligible as abbreviated or telegraphic versions of familiar constructions. "Mummy hair" and "Daddy car" seem only to omit the possessive inflection. Both "Chair broken" and "That horsie" become acceptable copular sentences if we leave the word order intact and fill in *is* and *a* or *the*. We have, therefore, analyzed all of the records in terms of English simple sentences by assigning each utterance to the sentence type it most closely approximates.

We have not yet hit on any good techniques for summarizing our compendious data, but one illustrative table (Table 5–7) will make a few important points. For each child we made an estimate of the mean length of utterances by counting morphemes from 100 consecutive utterances occurring in midmorning. From this count we thought it wise to omit the single-word rejoinders and exclamations, *No, OK, Yeah,* and *Oh,* since these are sometimes emitted many times in succession by speakers of any age; and if the small utterance sample happened to include such a repeating circuit, the estimate would be very unrepresentative. The estimates appear in Table 5–7 and the children's names appear in an order of increasing average utterance length. This order is related to the chronological age order but is not identical with it. An age-related increase in the mean length of utterances is, of course, one of the best-established facts in the study of child speech (McCarthy, 1954). There is, however, no reason to expect perfect correspondence with age. We conceive of developmental sequence as a Guttman scale with performances following an invariant order but not pegged to particular ages. The sequence can be covered at varying rates of speed; the rate would be a function of intelligence and learning opportunities.

When the analyzed records are ordered by mean utterance length, it becomes apparent that children all "reduce" English sentences in similar fashion. If the utterances of one child are, on the average, shorter than the utterances of another child, then of course, the first child will be omitting some morphemes that the second child is producing. However, utterances could be shortened by omitting any morphemes at all; there are many ways to abbreviate sentences, and it is perfectly conceivable that individual children would hit on different ways. They do not do so. We have checked all the records for progressive constructions (e.g., "I am going to town"). Without exception children whose mean utterance length is below 3.2 form this construction by omitting the forms of the verb *to be* (e.g., "I going"). We have checked sentences in which the verb would, for an adult, ordinarily require such a modal

Table 5–7

Estimates of Mean Utterance Length and Reports on Selected Grammatical Forms for Thirteen Children

Child	Age	Mean number morphemes	*Be* in progressive	Modal auxiliaries *will* or *can*
Andy	26	2.0	no	no
Betty	31½	2.1	no	no
Charlie	22	2.2	no	no
Adam	28½	2.5	no	no
Eve	25½	2.6	no	no
Fanny	31½	3.2	yes	no
Grace	27	3.5	yes	yes
Helen	30	3.6	yes	yes
Ian	31½	3.8	yes	yes
June	35½	4.5	yes	yes
Kathy	30½	4.8	yes	yes
Larry	35½	4.8	yes	yes
Jimmy	32	4.9	yes	yes

auxiliary as *will* or *can* (e.g., "I will park the car"). Children whose mean utterance length is below 3.5 invariably form these sentences by omitting modals ("I park the car" or "I go inside" or "I make a tower"). In general, it appears that children whose speech is not yet English are using grammars which are systematic derivatives of adult grammar and that the particular features of the derivative grammar are predictable from the mean length of utterance.

Table 5–8

Imitations of Spoken Sentences

	Eve, 25½	Adam, 28½	Helen, 30	Ian, 31½	Jimmy, 32	June, 35½
1. I showed you the book.	I show book.	(I show) book.	I showed you the book.	I show you the book.	C	Show you the book.
2. I am very tall.	(My) tall.	I (very) tall.	I very tall.	I'm very tall.	Very tall.	I very tall.
3. It goes in a big box.	Big box.	Big box.	In big box.	It goes in the box.	C	C
4. Read the book.	Read book.	Read book.	—	Read (a) book.	Read a book.	C
5. I am drawing a dog.	Drawing dog.	I draw dog.	I drawing dog.	Dog.	C	C
6. I will read the book.	Read book.	I will read book.	I read the book.	I read the book.	C	C
7. I can see a cow.	See cow.	I want see cow.	C	Cow.	C	C
8. I will not do that again.	Do—again.	I will that again.	I do that.	I again.	C	C
9. I do not want an apple.	I do—apple.	I do—a apple.	—	I do not want —apple.	I don't want a apple.	I don't want apple.
10. Do I like to read books?	To read book?	I read books?	I read books?	I—read book?	C	C
11. Is it a car?	'T car?	Is it—car?	Car?	That a car?	Is it car?	C
12. Where does it go?	Where go?	Go?	Does it go?	Where do it go?	C	C
13. Where shall I go?	Go?	—	—	C	C	C

C, correct imitation; —, no intelligible imitation obtained.

190

The abbreviation effect can be more directly studied in the utterances a child produces when he is asked to repeat a sentence said by an adult. For the last six cases we presented 13 simple sentences of various grammatical types and asked the subject to "Say what I say." Half of the sentences were presented at the end of the morning session and half at the end of the afternoon session. For each child a different random order

Table 5–9
Summary of Results with Sentence Imitations

a. *Mean lengths, in morphemes, of the model sentences and the imitations of each child*

Model sentences	Eve, 25½	Adam, 28½	Helen, 30	Ian, 31½	Jimmy, 32	June, 35½
5.2	2.2	3.1	3.7	3.5	5.0	4.9

b. *Number of morphemes correctly imitated in each of three serial positions**

	Eve	Adam	Helen	Ian	Jimmy	June	% of morphemes in model sentences correctly imitated
Initial position	4	9	6	9	12	12	70%
Middle position	5	3	8	7	11	13	64%
Final position	12	12	9	12	13	13	96%

c. *Percentages correctly imitated of morphemes in various syntactic classes†*

Classes having few members in English		Classes having many members in English	
Inflections	44%	Nouns	100%
Pronouns	72%	Adjectives	92%
Articles	39%	Main verbs	85%
Modal auxiliaries	56%		
Copular verbs (*to be*)	33%		

* The difference between initial and final positions is significant by sign test (two-tailed) with $P = .032$; the difference between middle and final positions is significant with $P = .062$; the difference between initial and middle positions is not significant.

† Using tests for differences between two percentages, the percentage correct in each of the classes with many members is significantly greater than the percentage correct in any of the classes with few members ($P < .001$, two-tailed test).

was presented. The sentences were spoken slowly and carefully and always by the same investigator. The child had the microphone directly in front of him, and so good recordings were made. Table 5–8 presents the first efforts of each child, and Table 5–9 a summary of the main results.

With increasing age children produce more imitations that are morphemically identical with the original. With increasing age the imitative utterances produced include larger numbers of morphemes—approaching the numbers in the model sentences. The morphemes produced are invariably in their original order. Omissions do not appear to be random or idiosyncratic. On the contrary, it looks as if, across children and across sentences, there is a consistent tendency to retain one kind of morpheme and drop another kind. The two sorts of morphemes contrast on several correlated dimensions. The morphemes most likely to be retained are morphemes that occur in the final position in the sentence; that are reference-making forms; that belong mainly to the large and expandable noun, verb, and adjective parts of speech;[5] that are relatively unpredictable from the context; and that receive the heavier stresses in ordinary English pronunciation. The morphemes least likely to be retained are those that occur in intermediate positions in the sentence; that are not reference-making forms; that belong to such small-sized grammatical categories as the articles, modal auxiliaries, and inflections; that are relatively predictable from context and so carry little information; and that receive the weaker stresses in ordinary English pronunciation. This does indeed seem to be telegraphic English. There is substantial support for our findings in the results with sentence repetition for 100 children at ages two and three obtained by Gesell and his associates (1940) and also in the work of Stutsman (1926).

Let us suppose that very young children speak a rather uniform telegraphic English. How do they come by it? It is conceivable that they hear it from adults; that they are imitating a "baby talk" which is an adult invention. We have on our tapes a large quantity of speech from mother to child; and while this material has not yet been transcribed or analyzed, it is quite clear that Eve's mother and the mothers of the other children do not usually use telegraphic English. The very young children are exposed to a much more complicated grammar than they use, and the older children to a somewhat more complicated grammar than they use.

While it seems safe to say that children do not learn their telegraphic English from adults, it is probably also safe to say that the average adult can do a good job of producing telegraphic English if he is asked to talk like a baby. We have even heard a three-year-old drop his more mature grammar in speaking to a two-year-old and produce a very good version of the two-year-old's speech. It is an old observation of linguists that the "baby talk" version of a language is very uniform from one adult to

[5] Aborn and Rubenstein (1956) have published evidence that, in six-word sentences, nouns are most frequent in final sentence position whereas function words tend to be most frequent in the fourth and fifth positions. This tie between position and part of speech is found also, and not by our intention, in the sentences we provided for imitation.

another. We can see good reasons why this should be so. If there is something about the operation of the child mind that causes each child to "reduce" English in a similar form, then adults everywhere could learn the same sort of baby talk from their own children. It is even possible, of course, that baby talk in all languages shows certain stable features, e.g., omission of low information, predictable forms. If, in addition, baby talk is a systematic transformation of adult simple sentences accomplished by the omission of certain kinds of words, then an adult should be able to throw some simple mental switch that activates the baby grammar.

A basic factor causing the child's reduction of adult sentences is surely an upper limit of some kind of immediate memory span for the situation in which the child is imitating and a similar limit of programming span for the situation in which the child is constructing the sentences. A comparison of the mean lengths of utterances produced as imitations (presented in Table 5–9) with the mean lengths of spontaneously produced utterances from the same children (presented in Table 5–7) shows that the paired values are very close and that neither is consistently higher. An increasing span for random digits is so reliably related to increasing age that it is a part of the Stanford-Binet test (e.g., a span of two digits at 30 months, three at 36, and four at 54 are the norms). Munn (1954) summarizes the results of many studies by saying: "That the memory span of children increases with age has been shown for all kinds of material investigated" (p. 413). We know from Blankenship's review of memory-span work (1938) and from Miller's discussion of "the magical number seven" (1956) that it is not yet possible to reduce the various measures of span to a common unit (bits) and thereby reconcile variations in the data. But there does seem to be ample indication that one or more memory spans show a steady increase in early childhood. It is this limitation of span in children for which the work of the descriptive linguist provided no parallel, and our obsession with linguistic technique long diverted us from recognizing the systematically derivative nature of child speech.

Span limitation is probably the factor compelling children to reduce adult sentences, but it does not, of course, account for the systematic tendency to drop one sort of morpheme and retain another sort. Because the two kinds of morphemes differ in numerous correlated respects, there are many conceivable explanations for the child's selective performance; and this will be so until the variables are experimentally separated. Here are a few of the many ways in which the story can now be put together. Perhaps the human mind operates on an unlearned "recency" principle, and English sentences (maybe also sentences in other languages) are nicely adapted to this principle in that the least predictable, most informative words usually fall into the final position. Perhaps, on the other hand, the "recency" effect in human serial learning is an acquired tendency to pay particular attention to material in final position, a tendency acquired because sentences are so constructed as to place in final position words carrying a lot of information. Perhaps it is differential stress that selects what the child will reproduce, and sentences are nicely adapted to this predilection in that the heavier stresses fall on the less predictable forms. Or perhaps it is some combination of these ideas.

CONCLUSION

This paper began with an argument that the correct English sentences produced by a child are not good evidence that he possesses construction rules since we can never be sure that a correct sentence is not directly copied from a model. It seemed to us that systematic errors and manipulation of invented words were better evidence as a child is not likely to have had exact models for these. In the second section of the paper we discussed techniques for inducing construction rules or a generative grammar from the child's natural speech. Since this speech, for Eve at least, is not good English, it can be argued that she had no models for it, and so it is legitimate to infer rules from such data. In the third section, however, we have seen that child speech can be rather well characterized as a systematic reduction of adult speech, and so, after all, there were models for Eve's sentences. She could have learned most of them by selective imitation if not by imitation per se.

Eventually children must do more than imitate and memorize if only because there is not enough time for them to learn as particular verbal responses all the sentences they will be able as adults to produce and evaluate grammatically. (For a detailed statement of this argument see Bruner, 1957, p. 156; or Miller, Galanter, and Pribram, 1960, pp. 146–147.) In addition to the logical argument that children must learn construction rules in view of their terminal linguistic achievement, there is much empirical evidence that children older than Eve do, in fact, learn construction rules. Some of this evidence is available to every parent in a child's systematic errors (*sheeps, I bringed*, etc.), and some of it has been collected in a controlled fashion by Berko (1958) and Brown and Berko (1960).

While children must and do eventually induce construction rules, it is not necessary that they do so from the very earliest age at which words are combined. Eve, after all, is not yet prepared to produce an infinite set of sentences, nor, so far as we know, is she able to distinguish all grammatical sequences from ungrammatical sequences. It is possible that for the earliest linguistic accomplishments one sort of learning theory will serve—a theory developed largely from the study of animal behavior—while for later accomplishments a completely different theory will be necessary—a theory permitting the inductive formation of syntactic classes that generalize far beyond obtained information. However, it is also possible that the induction of rules goes on from the very first. Eve, for example, produces such utterances as "Two chair" and "Kitty all gone" which could conceivably be either direct or selective imitations but might very easily be constructions resulting from over-generalized rules for the use of *two* and *all gone*. For a single example, we will show how Eve might be forming construction rules at the same time that she is practicing selective imitation without this construction process being clearly revealed in the present data. Selective reduction might cause Eve to imitate "That is a doggie" as "That doggie," "That is a horsie" as "That horsie," and "See the doggie" as "See doggie." At this point induction could operate and she might, because the context "That _____" is shared by "doggie" and "horsie," assume that the other context "See _____" can be shared and so form the utterance "See horsie." It is quite possible that the child reduces first, then forms inductive generalizations and makes new utterances on the model of his reductions.

It will often happen, if the above suggestion is correct, that a child will find forms syntactically equivalent which are not so for the adult. Suppose Eve heard the sentence "I see the man" and reduced it to "See man." The original demonstrates the nonequivalence of *see* and *that* since *see* occurs after a pronoun, and in addition, the original version does not justify adding *man* to the list starting with *doggie* and *horsie*. The reduced sentence, on the other hand, leaves *see* equivalent to *that* and suggests that *man* belongs with *doggie* and *horsie*. If a child induces a grammar from its own reduced sentences, it should generally lose the distributional detail provided by such morphemes as *an, the, will, do,* and /-z/. The result would be syntactic classes not identical with those of adult speech, few in number and large in size. In addition there would be loss of numerous semantic distinctions, e.g., the difference between "See the man" and "I see the man." It is important to note, however, that the gross sense of a sentence will usually be retained; e.g., in "See man" as in "I see the man" it is clear that man is the object of seeing. The crude sense of the sentence is generally recoverable from the child's reduction because one profound dimension of English grammar is perfectly preserved in telegraphese, and that dimension is word order.

For the present, then, we are working with the hypothesis that child speech is a systematic reduction of adult speech largely accomplished by omitting function words that carry little information. From this corpus of reduced sentences we suggest that the child induces general rules which govern the construction of new utterances. As a child becomes capable (through maturation and the consolidation of frequently occurring sequences) of registering more of the detail of adult speech, his original rules will have to be revised and supplemented. As the generative grammar grows more complicated and more like the adult grammar, the child's speech will become capable of expressing a greater variety of meanings.

REFERENCES

Aborn, M., & Rubenstein, H. (1956) Word-class distribution in sentences of fixed length. *Language*, 32, 666–674.

Barker, R. G., & Wright, H. F. (1954) *Midwest and its children*. Evanston, Ill.: Row, Peterson.

Berko, Jean. (1958) The child's learning of English morphology. *Word*, 14, 150–177.

Blankenship, A. B. (1938) Memory span: A review of the literature. *Psychol. Bull.*, 35, 1–25.

Brown, R., & Berko, Jean. (1960) Word association and the acquisition of grammar. *Child Developm.*, 31, 1–14.

Bruner, J. S. (1957) Review of K. W. Spence, *Behavior theory and conditioning*. *Contemp. Psychol.*, 2, 155–157.

Chomsky, N. (1957) *Syntactic structures*. The Hague: Mouton.

Francis, W. N. (1958) *The structure of American English*. New York: Ronald.

Gesell, A. *et al.* (1940) *The first five years of life: A guide to the study of the preschool child*. New York: Harper.

Guillaume, P. (1927) Le développement des éléments formels dans le langage de l'enfant. *J. Psychol. norm. path.*, 24, 203–229.

Harris, Z. S. (1951) *Methods in structural linguistics*. Chicago: University of Chicago Press.

Hill, A. (1961) Grammaticality. *Word*, 17, 1–10.

Hockett, C. F. (1958) *A course in modern linguistics*. New York: Macmillan.

Jespersen, O. (originally published 1905) *Growth and structure of the English language*. (9th ed., 1938) Garden City, N.Y.: Doubleday.

Lees, R. B. (1960) The grammar of English nominalizations. *Int. J. Amer. Linguistics*, 26, No. 3.

McCarthy, Dorothea. (1954) Language development in children. In L. Carmichael (Ed.), *Manual of child psychology*. New York: Wiley.

Maclay, H., & Sleator, Mary D. (1960) Responses to language: Judgments of grammaticalness. *Int. J. Amer. Linguistics*, 26, 275–282.

Miller, G. A. (1956) The magical number seven, plus or minus two: Some limits on our capacity for processing information. *Psychol. Rev.*, 63, 81–97.

Miller, G. A., Galanter, E., & Pribram, K. H. (1960) *Plans and the structure of behavior*. New York: Holt, Rinehart & Winston.

Munn, N. L. (1954) Learning in children. In L. Carmichael (Ed.), *Manual of child psychology*. New York: Wiley. Pp. 374–458.

Skinner, B. F. (1957) *Verbal behavior.* New York: Appleton-Century-Crofts.

Smart, W. K. (originally published 1925) *English review grammar.* (4th ed., 1957) New York: Appleton-Century-Crofts.

Smith, M. E. (1933) Grammatical errors in the speech of preschool children. *Child Developm.*, 4, 182–190.

Stutsman, R. (1926) Performance tests for pre-school age. *Genet. Psychol. Monogr.*, 1, 1–67.

Yngve, V. (1961) Random generation of English sentences. *Memo* 1961-4. Mechanical Translation Group, Center for Communication Sciences, Research Laboratory of Electronics, M.I.T., Cambridge, Mass.

COMMENTS ON THE PAPER BY BROWN AND FRASER

Charles N. Cofer

NEW YORK UNIVERSITY

In commenting on Brown and Fraser's paper, the first thing I want to say is that their material bears very directly on one of the central issues argued during the first conference. This was a complex issue, and I will try to formulate its several aspects before going on to sketch the relations to it of the observations reported by Brown and Fraser.

The issue was discussed at several points in the first conference, but it arose with its greatest force in conjunction with the discussion of Goss's paper (1961). In this paper, Goss applied his analysis of the acquisition and use of conceptual schemes to a child's act of writing something and suggested that verbal mediating responses might govern the form and the inflection of the sequence of words the child writes. For example, the child might say to himself, Goss suggested, that a sentence should have a subject, verb, object, preposition, object (or noun, verb, noun, preposition, noun) and use this scheme as he constructs the sentence, checking back against the scheme after the sentence is completed. There were several lines of attack on this notion:

a. One indicated that verbal labeling of this sort probably occurs but seldom, and in many cases, cannot occur because labels or rules cannot be formulated by the child or by adults that govern their choices.

b. It was further stressed, however, that choices of inflected forms are often correct, despite the absence of such verbalized knowledge and despite the novelty of the words that are so inflected.

c. The rapidity with which the inflected words can be transferred correctly to other linguistic environments requiring different inflections, occurring in many instances after a single experience, makes the applicability of simple principles of word association and of associative learning dubious.

Deese and Mandler formulated this point of view as follows:

The occurrence of a new word in a syntactic structure determines its position and possibly form in most other syntactic structures in that language.

This constraint cannot be explained in terms of the distribution of response probabilities or contingent probabilities between encoded units (Cofer, 1961, p. 78).

A part of the mystery that seemed (to me) to engulf this topic in the previous discussion of it was the presumed errorless transfer into inflected or syntactical form appropriate to a new linguistic environment by very young children. Similarly mysterious, there seemed to be a reluctance to accept the notion, brought out by Goss as well as by others, that such environments contain cues on which the transfer might be predicated, such cues having derived their pertinence from previous language experiences.

It seems to me that Brown and Fraser's paper contains evidence that removes some of this mystery. I am therefore moved to reexamine this or these questions. Young children use *regular* inflections more often than adults do; and it seems reasonable to suggest that, in the aggregate, their experience of hearing adult speech includes a higher frequency of regular inflections, even though, by themselves, some of the irregular inflections may be quite frequent. It is also clear that the application of syntactical rules to nonsense words is a skill that takes time to develop, i.e., children do better as they become older, and they showed differential rates of improvement with different parts of speech. I suggest that learning of inflectional and syntactical skills is akin to concept formation, and that its rate of occurrence may well be governed by such variables as number of instances, amount of feedback, ratio of positive to negative instances, reinforcement contingencies, and all of the other variables pertinent to concept formation. Labeling may not come until very late, if at all, in concept formation; but if it is introduced, it often facilitates concept formation. One point that needs to be made here on the question of labeling or rule formation is that linguists and grammarians often want to make relatively simple, exceptionless rules, or to encompass all contingencies in their statements; the requirements of ordinary language functioning are probably not so severe.

Personally, I think one of our major problems here is essentially the one Underwood formulates in another context in his paper for the present conference; this is the discovery of the functional stimulus. I would like to examine an example from the Brown and Fraser material and suggest some possible experimental approaches that, with young children as subjects, might have useful results.

Take the case of the plural morpheme. As is pointed out in the paper,

/s/, /z/, and /əz/ are used appropriately by children in the case of non-sense words like *bik*, *wug*, and *niss*. But these endings are systematically chosen on the basis of how the rest of the form ends, as in /k/, /g/, or /s/. Cannot these final phonemes serve as the cues on which the correct plural allomorph is selected? Three kinds of studies, it seems to me, are pertinent here.

One is articulatory. If one's voice is already in use in producing the voiced consonant /g/ as in *wug*, is it perhaps not easier to continue the voicing through the sibilant /z/, producing *wug*/-z/, than it would be to shift to a voiceless sibilant, producing *wug*/-s/? I cannot do the latter easily, as a matter of fact, without altering /g/ to /k/. Admittedly, this reflects linguocentrism, but in the case of young children being reared in a monolingual environment, it is probable that the models heard and the reinforcement contingencies experienced might, in this instance, lead to the habit sequence: back voicing—front voicing, a habitual relation which the child cannot verbalize. My suggestion may be too simple, of course, and there may be many exceptions in English to this sequence. The example is not important, however; the notion I would like to stress is that stimuli for subsequent linguistic responses may arise from prior ones, that prior arrangements of the articulators and the voice may facilitate later such arrangements, and that models and reinforcement contingencies are undoubtedly involved. And it would seem further that with ingenuity experiments could be arranged with young children, which might explore these matters. Take sound sequences which are not common in English. Can children be trained to use the earlier sound production as a cue for the later one? How long would it take? How widely would the skill generalize? How easily can it be differentiated from others? What is the range of variation within which the prior cue retains its discriminative value? Is it easier for sequences involving the continuation of a prior property, like voicing, to be learned than for a sequence involving discontinuous properties or change?

I think it is also important, as a second attack on these problems, to take the child who inflects words more or less correctly in natural environments and to vary systematically aspects of the linguistic pattern so as to identify the functional stimulus. Take *wuk* and *wug* and invent a game with two levers. One is the /z/ lever and the other the /s/ lever. On hearing *wuk* or *wug* the child is to respond to the appropriate lever for reward. He is reinforced for his correct selections but the distinctiveness of /g/ and /k/ here (and perhaps of other features of the stimulus pattern) is systematically varied, perhaps by methods of electronic production. Is the voicing of the consonant the functional cue? What variations in voicing make no difference in lever selection? What ones do?

As a final suggestion along these lines (and all three suggestions are closely interrelated), we should probably go to other languages as sources of materials. For example, I believe that there are two allomorphs (*lar* and *ler*) of the plural morpheme in Turkish and that their respective use is conditioned by the vowel in the preceding stem. Thus, items like *baš* and *dost* take the plural *lar*, becoming *bašlar* and *dostlar* (heads and friends), and any stem that contains a, o, u, i takes *lar*. Items which contain the vowels i, e, ö, ü, however, take the plural form *ler*, such as *dišler* (teeth), *eller* (hands), *ziller* (bells). It occurs to me that paired-associate training with children with various examples of the stems involving the two classes of vowel together with the appropriate plural ending and tests with previously unpresented stems with the child providing the suffix could answer a number of questions. How long does the training take? How well is the differentiation verbalized after different amounts of training? How well does the training transfer to new instances involving the vowel classes already presented? Will transfer occur to stems containing vowels which have not been presented at all? For example, would there be transfer of *lar* to stems containing /u/ after training which included, among the stems which take *lar*, only stems which contain /a/ and /o/?

The kinds of experiments I have suggested could be extended, of course, to include problems arising from syntactical rules as well as problems of morphology. Fundamentally, I think, as I have said, such experiments could isolate functional stimuli and answer basic questions concerning the acquisition, use, and transfer of the skills involved.

My last comment pertains to the point that the young children studied by Brown and Fraser use a reduced or telegraphic kind of English, from which function words or words contributing little information are deleted. I have no reason to doubt this finding and would agree with their interpretations of it. I think it would be of interest to re-present, a number of times, the model sentences which the child is to repeat in order to follow the course of acquisition of the various kinds of words of which the models are composed. But the most interesting association I have to the use of reduced English by children is that it is what I interpret Deese (1961) to have been saying last year in discussing adult memory. He said, in essence, that the subject constructs his recall by associating to what he does remember and, where necessary as in connected discourse, filling in the function words he sees as being needed. While the span limitation with young children is a factor to consider, such young subjects may be showing us, in their reduced speech, the essentials not only of communication but also of actual human memory.

Many years ago, I studied the learning of prose stories in college students. The errors the subjects made, as I interpreted them at that time, seemed to arise as a result of negative transfer effects from previous language habits. Looking over this material again after reading Brown and Fraser's paper, I would still maintain that conclusion. However, some of the evidence suggests also, I think, that the subjects *remembered* the material in telegraphic or abbreviated form and made English out of what they remembered as they recited. For example, if the "main" words (nouns, verbs, adjectives, adverbs) of a passage are scored, their learning is accomplished more quickly than the learning of the total passage (Cofer, 1941). Error analysis yields consistent findings (Cofer, 1943). For example, one sentence in one passage contained seven main words and five minor ones. Nine of the 24 subjects made no errors on the main words during the acquisition trials, while all subjects made errors on one or more of the minor words one or more times. The errors on the major words included *no omissions;* most of them were changes in verb form or substitutions of synonyms. One of the minor words was omitted by 19 subjects on one or more trials, and 13 subjects omitted another one. Other changes, of course, involved substitution errors. These data are only suggestive, but it seems to me that they do fit a notion of selective attention to and learning of the information-carrying items.

This is not direct proof, certainly, that adult memory is a construction based on a telegraphic version of the original material. To study this problem further and more directly we need subjects who can be made to tell us what they really remember of what they hear or read and not to put these memories into ordinary English. If we can get subjects to do this, it would not surprise me if their memories, aside from span factors and maturity of vocabulary, would resemble the reduced English of Brown and Fraser's youngsters.

REFERENCES

Cofer, C. N. (1941) A comparison of logical and verbatim learning of prose passages of different lengths. *Amer. J. Psychol.*, **54**, 1–20.

Cofer, C. N. (1943) An analysis of errors made in the learning of prose materials. *J. Exp. Psychol.*, **32**, 399–410.

Cofer, C. N. (Ed.) (1961) *Verbal learning and verbal behavior.* New York: McGraw-Hill.

Deese, J. (1961) From the isolated verbal unit to connected discourse. In C. N. Cofer (Ed.), *Verbal learning and verbal behavior.* New York: McGraw-Hill. Pp. 11–31.

Goss, A. E. (1961) Acquisition and use of conceptual schemes. In C. N. Cofer (Ed.), *Verbal learning and verbal behavior.* New York: McGraw-Hill. Pp. 42–69.

SUMMARY OF CONFERENCE DISCUSSION

One point which arose early in the discussion was a denial by Mandler and Deese that their formulation, as quoted by Cofer in his remarks, was meant to apply to children who are first beginning to learn a language. Jenkins reminded them that errors of children were cited as pertinent evidence in the first conference, but Mandler indicated he did not feel that Brown and Fraser's paper provides evidence negative to their viewpoint.

Several questions were raised concerning the experiments Cofer suggested. It was pointed out (Miller, Brown) that there are numerous languages in which consonant clusters can include both voiced and voiceless consonants. However, it is probable that a thorough study of the linguistic evidence would suggest that some sequences of articulation are more natural than others.

Brown felt that there is enough evidence that the voiced-voiceless grouping does not hold for the species to make experiment unnecessary, but that the grouping does almost always hold in English. However, the inflectional rules of English (plurality, the possessive, the third person present indicative of the verb, the simple past of the verb) go beyond any phonological formulation. On a phonological level the consonants /r/, /l/, /m/, and /n/ can go with either voiced or voiceless consonants, e.g., *pulls, pulse, blunt, bland.* However, when the final consonant is /s/ or /z/ functioning as an allomorph of plurality or possession, then /r/, /l/, /m/, and /n/ must take the voiced /z/, e.g., *pairs, gills, bums, buns.* Similarly when the final consonant is /t/ or /d/ functioning as a past tense allomorph, then /r/, /l/, /m/, and /n/ must take the voiced /d/, e.g., *purred, spilled, slammed, banned.* Consequently inflection is not simply phonology, and a child cannot properly inflect words from a knowledge of the final consonant clusters that are permissible in English. What is permissible is contingent on the function of the sound pattern. Jenkins suggested that such evidence as this points to the functional stimuli controlling certain verbal responses.

Miller referred to the aspiration in English of certain initial plosives as another instance in which cultural rules do not provide a satisfactory account of the stimulus. For example, most speakers aspirate the /p/ in *pin* but not in *spin.* It is difficult to believe that parents teach their children to do this, as the aspiration is not phonemic. Hence, how is this behavior reinforced? A few children aspirate the /p/ in both linguistic environments, and a few in neither. Wherein are the two cases different? How are these patterns learned? Musgrave asked whether the parents of these minorities aspirate the /p/ in ways similar to those of their children.

Brown added that, in English, vowels which occur before voiced consonants are longer (*need, mode*) than are the same vowels before voiceless consonants (*neat, mote*) and asked how the child comes to detect such differences which are not strictly necessary for distinguishing one word from another and how he learns to produce them. The answer may be that such differences are potentially informative, e.g., in a case where the final consonants in *need* and *neat* are not clearly distinguishable.

Miller stressed the point that redundancy aids perception through noisy channels, so that children must learn all these variations. Too serious a concern with the notion of the functional stimulus might generate speech that is overly simple. Brown pointed out that similarity between a child's and his parent's speech has functional value, and Melton that we often learn things that are not necessary. Brown added that the differentiation of patterns of stimuli can be learned to a very fine degree, i.e., there seems to be no "stop rule" on differentiation. Perhaps a process of attention is necessary.

Shepard, while admitting that there are different phonological patterns in the speech of parent and child, suggested that, following Chomsky,[1] there might be built-in machinery which enables the child to attend to similarities and ignore differences, i.e., innate mechanisms.

On the question of whether the child models his speech pattern on that of the parents Brown said he and Fraser had found little correction of children's speech by their parents. It was suggested that children may shape the parent's speech (Deese). Brown answered that there is considerable variation among parents in the degree to which they imitate the speech of their young children. Most parents use a considerably simplified English to very young children: short sentences, simple rather than complex or compound sentences, no passive construction or nominalizations. Some go further and copy minor ungrammaticalities of their children, e.g., "Some cookie" or "See horsie." Grandparents are often observed to go further in this indulgent direction. There is here an interesting problem of optimal linguistic "lead." A parent must speak a somewhat more complex English than his child if the child is to advance; but if the difference is large, advance may be slowed. Melton said there is frequent correction by older children of the speech of their younger siblings and playmates.

Mandler said there appear to be at least two mechanisms at work, reinforcement and correction. The latter is not adequately understood, since after correction children may go on using the incorrect form. He also deplored the frequent reference to imitation, indicating that we know very little about this process or the extent of its possibility in infants and young children. Mandler referred to unpublished observations that a 10-month-old infant can "imitate" lip-licking movements. This may suggest there are releasing mechanisms involved in imitative behavior at early ages.

There was discussion of the differential recall of function and content words as reported in Cofer's paper. Noble thought that function words

[1] The reference is to N. Chomsky, whom Shepard had heard make statements to this effect.

have low m values which might account for the difference. Melton stated that Slamecka (1961) may have data on errors made in the rote learning of sentences. Murdock added that with cloze technique, which Slamecka is now using, the words forgotten are function words. This did not accord with Deese's experience in immediate recall, but Murdock indicated different groups were used with the cloze procedure and with learning.

Miller pointed out that function words can often be very important to the significance of a message (e.g., the general arrived *from* or *with* his regiment), and Brown added that stress and intonation patterns can be used to call attention to function words when it is important that the listener distinguish them, e.g., "*a* book not *the* book."

Reduced or telegraphic English is often found in students' class notes or in the notes they make on blue books while writing examinations (Deese).

Brown used the differentiation between count nouns and mass nouns to show a way of demonstrating the varying usefulness of contexts in identifying the syntactic properties of a word. He was responding to the Mandler-Deese formulation, as quoted by Cofer, concerning a child's ability to encounter a word in a single context and then use it correctly in the other contexts. His point was that contexts are differentially "diagnostic." Therefore he would suggest modifying the Mandler-Deese statement to read "in a single *diagnostic* context." The following table shows contexts in which a count noun (*cat*) and a mass noun (*dirt*) could (X) or could not (0) be used.

	Count nouns (cat)	Mass nouns (dirt)
the + N + pl + V	X	0
the + N + V	X	X
A + N + V	X	0
N + V	0	X

For the distinction between count nouns and mass nouns there are three sorts of diagnostic or informative contexts and one kind of context that is uninformative for the purpose.

Miller indicated that the foregoing differs from the approach of Fries (1952), and Brown agreed, saying that functional or syntactic classes are supposed to be groups of words with identical privileges of occurrence but too little attention has been given to the details of these privileges. He believes, for instance, that most words have some idiosyncratic privileges of occurrence that distinguish them from other members of any large syntactic class in which the word may be placed.

Deese pointed out that grammatical category and occurrence do not always go together; we do not say "sticky grass." Brown reminded the group of Chomsky's (1957) "colorless green ideas sleep furiously" as a further example of such a disparity. Going on with his point concerning contexts, Brown indicated that for very young children one could not say that the affixation of terminal-voiced sibilants is a simple habit such as could be described by the rule: After a voiced terminal consonant, append /z/. This operation occurs in pluralization, in the formation of possessives, and in the inflection of the verb for third-person subjects. Jean Berko's research (1958) demonstrates that rules of this kind do not, in their various morphological settings, all begin to operate at the same age. It is rather the case that the rule will begin to operate regularly in one setting (e.g., the possessive) when it does not yet operate regularly in another setting (e.g., verbal inflection). In short, the learning of the same, simple phonological contingency seems to be specific to a syntactic function.

Brown went on to speak of Cofer's suggestion that concepts may operate in features of language behavior. Frequency is important here. Children do not use adverbs often or well before they go to school and probably also do not hear very many adverbs. In the two- to three-year-old group, there were very few regular, past-tense verbs. The irregulars "got" and "did" appeared. At the end of this age period correct regular inflections became common, and at the same time, the overgeneralized incorrect regularities appeared.

Actually, Brown said, relatively few errors, other than omissions, have been found in the speech collected by Fraser and himself. This surprised them, as they had thought that the process of inducing rules which generalize beyond the speech that has been heard would cause children to make numerous mistakes. However, they appear to be conservative. The proper names *Father* and *Mother* have similar privileges of occurrence rather early, but the child's name (e.g., *Evie*) does not seem to be added right away. Brown added: How does the child arrive at the point where he goes ahead and uses a given word as he does certain others? How does he form syntactic classes? Perhaps when the sample he has is of some size, he makes a syntactic class of an entire set; at some point he has enough cases and goes ahead. Or perhaps he puts some instances, like *Mommie* and *Daddy*, together first and then later adds others, such as his own name, one at a time. These are samples of the research hypotheses concerning learning suggested by the language-acquisition process.

Jenkins indicated that words might have to be of high frequency before they could be ordered to a class. When adults are given low-frequency adjectives as stimuli in a free-association test, they give noun responses as children do. On high-frequency words, adults tend to give responses which are in the same grammatical class as the stimulus. Children develop this latter pattern slowly (see Ervin, unpublished).

Brown pointed out that working with children to discover the contexts of a word is easier than it is with adults, because there are few words. Mandler reported some work he has been doing with stem completions under varying contexts. The subject is required to complete with single letters the two spaces following a consonant-vowel-consonant (CVC) combination. The CVC occurs within several contexts as well as by itself. For example,

1. The boys CVC—
2. The CVC— walks
3. The boy CVC—
4. The CVC— walked
5. The CVC—
6. The CVC— walk
   CVC—

The rank from 1 to 6 indicates the order of decreasing commonality of added letters among 84 subjects. A total of 14 CVCs were used. These represented two groups of seven each, a strong group of CVCs which in a pilot study had produced high commonality when presented without context and a group of weak CVCs which had produced low commonality. While the order of the contexts does not change materially for these two groups of CVCs, the "no context" condition produced commonality lower than any of the contexts for the weak CVCs, but produced commonality between ranks 2 and 3 for the strong CVCs. The two groups of CVCs were identical in mean Archer values, Noble's m', a, and a'.

Deese observed that with cloze or other completion tasks the effects of the forward contexts are more powerful than those of backward contexts. Musgrave reported the same observation (Musgrave, 1960) but added a question about the mechanism that accounts for greater commonality with contexts than without. She also remarked that context does not necessarily yield commonality greater than noncontext conditions (Jenkins and Cofer, 1957; Musgrave, 1958).

Mandler indicated some of the difficulties in explaining his results. For example, context 6 seems to have more contextual constraint on the responses than contexts 2 and 4, yet the latter yield greater commonality. Brown suggested that the part of speech (of the CVC) is indicated by the contexts, and since parts of speech take different endings, this might be a factor in the results. Shepard referred to Miller's study on redundant strings of letters (Miller, 1958), which suggests that what the subject had already done might influence what he does later. Postman thought the constraints represented in the contexts were not very clear.

Jenkins brought up a paper by Greenberg (1961) on linguistic universals. Greenberg points out that languages have interlocked features such as prepositions in "pre" or "post" positions. Looking at languages in this way, one can find types, based on the dominant pattern in a language. Thus, with subject always before object, we can get:

   I. Verb, Subject, Object
   II. Subject, Verb, Object
   III. Subject, Object, Verb

This kind of finding could be explored further using the techniques of Brown and Fraser. The 30 languages Greenberg used were from widely dispersed languages from different language families.

Shepard mentioned a paper by Yngve (1960) who, like Chomsky (1957), represented sentences by "tree structures" but who, unlike Chomsky, was particularly concerned with the order in which the "terminal" words of the structure are actually generated in time. On the assumption of a definite limit on the number of things that can be held in temporary memory at any one time, Yngve argued that the difficulty of a sentence will depend on the structure of its tree. Miller illustrated some of the types of tree-structures considered by Yngve. For example:

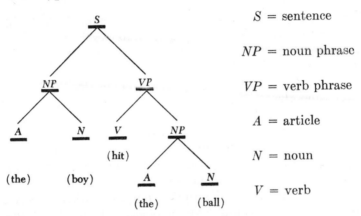

S = sentence

NP = noun phrase

VP = verb phrase

A = article

N = noun

V = verb

In English one can develop sentences either to the right or the left. An example of each follows:

Right-recursive   Left-recursive

Example: "The beauty of the color   John's father's car's color's
          of the car of the father of   beauty
          John."

According to Yngve's argument, the memory load of these two sentences would be very different. In a right-recursive structure the talker must remember only one grammatical obligation at a time in order to get out of the sentence without making a mistake. In a left-recursive sentence, he must remember to return and complete several of his grammatical promises. In fact, however, the two structures seem about equally difficult. A self-embedded sentence, difficult to recall after a single presentation, is illustrated by "The race that the car that the people that the man called sold won was held last summer."

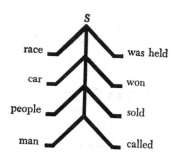

In the course of discussion Staats made methodological objections to the use of terms such as rules and strategies because they imply explanation and turn interest away from an experimental analysis of the independent variables involved. After observing that the child's verbal behavior, for example, comes to follow grammatical rules, which is itself a very important occurrence to establish by systematic observation, the task is then to make a functional analysis of the development of this behavior. The use of concepts like "rules" obscures this need. Brown said he thought associationists set themselves a very difficult theoretical task in so severely restricting the number of operations they would permit the organism to perform. Russell indicated he thought Brown was using terms for descriptive purposes, whereas S-R experimentalists look for mechanisms. Miller objected to the implication that we cannot observe behavior unless we have a notion as to the S-R mechanism. Mandler argued that we should observe first and then worry about specific mechanisms but stressed that both approaches are useful.

There was further discussion of these strategies, and Jenkins pointed out that naming can be important. He pointed to Wickens's (1938) experiment on aversive conditioning of a finger reaction which transferred when the hand was turned over, thus requiring a response antagonistic to the conditioned one. If the two responses are called avoidance responses, the fact that they are antagonistic is not a problem. Melton observed that terms like rules and strategies have some parallels in what we study in concept formation.

REFERENCES

Berko, Jean. (1958) The child's learning of English morphology, *Word,* 14, 150–177.

Chomsky, N. (1957) *Syntactic structures.* The Hague: Mouton.

Ervin, S. M. (unpublished) Age changes in word association.

Fries, C. C. (1952) *The structure of English: An introduction to the construction of English sentences.* New York: Harcourt, Brace.

Greenberg, J. H. (1961) Some universals of grammar with particular reference to the order of meaningful elements. Paper presented at S.S.R.C. Conf. on Language Universals, Dobbs Ferry, N. Y.

Jenkins, P. M. & Cofer, C. N. (1957) An exploratory study of discrete free association to compound verbal stimuli. *Psychol. Rep.,* 3, 599–602.

Miller, G. A. (1958) Free recall of redundant strings of letters. *J. Exp. Psychol.,* 56, 485–491.

Musgrave, Barbara S. (1958) Context effects on word associations using one-word, two-word and three-word stimuli. Paper presented at East. Psychol. Ass., Philadelphia.

Musgrave, Barbara S. (1960) The effects of verbal context factors on cloze and commonality scores. Unpublished M.A. thesis, University of Minnesota.

Slamecka, N. J. (1961) Proactive inhibition of connected discourse. *J. Exp. Psychol.,* 62, 295–301.

Wickens, D. D. (1938) The transference of conditioned excitation and inhibition from one muscle group to the antagonistic muscle group. *J. Exp. Psychol.,* 22, 101–123.

Yngve, V. H. (1960) A model and an hypothesis for language structure. *Tech. Rep. No. 369, Proc. Phil. Soc.,* 1960 (Aug. 15). Research Laboratory of Electronics, M.I.T., Cambridge, Mass.

Chapter 6

MEDIATED ASSOCIATIONS:
PARADIGMS AND SITUATIONS[1]

James J. Jenkins

UNIVERSITY OF MINNESOTA

The concern with mediate associations and mediation processes generally is ancient (as these things go in psychology), dating back at least to the British associationist philosophers. Research in the area has lagged far behind, of course, and is largely concentrated in the last twenty-five years. Even within this period it is easy to plot a rapidly accelerating curve of research endeavors and theoretical papers devoted to mediation, illustrating a growing concern with mediation phenomena and the adaptation of experimental tools, some new and some old, to the task of understanding the processes. This literature has been reviewed elsewhere (e.g., Jenkins, 1959; Kjeldergaard and Horton, 1960; Goss, 1961a, 1961b), and it is not my purpose to recapitulate it here.

The endeavor of this paper is to review some experimentation with which I have been closely involved, to illustrate ways in which the emphasis of our attack on mediation problems has shifted, and to propose a view of mediation which, I believe, suggests important directions for future research.

A FEW WORDS OF ORIENTATION

In our concern with research in mediation, I believe all of us have been attempting to demonstrate two major propositions: First (aimed at our doubting colleagues), mediation effects really can be found, and second (aimed at each other), mediation is "properly" inferred by X

[1] This paper was written with the support of the National Science Foundation under the grant, "The Role of Associative Models in Varied Symbolic Behaviors." Most of the Minnesota work discussed herein was supported either by the National Science Foundation under the current grant or by the Office of Naval Research which generously supported the Minnesota research program in verbal behavior from 1951 to 1957.

technique because the content of mediation "really is" Y. The first proposition has been rather firmly established; any counter contention faces too much evidence to survive. The second, while it has led us into much fruitful research, ought to be given less emphasis, for it blinds us from time to time to the extensive area of agreement we share by stressing the details in which we differ.

I refer here, of course, to a history of debate in which I, too, have played some part and must plead guilty along with my colleagues. The record of our predilections for particular forms of mediation is interesting in its variety. Cofer and Foley (1942) chose a Hullian model of implicit responses for their mediation process while they worked with word associations, both natural (Foley and MacMillan, 1943) and intentionally acquired (Foley and Mathews, 1943) and with logical categories such as synonyms and antonyms (Foley and Cofer, 1943; Cofer, Janis, and Rowell, 1943). On the other hand, Bousfield's pioneering work in recall processes (Bousfield, 1953; Bousfield and Cohen, 1955) was first organized around a set of Hebbian supraordinate structures. Jenkins and Russell (Jenkins and Russell, 1952; Jenkins, Mink, and Russell, 1958) and Deese (1959a, 1959b) took a cue from Bousfield with regard to the experimental situation but departed from his supraordinates to spark a concern with free associations as the key to mediators in structuring recall. Osgood (1952, 1953), who is perhaps as responsible as anyone else for much of the current thinking (either in agreement with or in opposition to his position), opted for "representational mediators" derived from the "detachable" portions of responses made in the presence of stimuli in the past. In addition, he recommended a particular instrument, the semantic differential, for the measurement of the mediators. Finally, Cofer (Jenkins and Cofer, 1957) and then Bousfield (Bousfield, Whitmarsh, and Danick, 1958), both taking new tacks, directed attention to the overlapping of associative hierarchies as the most appropriate inference base.

In all of this, we have tended to debate the fine points of "content of the mediation" (see, for example, the Bousfield-Osgood discussions of the previous conference and the paper by Wynne and Cofer, 1958) and have overlooked the very great consensus which has been achieved regarding the mediation process itself. I think we have made too much of disagreement.

The facts which were set forth in the Bousfield papers on supraordinate categories are still facts though our explanations of them change from time to time. I have no doubt that the words he used may be shown to be semantic differential similars, associates of each other, terms sharing high associative overlap, and of course, logically related. All of us, I suspect, would agree that as long as we operate within a natural language framework, all of our inference bases are confounded with hosts of overlapping processes, any or all of which may be intimately associated with the effects we observe. For example, though Russell and I often write *as if* a single associative response to a word is the effective agent in mediating response transfer, stimulus equivalence, or stimulus-response clustering, all we can seriously claim for the association is that it furnished an index which enabled us to choose words which "behaved" in a given way. Our excuse for using associations is that they have proved to be effective indices of the behaviors we wanted to study and they have made it possible to perform research which has helped uncover mediation phenomena in new situations and has drawn attention to the fact that some mediational phenomena are asymmetrical.

I would suggest that we minimize our debate and get on with two tasks which I see before us. The first is implied above. It is important that we know how our indices function with respect to each other in particular situations. We need studies of the strengths and weaknesses of each kind of measurement procedure, and we need to know how they are interrelated. Promising beginnings have been made on such problems by a number of investigators, for example, Cofer (1957), the Staats (Staats and Staats, 1959), and Flavell (Flavell, 1961a, 1961b; Flavell and Johnson, 1961), but much more work is needed both with natural language materials and laboratory materials where the subject's experience with the materials has been controlled.

The second task, I believe, is to press on in our experimental attack on the conditions of mediation; that is, we should attempt to discover how these implicit processes are acquired, how they are activated, how they are inhibited, and in general, how they are employed by the subjects.

In the remainder of the paper dealing with this second problem, I shall use the terms "mediation," "mediator," and "associative arousal" as general terms to avoid coming to grips with the first problem. The reader may construe the content of the "mediation" or "associative arousal" in any way he pleases. What will be assumed here is that the mediation process is a response process, that it may be implicit and unobservable, and that it has stimulus properties. The mode of inference concerning mediators used in the experiments reported here is ordinarily based on free-association behavior, but that is not critical to the argument.

RESEARCH IN MEDIATED LEARNING

The classic paradigm of mediate association as set forth by the British associationists is deceptively simple. Briefly, it was held that if an idea, A, was associated with another idea, B, and still another idea,

C, was also associated with B, then idea A would come to have some association with idea C. This was called a *mediate association* as opposed to an *immediate* association which arose from direct association through contiguity of the ideas in time or space. (In the remainder of this paper the neutral term "element" will be used in place of the "ideas," "images," and "brain states" found in the older literature. Thus, the foregoing would be rendered: If element A is associated with element B and element C is associated with element B, then element A will acquire some association with element C.)

A convenient and powerful way to test for mediate association is provided by a simple experiment using paired-associate learning lists. We may take natural associates as one pair of elements (say A and B). One member of the pair may be associated with a nonsense syllable (C) in paired-associate learning. We may then test for the presence of some association between the nonsense syllable and the other member of the natural pair by requiring the subject to learn a new list containing these elements and contrasting his performance with that of a control subject who did not learn the appropriate first list.

The experiment may be diagrammed and illustrated as follows:

Given (from norms):	A → B
Learn:	C → A
Test:	C → B

First list	*Second list*
ZUG—Table	ZUG—Chair
BOP—King	BOP—Queen
etc.	etc.

The experiment was conducted by Sacks and Russell in 1953 and enormous facilitation of second-list learning was found; the subjects learned it in virtually one trial.

The experiment may be criticized on the grounds that the subjects were "aware" of the relationship between the responses in the first and second lists. The criticism, while true, is irrelevant. The experiment constitutes a powerful demonstration of mediated learning. The paradigm employed takes the form of a chain.

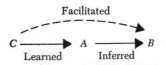

In an effort to escape from the "obviousness" of this experiment, Russell and Storms (1955) extended the chain by another inferred link.

Searching the norms, they discovered that they could assemble chains of two inferred links in which the first member rarely elicited the third member, though it elicited a second member which was closely associated with the third. Their experiment may be diagrammed and illustrated as follows:

> Given: A → B, B → C, A ↛ C
> Learn: X → A
> Test: X → C

> Given: Soldier → Sailor, Sailor → Navy, Soldier ↛ Navy
> Learn: ZUG—Soldier
> Test: ZUG—Navy

Significant facilitation in learning was found for the pairs in the second list for which mediation was assumed to be active. It should be noted that the assumed implicit term did not appear anywhere in the experiment and the subjects were not "aware" of the relationship between the first and second lists. In this experiment we may more clearly speak of associative arousal since other potential mediators may be assumed to exist, and it is clear that a variety of relationships may be postulated to exist between the key terms. Again, however, the explicit form of the experiment is that of a chain.

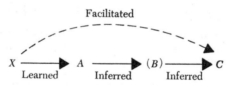

Following the Russell-Storms experiment, Bastian (1956) demonstrated that the effect found by Sacks and Russell could be repeated in the absence of the subjects' awareness by using mixed lists of associates, similars (based on ratings), and controls on the response side of paired-associate lists learned sequentially. He found that both associates and similars facilitated learning, though associates were also more facilitative than similars. We would include both of these terms under our broad term of associative arousal and thus conclude that the general mediation case is well documented and that in addition we have learned something about the efficiency of the two methods of inference.

At this point Ryan (1957, 1960) proceeded to test for mediation on the stimulus side of paired-associate lists. His experiment mirrors Bastian's in using mixed lists of associates, similars (determined from semantic differential ratings), and controls. He again found facilitation in second-list learning, though the amount of facilitation obtained with the associates and the similars was not as clearly different as it had been in Bastian's experiment. Here again, we may conclude that the general mediation case is well demonstrated and that the methods of inference are about equivalent.

Carlin (1958) then attacked the problem of predicting the amount of facilitation in the two experimental situations used by Bastian and Ryan by varying the strength of the associations involved. She employed high-, medium-, and low-strength associates as well as control words in duplicating the experiments. Her findings were dramatically different from our predictions of a proportionality between the strength of an associate and its presumed facilitative power in learning. All degrees of association produced significant facilitation in second-list learning as compared to controls but none was reliably stronger than any other.

We concluded that our inference base left something to be desired with respect to strength measures or that a situational variable operated to maximize associative arousal if it occurred at all. Storms (1956) had earlier suggested that "recency" operated to strengthen weak associates. He showed that if a subject is presented with a list of words which he is supposed to remember and then is given an association test, these words appear more often than usual as responses to appropriate stimuli in the test. We suspected that some such recruitment of strength might be going on with respect to the associative arousal process.

Our doubts concerning mediation as a neat, automatic, associative process directly inferred from normative data began to grow. In a series of studies as yet unpublished, Jerome Milstein, Joanne D'Andrea, and I have confirmed the work of Carlin and have in addition shown that even extremely weak associates, as determined by the norms (.2 of 1 per cent), can effectively mediate paired-associate learning.

About the same time Mink (1957) completed a series of studies on the generalization of an instrumental response from a stimulus word to its associate. The subject received a list of words to each of which he was instructed to press a lever. After a few trials, he was presented with a test list and told to press the lever to any words he had seen before. The test list contained the training words, associates of the training words, and control words. Mink found significantly more pressing to associates than to controls. When he further explored the situation, however, he made a surprising discovery. With unidirectional associates there was only one arrangement of words which would produce the generalization effect, and curiously, it was *not* the chaining arrangement we had been postulating in paired-associate learning.

Mink used two situations which may be diagrammed and illustrated as follows:

<table>
<tr><td align="center">I
(Equivalence)</td><td align="center">II
(Chaining)</td></tr>
<tr><td>Given: A → B
Learn: A → Press
Test: B → Press
Examples:
  Given: Eagle → Bird (and Bird ↔ Eagle)
  Learn: Eagle → Lever Press
  Test: Bird → Lever Press</td><td>Given: A → B
Learn: B → Press
Test: A → Press

Learn: Bird → Lever Press
Test: Eagle → Lever Press</td></tr>
</table>

Situation I repeatedly gave reliable evidence for generalization and situation II repeatedly did not. This apparently meant that mediation was taking place in the learning stage but not in the test stage. We were forced to consider that mediation might have to be "turned on or off" depending on its locus in a particular experiment, a prospect that was somewhat appalling. Mink's work was reconfirmed by Moss at UCLA (1960) and repeated many times at Minnesota with the same findings: Bidirectional associates always produce the generalization effect; unidirectional associates only produce the generalization phenomena when they are used in situation I.

Both the Mink and Carlin studies impelled us to retreat to the laboratory, build up controlled associative histories in our subjects, and systematically test all the reasonable mediation paradigms we could devise. Accordingly, this is what was done (see Jenkins, 1959).

MEDIATION PARADIGMS

It is evident that the simplest mediation paradigm consists of three elements so arranged that two of them are associated with the third. It is further clear that there are eight patterns of arrangements which satisfy this requirement and that only a few have been tested for mediation effects. The patterns are given in Table 6–1. Four of the paradigms may be designated as chaining paradigms (two are forward chains and two are reverse chains), two may be called acquired-stimulus-equivalence paradigms, and two may be called acquired-response-equivalence paradigms. Although some of them are unlikely candidates for mediation models, all were tested for mediation effects.

Kjeldergaard and Horton (1960), using very low-frequency English words as elements and the paired-associate learning method for each stage, studied 18 subjects in each of the paradigms. Materials were arranged so that each subject served as his own control; in the test list half the pairs that the subject learned were mediated and half were non-mediated. The over-all facilitation of the mediated pairs was highly significant. The investigators conducted t tests for individual paradigms and found that all but paradigm III (one of the reverse chain paradigms) showed significant effects of mediation. No differences between paradigms were significant however. The investigators had worked out a series of predictions of probable mediation effects based on a careful

Table 6–1
Three-stage Mediation Paradigms

	I	II	
Learn	A—B	B—C	Simple chains
Learn	B—C	A—B	$(A \rightarrow B \rightarrow C)$
Test	A—C	A—C	

	III	IV	
Learn	B—A	C—B	Reverse chains
Learn	C—B	B—A	$(A \leftarrow B \leftarrow C)$
Test	A—C	A—C	

	V	VI	
Learn	A—B	C—B	Stimulus equivalence
Learn	C—B	A—B	$(A \rightarrow B \leftarrow C)$
Test	A—C	A—C	

	VII	VIII	
Learn	B—A	B—C	Response equivalence
Learn	B—C	B—A	$(A \leftarrow B \rightarrow C)$
Test	A—C	A—C	

and ingenious analysis of the second-stage learning which seemed to be in accord with the differences which were observed between the paradigms, though of course the predictions lacked statistical confirmation.

Any consideration of mediation processes which accounts for the Kjeldergaard-Horton findings must include backward associative links. Fortunately, independent evidence for such backward associations following paired-associate learning is abundant (Feldman and Underwood, 1957; Jantz and Underwood, 1958; Storms, 1958; Murdock, 1956, 1958; Richardson, 1960). Throughout this paper it will be assumed that backward associations exist following paired-associate learning (see also Russell, 1955).

The findings of the Minnesota investigators were almost immediately confirmed by Cramer and Cofer (1960) using natural language materials for all eight paradigms.

Encouraged by their findings, we went on to a test of the reasonable four-stage paradigms which seemed to be of importance in the general questions of acquired stimulus and response equivalence.[2] The paradigms are given in Tables 6–2 and 6–3.

The four-stage paradigms are of particular interest because of the close resemblance which some of them bear to natural language models. Here again both equivalence and chaining paradigms may be found. Particular interest centers on the equivalence models both because of the theoretical importance they have in the explication of stimulus equivalence and response equivalence and also because they provide an

Table 6–2

Four-stage Paradigms Testing Acquired Stimulus Equivalence

	I	II	
Learn	A—B	B—C	Capacity of a chain to mediate stimulus
Learn	B—C	A—B	equivalence
Learn	A—D	A—D	
Test	C—D	C—D	

	III	IV	
Learn	B—A	C—B	Capacity of a reverse chain to mediate
Learn	C—B	B—A	stimulus equivalence
Learn	A—D	A—D	
Test	C—D	C—D	

	V	VI	
Learn	A—B	C—B	Shipley paradigms, "pure" stimulus
Learn	C—B	A—B	equivalence
Learn	A—D	A—D	
Test	C—D	C—D	

	VII	VIII	
Learn	B—A	B—C	Transfer of equivalent responses to
Learn	B—C	B—A	equivalent stimuli
Learn	A—D	A—D	
Test	C—D	C—D	

example of a minimal linguistic frame in which different elements may appear and offer an opportunity to study the degree to which these elements may be used in parallel fashion in a new setting.

A classic example of such an equivalence paradigm is the following:

Learn A → B
Learn C → B
Now learn A → D
Test C → D

It is here assumed that A and C become functionally equivalent stimuli during the first two stages. When a new response to A is learned in the

[2] The writer was assisted in this work by James Greeno, Philip Gough, David Hakes and Erwin Segal.

third stage, it should more likely occur to C in the test stage. It is presumed that the transfer is mediated by the implicit occurrence of B during both of the last two stages.

The case in which the functionally equivalent items shift position in the sequence is similarly the minimal case of language transformation.

$$A \rightarrow B$$
$$C \rightarrow B$$
$$D \rightarrow A$$
$$D \rightarrow C$$

Here, what were originally functionally equivalent stimuli must become functionally equivalent responses, an occurrence which is almost ex-

Table 6–3
Four-stage Paradigms Testing Acquired Response Equivalence

	I	II	
Learn	A—B	B—C	Russell-Storms paradigms, capacity of a
Learn	B—C	A—B	chain to mediate response equivalence
Learn	D—A	D—A	
Test	D—C	D—C	

	III	IV	
Learn	B—A	C—B	Capacity of a reverse chain to mediate
Learn	C—B	B—A	response equivalence
Learn	D—A	D—A	
Test	D—C	D—C	

	V	VI	
Learn	A—B	C—B	Transfer of equivalent stimuli to equiva-
Learn	C—B	A—B	lent responses
Learn	D—A	D—A	
Test	D—C	D—C	

	VII	VIII	
Learn	B—A	B—C	"Pure" response equivalence
Learn	B—C	B—A	
Learn	D—A	D—A	
Test	D—C	D—C	

clusively a linguistic event. While the eight possible four-stage equivalence paradigms could be discussed in detail, it is perhaps sufficient to state that they appear to furnish the most elementary approach to the development of functional classes in language and a beginning attack on the problems of linguistic transformations.

Following the Kjeldergaard and Horton procedure with some exceptions, 16 subjects were studied in each of the 16 paradigms. When the data were subjected to analysis, no mediation effects whatsoever were found. Furthermore, *no individual paradigm showed mediation effects significantly different from chance.*

At this point an agonizing reappraisal took place. While we had expected that many of the paradigms would show little if any facilitation, we were unprepared for the total collapse of the enterprise. The paradigms contained the same model as that used by Russell and Storms and subsequently confirmed by Cofer and Yarczower (1957) and Schulz and McGehee (1960) as well as the famous Shipley paradigm (Shipley, 1935) on which Hull (1939) had based his analysis of stimulus equivalence and on which Cofer and Foley (1942) and Osgood (1953) had built their theoretical extensions to language behavior. Yet the experiment had failed completely. Obviously, explanations were required, and we carefully reconsidered both our thinking about mediational processes and the experimental literature along with the particular details of the experiment itself.

EXPLANATION OF THE FAILURE TO FIND MEDIATION EFFECTS

Three explanations of the experimental findings seemed plausible.

1. The experimental situation did not build up enough associative strength to activate the mediational processes which would have been required to facilitate learning in the test list. This simple hypothesis seemed on the face of things most probable. It was clear that the amount of facilitation observed in the Russell-Storms experiment was much less than that seen in the Sacks and Russell, Bastian, and Ryan experiments. The added link in the associative chain apparently made the observation of facilitation much more tenuous than lowering the strength in a single-unit association problem. If only small effects could be obtained using natural language associations (which we believe to be much stronger than any association we can produce in the laboratory), then it seems reasonable to suppose that we had failed to mobilize sufficient strength to elicit and sustain the associative arousal process.

2. The experimental situation did not elicit and reinforce the specific mediational processes required. As we read the experimental literature again, we saw the Birge (1941) experiment in a new light. Birge had tried to show that the naming response can be used as an effective mediator by children. In her experiment children learned names for boxes with distinctive designs on the tops. Two boxes shared one name and two boxes shared another. After learning the appropriate names for the boxes, the child was presented with a pair of boxes with contrasting names and allowed to find candy repeatedly under one of them. Then he was presented with the other pair of boxes and allowed to guess which

one had candy under it. When the experiment was conducted in this fashion, the children chose randomly in the test stage (54 per cent correct, 46 per cent incorrect).

The experiment can be outlined as the Shipley paradigm:

> Learn: A → B (learn name to box)
> Learn: C → B (learn same name to other box)
> Learn: A → D (find candy under box)
> Test: C → D (find candy under other box)

When there was no explicit naming of the boxes in the third and fourth stages, there was no evidence for facilitation. When Birge introduced naming in the third stage, however, significant facilitation was found; with naming in the fourth stage still more facilitation was observed, and with naming in both the third and fourth stage maximum facilitation was found. While I had previously disregarded the Birge experiment as specific to children or a "weak" experiment, it now suggested an important consideration: The mediating process itself must be elicited and reinforced. Presumably, though the naming responses were readily available, the children were not using them as discriminative cues until the situation demanded it by requiring the name. Once the name was elicited, the desired association took place. Now this is assuredly mediation, though it loses some of its appeal because the mediator (or some portion of it) must be made explicit; but certainly we could teach the children to "name" subvocally if we were willing to repeat this kind of experiment several times with the same subjects. Our attention must be drawn to the fact that nothing in the single experiment reinforces the subject for behaving in a subvocal, mediating fashion. In the third stage there is no advantage in associative arousal since the boxes are clearly discriminable and the subject is allowed to see the candy placed under the box. The test trial which follows is a single performance trial and permits no "learning to mediate" to take place.

It is difficult to see in our own four-stage experiments what reinforcement would accrue to the subject for engaging in associative arousal. He has in effect three learning tasks in which such behavior will only *interfere* with his rote learning. It seems unreasonable to expect that he will suddenly begin to behave differently on the fourth task. Indeed if he learns by rote for three tasks, it will do him little good to attempt to utilize associative arousal on the fourth task in most of the paradigms. Consider in detail the Shipley paradigm:

> A → B
> C → B   *Hull's analysis:*
> A → D.......... A → (B) → D
> C → D.......... C → (B) → D

According to Hull's analysis, the mediation is effected in the third and fourth stages. As the subject learns A → D, he is said to build up a (B) → D connection since (B) occurs implicitly as an associative response following A. Then when the subject begins to learn the fourth list, C is supposed to elicit (B) because of previous training, and the (B) → D association is supposed to facilitate C → D learning. The work of Barnes and Underwood (1959), however, suggests that if (B) occurs as a response to A in the third stage, it constitutes an interfering response tendency and (B) will be inhibited or extinguished. If this is so, then little (B) → D strength will be established and in addition (B) may even be made less available as an associate to C. Thus, in the test trial even if C elicits (B), there is likely to be little (B) → D strength and little facilitation.

The Russell-Storms paradigm is a different case, however:

$$A \to B$$
$$B \to C$$
$$D \to A \qquad \textit{Russell-Storms analysis:}$$
$$D \to C\ldots\ldots\ldots\ D \to (A) \to (B) \to C$$

In this paradigm each link is explicitly reinforced, and there is little problem with interference until the test trial is reached. Here it would appear that we must either appeal to the strength of the links as before or make a general case of the reinforcement hypothesis and propose that the subject by this time has become a proficient rote learner and that mediating activities, having not been reinforced, are not going to appear suddenly.

3. Different experimental situations evoke different degrees or kinds of associative arousal. Two other successful demonstrations of four-stage mediation remain to be compared with the experiments here, those of Shipley (1935) and Wickens and Briggs (1951). Both of these are extensions of classical-conditioning experiments.

In Shipley's experiment a light was paired with a reflex eye blink in the first stage; a buzzer was paired with the same response in the second stage. In the third stage the light was paired with shock which induced finger withdrawal; in the fourth stage the buzzer was presented and the finger withdrawal was observed in the absence of the shock.

Wickens and Briggs, in a study designed to show that sensory preconditioning could be viewed as a special case of mediated generalization, used the same paradigm to transfer a conditioned response from one stimulus to another. They paired a tone and a light with the same verbal response and then shocked the subjects in the presence of the tone to elicit a GSR. They found evidence in the test stage of the transfer of the GSR to the light as a stimulus.

These studies suggest that there may be situational differences which are determiners of associative arousal. Critical importance may perhaps be attributed to the small number of stimuli used, perhaps to a difference in instrumental versus conditioned responses, or perhaps to the emotional involvement occasioned by the use of shock. In the Shipley experiment the mediator itself is a conditioned response of a reflex nature. Perhaps in such a situation what we have called associative arousal is automatic in the extreme. Perhaps it need have no "utility" for the subject. The Wickens and Briggs data, however, cannot be explained in this fashion since their mediator is a "voluntary" verbal response. Some considerations concerning situational differences in the conditioning experiment will be advanced in more detail below.

CHOICE OF EXPLANATIONS

In an effort to choose among the alternatives which we had proposed to explain the failure of our four-stage paradigms, James Greeno and I decided to test the Shipley paradigm with associative links taken from the natural language. If the Shipley paradigm could be demonstrated to work at least as well as the Russell-Storms paradigm when natural language associates were employed, we felt that this would argue for the explanation that our experiments with the four-stage paradigms had failed because too little associative strength had been involved in the separate links. Accordingly, natural associations of the form $A \rightarrow B$, $C \rightarrow B$ but neither $A \rightarrow C$ nor $C \rightarrow A$ were employed. An example of such a set is *Bird* $\rightarrow$ *Fly*, *Swatter* $\rightarrow$ *Fly* which are both associations of considerable strength but have the interesting property that *Bird* and *Swatter* are associatively unrelated. Other examples may appear more "reasonable" to the reader: *Table* and *Comfort* both elicit *Chair; Stars* and *Blue* both elicit *Sky*, etc. The experiment took the form:

First list	*Second list*
Bird—zug	Swatter—zug
Blue—hof	Stars—hof
etc.	etc.

Presumably the occurrence of the implicit response should mediate transfer. Thus *Bird* $\rightarrow$ (fly) $\rightarrow$ zug should facilitate *Swatter* $\rightarrow$ (fly) $\rightarrow$ zug. Mixed lists were employed so that subjects served as their own controls.

Analysis of the second-stage learning for 32 subjects showed no evidence for facilitation at any level of list mastery. Trial by trial the curves for mediated and control pairs were virtually identical. The explanation of the failure of the four-stage paradigms on the basis of weak interelement links did not seem adequate to account for the same finding when natural language terms and associations were used.

It might be argued of course that the Russell-Storms experiment was successful not only because of high strength of association but also because the associative activity took place on the response side. One might suppose that in the activity of trying to recall response terms, one might activate associative processes which would not have been activated if the terms had appeared on the stimulus side. To clear away this further hypothesis, the experiment described above was also conducted as a "response equivalence" experiment. The general form was:

First list	Second list
ZUG—Bird	ZUG—Swatter
HOF—Blue	HOF—Stars
etc.	etc.

Thirty-two subjects were studied in this experiment. No evidence for any mediational effect was discovered.

As matters stand at the present time, we believe that the results that we have achieved with the three-stage and the four-stage paradigms are valid; we think neither set of findings is random or accidental. We believe that the difference between the outcomes of these experiments points to a pair of powerful considerations with which we have not dealt previously: first, the reinforcement of specific mediation responses and, second, the general likelihood of eliciting mediational processes as determined either by the characteristics of tasks and situations confronting the subjects or by the subject's history of reinforcement for mediating in the specific situation.

Let us look at a few representative three-stage mediation models. In the simple chaining model, $A \rightarrow B$, $B \rightarrow C$, $A \rightarrow C$, the subject receives two learning tasks on which any mediating he does will be idiosyncratic and nonconstructive with respect to the third stage which is to come. When the third stage appears, however, there is high likelihood that the (B) element will be elicited either by direct association with A, backward association with C, or both. In any event, once it occurs, it offers the subject a "path" from A to C and "getting to C" is explicitly reinforced in the paired-associative learning situation. If the subject mediates, he is reinforced.

Now contrast this with the most similar four-stage paradigm:

$$A \rightarrow B$$
$$B \rightarrow C$$
$$A \rightarrow D$$
$$C \rightarrow D$$

Here we find the same two first stages in which no systematic media-tion will be reinforced. In the third stage according to traditional analy-sis, the implicit (B) is supposed to occur and become associated with D. But the odds seem against it. What is the utility of (B) here for the subject? It can only serve as a competing and interfering response. Then in the fourth stage when C is presented, what is the likelihood that the implicit (B) will be elicited? We must agree that it is not very strong. The C to (B) association is backward to begin with, which certainly implies reduced strength, and even if (B) is elicited, it can serve as a mediator only if it acquired an association with D in the previous stage, which seems doubtful. In short, when one takes a "reasonable" view of the four-stage situation and treats the implicit mediating response *as a response*, subject to reinforcement, interference, and inhibition, there is little reason to expect to find mediational facilitation.

The results when one considers the "equivalence" models are much the same. Let us take for example:

$$
\begin{array}{ll}
A \to B & A \to B \\
C \to B & C \to B \\
A \to C & A \to D \\
& C \to D
\end{array}
$$

In the three-stage model, the first two stages are, as before, rote-learned with some benefit from having a common response which usually is said to produce some positive transfer. Then in the test stage both A and C should tend to have a high probability of eliciting (B), and (B), once elicited, provides a reinforced path to get from A to C. [A to (B) by a forward association and (B) to C via a backward association.]

In the four-stage model we encounter the same problem we found above. The only way in which the model can produce mediated facili-tation is if the implicit (B) term can be elicited and associated with response D in the third stage. Since there is no reason to believe that this will occur (if we believe that the response must be reinforced), there is no reason to expect that mediated facilitation will be found in the fourth stage of learning.

While this approach seems to account for the differences found in our experiments on three- and four-stage paradigms (albeit, after the fact), how can we account for the Shipley and Wickens and Briggs find-ings for a four-stage paradigm? At this point I see two alternatives. Perhaps the role of mediation in classical conditioning is different from its role in instrumental learning, or perhaps differing situations in which learning and performance are carried on are intrinsically more or less favorable to associative arousal. Fortunately, a nice comparison of clas-sical "semantic" conditioning and instrumental "semantic" conditioning, both of which rely on a performance test of mediation, is available in the experiments of Razran (1949) and Mink (1957).

COMPARISON OF AN INSTRUMENTAL AND CONDITIONING SITUATION

While Mink's work has been discussed earlier, we may again summarize it here. Using a lever press as his instrumental response, Mink taught subjects to press to a small number of words. Subjects were then given a test list which contained the original words, associates of the original words, and control words. His measure of generalization was the extent to which subjects pressed more to associates than to controls. Using unidirectional associates, he found that generalization occurred in one paradigm but not in another. Mediation seemed to occur in the learning stage.

Successful paradigm	*Unsuccessful paradigm*
Given: A → B	A → B
Learn: A → C	B → C
Test: B → C	A → C

On the other hand Razran maintained that the generalization of salivary conditioning depended on semantic mediation in the test stage and reinforced his observation by showing that if one conditioned *Yankee*, one got little generalization to *Doodle*, but if one conditioned *Doodle*, there was appreciable generalization to *Yankee*. His results may be contrasted to Mink's:

A → B
Given: (Yankee-Doodle)

Unsuccessful generalization	*Successful generalization*
Condition: A → C	B → C
Test: B → C	A → C

His successful paradigm is, of course, the so-called Shipley-Lumsdaine paradigm which was already known to be effective with nonsemantic materials and a different conditioned response (see Shipley, 1933; Lumsdaine, 1939).

Razran's argument, which was based on assumed rather than observed associative structures, has been confirmed by the recent work of Whitmarsh and Bousfield (1961). These investigators recently collected associations of college students to the Razran words and showed that the overlap of associative hierarchies (from test word to stimulus) correlated highly with the measured amounts of salivary generalization obtained by Razran. The writers were kind enough to lend me their data, and, to make the argument clearer, I have plotted the simple association strengths between the test and stimulus words against the amount of generalization of response. The plots are presented in Figures 6–1, 6–2, and 6–3. Inspection of the figures shows that Razran was in the main correct. One must first, of course, disregard the appreciable generalization found for stimuli and test words which are formally similar (same letters). Aside from that, generalization may be seen to depend on the capacity of the test

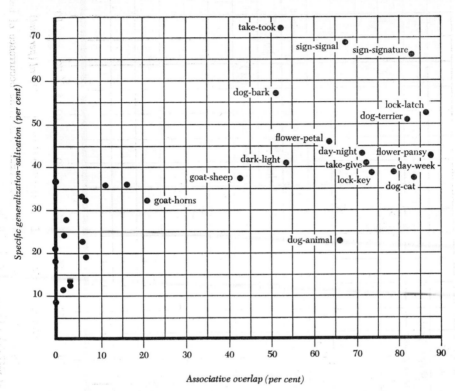

FIG. 6–1. The relation of semantic generalization to associative overlap between test stimuli and conditioned stimuli.

word to elicit the stimulus word to which the primary conditioning occurred. It is clear that this is the reverse of Mink's finding.

How may we account for the differences seen to exist between the Mink and the Razran findings? My first impulse was to say that this was a fundamental difference between operant and respondent behavior, but a little reflection convinced me that this remark was singularly useless in advancing our understanding of mediation processes. What was needed was a careful comparison of the two studies with special attention to the differences in the subject's activities in the two stages of the experiments.

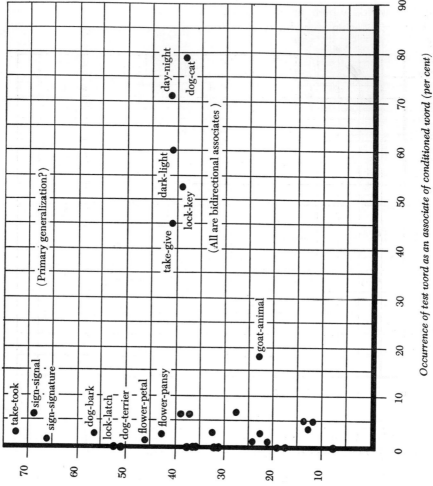

Specific generalization–salivation (per cent)

take-took

sign-signal
sign-signature

(Primary generalization?)

dog-bark

lock-latch
dog-terrier
flower-petal

flower-pansy

take-give

dark-light

lock-key

(All are bidirectional associates)

day-night

dog-cat

goat-animal

Occurrence of test word as an associate of conditioned word (per cent)

Fig. 6–2. The relation between semantic generalization and the occurrence of test stimuli as associates of conditioned stimuli.

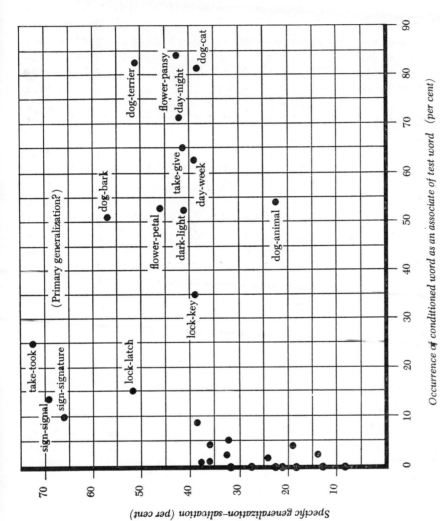

Fig. 6–3. The relation between semantic generalization and the occurrence of conditioned stimuli as associates of test stimuli.

229

In the instrumental situation in the first stage the subject was presented with a set of words one at a time at a two-second interval for very few trials. He was told that he was supposed to try to remember the words so that he could recognize them later. He was also told to press a lever as rapidly as he could as each word appeared. It is our impression that the subjects were focused on the words and trying to learn them as they had been instructed to do. They pressed the lever quickly and almost automatically as each word appeared. In short the words seemed to be central to the task, and the lever press peripheral to the task. Typically, the learning trials were stopped before the average subject would have been able to recall the complete list (two learning trials with 12 words).

We know from a variety of studies (Jenkins and Russell, 1952; Jenkins, Mink, and Russell, 1958; Deese, 1959a, 1959b) that recall is structured in a fashion indexed by association. It seems a fair inference that there is marked associative arousal in the effort made to learn words for recall. We may assume that the subject's associative processes were well activated by the task and, since the subject was at the same time engaged in another response, we may further assume that the stimuli provided by the associative arousal became related to the motor response of lever pressing. It should be noticed that the response activities of the subject are noninterfering and that there is no reason to expect that one would be inhibited because of the activation of the other. If we accept simple contiguity learning, the two kinds of response processes become associated; and the necessary mediational step in the successful Mink paradigm is effected at this point.

In contrast let us look at the first stage of the human conditioning study.

The stimuli-to-be-conditioned are presented a number of times, intermittently, for periods of one to two seconds, while the Ss are eating small 8-shaped pretzels or tea sandwiches or sucking at lollipops or peppermint candy. . . . The eating periods last from two to four minutes with one to two minute rest intervals between them, and ten to fifteen of such eating periods constitute an experimental training session. . . . The multiple intermittent presentations of the stimuli-to-be-conditioned are intended to secure a maximum of attention for the stimuli. . . .

A very special characteristic of the writer's technique is that of misinforming the Ss about the nature of the experiment. This misinformation is a *sine qua non*, if the disrupting subjective attitudes in the wake of the Ss' knowledge-expectancy of being conditioned are to be controlled. Fortunately, with the method outlined, disguise has not been too difficult. Telling the Ss that the experiment aims to study "the effects of hunger on eye-fatigue," or "upon memory" and actually giving a few "sham" memory or eye-fatigue tests has been most commonly and successfully used in the last few years. Occasionally, an S will "catch on," and then the practice has been to assign him to another study. . . . (Razran, 1949, p. 643.)

In the particular experiment we are discussing, the stimuli were presented for 1 second with an interval between exposures of ½ or 1½ seconds. Fifteen 3-minute training sessions were used with intervals of ½ or 1½ minutes between them. The procedure permits 1,350 training presentations which means that each stimulus was probably presented 192 times in the seven-word experiment and 270 times in the five-word experiment. While Razran does not report which of the sham instructions he used, it seems clear that with so few stimuli (within the average immediate memory span) even the "memory test" instructions should produce little associating with such a massive number of trials. If the subjects are attending to and repeating the stimuli to themselves, the situation may even approximate a satiation situation rather than an associating situation (see Lambert and Jakobovits, 1961).

In short, in the conditioning experiment the subject is misdirected, is engaging in another activity (eating) which he has been told is an integral part of the experiment and has no task to perform which is likely to arouse associative processes with respect to the stimuli. The words themselves appear to be either incidental to his task or, if viewed differently, to be candidates for semantic (and associative) satiation.

Thus, in comparing the first stages of the two experiments, it appears that the instrumental situation is conducive to arousal of the associative or mediating processes and that the conditioning situation is less so.

The second stage of each experiment correspondingly furnishes an interesting contrast. In the instrumental situation the second stage is explicitly a test list. The subject was directed to press a lever if he saw a word that he thought he had seen on the training list. He was told not to press if he was sure that he had not seen the word before. This constituted a discrimination situation. While we know less about this situation with respect to its arousal of associative processes, it seems reasonable to believe that the discrimination task does not effect a general arousal of mediating responses. (Some evidence regarding this assertion will be presented below.) When a learning list word appears, both the instructions and the previous training combine to elicit a lever press.

When an associate appears in the test list, the response tendency which it acquired in the first stage is sufficient to precipitate the observed pressing response in about one-fifth of the presentations. No mediating activity needs to be assumed in the test list itself, and indeed, Mink's work with the other paradigm indicates that no associative arousal takes place.

(One can render a slightly different account of the test-list behavior, however, which, though gratuitous and grossly inferential, has implications regarding another form of mediation. One general response which should discriminate the group of learned words from the others presented is the learned response of lever pressing itself. The subject is so to speak reinforced for capitalizing on this response as a discriminator. If he sees a word, recognizes it, and at the same time discriminates or "becomes aware of" his own response tendency to lever press, presses, and "knows that he is correct," we can argue that he is reinforced for pressing in the presence of the response tendency to press. While this somewhat mushy and intuitive analysis is not required, it adds further suggestions for future examination.)

In Razran's second stage, training sessions are interspersed with testing sessions. (The subject receives 450 more reinforced presentations of the conditioned stimuli.) In the actual test the test words are presented to the subject for one minute while salivation is measured by the cotton-roll technique. Five such measures are made for each conditioned stimulus, each test word, and each control word. We have no data concerning associative processes in such a situation, but it seems likely that in 60 seconds of staring at the word the associative processes would be activated much as in a free association test. Presumably, if the conditioned stimulus is in the associative hierarchy of the subject, it will be elicited as a mediating response and will serve as implicit stimulus for the salivary response. We might well expect such elicitation to be strengthened by "recency" effects (see Storms, 1956).

In comparing the second stages of the two experiments, therefore, it is suggested that the instrumental situation does not arouse general associative responses while it is suggested that the conditioning situation does.

Over-all, there appears to be little reason to appeal to the difference in the nature of the response involved in the two types of experiments in explaining the different outcomes. The situations employed and the general nature of the subject's task appear sufficient to account for the difference in effectiveness of the two paradigms in the two situations. One is structured to provide maximum associative arousal in the first stage, leading to the success of the equivalence paradigm with first-stage mediation. The other minimizes associative arousal in the first stage but presumably offers an opportunity for arousal in the second stage and leads to the success of the chaining paradigm.

Further Evidence: Instrumental

Further evidence for the analysis given above may be found in other experiments. Much of the literature on semantic conditioning is useless for this purpose because the materials used are bidirectionally associated, the associative structures are unknown, the procedures used do not make a stage-by-stage analysis possible, or the data reported are insufficient for our purpose. For the instrumental case, however, a set of studies is available.

Martin (1960) in a series of 11 experiments did much to elucidate the critical variables involved in the Mink experiment. Most importantly for our purposes here he demonstrated that if the subject is forced to discriminate in the first stage of the experiment, the amount of generalization found in the second stage is dramatically reduced. He presented subjects with a "learning list" of words only half of which were to receive the lever press response. The subject had to learn which stimuli he was to respond to. He was "informed" by a buzzer when he had made a correct lever response. After the subject had learned this task, he was presented with the standard test list and instructed to press to any words which he thought he had seen before. Under this training condition, the amount of lever pressing to associates of words to which he had been trained to press declined from 21 to 7 per cent. It seems clear that the discrimination task involved in the learning stage minimized the associative arousal which was present in the uncomplicated form of the experiment.

In another experiment Martin demonstrated that the chaining paradigm could be made effective if the second stage of the Mink experiment was converted into a learning task. After the "standard" learning stage, he told subjects that they were now to learn which stimuli to press to in the second list. Subjects were informed of correctness by a buzzer following a correct response. Half of the associated words and half of the control words were made "correct," and the other half of the associates and controls were made "incorrect." The correct associates were more rapidly learned as appropriate stimuli than were the correct controls, and the incorrect associates were more frequently responded to than the incorrect controls. Here it appears that the mediating process is being reinforced in the case of the correct associates, and this not only makes them easier to learn but also makes it more difficult to suppress responding to the incorrect associates which now apparently elicit their associate words which were stimuli for responding in the learning list.

While Martin's work is too extensive to report in detail here, it can be seen that it provides support for the ideas that the discrimination situation minimizes associative arousal and that the mediating process may be reinforced under the appropriate conditions.

Recently, Carol Cohen, Virginia Blomholm, and I have found that if a short list of words is used in the learning stage of the Mink experiment, the requirement of the lever press in that stage is critical with respect to finding generalization in the test stage. Only 8 words were used instead of 12 words used by Mink and Martin. One group of subjects was directed to remember the words but did not receive the instructions to press the lever; the other group of subjects received the usual instructions. Prior to the test list presentation, the first group of subjects was given practice in lever pressing (with no words present) to equate for any motor habit difference. Significant generalization effects were obtained in the second group as usual, but no evidence for generalization was found in the first group. (The median generalization score for the first group was in fact zero.) This finding lends support to our analysis which requires the presence of the lever press at the time the associative arousal is presumed to occur.

Turning to other more or less instrumental experiments, it is tempting to apply the current analysis to the studies of learning of synonyms and antonyms (such as those of Foley and Cofer, 1943, and Cofer, Janis, and Rowell, 1943); but the associative patterns appear to be either mixed or bidirectional so a study of the locus of mediation is not possible.[3]

One example in this area which utilized list recall without respect to order is of some interest, however.

Goodwin, Long, and Welch (1945) performed an experiment involving the nonordered recall of lists of words. Subjects after practice in recall tasks were assigned to two equated groups. One group received four exposures in different random orders of a list of specific words before being presented with a list of appropriate generic terms which they were to recall after one trial. The control group received four exposures of a list of unrelated words and then was given the list of generic terms to recall. The controls performed at the same level as on the initial practice list while the experimental group was significantly superior in number of items recalled. A study of the lists suggests that the words in the experimental list were stimuli for the words in the test list as associates. We suspect that the words in the test list were already associatively aroused when that list was presented for recall. The fact that the second list consisted of generic terms (*animal, color, number, fruit,* etc.) probably aided the subjects in discriminating what otherwise might have been potentially intrusive responses from the associative hierarchies involved. A number of interesting experimental possibilities are immediately apparent.

---

[3] It should be remarked, however, that the criticism that the subjects "caught on" in these experiments is irrelevant and obscures a very important finding. If the associative tendencies of the subject are so strong that even he is aware of them and can utilize them, not only in the sense of telling the experimenter that he has "caught on," but also in the task of producing more members of the test list, then this is a very powerful form of mediation indeed.

Further Evidence: Conditioning

On the conditioning side of the analysis, it is more difficult to find data which support the argument. The experiment performed by Riess (1946) in which conditioning generalization gradients over homophones, synonyms, and antonyms were studied for four age groups would be of enormous interest if we had the relevant associative data for these groups. In the absence of such data the analysis is wholly speculative and will not be attempted here. The experiment is a model, however, which suggests work to be performed when association norms for children become available.

A study by Diven (1937) at first glance appears to confound the analysis presented for the Razran data above, but a closer study of the situation shows that it is in agreement with the general line of argument. Diven obtained more generalization of the conditioned response to associates of the original stimulus (in some cases) than to the original stimulus itself. His procedure, however, was to present the word, *instruct subjects to associate silently to it,* and then present the unconditioned stimulus. In the final analysis the experiment seems to show that associations can be activated by asking the subjects to associate (which is hardly surprising) and that the silent associates do serve as conditioned stimuli (which is of considerable importance).

A set of very careful studies by Branca (1957) on semantic generalization of shock-induced GSRs seems to be of most importance to the view expressed here. Branca's work began with a very interesting finding. He ran his early studies on a poorly motivated group of subjects (patients and aides in hospitals) and carried training trials to the point where he got GSRs of appreciable magnitude only to the conditioned stimulus; the neutral stimuli barely elicited a response. Under these circumstances when the test stimuli were presented to evaluate semantic generalization, no GSRs occurred. It was as if the subjects "had decided" that they were being shocked on only the conditioned stimulus and ceased "attending" to anything else.

In Branca's major study, college students were used as subjects, and he stopped the training trials and switched to test trials before the neutral stimuli had lost their capacity to elicit at least some GSR.

In five experiments Branca found that generalization of the conditioned response was almost completely predictable (93 per cent) on the basis of the subject's expectation of shock.

The possibility that generalization here resulted from recognition of relationships among the experimental stimuli was suggested in the verbalizations of the Ss. In every case of a significantly large GSR to a stimulus testing generalization, S later expressed awareness of the intended relationship between the experimental stimuli, and in every case this knowledge was followed by the inference that shock would follow the appearance of the test-stimulus (Branca, 1957, p. 547).

The wholesale recognition of the relationship between the stimuli and the expectation of shock implies that the test stimulus associatively elicited the conditioned stimulus and the defense reaction associated with the shock. When the subjects did not see the relation (i.e., the test stimulus did not elicit the conditioned stimulus), there was no evidence for the conditioned response. This finding furnishes support for the analysis of the Razran experiment even though the conditions of the experiment were drastically different.

The relevance of Branca's findings for our purpose may be illustrated by two of his experiments. In one a picture of a hat was the conditioned stimulus and the word *hat* was the test stimulus. Only 1 of 10 subjects showed significant generalization to the test stimulus. (Keller, 1943, similarly failed to find appreciable generalization from picture to word in this situation.) In line with our argument that the test stimulus must elicit the original stimulus if it is not already associated with the response, it seems apparent that the likelihood that the word *hat* will elicit a particular image is very small and hence little generalization is to be expected. The *one* subject who showed generalization reported:

I knew it was about conditioning . . . it was conditioning about word relationships. When I saw the word it took me by surprise and all I could think of was the picture of the hat. The shock came after the picture so naturally when I thought of the picture I thought the shock would come too (Branca, 1957, p. 547).

In Branca's second experiment the conditioned stimulus was the word *hat* and the test stimulus was the picture of a hat. In this situation 7 of 12 subjects showed significant generalization of the unconditioned response. The writer has unpublished data showing that the most common associations to simple pictures are the same as those to the name of the picture, implying that the verbal response of naming is central in the associative arousal. Thus, we would expect the common response to a picture to be the name of the picture; and in this case when the test stimulus of the picture of the hat is presented, we would expect that the conditioned stimulus *hat* would be elicited and the unconditioned response would follow. The findings support the analysis.

The question must be asked why the word *hat* did not become conditioned during the presentation of the picture as a conditioned stimulus in the first experiment. There is no shift in procedure from training to testing trials and no ready explanation of why the subject should not have been associatively occupied when the shock came on in the training series. Branca prefers the explanation that the second experiment "primed" the subjects for the test trial since the presentation suddenly went from words to pictures whereas in the first experiment words and pictures were scattered throughout the experiment.

While the over-all findings of Branca's studies are in accord with the point of view offered in this paper, it is clear that more work on the situational characteristics which are favorable to associative arousal is needed to provide a full account of the data.

DIRECTIONS FOR RESEARCH

It is no doubt apparent to the reader that support of the view espoused in this paper would be increased if it were possible at this point to return to the four-stage paradigms (or selected examples) and "make them work." If the analysis is correct, how might this be done? Unfortunately, there has been no opportunity to test the suggestions below but they are given tentatively here as possible answers to the above question.

Reinforcing Mediating Responses

It has been asserted that mediation or associative arousal is a response. Unless it is reinforced, it should be extinguished or inhibited. How can one prevent this outcome which presumably blights mediational phenomena?

Elicit and Reinforce the Mediator. For example, when the subject begins the third stage of the Shipley paradigm, he may be required to verbalize his previously learned response. By making the presumed, implicit, hypothetical response observable, explicit, and reinforceable, we should be able to "sledge-hammer" our way to a demonstration of four-stage mediation.

Repeat the Learning Stages. A more subtle means of arriving at the same end might be to repeat on several occasions the first three stages of learning. The subjects should build up higher strengths of association and maintain competing responses at equal strength. Both outcomes should favor the development of new associations involving implicit terms. In the Shipley model, for example, the subject might learn $A \to B$, $C \to B$, $A \to D$, $A \to B$, $C \to B$, $A \to D$, etc., until these are all at high strength and there have been ample opportunities for $(B) \to D$ and even $A \to (C)$ associations to form. The test-stage $C \to D$ should be facilitated.

Capitalize on Reference. We assume that names are verbal behaviors which retain high strength even though they may be emitted infrequently. Presumably, we have been aperiodically reinforced for maintaining naming terms in the face of all sorts of other potentially interfering responses made in the presence of the same stimuli. This suggests that we might do well to take Birge's device of naming as our first two stages. If the situation can be arranged so that the names are "useful" in the third stage (i.e., the stimuli to which names have been learned are physically similar so that the name plays an important role in stimulus identification), we ought to expect mediation in the fourth stage. If we wish to expand this further, we could go to motor responses in the third and fourth stages which should result in less interference than if we used new verbal responses and a greater opportunity to "use" the verbal mediator.

Prime the Mediators. We know from the work of Storms (1956) and Segal and Cofer (1960) that the strength of a particular associative pair may be increased (under certain circumstances) by the prior presentation of the response term as an item to be recalled. If we "primed" the subjects in the natural language form of the Shipley experiment given above, we should expect to activate the mediators which were so "silent" in the experiment reported. Thus, we might present a list of B terms first for recall, and then have the subjects learn the two stages required in the experiment.

Recall task	*List of B terms*
Learn	A → (B) → D
Learning test	C → (B) → D

A more direct alternative would be to have the subjects "learn" the A → B and C → B lists in immediate succession before the A → D, C → D learning. We know from other work that the subjects would "learn" the tests in one trial and the rapid sequence should alert them to the possibilities of mediation or at least "warm up the mediators."

Instruct the Subject to Use Responses as Mediators. We must not overlook the role of specific instruction in attempting to understand the mediational paradigms. If we are truly interested in what the subject *can* do, then one expedient we may follow is to tell him what to do and see if he can do it. In the Shipley paradigm, for example, we could use sets of instructions of a more and more specific nature directing the subject's attention to the possibility of using the first set of responses (B terms), which he already has available, to help transfer the second set of responses. The extreme case would be the discussion of the paradigm itself prior to the beginning of experimental work.

While the problem of what constitutes an adequate control for such techniques is a difficult problem, interparadigm comparisons could be readily made and should be very instructive.

Reinforcing Mediation Itself

An alternative to reinforcing particular responses which may serve as mediators is to reinforce the subject for engaging in mediation activity. In the past we have done virtually the opposite. In our work with the four-stage paradigms we had the strong feeling that subjects were being reinforced for keeping their learning as "rote" as possible. One wonders what would happen to the experienced subject who has learned, say, 25 lists of unrelated pairs when he is presented with the Sacks-Russell or Russell-Storms lists to learn. I would be willing to wager that little evidence for mediation could be found. On the other hand, we would expect that given the relevant experience on other lists in which mediation is helpful, the subject would show even greater mediation effects. Two techniques suggest themselves.

Laboratory Experience with Mediation. We might structure a subject's approach to a particular mediation problem or paradigm by leading him through a series of tasks in which he is reinforced for mediating. Such a series might begin with a list of pairs to be learned which are high-strength associates, next the subject might be given a low-strength associate list, then he could be presented with the Sacks-Russell lists, then with lists employing mediation on the stimulus side, then with lists as remote as the Russell-Storms lists, etc. In short he might be led up a hierarchy of more and more remote mediational activities in such a way that he was reinforced for the activity itself at each stage.

Instructions. Since the above activity is expensive and time consuming, we might here appeal to instructions as we did above. If we are interested in what the subject *can* do, then we can instruct the subject with suitable examples concerning the process we want him to engage in.

A Study of Situations and Tasks

In the course of the paper, it has been asserted over and over again that different situations and different tasks have differential effects on the activation of associative arousal or mediation processes. It is further clear that a paradigm for mediation is only completely understood in the context of the tasks and situations involved. Thus, if we study three-stage paradigms I and VII, we have three different findings depending on which situation-task complex we are talking about:

I	VII
A → B	A → B
B → C	A → C
A → C	B → C

In verbal paired-associate learning, both paradigms show facilitative effects; in instrumental generalization, VII shows generalization but not I; and in salivary conditioning, I shows generalization but not VII. Clearly, we must study paradigms in the context of situations and tasks.

A *Hierarchy of Tasks.* We may, I think, postulate a general ordering of tasks on the basis of their ordinary capacity to evoke associative arousal (realizing, of course, that in any given case this may be manipulated by instruction and reinforcement). I suspect this ordering ought to relate to the degree of incidental learning found in these situations if we accept Postman's (1955) analysis of the process. A hypothetical dimension of arousal is given in Figure 6–4. No special brief is held for any given entry being at a particular value relative to some other given entry. The intent of the diagram is to suggest that there are graded series of tasks with respect to associative arousal, most probably ranging from irrelevant discrimination tasks ("Circle the word with the most letters.") to recall tasks ("Remember these words in any fashion and any order that you can."). I believe this is a very important aspect to which we must attend in designing further studies of the mediation processes.

Cofer's remarkable success with the Maier two-string problem and his findings with an ingenious "verbal chains" experiment (Cofer, 1951) support the view that situations which require problem-solving and hypothesis formation are sensitive to associative arousal factors. In the first situation Cofer showed that learning an appropriate serial list, which was reinforced on several days before the experiment, was related to "pendulum" solutions (the "good-Gestalt solutions") of the two-string problem. In the second situation a chain of associates was imbedded in a set of irrelevant words in such a way that the first word of the chain could be repeatedly reinforced. Then the subject was presented with a new card with four words and asked to choose one. One of the words was an associate of the word on the first card. He was not informed whether his choice was correct or not but was presented with the next card to make another choice and so on. Given these circumstances, subjects overwhelmingly chose words associated with the word reinforced on the first card.

Such situations through their absence of specific instruction force the subject to structure the problem himself and the structure apparently conforms to what would be expected on the basis of normative data or learned associates.

SUMMARY

This paper attempts to illustrate the shift in emphasis of one line of investigation in the pursuit of greater understanding of mediation phenomena. It was taken for granted that mediation phenomena may be

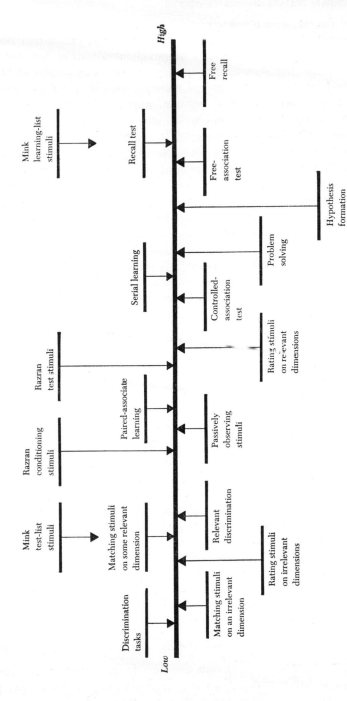

FIG. 6-4. A hypothetical dimension of associative arousal.

241

observed under at least a few prescribed conditions. It was urged that we not concentrate on the "content" of mediation but rather on the conditions governing its occurrence. A chronological record of one research project was presented showing the changing emphasis from (1) "Does mediation exist?" to (2) "What are the juxtapositions of experiences essential to produce mediation phenomena?" (paradigm studies) to (3) "What are the juxtapositions of what kinds of experiences which will produce mediation phenomena?" Attention was especially directed to situational and task variables which seem to be important in determining whether or not associative arousal will play an important role in any particular paradigm.

Three directions of future research were outlined: reinforcing particular mediational responses, reinforcing the mediating activity itself, and exploring the "natural" capacity of tasks and situations to elicit associative arousal and consequent mediational phenomena.

REFERENCES

Barnes, Jean M., & Underwood, B. J. (1959) "Fate" of first-list associations in transfer theory. *J. Exp. Psychol.*, **58**, 95–105.

Bastian, J. R. (1956) Response chaining in verbal transfer. Ph.D. thesis, University of Minnesota.

Birge, Jane S. (1941) The role of verbal responses in transfer. Ph.D. thesis, Yale University.

Bousfield, W. A. (1953) The occurrence of clustering in the recall of randomly arranged associates. *J. Gen. Psychol.*, **49**, 229–240.

Bousfield, W. A., & Cohen, B. H. (1955) General review of a program of research on associative clustering. In J. J. Jenkins (Ed.), *Associative processes in verbal behavior: A report of the Minnesota Conference.* Minneapolis: University of Minnesota, Department of Psychology. Pp. 64–83.

Bousfield, W. A., Whitmarsh, G. A., & Danick, J. J. (1958) Partial response identities in verbal generalization. *Psychol. Rep.*, **4**, 703–713.

Branca, A. A. (1957) Semantic generalization at the level of the conditioning experiment. *Amer. J. Psychol.*, **70**, 541–549.

Carlin, Jean E. (1958) Word-association strength as a variable in verbal paired-associate learning. Ph.D. thesis, University of Minnesota.

Cofer, C. N. (1951) Verbal behavior in relation to reasoning and values. In H. Guetzkow (Ed.), *Groups, leadership and men.* Pittsburgh: Carnegie Press. Pp. 206–217.

Cofer, C. N. (1957) Associative commonality and rated similarity of certain words from Haagen's list. *Psychol. Rep.*, **3**, 603–606.

Cofer, C. N., & Foley, J. P., Jr. (1942) Mediated generalization and the interpretation of verbal behavior: I. Prolegomena. *Psychol. Rev.*, **49**, 513–540.

Cofer, C. N., Janis, Marjorie G., & Rowell, Mary M. (1943) Mediated generalization and the interpretation of verbal behavior: III. Experimental study of antonym gradients. *J. Exp. Psychol.*, 32, 266–269.

Cofer, C. N., & Yarczower, M. (1957) Further study of implicit verbal chaining in paired-associate learning. *Psychol. Rep.*, 3, 453–456.

Cramer, Phebe, & Cofer, C. N. (1960) The role of forward and reverse association in transfer of training. *Amer. Psychologist*, 15, 463. (Abstract)

Deese, J. (1959a) On the prediction of occurrence of particular verbal intrusions in immediate recall. *J. Exp. Psychol.*, 58, 17–22.

Deese, J. (1959b) Influence of interitem associative strength upon immediate free recall. *Psychol. Rep.*, 5, 305–312.

Diven, K. (1937) Certain determinants in the conditioning of anxiety reactions. *J. Psychol.*, 3, 291–308.

Feldman, S. M., & Underwood, B. J. (1957) Stimulus recall following paired-associate learning. *J. Exp. Psychol.*, 53, 11–15.

Flavell, J. H. (1961a) Meaning and meaning similarity: I. A theoretical reassessment. *J. Gen. Psychol.*, 64, 307–319.

Flavell, J. H. (1961b) Meaning and meaning similarity: II. The semantic differential and co-occurrence as predictors of judged similarity in meaning. *J. Gen. Psychol.*, 64, 321–335.

Flavell, J. H., & Johnson, B. Ann. (1961) Meaning and meaning similarity: III. Latency and number of similarities as predictors of judged similarity in meaning. *J. Gen. Psychol.*, 64, 337–348.

Foley, J. P., Jr., & Cofer, C. N. (1943) Mediated generalization and the interpretation of verbal behavior: II. Experimental study of certain homophone and synonym gradients. *J. Exp. Psychol.*, 32, 168–175.

Foley, J. P., Jr., & MacMillan, Z. (1943) Mediated generalization and the interpretation of verbal behavior: V. "Free association" as related to differences in professional training. *J. Exp. Psychol.*, 33, 299–310.

Foley, J. P., Jr., & Mathews, Mary A. (1943) Mediated generalization and the interpretation of verbal behavior: IV. Experimental study of the development of inter-linguistic synonym gradients. *J. Exp. Psychol.*, 33, 188–200.

Goodwin, J., Long, L., & Welch, L. (1945) Generalization in memory. *J. Exp. Psychol.*, 35, 71–75.

Goss, A. E. (1961a) Early behaviorism and verbal mediating responses. *Amer. Psychologist*, 16, 285–298.

Goss, A. E. (1961b) Verbal mediating responses and concept formation. *Psychol. Rev.*, 68, 248–274.

Hull, C. L. (1939) The problem of stimulus equivalence in behavior theory. *Psychol. Rev.*, 46, 9–30.

Jantz, E. M., & Underwood, B. J. (1958) R-S learning as a function of meaningfulness and degree of S-R learning. *J. Exp. Psychol.*, 56, 174–179.

Jenkins, J. J. (1959) A study of mediated association. *Studies in verbal behavior*. Rep. No. 2, NSF Grant, University of Minnesota.

Jenkins, J. J., Mink, W. D., & Russell, W. A. (1958) Associative clustering as a function of verbal association strength. *Psychol. Rep.*, 4, 127–136.

Jenkins, J. J., & Russell, W. A. (1952) Associative clustering during recall. *J. Abnorm. Soc. Psychol.*, **47**, 818–821.

Jenkins, Patricia M., & Cofer, C. N. (1957) An exploratory study of discrete free association to compound verbal stimuli. *Psychol. Rep.*, **3**, 599–602.

Keller, Margaret. (1943) Mediated generalization: The generalization of a conditioned galvanic skin response established to a pictured object. *Amer. J. Psychol.*, **56**, 438–448.

Kjeldergaard, P. M., & Horton, D. L. (1960) An experimental analysis of associative factors in stimulus equivalence, response equivalence and chaining paradigms. *Studies in verbal behavior*. Rep. No. 3, NSF Grant, University of Minnesota.

Lambert, W. E., & Jakobovits, L. A. (1960) Verbal satiation and changes in the intensity of meaning. *J. Exp. Psychol.*, **60**, 376–383.

Lumsdaine, A. A. (1939) Conditioned eyelid responses as mediating generalized conditioned finger reactions. *Psychol. Bull.*, **36**, 650. (Abstract)

Martin, J. G. (1960) Mediated transfer in two verbal learning paradigms. Ph.D. thesis, University of Minnesota.

Mink, W. D. (1957) Semantic generalization as related to word association. Ph.D. thesis, University of Minnesota.

Moss, S. A. (1960) A study of the semantic generalization effect. Ph.D. thesis, University of California.

Murdock, B. B., Jr. (1956) "Backward" learning in paired associates. *J. Exp. Psychol.*, **51**, 213–215.

Murdock, B. B., Jr. (1958) "Backward" associations in transfer and learning. *J. Exp. Psychol.*, **55**, 111–114.

Osgood, C. E. (1952) The nature and measurement of meaning. *Psychol. Bull.*, **49**, 197–237.

Osgood, C. E. (1953) *Method and theory in experimental psychology.* New York: Oxford.

Postman, L. (1955) An analysis of incidental learning. In J. J. Jenkins (Ed.), *Associative processes in verbal behavior: A report of the Minnesota Conference.* Minneapolis: University of Minnesota, Department of Psychology. Pp. 102–135.

Razran, G. (1949) Semantic and phonetographic generalizations of salivary conditioning to verbal stimuli. *J. Exp. Psychol.*, **39**, 642–652.

Richardson, J. (1960) Comparison of S-R and R-S learning of paired-associates. *Psychol. Rep.*, **7**, 225–228.

Riess, B. F. (1946) Genetic changes in semantic conditioning. *J. Exp. Psychol.*, **36**, 143–152.

Russell, W. A. (1955) Bi-directional effects in word association. In J. J. Jenkins (Ed.), *Associative processes in verbal behavior: A report of the Minnesota Conference.* Minneapolis: University of Minnesota, Department of Psychology. Pp. 1–11.

Russell, W. A., & Storms, L. H. (1955) Implicit verbal chaining in paired-associate learning. *J. Exp. Psychol.*, **49**, 267–293.

Ryan, J. J., III. (1957) An experimental comparison of response transfer facilitated by meaningfully similar and associated verbal stimuli. Ph.D. thesis, University of Minnesota.

Ryan, J. J., III. (1960) Comparison of verbal response transfer mediated by meaningfully similar and associated stimuli. *J. Exp. Psychol.*, **60**, 408–415.

Schulz, R. W., & McGehee, Nan E. (1960) Mediation in verbal paired associate learning. Paper read at Midwest. Psychol. Ass., Chicago.

Segal, Sydney J., & Cofer, C. N. (1960) The effect of recency and recall on word association. *Amer. Psychologist*, **15**, 451. (Abstract)

Shipley, W. C. (1933) An apparent transfer of conditioning. *J. Gen. Psychol.*, **8**, 382–391.

Shipley, W. C. (1935) Indirect conditioning. *J. Gen. Psychol.*, **12**, 337–357.

Staats, A. W., & Staats, Carolyn K. (1959) Meaning and *m*: Separate but correlated. *Psychol. Rev.*, **66**, 136–144.

Storms, L. H. (1956) Backward association in verbally mediated learning. Ph.D. thesis, University of Minnesota.

Storms, L. H. (1958) Apparent backward association: A situational effect. *J. Exp. Psychol.*, **55**, 390–395.

Whitmarsh, G. H., & Bousfield, W. A. (1961) Use of free associational norms for the prediction of generalization of salivary conditioning to verbal stimuli. *Psychol. Rep.*, **8**, 91–95.

Wickens, D. D., & Briggs, G. E. (1951) Mediated stimulus generalization as a factor in sensory pre-conditioning. *J. Exp. Psychol.*, **42**, 197–200.

Wynne, R. D., & Cofer, C. N. (1958) On meaning, association and transfer. (Unpublished manuscript, privately circulated.)

COMMENTS ON PROFESSOR JENKINS'S PAPER

George Mandler

UNIVERSITY OF TORONTO

Over the past few years, the weight of evidence for the mediation hypothesis has made the phenomenon more than a curiosity; it approaches the status of established fact. It is this weight and persistence that makes it possible for Professor Jenkins to do something few psychologists should or would dare to offer, and even fewer would hope to have accepted. He is able to present a line of argument and theoretical discussion based to a large extent on a massive negative finding—the failure of the four-stage mediation paradigm. This can be done only when the weight of past evidence and past experience is such that we know that these negative findings must lead to a reexamination of the general hypothesis, not to any puny carping about design or procedure. Professor Jenkins knew there was something wrong because he had known how to do it right for so many years.

In the first part of my discussion I want to comment on some of the problems raised by Professor Jenkins within the framework of the mediation models—particularly one based on word-association norms. In the second part I want to depart from the mediation mold, take a second

246 VERBAL BEHAVIOR AND LEARNING

look at the model in general, and suggest some alternative ways of handling these phenomena. In general, I interpret my role as a critic and will, therefore, stress disagreements.

Let me start with a quibble that was already rife at the last ONR conference. I am still somewhat unhappy about the use of the Minnesota norms—or any population norms—to infer the operation of associative links for individual subjects. I am sure that Professor Jenkins will agree that if he knew the hierarchy of associates for any particular subject used in his experiments, he should and would be on safer grounds to infer the presence of particular associative mediating links. As it is, any subject might have as a dominant associate not the one that is supposed to be doing the linking, but some other, low probability associate. The short cut of assuming the population norms for the subject population probably decreases the power of his findings, but in the absence of specific evidence that the same results could be obtained when the idiosyncratic norms of each subject are used, I would want to hedge a little bit about the generalizability of his results. Such reservations cast a shadow over Carlin's results which showed that strength of the association has little to do with the mediation effect. It is still possible to believe that it does by arguing, first, that the Minnesota norms have not been shown equivalent to the hierarchy of association continuously elicited either by individual subjects or populations; second, that there is no evidence what the actual hierarchy of the Carlin population was; and finally, that strength of associations may not affect such gross measures as speed of learning, but may appear in more fine-grained analyses, such as reaction times.

One small aside in this connection. In a field such as verbal learning, where individual differences in past verbal experience loom large, I would prefer to see more individual data analyses. For example, it would be most interesting to know in what percentage of Professor Jenkins's subjects we do find a mediation effect, and whether these subjects can be distinguished in terms of their understanding of the instructions, their past history, and so forth. In using group data, we usually assume that the effect of the interaction between the uncontrolled variables and the dependent variables will be symmetrical around the mean or median. Basic to this assumption is the symmetry of the uncontrolled variables— usually defensible in the case of experimenter error, experimental variations, genetic factors, and others. In the case of individual differences in verbal predispositions such a symmetry about the mean is difficult to defend, and some examination of individual data might reveal interactions between individual differences and the dependent effects.

We now come to the major problem, the road from the negative results on the four-stage paradigms to their "explanation" and to the "next steps" that Professor Jenkins suggests. I was particularly excited about the suggestion that there is something in all this business about "actually responding" and "eliciting or arousing the mediation process." He has put into words and provided presumptive evidence for something that I have for some time intuitively accepted. However, I doubt that he has provided more than some equally intuitive appeal. A similar phenomenon appears in the studies on the effect of meaningfulness on paired-associate learning. We know now that meaningfulness on the response side is more powerful than it is on the stimulus side and also that "pronouncing" is more powerful than "just looking." Somehow the "actual responding" seems to have something to do with mobilizing the meaningfulness and familiarity to associates in paired-associate learning just as "responding" seems to have something to do with arousing the associates or mediates in the Jenkins experiments. I cannot find any way satisfactorily to describe what "actually responding" means. Does it have something to do with attention, with activation and effort? Or should we take our cue from Professor Underwood's paper and suggest that when the subject "makes a response" we know what the functional response is (it is likely to be pretty close to the nominal response), but that we know less about the functional stimulus. By having the subject "actually" respond (e.g., by pronouncing) we can make some attempt to assure a greater coincidence between nominal and functional stimulus.

Another problem that I encountered is that every now and then Professor Jenkins seems to slip into a homunculus-like theory of behavior. I am perturbed by the impression of some little man who sits somewhere between the experimental materials and the behavior and decides when to "just rote learn" or when to "mediate." How does the subject make decisions of this kind, e.g., what the "utility" of doing something or other is or might be. I was also puzzled by the operation of "reinforcement" in these experiments. If mediation can be reinforced and reinforcement has the usual properties, then nonreinforcement should lead to extinction of mediation, partial reinforcement (probably typical of the effect postulated by Professor Jenkins) should lead to greater resistance to extinction, and all the other consequences of a respectable reinforcement concept should be demonstrable. But when subjects switch back and forth in their use of mediation, I wonder whether we should use reinforcement classically or rather some other term in the order of "decision making"; i.e., when one particular response does not lead to a result, you use another one. Maybe we ought to restrict the term "reinforcement" to those stop rules where the term can be used in all its theoretical splendor and use some other term to indicate that the organism has switched from one response mode or strategy to another as a result of lack of success with the first one.

One final comment within the framework of Jenkins's search for the fly in the four-stage ointment. Some of his suggestions for eliciting priming or for arousing associative and mediating processes make the whole enterprise sound awfully close to a concept formation experiment. Not that this is "bad," but I have the feeling that many of his "next steps," such as reinforcing mediation, priming, instructing the subject to use responses as mediators, and prior experience with mediation—particularly when considered in conjunction—suggest that the mediation experiment becomes a situation in which the experimenter has some notions how to proceed, what the best strategy for learning the fourth stage *might* be. The experimenter then tries to find out if the subject—given minimal or maximal cues about the hypothesized process—can duplicate these notions, can find out "what the concept is." The question then becomes not whether the mediation hypothesis explains these phenomena, but rather whether the subject can guess our theory. If he can and does, then he goes through the same steps that we went through in constructing the materials, and, lo and behold, he learns. But what he has learned is our theory, or possibly one particular way of solving these problems—I wonder whether he has demonstrated the validity of the theory. If we look at a theory as a way to program the organism, a series of steps that mediate between input and output, the question in these suggestions seems to switch from trying to discover what the program is or might be to determining what kind of program we can put *into* the machine.

The mediation hypothesis also assumes a rather peculiar role in this tendency toward concept formation in relation to the norms problem. I have assumed in my earlier discussion that mediation occurs "automatically"—certain words arouse others, which in turn serve as adequate stimuli for the third link. If it turns out that the mediation hypothesis operates regardless of the associative hierarchy of the individual subject, i.e., it operates according to population norms, then the "links" used by the subject are somewhat independent of the associations built up in his past history. In that case, associative arousal and linking are not automatic but rather presuppose some directed search by the organism for the "expected" or "proper" normative associations which then provide the link.

I would like to suggest now that, rather than trying to repair the mediation model, we might reexamine the first point that Professor Jenkins dismissed at the beginning of his paper. He suggested that the various mediation models could be looked at as equivalent and that little profit would be gained from internecine warfare within the different interpretations of the mediation model. What might be the case, however, is that the very things that these various mediation models have in common is what has misled us in the interpretation of his results. What they apparently have in common is the assumption that the organism uses the associative model to process inputs; i.e., if element A is associated with element B, and element C is associated with element B, then element A will acquire some association with element C. The operative rules suggest that the organism processes input in line with two operations— *contiguity* and *order*, though the latter has some weak bidirectionality (backward association). I would like to examine the possibility that, in handling verbal material in particular, the organism operates on quite different rules, in the case of the adult subject in terms of logical or quasi-logical rules. By quasi-logical I mean rules that could be established on the basis of plausible reasoning without conforming—and sometimes even violating—the rules of symbolic logic.

Take as an example the simple chaining paradigm; this paradigm embodies the rules of transitivity if we transcribe the paired-associates in terms of the conditional. If we assume that the organism interprets the presentation of A to be always called B as "if A then B" and so forth, the paradigm reads

$$\begin{array}{ll} & \text{If A then B} \\ \text{and} & \text{if B then C} \\ \text{then} & \text{if A then C} \end{array}$$

In the diagram presented below, A, B, and C are elements, and arrows indicate the implication relationship. Thus, the chaining or transitivity paradigm looks like this:

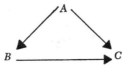

Now it is interesting to note that of the eight paradigms used in the three-stage mediation experiment, all but two (namely, III and IV) are transitivity paradigms, albeit with the order of presentation of the three units transposed. Numbers III and IV look like this:

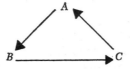

a relation which has no syllogistic status (CA does not "follow" from AB and BC) and behaviorally might best be called "ring around the rosy." Interestingly enough these two paradigms show either no or very little mediation in the Kjeldergaard and Horton experiment (1960).

If we look at the four-stage paradigm situation, the relations built into the Shipley and Russell-Storms paradigms, for example, do not offer any logical or quasi-logical rules for arriving at the test stage— not even anything as appealing as the "ring around the rosy" situation:

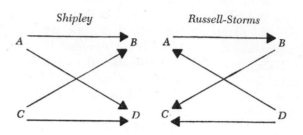

We find that to devise any rules for arriving at the C-D relation becomes rather complicated. I am not surprised that Professor Jenkins suggests that a concept formation set might be most useful.

Recently we completed a study (Mandler and Cowan, 1962) in which we examined learning effects associated with all 16 paradigms composed of three elements. In the two structures relevant to the Kjeldergaard and Horton results, we found comparable results. In our study we used three low-association-value CVCs as elements. A trial consisted of the presentation to the subject of the six possible combinations of the three elements each on the face of one of six cards. On the reverse side of the cards we placed a checkmark for some of the pairs and not for others. The subject's task was to predict whether a particular card had a checkmark on the back or not. Subjects were given 15 trials with the order of pairs within trials randomized. The assignment of checkmarks to particular pairs followed the paradigmatic model, such that in the case of the transitivity paradigm the cards with elements AB, BC, and AC would have checkmarks and the remaining cards would not; in the case of the other paradigm the cards with AB, BC, and CA would have checkmarks and the remaining ones not. Our subjects learned the transitivity paradigm significantly faster.

These analyses suggest that, instead of contiguity, we might look to rules and logical and quasi-logical relations for the exploration of these paradigms. Before I am misunderstood, however, let me emphasize that this substitution for contiguity is not a plea to throw contiguity out the window. Rather, it is possible that verbal behavior in adult subjects, having been subjected for many years to the rules and regulations of ordinary language, might be better analyzed in other terms. For this reason I find Jenkins's analogy with the Shipley experiment somewhat strained. It also leaves us the task to discover how these rules are established, and I believe that here contiguity will reclaim its honored place.

Now as far as the problem of directionality is concerned—a problem which is also implicit in the conditioning model for verbal learning—I have a tentative suggestion for an alternative way of looking at the phenomenon of forward and backward associations. Endel Tulving and I have recently explored the following notions for interpreting directionality in the word-association experiment. We find it useful to consider words, concepts, or other verbal response units as n-dimensional spaces, and to view associative linking between two units as the overlap between their corresponding spaces. The size of a space might be conceptualized as representing the number of associations a unit evokes, or frequency of usage or acquaintance, or some other—as yet unknown—variable, or it may be a function of some combination of such variables.

We assume that the probability that a particular unit, word A for example, will elicit another unit, word B, as an associate, is a function of the overlap between A and B relative to the total size of A. Given this assumption, certain conclusions follow: (1) When the sizes of A and B are fixed, the probability of one of these units occurring as an associate to the other is a direct function of the amount of overlap. (2) When the size of overlap between A and B is given, the probability of B as an associate to A is an inverse function of the size of A (and independent of the size of B!). (3) Whenever the probability of A occurring as an associate to B is larger than the probability of B occurring as an associate to A, then the space of A must be larger than B. Perfect bidirectionality can occur only in the case of words of equal space.

In the concrete example from Professor Jenkins's paper, we can apply these notions to two words: "Bird" and "Eagle." We make the reasonable assumption that "Bird" has a larger space than "Eagle." Given any overlap between the two, the amount of "Bird" space contained in "Eagle" relative to the total "Eagle" space is larger than the relative amount of "Eagle" space in "Bird." Diagrammatically, this situation is presented in the following figure:

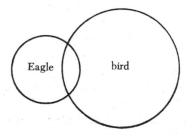

The diagram shows that "Bird" should be a more probable associate to "Eagle" than "Eagle" is to "Bird."

In the case of paired-associate learning of elements that start with spaces of equal size, have no overlap and, therefore, no associative probability on each other, we assume that contiguity leads to overlap and that overt responding of the "response" item B establishes a larger space for it than for the "stimulus" item A. This would account for the relatively weaker B-A association. Another possibility is that the functional A may be different from the nominal A (in Underwood's terminology). In particular, this may be the case when A is not pronounced, and it would lead to the same prediction since the overlap produced by contiguity is not between A and B but between some A' and B, and the probability of A (given B) would necessarily be reduced. Finally, it is of interest to note that, if we assume that paired-associate learning of "nonsense" CVCs produces a spatial arrangement such that B is not only larger but also that all of A is contained in B, we have established a point of contact with the logical model described earlier. In this case (A contained in B) the probability model is isomorphic with the logical concept "If A then B" or "All A are B" which was one of the input transformations suggested for the paired-associate situation.

Returning to the mediation studies and the trend to make them into concept formation experiments, it is obvious that the logical and quasi-logical transformations go even further in that direction. I am suggesting certain habitual conceptual transformations of input in the case of adult subjects. If the mediation phenomena are "conceptual" (either in associative or logical terms) one of the problems with the four-stage paradigm might be that it overtaxes the informational capacity of the organism. The amount of information to be used by the time the last stage is reached might be more than the organism can "hold." The success of the Russell and Storms experiment (1955) with preestablished normative associations may be a function of the easier availability of the first stages which have been overlearned and well established prior to the experimental procedure. In any case, Professor Jenkins's suggested further research should shed some light on this problem regardless of whether subjects are "associating" or "concept forming."

REFERENCES

Kjeldergaard, P. M., & Horton, D. L. (1960) An experimental analysis of associative factors in stimulus equivalence, response equivalence and chaining paradigms. *Studies in verbal behavior.* Rep. No. 3, NSF Grant, University of Minnesota.

Mandler, G., & Cowan, P. A. (1962) Learning of simple structures. *J. Exp. Psychol.,* **64,** 177–183.

Russell, W. A., & Storms, L. H. (1955) Implicit verbal chaining in paired-associate learning. *J. Exp. Psychol.,* **49,** 287–293.

SUMMARY OF CONFERENCE DISCUSSION

Mandler's emphasis on the hierarchy of associative responses as it may exist in the individual (as opposed to group norms) occasioned some protest. Deese asked how such an individual hierarchy could be obtained, and Mandler suggested using the m method. Jenkins pointed out that in his case studies (Peterson and Jenkins, 1957) the responses of the low-commonality subject could best be predicted by the group norms because his individual protocols varied too much from day to day. Also, associative relations can be built in, if necessary, as Horton and Kjeldergaard did.

Melton thought perhaps the common associations could be primed, so that they would be available in all subjects. By priming here he means having the subject learn a list of paired-associates composed of word-association stimuli and their most popular responses. Cofer warned that any priming procedure less explicit than this might well not work. He mentioned that Storms (1958) achieved only a relatively small change with his priming operation.

Postman was concerned that work with the individual subject would deprive us of control base lines; Mandler thought the control groups could be based on group norms with the experimental ones based on individual hierarchies. Or the control and experimental conditions could be run at widely separated intervals, despite all the problems such a procedure entails.

Mandler thought it important to look especially at the individual cases in which the paradigms (mediation) do not work. Russell wondered if he was saying that the group data lack power or that different conclusions would come from observing the individual rather than the group. Mandler went on to ask what it means to say that there is a potential response (with a specific, norm-based probability) in the subject's hierarchy? Is he making it implicitly, overtly?

Goss said there is some evidence in Norcross's thesis (1957) for acquired distinctiveness or a mediation effect when the subject made the response but not when he did not make the response. Mandler wanted to know what this effort variable is, if that is what it is; implicit responding seems to be important in Jenkins's studies.

There was discussion of the possibility of extinguishing a mediating response, or of a *class* of mediating responses which might extinguish if it is not reinforced. Mandler said, as in his paper, that a partial reinforcement schedule may be in operation, but Jenkins said this could hardly be the case with new responses. Postman wondered how a *class* of responses could be extinguished; what is meant by a class? How could the organism make this kind of discrimination? Jenkins pointed out that a subject given list after list shows little interaction in the responses between lists. Concerning extinction, Staats mentioned Wertheimer's (Wertheimer and Gillis, 1958) experiments on satiation of verbal meaning as perhaps relevant to the question of whether mediating responses might extinguish; there could be extinction in the one situation but not in others. Deese wondered whether subsequent learning is affected by prior satiation of meaning, and Jenkins said that Wallace Lambert has such information.

Deese thought we might avoid the use of terms like discrimination, extinction, and inhibition which we import from other areas; but this suggestion met objections (Underwood, Wickens), including the idea that such concepts should cut across fields. Mandler felt the term reinforcement makes trouble here. Postman pointed out that, if the mediator extinguishes, tests can be made to show that this is the case; the response should not be available at all, as it would be if voluntary inhibition is what is involved. Melton said we have data only on the repeated extinction of a single response, not on classes or modes of responses. Staats argued that if mediators can be strengthened through reinforcement, they should be capable of extinction; but Deese pointed out that people have extensive histories, in the natural language, of reinforcement and extinction of classes of response and should be at a stage of almost instantaneous changeover (cf. Verplanck, 1942). Murdock said that in his own thesis (Murdock, 1952) he still obtained significant mediation effects in a three-stage paradigm despite extinction or inhibition of mediating responses. Musgrave reported her own experiences as a subject required to repeat an association test many times. She soon learned to forego her initial, rather long, response words and to use short ones, easy to write.

There was criticism of Mandler's paradigms because they do not account for order (Murdock). Goss indicated that Mandler's paradigms do not adequately describe the lists used by Jenkins, because in such lists there are several units, not just one. But Mandler said he was talking about a structure which takes input and transforms it; Goss objected to this statement, saying that not structure but the links within the structure accomplish the transformations. We need the associations. Deese agreed with Goss. But Mandler argued that if the subject has two of the links or terms in the transitivity case, he can fill in the third, syllogistically.

There were various criticisms directed to the experiment by Mandler and Cowan which explored the point, what is the stimulus the subject uses? Mandler said the task was like a concept formation problem, or at least some subjects could attack the task that way. Shepard pointed out that other subjects might approach it differently. Jenkins thought that in the situation described for the Mandler-Cowan experiment the Shipley-Lumsdaine paradigm should work. Others (e.g., Miller) were not convinced of this.

Mandler stated a formulation which he believed was involved in some of Postman's earlier comments concerning the paradigms displayed in Jenkins's Table 6–1. In paradigms I and VII, we have the following:

I	VII
A → B	B → A
B → C	B → C
A → C	A → C

Paradigm I, so far as the stimulus (A) is concerned, is an interference paradigm; in the last two stages of paradigms I and VII, B-C, A-C, we have a facilitation condition, while the first two stages of paradigm VII involve interference (B-A, B-C). The question is: How can one evaluate mediation effects when both interference and facilitation are involved? Jenkins answered by saying that there are always controls. In paradigm I the last stage for the experimental condition looks like

this: $A \xrightarrow{B} C$ whereas the controls, following the first two stages, have an irrelevant B interfering. The facilitation effects are due to the bridge between A and C (in paradigm I), overcoming the interference effects. It was pointed out, however, that this is no guarantee that the "facilitation effect" is actually positive; it may simply be less negative than the control cases, as there is no comparison with some absolute level.

Wickens observed that these kinds of experimental designs which used mixed lists (consisting of both mediated or experimental and control pairs) argue against the possibility that the subject discovers a rule; Jenkins confirmed this comment by saying that no subject in any of the eight paradigms could tell the experimenter what was going on in the experiment. The mediation effects obtained are minimal, because they are not given much of a chance to operate. Deese felt, however, that interference effects could be maximizing the differences, particularly if the subject is using a rule.

To Postman's further expressions of concern about the evaluation of transfer in these various paradigms, Jenkins answered that all of them have both positive and negative transfer aspects to them.

Postman expressed concern, also, about response familiarization and stimulus familiarization across paradigms; Jenkins said that inter-paradigm comparison is complicated. The paradigm that works best, A-B, C-B, A-C, raises the problem of the availability of C. In all paradigms there is familiarization, however.

Musgrave asked if in any experiments the mediate links had been presented overtly, referring to Pan's study (1926) in which contextual factors led to interference. Postman thought that the use of highly practiced subjects might be preferable to the use of unpracticed ones. Jenkins said practiced subjects could probably separate the lists, "unregistering" the last one before undertaking the next one.

Miller was concerned as to the role of the content in mediational effects and thought the content of what goes on might represent an important condition. Jenkins thought not. The time required for mediation processes was a point raised by Staats; Underwood was persuaded as to the importance of time and hypothesized that with unlimited time the four-stage paradigms might work. Of course, he added, mediators could produce interference.

Jenkins went back to discuss the problem of the norms, observing that they do work and that the variability in free association responses from low-commonality subjects is very great. There was further discussion of the point that K-R stimulus-response frequency does not have much influence on the learning of such pairs, above very low frequencies. Postman said this was found not to be true if the stimuli were low-frequency words (Postman, 1962).

There was comment concerning the issue raised by Mandler as to what is meant by the phrase in relation to mediation, "actually implicitly occurring." We mean, evidently, that something is going on, but we must devise ways to discover if it actually is. Shepard asked if anyone had attempted to condition the GSR to a word supposed to be a mediator. Jenkins said that it had been done, but not "cleanly" enough; Branca's data are not clear as to interpretation. Besides he rejected his data because of the subject's awareness of what went on in the experiment.

Mandler thought a response other than GSR would be preferable, and he suggested some small muscle responses.

Jenkins, referring to mediation theory, said we have moved from a wholly automatic conception of it to a more complex one; it is and it is not there under various conditions. He felt that the Mandler and Cowan experiment would more readily yield to an analysis in terms of functional stimuli than to a mediation interpretation.

REFERENCES

Murdock, B. B., Jr. (1952) The effects of failure and retroactive inhibition on mediated generalization. *J. Exp. Psychol.*, **44**, 156–164.

Norcross, K. J. (1957) The effects on discrimination performance of the similarity of previously acquired stimulus names. Ph.D. dissertation, University of Iowa.

Pan, S. (1926) The influence of context upon learning and recall. *J. Exp. Psychol.*, **9**, 468–491.

Peterson, M. J., & Jenkins, J. J. (1957) Word association phenomena at the individual level: A pair of case studies. *Tech. Rep. No. 16*, Contract No. N8onr-66216, Office of Naval Research and University of Minnesota.

Postman, L. (1962) The effects of language habits on the acquisition and retention of verbal associations. *J. Exp. Psychol.*, **64**, 7–19.

Storms, L. H. (1958) Apparent backward association: A situational effect. *J. Exp. Psychol.*, **55**, 390–395.

Verplanck, W. S. (1942) The development of discrimination in a simple locomotor habit. *J. Exp. Psychol.*, **31**, 441–464.

Wertheimer, M., & Gillis, W. M. (1958) Satiation and the rate of lapse of verbal meaning. *J. Gen. Psychol.*, **58**, 79–85.

Chapter 7

PURPOSE AND THE PROBLEM
OF ASSOCIATIVE SELECTIVITY

Wallace A. Russell

UNIVERSITY OF MINNESOTA

Since Gibson's (1941) critical review of the concept of set, it has been apparent that the term has meant many things to many people. Confusion over the usage of the word has been so deep that in some circles it has become equivalent to an admission of ignorance to suggest that an observed bit of behavior was due to the subject's set. Nevertheless, the inevitability with which the term, or one of its many variants, intrudes itself into otherwise meaningful discussions attests to the reality of at least some of the effects which it has been called in to explain. In the area of verbal learning and verbal behavior, scarcely an investigator has failed to mention the possibility that sets, intentions, selector mechanisms, response biases, *Aufgaben*, motives, purposes, or what have you, might drastically affect performance in his experimental task. In symposia such as this one, it seems that one current of discussion inevitably eddies about the manner in which the use of language is selectively directed, how certain verbal structures are "tuned," or "primed," how certain "schemata" are adopted, or how particular "supraordinate categories" are activated.

There are wide individual differences among investigators with respect to their willingness to introduce special constructs to account for the behavioral selectivity which is usually attributed to set. Most often, however, the attempt is made when the usual operation of recognized associative principles fails to occur. It may be a matter of stimulus selectivity, in which a subject responds to one aspect of a situation and not to another even though it is known that the ignored stimulus elements have in the past been capable of eliciting some response. There may be response selectivity, that is, an instance in which a particular stimulus evokes one response rather than another with which it has been strongly associated. More recently, studies at the University of Minnesota (Martin, 1960) have suggested a phenomenon which might be called mediational selectivity. Previous work had shown that implicit word associations could operate as mediators to influence behavior in a wide variety of situations involving recall, learning, perception, and generalization. The findings of Martin and others emphasize that these mediational processes are by no means automatic and inevitable. Rather they are characterized by a high degree of selective use. It is tempting to say that under appropriate "sets" mediational paths based on word associations are effective behavior determinants but that under others they may not be utilized at all.

To hold that sets are operating to produce associative selectivity in these recent studies is, of course, an example of using the term in its usual ambiguous sense, and it may be quite accurately interpreted as a confession of ignorance. Obviously, one thing that must be done is to explore the conditions which give rise to the selective utilization of word associations in these situations. At the same time, it might prove profitable to recognize that these findings are but another occurrence of a long line of such occurrences in verbal behavior research. Seldom do associative processes seem to operate unselectively, that is, without reference to conditions other than the associative strengths existing among the observable stimulus and response elements of the situation. Rather, selector mechanisms of one sort or another seem to influence behavior generally, and to be worthy objects of study in their own right. Most usually, associatively oriented investigators have looked upon such variables as nuisance factors, to be controlled as rigorously as possible while the more traditional determinants of behavior were fully explored. It may be that the variables neglected in this way are more central to verbal behavior theory than some of those attended to. At least it can do no harm to look again at the foggy terrain of set and related constructs, to see if a direct examination can now dispel some of the mist and offer constructive suggestions for exploring the role of variables governing the selective use of the verbal repertoire.

If anything is to be learned from experience, however, it is apparent that one should not approach the problem of associative selectivity with the presumption that there is anything unitary about set. The problem is multiple. In some cases it involves effects that only very minutely restrict the perceptual or response range of the subject. In other cases, the restriction may be very marked, as in the case of "intentional" versus "incidental" learning. Similarly, some considerations of set involve very short intervals of time. Others involve quite long periods. It is unlikely that such a multifaceted problem would have a single solution. As a beginning, it should be quite enough to examine some limited aspect of the total problem. In line with this reasoning, the present paper will consider some of the possible selector mechanisms which have specific relevance for goal-seeking, or purposeful, behavior.

Even when restricted to purposeful behavior, a consideration of selector mechanisms presents a task of classic proportions. Perhaps no fact has provided more difficulty for systematic psychology than has the obvious one that behavior can frequently be described in terms of some conceived end toward which it is directed. It has led some theorists to assume that purposefulness is an irreducible characteristic of all behavior, a characteristic not to be explained, but to be introduced as a basic postulate from which other consequences are to be derived. Other, more teleophobic systematists have felt impelled to ignore the fact, and to proceed with the investigation of variables untainted by purposive connotations in the apparent hope that, if no one talked about purpose, it would aimlessly drift away. Obviously, one cannot undertake a discussion of purposeful behavior without recognizing this prickly situation and providing the reader with some general guides for its use in each particular context.

First of all it should be made clear that, as it is used here, purpose has nothing necessarily to do with drive. Traditionally, of course, the topic of motivation has dealt with both the activation and direction of behavior, and it has been customary to link the first characteristic with the second when dealing with motives. That is, an organism is assumed to become "*activated*," or aroused, by a drive and to be *directed* in some way toward a situation which will satisfy or reduce the drive. Judson Brown (1961) has advocated a clear distinction between these activational and directional functions, with the term drive to be reserved for the activational function only. The directional character of behavior he attributed to the associative predispositions of an organism. The interest of this discussion of purpose clearly falls on the directional side of this dichotomy, and, having recognized the dichotomy, there is no logical basis for insisting that goal-seeking, or purposeful, behavior also implies a drive of some sort. If we are concerned with the directional character of behavior for itself, there is no a priori demand that it be linked in any way to the arousal or reduction of drive.

Having conceptually separated purpose from drive because of the clearly directional function of the former, however, by no means completes the picture. The term purpose would still be entirely uninteresting if it referred to all associatively directed behavior. In that case it would merely be a synonym for the ability of stimuli to elicit particular responses. The fact that behavior descriptively has direction can be accounted for at several levels, with only the most complex cases having characteristics that seem to warrant the use of the term purpose. As a rough approximation these levels, from simple to complex, might order themselves as follows:

1. *Reflex level*. Specific stimuli may regularly elicit particular responses. This simple fact may give apparent direction to behavior, or at least demonstrate a kind of adaptivity that tempts description in directive terms. Appropriate facial stimulation of an infant, for instance, produces sucking responses which have adaptive value. The directionality which may be attributed to such behavior would seem to be only a product of its nonrandomness. The mere occurrence of the response makes some consequences more likely than others. At this level there is little profit in speaking of direction in behavior, and no reason to regard it as purposeful.

2. *Orientation (tropism)*. Although it occurs in the presence of more or less specific stimuli, the form of a reflex response as considered above is relatively unrelated to the external environment. The patellar reflex occurs, but the leg motion involved does not bear a constant relation to or is not significantly "aimed at" any surrounding object. Oriented responses do occur, however, and represent a somewhat more significant case of directed behavior. Tropistic reactions illustrate this case well. Blowfly larvae creep away from a light source. Sunflowers orientate toward the sun. In such cases the reaction is describable with reference to the location of a source of stimulation, and where there is locomotion it is genuinely directed toward or away from some stimulus source. In spite of its highly directed character, such behavior is not here held to be purposeful, however, since it can be entirely accounted for in terms of the nature of the stimulus source and the necessary reactions of the organism in its presence.

3. *Approach and withdrawal (goal directedness)*. Schneirla (1959) has proposed that "*approach* and *withdrawal* are the *only* empirical, objective terms applicable to *all* motivated behavior in *all* animals." He then proceeds to elaborate a theory to account for the *towardness* or *awayness* of behavior in organisms from amoeba to man. As a theory of *motivated* behavior it is interesting in that the focal point is an account of directionality, the traditional aspect of motivation which Brown (1961), by contrast, has relegated to the nonmotivational associative predispositions of the organism. Schneirla's formulation is most relevant to this discussion because of the essentially directional characteristics of purpose. He assumes basically that "low intensities of stimulation tend to evoke approach reactions, high intensities withdrawal reactions with reference to the source." Out of this underlying generalization, he proposes to derive the most superior types of adjustment which are to be found. Most pertinent here is his recognition of different levels or orders

of directedness. The amoeba moving toward the source of a directed weak light, seen here as a tropism, is judged to demonstrate lower level, less specialized processes than the rat which comes into the open only when food is placed before it. The rat's approach to food is a goal-directed response to an incentive and not, as was the amoeba's, a "forced protoplasmic reaction." Such incentive-oriented responses, presumably whether learned or not, take the problem of directionality beyond the tropistic level. Schneirla suggests that his rat was behaving purposively. In the discussion below, however, it will be seen that there are reasons to refer to approach or withdrawal behavior occurring in the presence of an observable, external-eliciting stimulus as goal-directed rather than as definitionally purposeful. To be sure, approach and withdrawal, particularly when the result of learning experience, involve processes far different from those operating in tropistic behavior. Nevertheless, as long as there is a plausible explanation for the occurrence of such behavior in terms of differential overt associative responses to objectively present, external stimuli, it would seem to add only an adjective to say that it was purposeful.

4. *Seeking and avoiding.* Schneirla (1959) does recognize processes which are of a "higher evolutionary and developmental order" than approach and withdrawal. These occur when an organism may descriptively be said to be looking or searching for something which is not physically present, or equally when it is seen to be avoiding something which is not present. It is in connection with such situations that the term purpose may be most meaningfully introduced in this discussion, for in them the selective character of the behavior shown is more likely to be attributed to the operation of some state or mechanism within the organism, rather than to be interpreted as a simple case of differential responding to external stimuli. When such hypothesized states or mechanisms are attributed characteristics which force the organism to behave in such a way that the behavior is describable with reference to some anticipated end, then it would seem that the term purposeful could be significantly applied to the behavior so mediated. And it is to such behavior and the possible selector mechanisms which may be operating in them that this paper is directed.

By way of further clarification, consider the following illustration: Professor Olson leaves home at the usual hour on a weekday morning. He drives along the usual route toward his office at the university until he reaches an intersection, where instead of going straight through to his office as is his custom, he turns right and drives along a relatively strange route in a southerly direction. Some distance along, the road is blocked by construction, and Professor Olson veers onto a street he has never traveled before, but continues his general southerly course until he eventually turns back onto the previous route and shortly arrives at a hospital where, promptly at nine o'clock, he holds a prearranged consultation with a group of hospital staff members.

At a descriptive level, few would argue against the statement that Professor Olson's behavior was purposeful. He was traveling this strange route in order to get to the site of his consultation appointment. This anticipated end in some way conditioned his behavior, making him abandon the well-learned path to his regular office and allowing him to make certain responses in a new situation and to stop his travel at a particular place and time. He was obviously seeking the hospital, and while his behavior was by no means independent of his external environment, his personal conception of his objective was undoubtedly the critical factor selecting out the responses which occurred.

To recognize that Olson's behavior may be efficiently described in terms of the anticipated end toward which it was directed, or even to admit that behavior describable in this way may meaningfully be called purposeful, has, of course, done nothing to advance an explanation of his actions. It has merely, and hopefully, clarified the kind of behavior to be examined here with reference to the operation of sets or selector mechanisms.

The formulation of purpose as occurring when behavior is selectively influenced by some internal condition so that the behavior may be described in terms of an anticipated end has, however, a number of implications. As already mentioned, it does not demand that such a "purpose" mechanism be accompanied by an increase in drive or arousal level, nor does it demand that the realization of the anticipated goal be reinforcing or drive-reducing. If the direction given to behavior by such mechanisms is to be considered motivational in nature, as it has been by Schneirla, then it is of a nondynamic sort that might better be designated as symbolic or cognitive motivation. One could imagine instances, of course, where drive changes might accompany purpose conceived in this way, but the notion does not demand this.

This view of purpose is more restrictive than many which have been proposed. Schneirla, as noted, would call all goal-directed behavior purposeful, while this proposed usage would not automatically apply to goal-directed behavior which occurs in the presence of the goal. It would be applicable to goal-directed behavior occurring in the absence of the goal, and, of course, might apply to behavior occurring in the presence of the goal if the latter could be shown to be influenced by an anticipation or a conceptualization of the goal. Furthermore, the criterion of docility, first suggested by Tolman, and still frequently cited, would not be adequate to infer purpose under this suggestion. That responses are learned when followed by certain events, and that this consequence may then lead to a certain "docility" of the organism with respect to such reinforcing events, is a matter of more relevance for the learning of associations than for the problem of their selective use.

It must be confessed that the present proposed usage places purpose quite clearly into Koch's (1956) little-esteemed "extrinsic mold." Purposeful behavior is that which is directed toward some end. It is quite meaningful to say that, descriptively, the behavior occurs "in order to" achieve something. Koch's "intrinsically" regulated behavior would by this view be quite purposeless. In fact, if the topic of motivation is concerned with the activation and direction of behavior, it is difficult to see how intrinsic behavior, as described by Koch, could be seen as posing any problem within the scope of motivational psychology.

There is a final implication which should be mentioned. It is that the present view of purpose would fall midway between those extreme positions which hold either that all behavior is purposeful or that no behavior is purposeful. The regulating mechanisms which are suggested obviously are not of the sort which would universally be crucial determinants of behavior. It is even questionable if genuine seeking behavior is to be found very far down the mammalian scale. This view, then, would reserve the use of the term purpose for only those situations where the operation of (Schneirla's) processes of a "high evolutionary and developmental order" lead to the seeking or the avoiding of some anticipated situation.

The characteristics of purpose which have been implied thus far, however, do not deal with its positive properties as a behavior determinant. If the formulation is to have substance, a direct attack on this issue must be made. It cannot be accomplished on the basis of incidental evidence. It is the theme of this paper that purposive processes warrant experimental analysis in their own right, and not only as their operation forces consideration through their appearance in investigations designed primarily to investigate other variables. Homely illustrations about the daily life of Mr. Jones (Peters, 1958) or Professor Olson, even when coupled with scattered hints from experimental sources, do not establish the hypothesis of purpose mechanisms in any systematic way. Even the rough guides for the use of the term which have just been reviewed are essentially empty from a functional point of view. But perhaps such material can serve as the starting point for empirically meaningful questions.

Certainly, there is the necessity for determining the origin and quality of the "conceived or anticipated end" with respect to which behavior is said to be directed. What occurs psychologically when a purpose or intention becomes operative? A goal is set, but this goal must be distinguished from any actual object or event which it may in some way symbolize. It is a cognition of the organism, but to the psychologist the character of this cognition is anything but obvious. It may, among other possibilities, be viewed as an unanalyzable S-S expectancy, or as having a counterpart in an anticipatory response-stimulus mechanism (r_g-s_g). Very likely, however, it involves much more elaborated processes than either of these, processes which may or may not be reportable by the subject, and which are probably reliant upon general mediational or "meaning" functions which are the frequent subject of investigations by many investigators in the area of verbal behavior. At any rate, a satisfactory account of the character of purpose as a psychological concept is a major theoretical challenge.

More central to the present problem is the question of how the purpose mechanism, whatever its source and character, exercises its regulatory influence upon behavior. Here lies the relation of purpose to the larger problem of set. When one is acting purposefully there is a selectivity in the use of the behavioral repertoire which is analogous to the general biasing of responses which is a common feature of the situations in which the vague concept of set is likely to be involved. A consideration of what selective mechanisms may be aroused by purpose does not require the construct of purpose itself to be highly specified in other respects. It can be postulated as a governing device operating upon the associative repertoire of the organism, and questions concerning this governing function may be raised in the absence of information concerning the more qualitative characteristics of purpose.

This line of consideration is highly reminiscent of the position of the researchers of the Würzburg School, who held that behavior was affected by the joint operation of association and a less highly specified "determining tendency." It has sometimes been held that their view anticipated Hull's basic formula for the determination of behavior by the combination of habit factors (H) and a general drive factor (D). However, the essential characteristic of the determining tendency was a selective-directive function rather than an arousal or D function. Determining tendencies were invoked to account for such findings as the modification of word associations following the instruction to respond with opposites or the fact that the stimuli 2 and 5 might elicit as responses the numbers 3, 7, or 10, depending upon a set of the subject to subtract, add, or multiply. It was much more closely related to the present proposal of a purpose mechanism than to Hull's concept of drive. Should the selective functions of purpose, contrary to the position of Brown on directionality but consistent with the Würzburg hypothesis, prove to involve processes unlike those of habit functions, then the possibility emerges for behavior to be viewed as a function of all three constructs—habit, purpose (or set), and drive.

An obvious line of inquiry lies in the possibility of tests to determine empirically whether the selective consequences of purpose can be reduced to the operation of habit functions operating implicitly. Such an approach would involve an application of the currently popular mediation hypothesis. This is the hypothesis that implicit responses and stimuli, functioning in conformity to the principles known to apply to their overt counterparts, serve as mediators of effects not explicable in terms of the relationships existing between the observable stimuli and responses in a situation. This hypothesis has been immensely fruitful in the recent experimental study of the so-called higher mental processes and has clear relevance to the present problem. May set be conceived as a complex of implicit stimuli, produced by covert responses, which evoke other responses and thus selectively determine what behavior will occur? Is purpose a special case of this phenomenon?

Osgood (1957) has been a foremost proponent of the mediation hypothesis. In his treatment of the motivational dynamics of language behavior he has applied himself to the problem of set and has suggested how implicit stimuli from a variety of sources might "tune up" a class of meanings or participate in the selection of overt responses. The list is an impressive one. The arousal of a drive state brings with it implicit cues or drive stimuli. If the drive has been active at the time of occurrence of particular meanings and overt responses, these *drive-related* cues might be expected to increase selectively the probability of occurrence of such responses when the drive state was high. Thus thoughts or activity associated with hunger should be more likely when the individual has been deprived of food. Additionally, "Contextual cues, such as the instructions given by an experimenter, the presence of a member of the opposite sex, or even private association sequences, may also be associated with the same meanings and serve to make others more probable. This is what I believe most people call *set.* . . . " Also, " . . . incomplete information in the stimulus display itself may have a selective effect upon alternative meanings—I use the term *hint* for this sort of control."

For Osgood, then, stimuli from drive states, instructions, context, and the stimulus display may selectively affect the response hierarchy at any moment. But the effects are all presumed to be due strictly to the combined associative characteristics of all these stimuli.

As plausible as Osgood's treatment may be, it has a technical difficulty that results from the very number of hypothesized stimulus sources which are considered. It is that even if the associative hierarchies of each stimulus source operating alone were known, there is still the problem of predicting the resultant when they are all simultaneously operating. Until this can be done with some accuracy, it will be difficult to test his predictions in complex cases.

The mediational account of set in Osgood (1957) is also limited by the fact that it gives almost no reference to the selectivity that occurs specifically in goal-seeking behavior. The cue sources which he does mention would seem to be very crude tools to account for goal striving, although they could, of course, be among the factors involved. It is interesting that Osgood did not mention the cue effects of stimuli that occur as the result of anticipatory goal responses. To be sure, such responses have usually been considered in terms of their possible arousal or reinforcing properties in studies of incentive effects. But Hull (1930) has recognized their cue properties as well, and when represented in their usual symbols (r_g-s_g) the relevance to the mediation hypothesis is obvious. The r_g-s_g mechanism provides a promising basis for inferring a stimulus source that has unique reference to the goal and hence might serve as a mediator of responses relevant to it. The major problems in connection with its use are the basic ones of determining if r_g-s_g has the formal properties of a response and a stimulus and of ascertaining that s_g has an associative hierarchy capable of adding to the total habit strength of the responses which it must selectively regulate.

The r_g-s_g mechanism, dealing primarily with capacity of s_g to elicit a restricted range of responses, seems to be primarily a vehicle of response selection. It has the capability, nonetheless, to act as an indirect stimulus selector. It might be hypothesized, for example, that a given r_g-s_g could be conditioned to elicit an *orienting* response which in turn would greatly restrict the range of cues with which the organism would come in contact. Such a response could very well mediate behavior which would be described as "paying attention" to particular stimuli.

A serious application of the mediation hypothesis would surely suggest experiments which could confirm or disconfirm its applicability to purpose. There are, in addition, other less rigorously formalized positions which might guide research in this area, and which would start from the position of establishing unique nonhabit functions for purpose rather than with the assumption that an extension of association theory would account for the phenomena involved.

A simple illustration of a position attributing a unique function to a selection process is that of Bruner, Matter, and Papanek (1955) and Easterbrook (1959). Their interpretations of motivation and emotion, respectively, hold that the effect of an increase in the state involved is to narrow the range of stimuli to which the subject will respond. Normally they would expect the most efficient behavior to occur at intermediate levels of motivation or emotion. At these levels subjects would not be responding to extraneous stimuli but would be utilizing enough environmental stimuli to perform at a high level. Too many stimuli responded to at low levels of excitation and too few at high levels would both result in less efficient behavior. These formulations are simple in that they involve assumptions only about stimulus selectivity; but the assumptions are different from those customarily made about drive or habit, and they are testable.

Another view, considerably more involved, is that of Rapaport (1960) who has extended the psychoanalytic theory of motivation to deal with problems of purposeful and other forms of selectivity. He holds that internal or external excitations (stimuli?) may attract attention cathexes proportionate to their intensity. Attention cathexes on their part represent a quantum which may be attracted to stimuli selectively and momentarily. Attention cathexes are held to produce the conscious experience of stimulation, to produce directed motivation (as in Lewin's quasi needs), and even to give rise to a "memory trace" (association?). Although the concept of attention cathexis is broad rather than clear, it has been used by Rapaport (1960) and Rouse (1959) to predict characteristics of attention span, immediate memory, incidental learning, and "primacy" effects in association. The effects it is held to have upon behavioral selectivity are nonassociative in nature, yet they are seen as operating upon an underlying associative repertoire.

More radical than the previous positions is that of Miller, Galanter, and Pribram (1960). In their book *Plans and the Structure of Behavior* they develop an analogy between the performance of electronic computers and the human brain. For them the concept of association is replaced by that of the TOTE unit. The TOTE unit, they say, "incorporates the important notion of feedback, is an explanation of behavior in general, and of reflex action in particular, fundamentally different from the explanation provided by the reflex arc." The letters TOTE stand for test-operate-test-exit, words which describe the way in which behavior is governed by tests of congruity between "image" and environment. When action has produced congruity, the organism may go on (exit) to another phase of a *Plan*. A plan has characteristics somewhat analogous to purpose as here defined. The question of how plans are carried out by *strategy* and *tactics* seems comparable to the present question of how the purpose mechanism selectively operates to shape behavior to an anticipated end. An important difference, however, lies in the assumption of Miller, Galanter, and Pribram that *all* behavior represents the execution of some plan; i.e., all behavior is purposeful. As with others who have held such positions, this assumption leads them to concentrate more on the consequences of purpose than on the question of how these selective effects are produced. Nevertheless, their novel position is one which may be capable of generating hypotheses concerning unique functions for plans or purposes.

This brief scanning of some of the theoretical frames within which the selective characteristics of purpose might be treated is sufficient to demonstrate that there are a number of avenues along which investigation might proceed. It also indicates the primitive state of development of both theory and research on purpose. All of the formulations are tentative and incomplete, and they are all in need of a firm empirical base. While they all imply an important selective role for purpose mechanisms, they all suffer from the lack of a solid understanding of the precise empirical phenomena they would presume to explain. Research designed to establish experimental facts concerning the role of purpose in stimulus selection, response restriction, and the differential use of mediational modes seems most necessary. The various theoretical positions suggest possibilities along this line, but there can be no confidence that, even taken together, they cover the range of effects that direct observation would reveal.

Even while theoretically inspired research is being carried on to confirm or disconfirm the implications of proposed purpose mechanisms, it would, in the light of these last considerations, seem worthwhile to undertake research exploring the consequences of the laboratory manipulations usually associated with research on purpose in a more theoretically neutral fashion, using the experimental tasks that seem most likely to reflect the influence of any possible selective processes.

A careful analysis of intentional and incidental learning in conjunction with manipulations designed to affect purpose might provide a promising starting point. Differences between these two kinds of tasks might well be related to the degree of associative selectivity operating. Postman (e.g., 1956, 1960) has worked extensively on closely related problems, and many of his tasks could lend themselves to the investigation of these issues. Experiments that presumably would be relevant to purpose include the study of (1) performance on the intentional and incidental tasks under differential-incentive conditions, (2) performance following a wide range of intention-producing instructions, and (3) performance under conditions where the subject is allowed a choice of objectives. Bahrick (1954) has reported an experiment to suggest that incidental learning decreases with increased incentives, but his limited study only scratches the surface of the possible manipulations under this heading. Postman and Senders (1946) have provided examples of research with different intention-producing instructions and to some extent with conditions where the subject chooses his own objectives. Both areas need further work focused on the present issues, however, and each may call for the devising of novel experimental tasks which offer the subject a wider range of possible objectives and responses than do the well-known laboratory tasks.

All of these manipulations and tasks could be studied with special reference to stimulus selection on the one side and response selection on the other. The first would tend to occur when the subject is given the "option" of observing or not observing a particular stimulus, while the latter would be most apparent when some required orienting task insured that all stimuli had at least been observed, even though they are responded to selectively.

This kind of empirical approach to the issue of the selective use of *mediational* processes could be made by employing tasks in which there are opportunities for various paths of mediation to occur. The possible differential use of, say, associative versus semantic mediation under differing conditions of "purposefulness" might prove very worthwhile. It is likely, too, that selective processes other than those related to purpose mechanisms would account for much of the variance in such situations. The subtle ways in which a subject might become selectively attuned to particular modes of mediation represent a problem in the larger domain of set of which purpose is only a part.

Studies along these suggested lines might carry the investigator into problems which seem far removed from the usual topics of verbal behavior research. On the other hand, a general solution to the problem of associative selectivity produced by purpose mechanisms might prove to have a direct and double relevance for those interested in verbal behavior. First, it is entirely possible that the effects of purpose are attributable in a larger degree than one might expect to linguistic mediation. This would make it an area in which to apply verbal behavior theory. Second, it is very probable that a knowledge of purpose mechanisms would provide another key in accounting for the organization and content of linguistic productions. As such, it would be a tool in the explanation of verbal behavior.

REFERENCES

Bahrick, H. P. (1954) Incidental learning under two incentive conditions. *J. Exp. Psychol.*, **47**, 170–172.

Brown, J. (1961) *The motivation of behavior.* New York: McGraw-Hill.

Bruner, J., Matter, J., & Papanek, M. (1955) Breadth of learning as a function of drive level and mechanization. *Psychol. Rev.*, **62**, 1–10.

Easterbrook, J. A. (1959) The effect of emotion on cue utilization and the organization of behavior. *Psychol. Rev.*, **66**, 183–201.

Gibson, J. J. (1941) A critical review of the concept of set in contemporary experimental psychology. *Psychol. Bull.*, **38**, 781–817.

Hull, C. L. (1930) Knowledge and purpose as habit mechanisms. *Psychol. Rev.*, 37, 511–525.

Koch, S. (1956) Behavior as "intrinsically" regulated: Worknotes towards a pre-theory of phenomena called "motivational." In M. R. Jones (Ed.), *Nebraska symposium on motivation.* Lincoln, Nebr.: University of Nebraska Press. Pp. 42–87.

Martin, J. G. (1960) Mediated transfer in two verbal learning paradigms. Unpublished doctoral dissertation, University of Minnesota.

Miller, G. A., Galanter, E., & Pribram, K. (1960) *Plans and the structure of behavior.* New York: Henry Holt.

Osgood, C. E. (1957) Motivational dynamics of language behavior. In M. R. Jones (Ed.), *Nebraska symposium on motivation.* Lincoln, Nebr.: University of Nebraska Press. Pp. 348–424.

Peters, R. S. (1958) *The concept of motivation.* London: Routledge and Kegan Paul.

Postman, L., & Adams, P. A. (1956) Studies in incidental learning: IV. The interaction of orienting tasks and stimulus materials. *J. Exp. Psychol.*, 51, 329–333.

Postman, L., & Adams, P. A. (1960) Studies in incidental learning: VIII. The effects of contextual determination. *J. Exp. Psychol.*, 59, 153–164.

Postman, L., & Senders, V. L. (1946) Incidental learning and generality of set. *J. Exp. Psychol.*, 36, 153–165.

Rapaport, D. (1960) On the psychoanalytic theory of motivation. In M. R. Jones (Ed.), *Nebraska symposium on motivation.* Lincoln, Nebr.: University of Nebraska Press. Pp. 173–247.

Rouse, R. O. (1959) Proactive inhibition as a function of degree of practice of the two tasks. *Amer. Psychologist*, 14, 385. (Abstract)

Schneirla, T. C. (1959) An evolutionary and developmental theory of biphasic processes underlying approach and withdrawal. In M. R. Jones (Ed.), *Nebraska symposium on motivation.* Lincoln, Nebr.: University of Nebraska Press. Pp. 1–42.

COMMENTS ON PROFESSOR RUSSELL'S PAPER[1]

Arthur W. Staats

ARIZONA STATE UNIVERSITY

Russell has very well posed the difficult problems in dealing with "purpose" and "set" within an objective framework. The conceptual and experimental difficulties are described, and alternative strategies are presented. This effort should rekindle interest in these areas of complex

[1] This work was supported by the Office of Naval Research under Contract Nonr-2794(02), by the Office of Education, Cooperative Research Program, under Contract 1048, and by the National Institute of Mental Health under Contract 2381(02).

human behavior and should stimulate experimental or conceptual work which will attack the various problems.

Russell concludes that the consideration of the various theoretical frames indicates that, "There are a number of avenues along which investigation might proceed," (p. 269) and states, "It would . . . seem worthwhile to undertake research exploring the consequences of the laboratory manipulations usually associated with research on purpose in a more theoretically neutral fashion, using the experimental tasks that seem most likely to reflect the influence of any possible selective processes" (p. 269).

In the first part of my comments dealing with the complex topic of purpose, I would like to make a case for an S-R approach, and later describe some of our research which I think is relevant to the problem of set.

First, however, I would like to include myself among those whom Russell describes as teleophobic in attempting to "proceed with the investigation of variables untainted by purposive connotations" (p. 260), although I do not feel it is necessary, in a sense, to ignore the behaviors involved, hoping the problems will "aimlessly drift away." As Russell points out, "Perhaps no fact has provided more difficulty for systematic psychology than has the obvious one that behavior can frequently be described in terms of some conceived end toward which it is directed" (p. 260). It appears to me, however, that there are difficulties in addition to the complexity of the events involved. The additional problems stem from the terms and approaches which have been applied to the area, which still continue to survive, and which I think obtrude their unproductive implications. For example, the terms "goal-directed," "goal-seeking," "behavior which occurs in order to achieve something," and so on, suggest that there is some influence by the goal itself—some future causality. A step away from this approach, with its obvious conflict with the demand for a demonstrable type of relationship between antecedents and consequents, is the idea that there is a "purpose" or "conception" or "intention" which precedes the behavior. This allows for an acceptable direction of causality but has mentalistic overtones, unless the antecedent variables are specified—and may be only one step away from a teleology if there is the implication that the as-yet-to-be-realized goal influences the intention. While it is true that Russell does not use the purposive terms with teleological connotations, I think that an analysis of the drawbacks in the use of such terms is productive here because of their implications for many people and because they are indeed unnecessary. The introduction of purposive terms does seem to include the goal as an event to be considered. And in relatively uncharted territory, depending upon how the problem is defined, different approaches and methods are indicated.

When the conceived end, or purpose, is considered as a behavior, however, other implications follow which are not mentalistic or teleological. The indication then is that the task is (1) reliably to describe the behavior involved, and (2) to establish the independent variables of which it is a function. In addition, (3) as a stimulus producing occurrence, a behavior can have a "causing" or "determining" status. That this is more than word magic will, I hope, be shown as we go on.

Russell describes several levels, or complexities, of behaviors with respect to a stimulus condition. Thus, there are simple reflexes and tropistic responses whose relation to the stimulus is clear. And he states, when describing an organism's approach response to the presence of a reinforcing stimulus, "As long as there is a plausible explanation for the occurrence of such behavior in terms of differential overt associative responses to objectively present, external stimuli, it would seem to add only an adjective to say that it was purposeful" (p. 262). It might help to add only that these occurrences are *best* described by referring to the *past* occasions where the organism's approach to the visual stimulus has been followed by reinforcement, e.g., the operations for producing a discriminative stimulus for an approach response. It might indeed detract here to use the term goal-directed since this suggests the improper method of examining the relationship of the goal as a goal to the behavior.

On the other hand, when the organism behaves in a manner described as looking for something which is not present, Russell feels that the term purposive is appropriately used. It is then that

The behavior shown is more likely to be attributed to the operation of some state or mechanism within the organism, rather than to be interpreted as a simple case of differential responding to external stimuli. When such hypothesized states or mechanisms are attributed characteristics which force the organism to behave in such a way that the behavior is describable with reference to some anticipated end, then it would seem that the term purposeful could be significantly applied to the behavior so mediated (p. 262).

Thus Russell considers the term purposive as an inferred process of some type which mediates behavior. Whether the term can be productively or significantly applied in even this manner, however, is questionable.

Russell describes an example of this mechanism in the case of Professor Olson who gets up in the morning, drives on the route to his regular office, meets a road block, changes direction, detours through unknown streets until he meets a familiar route again, and arrives at the hospital where he has an appointment. This behavior can be termed purposeful—behavior in order to get to the hospital, behavior with an anticipated end, behavior which seeks the hospital, behavior under the control of a personal conception of the objective.

Russell adds that this type of description of Professor Olson's behavior does not provide an explanation of his actions but only clarifies what type of behavior will be considered under the term purposive. However, it does seem that some of the purposive terms tend to lead one away from consideration of the possible S-R processes involved and from the independent variables responsible for these processes. The hypothetical case of Professor Olson would not be so recondite if described in more detail in S-R terms. Upon arising in the morning Professor Olson opens his appointment book and texts the page for that day with the response, I HAVE TO BE AT SUCH AND SUCH HOSPITAL AT NINE O'CLOCK. I WONDER HOW I GET THERE. This verbal sequence then provides the stimulus controlling the responses of finding and scanning a map of the city. Tracing the route between his house and the hospital, he responds verbally, saying, TAKE MY USUAL ROUTE UNTIL I COME TO SEVENTH AVENUE. THEN RIGHT TO . . . etc., etc. Once in his car he drives for a time and then looks at the street signs, saying, I TURN RIGHT AT SEVENTH AVENUE. When the appropriate sign appears he texts it as SEVENTH AVENUE, and this verbal response then controls the motor response of turning the car to the right. The professor then drives until the road block appears. At this time he responds, I'LL GO SOUTH FOR A BLOCK AND THEN CONTINUE EAST SINCE THAT WILL PARALLEL THIS STREET AND EVENTUALLY GET ME TO HIGHLAND BOULEVARD WHICH TAKES ME TO THE HOSPITAL. He continues on, texts HIGHLAND BOULEVARD, turns toward the hospital, reaches the hospital, responds to the stimuli present by looking around, sees an open place at the curb, parks the car, goes into the hospital, looks around, texts the directory with DR. MORRIS, ROOM 329, and goes to this office in a still complicated sequence of verbal and motor behaviors.

Some of the texting responses involved in this sequence could be replaced by the individual's own verbal response sequences—and if the sequence occurred frequently enough, the behavior chain would occur without the support of the verbal behavior. That is, the motor behaviors involved, since they also produce certain visual stimuli (in some cases proprioceptive stimuli would be effective), would come to control the behaviors—thus, each motor behavior would result in arriving at a visual stimulus situation which would control the driving responses involved, and so on.

Although this is a hypothetical example, it seems to me, following this description, that the end or goal in this, or any situation of this type, would be irrelevant—and that use of purposive terms even in description of the behavior is misleading. If someone had placed a bomb in the office in which Professor Olson was to have the appointment—he would still go there. The determinants of Professor Olson's behavior are the past training circumstances concerned with the motor and verbal behaviors involved, and the manner in which they "mediate" the final behavior of entering the office.

The fact that the professor upon request could state that he was going to the hospital for an appointment would not change the situation. This behavior also is under the control of past events, actually the same ones as those which have already been mentioned. Certainly, this verbal behavior cannot be called the "goal" of the professor although it may enter into his getting to the hospital. It is simply verbal behavior under the control of the appointment book notation.

However, this is a very complex case, and perhaps an experimental example would be helpful here. Judson, Cofer, and Gelfand (1956) used Maier's two-string problem as the task for the subjects. Prior to being introduced to the problem, however, the subjects received pretraining on a separate learning task. This task involved learning lists of words in serial order. For one group of subjects the words ROPE, SWING, and PENDULUM were inserted in that order into one list. Thus, this group of subjects learned this sequence of word responses. Other groups of subjects did not learn these words in that manner.

It would be expected that the group of subjects for whom the response sequence ROPE-SWING-PENDULUM had been established, on encountering the Maier two-string problem, would tend to respond with ROPE (or STRING) to the cord involved in the problem. The response ROPE would produce stimuli which would elicit the response SWING, and SWING would elicit PENDULUM. It would also be expected that the sequence ROPE-SWING-PENDULUM would mediate the motor responses of constructing a pendulum, using the cord and swinging it. (A schematization of this is presented in Figure 7–1.) Thus, subjects who had this verbal sequence of responses established in good strength should be more likely to solve the problem. In general, the results of the experiment substantiated this prediction.

Although this is an experiment in reasoning or problem solving, the same elements are present as in the case of Professor Olson. The goal, or end, here is in reality the *present* instructions to tie the string together; these instructions perform a similar function as did Professor Olson's appointment book; that is, they mediate observing responses to the strings, etc., and the verbal and motor response sequences then unfold. This example indicates, I believe, that the purposive terms are misleading. The same events are studied without recourse to these terms or interest in the function of a goal.

The example of Professor Olson is much more complex in the training variables which must have been involved, in the controlling stimuli which were effective, and in the behavioral repertoires displayed. For example, each link in the verbal response sequences involved would be expected to be a hierarchy instead of a straightforward elicitation of the next response and no other. Thus, rather than as a smooth chain of verbal and instrumental responses, the chain would more realistically be described as showing the relative strengths of competing responses involved at each stimulus point. In addition, the picture of verbal behavior described is oversimplified, since it included only operant word responses and no mediating responses of the "meaning variety," which are developed under the principles of classical conditioning. If Professor Olson

Instructions

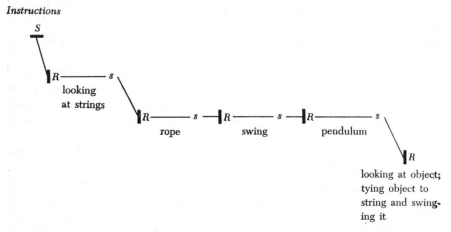

FIG. 7–1. Schematization of the Judson, Cofer, and Gelfand study of problem solving in which the stimulus of the instructions sets the occasion for the Ss response of looking at the strings. The visual stimulus of the strings tends to elicit the verbal response ROPE, which is the initial response in the previously established verbal chain ROPE-SWING-PENDULUM for experimental group Ss. This sequence then mediates the problem solving behaviors.

had had previous experience of an aversive nature at hospitals, for example, his textual sequence of responses to the appointment book would also elicit a negative meaning response, which would tend to elicit avoidant responses. As a consequence, it might be seen that the alacrity of Professor Olson's behavior would be missing.

The above is meant only to suggest that a description in terms of behavior principles can be made without resort to a purpose mechanism. As Russell points out, analyses of such "homely illustrations" do not constitute experimental hypotheses, but they can serve as a starting point. In this respect, however, since the above description is based upon principles which have arisen in controlled study, the nature of the independent variables underlying the complex purposive behavior is thereby suggested. That is, if one wishes to know how the individual responds verbally in a certain manner to the visual verbal stimuli in an appointment book, Skinner (1957) describes this; and there is ample evidence as to how visual discriminative operants are established and, specifically, how texts are formed according to the principles of reinforcement (Staats, Staats, Schutz, and Wolf, 1961). Since these textual responses themselves produce stimuli, the manner in which they can come to control motor behaviors should follow the same principles as those involved in bringing any behavior under stimulus control. And from a practical standpoint, if one is interested in developing purposive behavior, relevant training variables and verbal and motor repertoires are suggested. It is this which makes a description in terms of behavior principles more than an idle pastime or a retreat to mentalism. This is not to suggest that these complex cases have been experimentally approached—it indicates only potential.

Russell indicates that stimulus-response processes are possibly involved in purpose and suggests, in addition, that meaning functions are likely to be involved. He then presents the problem of "how the purpose mechanism, whatever its source and character, exercises its regulatory influence upon behavior" (p. 265).

On a general level, following from the previous S-R description, it could be said simply that the regulatory function occurs in the same manner as that in which any stimulus control occurs. That is, if what is called the purpose mechanism consists of chains of verbal and motor responses (some of which get the organism into new environmental stimulus conditions), then the resulting stimuli have the usual function in eliciting the final response.

In discussing this regulatory function, dealt with under the descriptive term set, Russell does describe Osgood's mediating response (1957) and Hull's fractional anticipatory goal response (1930). Russell suggests that study of these types of habit mechanisms may be one way of approaching the topic, but points out that Osgood's treatment has drawbacks.

As plausible as Osgood's treatment may be, it has a technical difficulty that results from the very number of hypothesized stimulus sources which are considered. It is that even if the associative hierarchies of each stimulus source operating alone were known, there is still the problem of predicting the resultant when they are all simultaneously operating. Until this can be done with some accuracy, it will be difficult to test his predictions in complex cases (pp. 266–267).

However, the difficulty here seems to lie more with the complexity of the events under question, rather than with the attempt to deal with these events with behavior principles. Prediction of the complex case, even when the principles have been ascertained, is a practical problem and rests upon knowledge of the independent variables involved. The physicist cannot predict the flight of a feather because he does not have the appropriate information though he knows the principles which are operative. On the other hand, on the basis of the principles, he can manipulate independent variables to produce many important results.

The same types of possibilities are present in the areas of study under consideration. Although some complex set behaviors could not be predicted in everyday life because many unknown variables are operating, it is not unreasonable to expect that when the principles are well understood, it will be possible to manipulate variables to produce the desired behavior in this area.

Specific knowledge of the principles, of course, will stem from a piecemeal attack on the complex case, broken down and studied in the laboratory, as Russell points out. The question at this point is what basic principles and methods to apply in the laboratory study of set. Are behavior principles the most likely prospects for success in this task? I think so, and I would like to present several studies which we have conducted in a program of a piecemeal approach to one problem of set.

Russell describes sets in verbal learning and verbal behavior as "the manner in which the use of language is selectively directed, how certain verbal structures are 'tuned,' or 'primed,' how certain 'schemata,' are adopted, or how particular 'supraordinate categories' are activated" (p. 258). In Russell's description, it seems to me there are two separable types of events: (1) the "verbal structures," "categories," or "schemata"; and (2) the way in which these are "tuned," "primed," or "activated."

In our laboratory, we too have been interested in dealing with these two types of events, but we have approached these topics by working with the operant conditioning of word classes. A word class may be considered a verbal structure or category, and operant conditioning, in this case, can be considered in terms of its activating or tuning effect. Although the principle of operant conditioning has been frequently tested in the area of verbal behavior (see Krasner, 1958; Salzinger, 1959), the variables underlying the formation and function of the word classes or verbal structures involved (i.e., the set mechanisms) have received scant attention.

For example, in Salzinger's article summarizing studies of the operant conditioning of word classes, it is suggested that responses making up a word class are those which may be substituted for one another, are followed by the same reinforcement, or are emitted in the presence of the same discriminative stimulus. This does not appear (see Staats, 1961) to be an adequate rationale for the fact that the reinforcement of one word response strengthens other members of a class of words. Therefore,

I would like to present what I consider to be a more detailed conceptual and experimental analysis which, at the same time, represents an analysis of a certain type of set.

Cofer and Foley (1942), Mowrer (1954), Osgood (1953), and Staats and Staats (1959) have discussed word meaning in terms of Hullian concepts as an implicit, mediating response. According to this interpretation, when a word is contiguously presented with a stimulus object, some of the unconditioned responses elicited by the object will be conditioned to the word. These responses when stably conditioned become the meaning of the word. First-order conditioning of meaning has been demonstrated by Staats, Staats, and Crawford (1958). Additional support for the contention that the concept of meaning may be treated as a conditioned response is given by a series of studies (Staats and Staats, 1957; Staats, Staats, and Heard, 1961) in which conditioning was accomplished by pairing a word which already elicited a meaning response with the verbal stimulus to be conditioned to elicit that meaning, i.e., a higher-order conditioning paradigm. Both connotative and denotative meaning responses were conditioned.

In addition, suggestions concerning the nature of the conditioned meaning response have been offered elsewhere (Osgood, 1953; Staats, 1961), and it will suffice to point out here that the conditioned response may be considered an autonomic response, an implicit motor response, or the conditionable portion of a sensory response. Thus, when a word is paired with an unconditioned stimulus eliciting a motor, autonomic, or sensory response, part of the response is conditioned to the word.

On the other hand, word responses also come under the control of stimulus objects, according to the principles of operant conditioning (Skinner, 1957). That is, a word response reinforced in the presence of a stimulus (and not in its absence) will come to be elicited (or controlled) by that stimulus. In this process, the word response comes to be elicited by the motor, autonomic, or sensory response produced by the stimulus (including those parts of the response which are conditionable as meanings). Thus a word as a stimulus-producing response comes to elicit a conditioned meaning response, but in addition, this same response comes to elicit the word response. This is depicted in Figure 7–2. The word BALL is elicited by the sensory response elicited by the object ball. In addition, BALL as a response elicits the conditionable parts of that sensory response.

At this point, the class of words consists of only one member. However, not only will the word BALL be reinforced in the presence of the stimulus object (or similar objects), but other responses will also be similarly treated, e.g., ROUND, CIRCULAR, SPHERICAL, ORANGE, BALLOON, and so on. Stimuli produced by these responses will also be paired with the objects in the classical conditioning of meaning. If in language learning, groups of words come to elicit the same meaning response component on the basis of being paired with the same or similar stimulus objects, and if the same meaning response component, through the stimuli it produces, comes to control the emission of each of the word responses in the class,

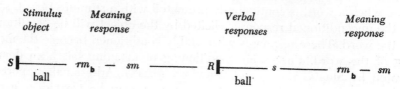

Fig. 7–2. The stimulus object ball elicits a sensory (meaning) response which, in the process of tacting, has come to elicit a verbal response BALL. The word BALL has been classically conditioned to elicit the same meaning response by being paired with the object ball. The object ball also elicits sensory responses which are not conditionable and which control the word response BALL, but this is not depicted.

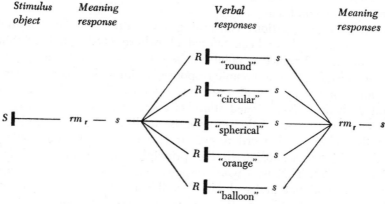

Fig. 7–3. A number of verbal responses have been operantly conditioned in the presence of the same or similar round objects which elicit the round meaning response. Thus, the verbal responses tend to be elicited by that round meaning component. The same word stimuli have also been paired with similar round objects and have come to elicit the round meaning response. Consequently, any object (or word) which elicits the round meaning response will tend to elicit the various verbal responses. This constitutes the verbal habit family for "roundness."

then a mechanism would exist which would constitute a verbal structure or set on the basis of which operant conditioning of the class could occur. This verbal structure may be called a verbal habit family, using a Hullian-type terminology. The verbal habit family for "roundness" is schematized in Figure 7–3.

In the various studies of the operant conditioning of word classes, conditions are manipulated so that the subject emits words. When a word response which is a member of the class the experimenter has chosen occurs, the experimenter presents some reinforcing stimulus. It is found that the frequency of the emission of the other members of the word class increases. This occurrence can be accounted for on the basis of the verbal habit family in the following manner. When the word response is reinforced, both the word response and the meaning response elicited by the word would be conditioned to the cues of the situation. However, since the meaning response component would also tend to elicit each of the word responses in the class, strengthening the tendency of the situation to elicit the meaning response would raise the probability that each of the word responses would be emitted. Each time one of the members of the class was emitted and reinforced, the strength of the habit family in that situation would, in this manner, be increased. This would not be the case for any word emitted in the situation and not reinforced, i.e., a nonclass word.

On the basis of this rationale, a study (Staats, Staats, and Finley, 1961a) was recently completed in which a group of 40 words was selected, each of which possessed positive evaluative meaning, that is, each one of the words elicited a "positive evaluative" meaning response component, although the various words also elicited other meaning responses. Each of these words was presented on a card with three other words of unsystematic meaning. Randomization procedures were followed with respect to the position of the words on the cards, as well as the order of the cards. The subjects in the experimental group were presented with each card, were directed to select one of the four words, and were socially reinforced by the experimenter upon selecting one of the positive meaning words. Control group subjects were not reinforced. Figure 7–4 presents the results, which indicate that a group of word responses, each of which elicited a common meaning response component, could be operantly conditioned as a class.

Consideration of the verbal habit-family model, however, leads to the expectation that any group of words which elicited a common response, if that response also tended to elicit each of the word responses, would condition as a class, i.e., be susceptible to set phenomena. An example of this may be found in the word-association norms of Russell and Jenkins (1954). The word SLEEP elicits BED, DREAM, COMFORT, and DEEP as associates to varying degrees. BED, DREAM, COMFORT, and DEEP in turn also elicit SLEEP. This response class is shown in Figure 7–5. Thus, it would be expected that reinforcing an individual every time he emitted one of the words that elicits SLEEP would strengthen the response SLEEP to the stimulus situation. The situational stimuli would thus tend to elicit SLEEP and thereby increase the probability that the associates to SLEEP would occur in the situation. Because of the few words involved in this class, of course, it would be difficult to condition the class operantly. However, a large number of subjects in an experiment of this type might be used to demonstrate the effect. Or a word class of this type which included more members could be formed in the laboratory.

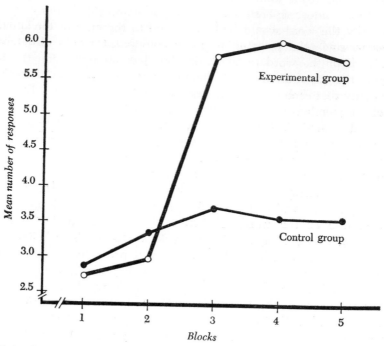

FIG. 7–4. The mean number of positive word responses for the five successive blocks of items for experimental and control group Ss.

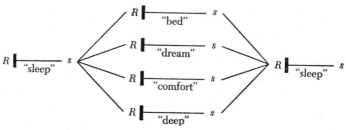

FIG. 7–5. The "sleep" word response class.

Russell and Storms (1955) have shown that the implicit word associates of a stimulus word elicited upon presentation of the stimulus word may have a learning function. That is, subjects were able to acquire an A-D association, where A-B, B-C, and C-D associations already existed. It could thus be concluded that presentation of A tended to elicit B implicitly, B tended to elicit C, and C tended to elicit D.

On the basis of implicit chains of verbal responses, it would be expected that any serial chain of word associates, i.e., word responses, would demonstrate set characteristics in the operant conditioning situation. That is, if the first response in a chain were emitted, its word associates, the next several responses, would be elicited implicitly. The occurrence of reinforcement would then strengthen the tendency for all of the implicit responses to be elicited by the situation. If the next response in the chain occurred, the same process would be repeated and would make it even more likely that the third response in the chain would be elicited. Each succeeding word response in the chain, when it occurred, would further increase the likelihood that the next response would be elicited. The Pledge of Allegiance would constitute such a word class for an individual raised in the United States, as would poems, rituals, and shorter word-association chains.

It would also be expected that a serial chain of responses would constitute a word class in an operant conditioning situation even when not emitted in the serial order. That is, when a series of word responses are chained in a serial learning task, associations are formed between words other than those which are directly contiguous (Postman and Egan, 1949).

However, the closer the order to that in the serial learning task, the stronger the associations would be and the greater the extent of operant conditioning expected.

These expectations were tested in the following study (Staats, Staats, and Finley, 1961b). The subjects separately learned two serial lists by the paired-associate method of anticipation. The items on the lists were nonsense words, e.g., HUFOD, TEBAM, SOZOG. Later, the first words from each of the lists was placed upon one card, the two second words on another, the third on another, and so on. Then, in the serial order, the cards were individually presented to the subject with instructions to select one word. The word responses in one of the lists (the list opposite to that which was chosen on the first card) were then reinforced. The reinforcer was a pencil tap as a "point," as used by Verplanck (1956). Of the three subjects so treated each selected 9 or more words from that list out of the possible 11—a statistically significant performance in each individual case—for a mean of 9.67. This procedure was replicated for six additional subjects with one change. The order of the presentation of the words in the operant conditioning phase of the experiment was 1-3-5-7-9-11-2-4-6-8-10-12. The mean number of words from the reinforced list was 7.50. Another group was run in which the order of presentation of the words was random. The mean for this group was 6.67. And finally, for a control group where the word response sequences were not established at all, the mean number of responses selected from the reinforced list was 5.67. The results for the four groups are shown in Figure 7–6. Thus, the extent of operant conditioning of the groups was greatest for subjects operantly conditioned in serial order, next greatest for subjects presented the alternate order, next for subjects receiving the random order, and least for the control subjects. A regression analysis of the treatment condition indicated a linear trend significant at the .005 level.

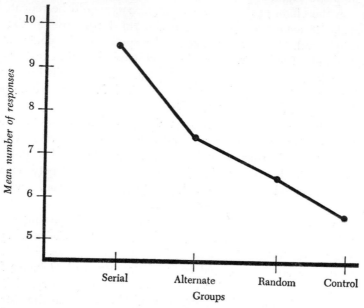

Fig. 7–6. Mean number of correct word responses for each of the serial learning study treatment groups.

That is, the conditionability of this class of word responses was dependent upon the strength of associations between the words. In other terms, it could be said that the effect of set depended upon the strength of associations. The serial training procedure produced a class of word responses for an operant conditioning situation.

In addition to this type of word response class, any words which occur frequently in contiguity with each other should condition as a class. Take, for example, the word associates to a stimulus word in word-association norms. Many of them are interassociated, e.g., in the word responses to MUSIC there are SWEET and SOFT, but SWEET and SOFT also elicit MUSIC. In addition the word LOUD, although not elicited by MUSIC, is elicited by SOFT. Thus, LOUD would tend to occur as a response to

MUSIC, since it is mediated by the response SOFT. Now LOUD as a stimulus word has as its associates a number of responses which are also direct associates to MUSIC, as well as the word MUSIC itself. This complex network of interrelated associations is illustrated in Figure 7–7. If complete word-association norms were available for these words, additional inter-associations would be seen.

Such a group of words should thus operantly condition as a class. This was tested (Staats, Staats, and Minke, 1961), using the methods of operant conditioning already described, for the word associates to

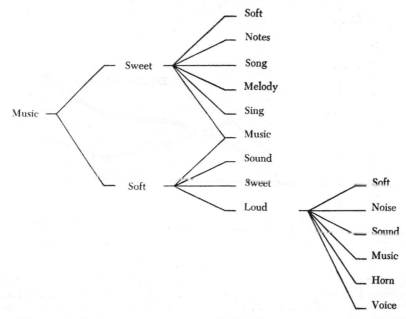

FIG. 7–7. Some of the interassociations established between the word associates to MUSIC.

MUSIC. That is, 25 associates to the word MUSIC were taken from Russell and Jenkins (1954), and each was presented with two nonmusic words on a card to two groups of subjects. All subjects were instructed to select one of the three words. In the experimental group the selection of a music word was followed by the reinforcement of the pencil-tap point, but no responses were reinforced in the control group. The results indicated that the number of MUSIC word responses significantly increased, and in a linear fashion ($p < .01$), for the experimental group relative to the control group. The results are shown in Figure 7–8.

On the basis of this evidence, which is not yet complete, it is now possible to analyze this aspect of the problem of set in greater detail.

Salzinger stated that word classes are formed when the same discriminative stimulus controls the various words. This statement is incomplete, if
not incorrect, on several grounds. First, the same S^D does not control
all the words in the classes which have been operantly conditioned; e.g.,
not all living-thing words are controlled by the same stimulus. Even if
Salzinger's statement was accepted there would still remain the question
of why word responses controlled by one stimulus should behave as a
class in a situation in which this S^D was not present. When the S-R
principles are considered in greater detail, however, the picture becomes

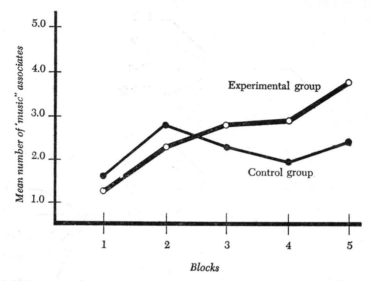

FIG. 7–8. Mean number of MUSIC associates emitted in each block of five trials for
experimental and control group Ss. The experimental Ss were reinforced upon each
emission of an associate to MUSIC, while none of the responses of the control Ss were
reinforced.

clearer. Words may not be controlled by the same specific S^D but by
several S^D's which occur in conjunction. For example, a symphony concert
is a complex stimulus situation in which such words as LOUD, SOFT, SWEET,
MUSIC, HORN, NOTES, MELODY, and so on, are likely to occur, controlled
by the various specific stimuli. As a consequence, word associations will
be formed between the word responses, and they will function as a
class in the manner described. The same associations, however, could also
be formed on the basis of reading an account of the symphony, so that
tacting would not necessarily be involved in the formation of the
verbal structure.

Another statement of Salzinger's was that words reinforced by the
same stimulus would function as a class. Again this is incorrect, or at

least incomplete. First, many word responses are reinforced by the same social reinforcers but are not in the same response classes. On the other hand, food-word mands, such as MILK PLEASE, BREAD PLEASE, and so on, are reinforced by different stimuli and yet they are in the same class. In the terms developed herein, however, the interpretation of the development of this class of words might be that salivation would come to elicit all food words and be elicited by all of them—thus, forming a verbal habit family. On this basis, a class of food words should be capable of operant conditioning.

I have used a particular research series to demonstrate the application of S-R principles and methods to the problems of set. The problem is one in verbal learning, involving both verbal structure (or set), as well as the activation of the structure; it hews closely to the aspects of set which Russell describes. The problem selected also indicates that the use of the term set is largely arbitrary, since operant conditioning of word classes has been studied without recourse to the term. I hope the above examples also additionally serve to indicate that verbal behavior is *one* field and that the principles studied in the various subareas of operant conditioning, paired-associate and serial learning, word-association norms and mediation, and semantic conditioning and mediation are all operative when complex cases are considered in detail. Especially, I am interested in indicating that operant conditioning is not a new and separate area in verbal learning. It depends upon principles and results available in other fields.

Although the complex behavior in everyday life may be difficult to predict since a number of S-R mechanisms are involved, the mechanisms may be capable of separation and thus be susceptible to investigation in the laboratory. Such investigation, on the other hand, should eventually yield the customary products of prediction and control.

I don't wish to give the impression that the research summarized is the only or the first attempt to attack the various problems of set with S-R principles. A number of other studies furnish the same type of evidence. For example, using anagrams and water-jar problems, Maltzman and associates (1953) have indicated that Hullian concepts of response hierarchies and drive are applicable in indicating some of the characteristics of the selective mechanisms. Maltzman and associates (1958), following an earlier attempt using the two-string problem (Staats, 1955), have shown that verbal responses to problem-solving objects are an index of later performance in the problem. Adamson (1959) has shown that schedule of reinforcement of anagram solutions affects the persistence of the solution (i.e., the rigidity of set). And the S-R verbal mechanisms involved in a number of verbal set behaviors have been studied by Bousfield and associates and Cofer and associates (see Bousfield, 1953; Bousfield and Cohen, 1953; Bousfield, Whitmarsh, and Berkowitz, 1958; Judson and Cofer, 1956; and Havron and Cofer, 1957).

On the basis of these demonstrations, I would suggest a redefinition of the problems of set and purpose which would deny a special mechanism, or category of behavior. While recognizing the need to deal with complex behaviors of the type described by Russell, it seems that S-R principles will suffice. In these terms, the problem is first an adequate description of the behaviors involved, second an analysis of the S-R mechanisms, and third a laboratory isolation and simplification of the interacting mechanisms. Certainly, S-R principles are potentially, at least in combination, capable of the complexity seen in human behavior in everyday life. That is, stimulus events vary in type (i.e., exteroceptive, interoceptive, and proprioceptive) and are capable of variations in the strength with which they elicit or control responses. Chains or sequences of behavior are capable of extensions in terms of the number and types of units involved, and the individual units are capable of combination into hierarchies. Thus, there may be hierarchies of stimuli which elicit chains of responses which mediate hierarchies of other responses. In addition, verbal behaviors, as one type of response, allow for the long-term direction of behavior which leads to labels of "purposive," and so on. Although there are infinite variations in complex human behaviors, the S-R mechanisms which have already been established are capable of combination into infinitely varied arrangements.

One further point. As Russell points out in mentioning teleophobia, purposive terms and the behavior involved have been excluded by many S-R investigators as legitimate areas of study. In fact, because of the mentalistic misuse of such terms as meaning, images, thinking, and even some types of overt language behaviors, such events were also rejected as appropriate subject matter for study. And possibly rightly so, since events which cannot be approached objectively should perhaps be overlooked in favor of more simple and basic events. Probably early experimental approaches to behavior could handle only simple behaviors with simple organisms. However, as time passes, behavioristic psychology, building upon the more basic principles, has already objectively approached some of these formerly taboo areas, as well as the area under discussion—and with success. The progression of this approach has been in the best tradition of science, beginning with the more simple events investigated in well-controlled circumstances, and advancing to consideration of the more complex cases as methodology develops. Because of this history, and the well-established principles which have been produced, when there is a choice concerning which methodology and principles seem most applicable to a new area of behavior, it seems reasonable to apply first those of the S-R approach.

REFERENCES

Adamson, R. (1959) Inhibitory set in problem solving as related to reinforcement learning. *J. Exp. Psychol.*, 58, 280–282.

Bousfield, W. A. (1953) The occurrence of clustering in the recall of randomly arranged associates. *J. Gen. Psychol.*, 49, 229–240.

Bousfield, W. A., & Cohen, B. H. (1953) The effects of reinforcement on the occurrence of clustering in the recall of randomly arranged associates. *J. Psychol.*, 36, 67–81.

Bousfield, W. A., Whitmarsh, G. A., & Berkowitz, H. (1958) Partial response identities in associative clustering. *Tech. Rep. No. 27.* Contract No. Nonr-631(00), Office of Naval Research and University of Connecticut.

Cofer, C. N., & Foley, J. P. (1942) Mediated generalization and the interpretation of verbal behavior: I. Prolegomena. *Psychol. Rev.*, 49, 513–540.

Havron, M. D., & Cofer, C. N. (1957) On the learning of material congruent and incongruent with attitudes. *J. Soc. Psychol.*, 46, 91–98.

Hull, C. (1930) Knowledge and purpose as habit mechanisms. *Psychol. Rev.*, 37, 511–525.

Judson, A. J., & Cofer, C. N. (1956) Reasoning as an associative process: I. "Direction" in a simple verbal problem. *Psychol. Rep.*, 2, 469–476.

Judson, A. J., Cofer, C. N., & Gelfand, S. (1956) Reasoning as an associative process: II. "Direction" in problem solving as a function of prior reinforcement of relevant responses. *Psychol. Rep.*, 2, 501–507.

Krasner, L. (1958) Studies of the conditioning of verbal behavior. *Psychol. Bull.*, 55, 148–170.

Maltzman, I., Brooks, L. O., Bogartz, W., & Summers, S. S. (1958) The facilitation of problem solving by prior exposure to uncommon responses. *J. Exp. Psychol.*, 56, 399–406.

Maltzman, I., Fox, J., & Morrisett, L., Jr. (1953) Some effects of manifest anxiety on mental set. *J. Exp. Psychol.*, 46, 50–54.

Mowrer, O. H. (1954) The psychologist looks at language. *Amer. Psychologist*, 9, 660–694.

Osgood, C. E. (1953) *Method and theory in experimental psychology.* New York: Oxford.

Osgood, C. E. (1957) Motivational dynamics of language behavior. In M. R. Jones (Ed.), *Nebraska Symposium on Motivation.* Lincoln, Nebr.: University of Nebraska Press. Pp. 348–424.

Postman, L., & Egan, J. P. (1949) *Experimental psychology: An introduction.* New York: Harper.

Russell, W. A., & Jenkins, J. J. (1954) The complete Minnesota norms for responses to 100 words from the Kent-Rosanoff Word Association Test. *Tech. Rep. No. 11,* Contract No. N8onr-66216, Office of Naval Research and University of Minnesota.

Russell, W. A., & Storms, L. H. (1955) Implicit verbal chaining in paired-associate learning. *J. Exp. Psychol.*, 49, 287–293.

Salzinger, K. (1959) Experimental manipulation of verbal behavior: A review. *J. Gen. Psychol.*, 61, 65–94

Skinner, B. F. (1957) *Verbal behavior.* New York: Appleton-Century-Crofts.

Staats, A. W. (1955) A behavioristic study of human problem solving. Ph.D. dissertation, University of California, Los Angeles.

Staats, A. W. (1961) Verbal habit-families, concepts, and the operant conditioning of word classes. *Psychol. Rev., 68,* 190–204.

Staats, A. W., & Staats, C. K. (1959) Meaning and (m): Separate but correlated. *Psychol. Rev., 66,* 136–144.

Staats, A. W., Staats, C. K., & Crawford, H. L. (1958) First-order conditioning of word meaning. *Tech. Rep. No. 6,* Contract No. Nonr-2305(00), Office of Naval Research and Arizona State University.

Staats, A. W., Staats, C. K., & Finley, J. R. (1961a) Operant conditioning of a semantically identified word class. *Tech. Rep. No. 14,* Contract No. Nonr-2794(02), Office of Naval Research and Arizona State University.

Staats, A. W., Staats, C. K., & Finley, J. R. (1961b) Operant conditioning of serially-chained verbal responses. *Tech. Rep. No. 19,* Contract No. Nonr-2794(02), Office of Naval Research and Arizona State University.

Staats, A. W., Staats, C. K., & Heard, W. G. (1961) Denotative meaning established by classical conditioning. *J. Exp. Psychol., 61,* 300–303.

Staats, A. W., Staats, C. K., & Minke, K. A. (1961) Operant conditioning of a class of word associates. *Tech. Rep. No. 18,* Contract No. Nonr-2794(02), Office of Naval Research and Arizona State University.

Staats, A. W., Staats, C. K., Schutz, R. E., & Wolf, M. (1961) The conditioning of textual responses utilizing "extrinsic" reinforcers. Unpublished manuscript completed under Contract 1048, Office of Education, Cooperative Research Program. Available from authors.

Staats, C. K., & Staats, A. W. (1957) Meaning established by classical conditioning. *J. Exp. Psychol., 54,* 74–80.

Verplanck, W. S. (1956) The operant conditioning of human motor behavior. *Psychol. Bull., 53,* 70–83.

SUMMARY OF CONFERENCE DISCUSSION

The discussion revolved around three major issues. First, there was objection to Staats's treatment of purpose in S-R terms, because of the belief that it either ignored or obscured important aspects of the problem. Second, there was discussion of his application of the conditioning paradigm to verbal responses and of the nature of the processes involved in his experiments. Third, concern was expressed about the applicability of S-R principles, including reinforcement, to the processes designated by such terms as set, *Aufgabe,* rules, and the like.

The first point was stressed by Jenkins, Deese, and Mandler. The importance of instructions in an experiment like the one by Judson, Cofer, and Gelfand, it was felt, was ignored by Staats. A subject must be told that he is to solve a problem before the analysis represented by Figure 7–1 would apply. Jenkins observed that if he gave a subject a box of crayons and a picture of the Maier problem, the subject would probably color the picture rather than try to work out methods of tying the two strings together. Parallel to this argument was the assertion that Professor Olson's looking at his appointment book was insufficient to account for the purposive character in his behavior. What is involved, as Deese suggested, is the problem that the Würzburg School faced (cf. Humphrey, 1951, chaps. 3–5) and conceptualized in such terms as *Aufgabe, Bewusstseinslagen*, determining tendency, and so on. Mandler asked why Professor Olson looked at his appointment book. Waking in the morning is hardly an adequate stimulus for such an act. Mandler argued that there are at least three defects in Staats's analysis of Olson's behavior: (1) It does not account for his looking at the appointment book; (2) it does not tell us why he looked at the map, or (3) why he stopped looking at it. Olson can probably figure out many ways of reaching the hospital; why does he stop when he finds one? What are the reinforcement contingencies for looking at the map? If this kind of terminology is to be used, it should explain the behavior. In reply to all these criticisms, Staats indicated that Olson's behavior is, of course, complexly controlled and that each of these questions could be answered in S-R terms, but a more detailed account would be necessary. Wickens noted that Staats had said that many stimuli affect Olson's behavior, not all of which had been discussed.

Russell observed that the main feature he had emphasized in Olson's behavior was the fact that he turned off the habitual route on the day in question. Staats felt that his presentation provided a feasible empirical approach to the study of such problems, but Russell expressed the fear that Staats's S-R commitment could blind him to the operation of important variables. Deese emphasized that Russell described the behavior without prejudice, whereas Staats is oriented to certain features of it. Russell pointed out that his description avoids teleology by using terms like anticipated goal or concept of goal and that he thought the problem of stimulus selection the real one here. There is an associative repertoire, but some principles, like *Bewusstseinslagen*, are needed to account for the fact that Olson responds to certain stimuli at one time and to different ones on other occasions. Martin's results which show failures of responding to mediational stimuli and Underwood's concept of stimulus selection suggest that such principles are necessary. Jenkins added that we ought to find out under what range of instructions results similar to those of Judson, Cofer, and Gelfand would be obtained.

The second point of the discussion arose (and it was with some relief that the participants left Professor Olson's case) when Goss objected to the term "operant conditioning" as used in Figure 7–3. He thought that Staats meant classical conditioning, as historically (Allport 1924;

Dashiell, 1928), classical conditioning has been invoked to account for name learning. Staats presented a further analysis as follows. If a child's mother speaks the word *ball* (CS) in the presence of a ball (UCS), the visual response (UCR), or a fractional portion of it, that is made to the ball can become conditioned to the sound of the word *ball*. The fractional part is the r_m for the word *ball*. Later, when the child's verbal response of the word *ball* in the presence of an actual *ball* is reinforced, the s_m which arises from the r_m made to the actual ball will acquire the capacity to evoke the verbal response *ball* from the child. The latter part of this analysis, which is what Staats meant by operant conditioning, applied to the verbal responses in the hierarchy of Figure 7–3; Mandler pointed out the pertinence of this discussion to the Bousfield-Osgood controversy of the first conference (Cofer, 1961, chap. 4).

Mandler asked what would happen if, when the ball is shown, the child is told "it's *not* a ball." Staats responded that if the stimulus "not a ball" was systematically paired with the ball, the verbal stimulus "not a ball" would come to elicit the meaning response elicited by ball on an unconditioned basis. Mandler wondered if such analyses are sufficiently complex to apply to actual situations.

As to Staats's experiments, Deese pointed out that the subject's *purpose* is to obtain points which the pencil tap signifies. The experiment involving the learning of two serial lists and the subsequent reinforcement of the subject's choice of items from one of the lists occasioned a good deal of discussion. Postman pointed out that the serial test is a test of retention, the alternating and random procedures a test of retention under interference conditions. Staats responded that that is indeed the point. The variables and principles studied in retention are the same as those which, in part, account for the formation of word classes which will condition operantly. Noble said that the alternating method was similar to the method of derived lists as developed by Ebbinghaus (1885). Jenkins regarded the method of operantly conditioning word classes as a method for probing response pools. Staats said that the results of the studies under question indicated that implicit responses (of a meaning or word-response nature) could be strengthened by the use of the method of reinforcement, thus strengthening a class of word responses associated with the implicit response. The experiments indicated some of the variables involved in the formation of word classes which will operantly condition.

Mandler felt that none of these ideas helped to explain the mechanism of operant conditioning of classes. How would they help to understand the conditioning of plural responses or of words beginning with a particular initial letter? Staats noted that the case of the operant conditioning of such classes of words was simply the strengthening of the part response, e.g., the s sound at the end of many plural words. Mandler suggested that such experiments examine the conditions under which it is appropriate to emit certain classes of responses (Skinner, 1957; Matarazzo, Saslow, and Pareis, 1960; Dulany, 1961). Jenkins applied Dulany's notion to the case of plurals; the subject continues to make responses from a form class until he runs out of items, after which he moves to another one. Jenkins indicated that this is a method for finding classses. Mandler indicated that he would like to know how classes are formed.

The third issue of the discussion was introduced by Russell who expressed disappointment that strategies of attack on the problem of purpose had not been discussed and that purpose had been dismissed, at least by some, as necessarily an S-R chain. He felt that more work is needed on the descriptive aspects of purpose and that the mediation hypothesis could be one of several fruitful sources of research possibilities. Melton observed that the basic question is whether such notions as set and determining tendency, which have more breadth than the concept of response, can be handled in terms of principles of habit formation, deterioration, forgetting, etc., which are appropriate to the single association. He added: Can we apply the concepts of stimulus and response to set? And, referring to the experiments by Kendler (cf. Kendler and Kendler, 1962) and by Luchins (1942), he answered that it is being done to some extent. He has work currently under way which is designed to develop search strategies in subjects who must look for a target. He has no data so far (Deese indicated that he had failed in a similar attempt; cf. Deese and Ormond, 1953) but wondered if this is a good direction to follow.

Deese pointed out that neither Luchins (1942) nor Duncker (1945) was an S-R theorist and that the source of their ideas was not S-R theory. But Luchins showed set to grow with repetition, thus illustrating an S-R principle, Melton replied. Miller objected that Luchins did not reinforce a response but rather a rule, and that S-R theorists wince when it is proposed that a rule or anything like it is reinforced. Deese added that S-R theorists may object to the notion of reinforcing a response that is not made. Miller could not see how reinforcement of a rule could be compatible with a peripheralist interpretation of response. Goss and Noble objected to these allegations relative to S-R theory, Noble indicating that the important point is that the response be identifiable rather than that it is peripheral or central.

Russell emphasized that there are other problems. He stressed that response selection can occur one way one time and a different way another time. Why does selection vary this way? He doubts that the r_g-s_g mechanism is well enough understood to be applicable to this problem or that it can be easily extended to the human case. Melton indicated that Russell desires experimenters to identify and manipulate sets by independent operations to avoid circularity. Russell agreed, saying that was why he had mentioned the experiments involving incidental learning and incentive change conditions.

Mandler said that as the increased incentive of the Bahrick (1954) experiment reduced incidental learning, it appears that energizing the organism also reduces the range of stimuli it will notice. The maintaining state of the organism not only leads to locomotion but makes a difference as to what it registers. Russell mentioned that Kausler, Trapp, and Brewer (1959) did not verify Bahrick's findings. Noble cited Berlyne's theory of attention (1951), and there was reference to another study of incidental learning by Bahrick (1957).

REFERENCES

Allport, F. H. (1924) *Social Psychology.* Boston: Houghton-Mifflin.

Bahrick, H. P. (1954) Incidental learning under two incentive conditions. *J. Exp. Psychol.,* **47,** 170–172.

Bahrick, H. P. (1957) Incidental learning at five stages of intentional learning. *J. Exp. Psychol.,* **54,** 259–261.

Berlyne, D. E. (1951) Attention, perception and behavior theory. *Psychol. Rev.,* **58,** 137–146.

Cofer, C. N. (1961) *Verbal learning and verbal behavior.* New York: McGraw-Hill.

Dashiell, J. F. (1928) *Fundamentals of objective psychology.* Boston: Houghton-Mifflin.

Deese, J., & Ormond, E. (1953) Studies of detectability during continuous visual search. *USAF Tech. Rep.,* WADC-TR-53-8.

Dulany, D. E., Jr. (1961) Hypotheses and habits in verbal "operant conditioning." *J. Abn. Soc. Psychol.,* **63,** 251–263.

Duncker, K. (1954) On problem-solving. (Trans. by L. S. Lees.) *Psychol. Monogr.,* **58,** No. 270.

Ebbinghaus, H. (1885). *Über das Gedächtnis.* Leipzig: Duncker & Humblot. (1913) H. Ruger & C. Bussenius (Trans.) New York: Teachers College.

Humphrey, G. (1951) *Thinking: An introduction to its experimental psychology.* New York: Wiley.

Kausler, D. H., Trapp, E. P., & Brewer, C. L. (1959) Intentional and incidental learning under high and low emotional drive levels. *J. Exp. Psychol.,* **58,** 452–455.

Kendler, H. H., & Kendler, T. S. (1962) Vertical and horizontal processes in problem solving. *Psychol. Rev.,* **69,** 1–16.

Luchins, A. S. (1942) Mechanization in problem solving. *Psychol. Monogr.* **54,** No. 248.

Matarazzo, J. D., Saslow, G., & Pareis, E. N. (1960) Verbal conditioning of two response classes: Some methodological considerations. *J. Abnorm. Soc. Psychol.,* **61,** 190–206.

Skinner, B. F. (1957) *Verbal behavior.* New York: Appleton-Century-Crofts.

Chapter 8

ONE-TRIAL LEARNING

Leo Postman

UNIVERSITY OF CALIFORNIA

When theoretical assumptions and experimental methods prove useful in the laboratory, they begin to be taken for granted. Periodic challenges to such firmly entrenched conceptions are to be welcomed. If the attack is successful, it prevents the perpetuation of an error; if it fails, it may nevertheless perform a useful function by forcing a reexamination and clarification of prevailing views. New experimental and analytic techniques developed in the course of the controversy may prove of lasting value regardless of the outcome of the debate. The current attack on the traditional conception of associative strength by exponents of one-trial learning (Estes, 1960; Rock, 1957) may have such beneficial effects in the long run. However, as we shall try to show, the facts and arguments which have been put forth thus far have failed to inflict decisive damage on the theory of incremental growth or to put the all-or-none hypothesis on a firm empirical footing.

BASIC ISSUES

Acquisition. The question at issue is whether associative strength increases by successive increments as a function of practice or changes in all-or-none fashion from zero to maximum. The fact that the number of correct responses increases with trials is consistent with both positions. On the incremental assumption each trial adds to the strength of the associations. According to the all-or-none hypothesis, each repetition provides an opportunity for new associations to be established in a single trial. The finding that items within a series are acquired at different rates also presents no basic difficulty for either interpretation. The rate at which habit strength grows may be expected to vary from item to item. Alternatively, the organism's input capacity restricts the number of different associations which can be established on a single trial. Whatever makes for differences in difficulty among items can be expected to influence gradual and all-or-none learning alike.

295

The common facts of acquisition do not permit a ready decision between the opposing points of view. Sharply different predictions are generated, however, when the effects of trials prior to the first correct response are considered. The incremental hypothesis clearly implies that habit strength is gradually increasing during these trials. The first correct response occurs when associative strength has been built up to the level required for performance. By contrast, the all-or-none hypothesis leads to the prediction that no learning occurs on the trials preceding the first correct response. An association must be either at zero or at full strength. The strength must be assumed to remain at zero as long as the subject continues to make errors; the appearance of the first correct response signals the shift from zero to full strength. Thus, we can seek a decision between the two conceptions of associative growth by investigating the effects of early unsuccessful trials on subsequent performance. The recent studies which we shall consider are based on precisely this line of reasoning.

Retention. The two theoretical views also lead to different deductions about the conditions of retention. According to incremental theory, retention varies directly with the degree of overlearning; i.e., associative strength continues to grow gradually beyond the point at which the correct response occurs for the first time. The probability of recall is then a direct function of the level of habit strength at the end of practice. In fact, resistance to forgetting may be used as a measure of habit strength. All-or-none theory, on the other hand, must predict that retention is not related to the degree of overlearning. Since the association is at full strength at the time of the first correct response, additional practice cannot strengthen it further and hence cannot increase resistance to forgetting. The evidence obtained in conventional studies of rote learning clearly supports the incremental interpretation. The positive relationship between degree of overlearning and retention is exhibited directly by the results of successive-probability analyses (Underwood, 1954): The more frequently an item has been anticipated in the past, the higher is the probability that it will be given correctly on the next trial. This relationship applies not only to retention from one acquisition trial to the next but to long-term recall as well (e.g., Underwood and Richardson, 1956). It is not surprising that exponents of the all-or-none hypothesis have begun to reexamine the classical relationship between the number of reinforcements and retention to determine whether or not it is "an artifact of the confoundings [e.g., between reinforcements and test trials] inherent in the usual experimental paradigm" (Estes, 1960, p. 220).

If the relationship between overlearning and retention is found to hold, it is possible to make a distinction, as Rock (1957) has done, between the effects of repetition on the "formation" and on the subsequent fixation of associations. He suggests that associations are formed in one trial, but once formed are strengthened by repetition. The distinction appears plausible but it greatly complicates the theoretical picture. It is admitted that associations are not at maximal strength at the time of their "formation." Instead, some intermediate amount of strength is attained in a single trial. Thus, the all-or-none conception is transformed into a some-or-none hypothesis. But how much is some? The ultimate usefulness of this version of one-trial theory will depend on the precision of the criteria for identifying the point at which an association is "formed," but not yet strengthened by repetition. Rock himself remains obscure on this point. In discussing the criterion for the existence of a "formed" association he suggests that "it probably makes more sense—in terms of what we usually mean by associative learning—not to define success by the easy test of immediate memory, but rather by the traditional [?] delayed test" (1957, p. 192). The statement implies that there are degrees to which associations can be "formed" since a test of immediate memory is not considered sufficiently sensitive. If so, the distinction between a one-trial and incremental conception has been all but obliterated. The un-amended all-or-none hypothesis is more parsimonious and more precise than Rock's two-stage theory, and also more vulnerable to disproof.

Response Competition. If the all-or-none conception of associative strength is correct, the probability of any given response to a stimulus must be either 0 or 1. It follows that it is impossible for more than one response to be associated with a stimulus. For example, if a subject first learns A-B and then A-C, the probability of B changes from 1 to 0, and that of C from 0 to 1. Thus, as Estes (1960) has clearly recognized, the concept of habit-family hierarchy is inconsistent with the all-or-none hypothesis. The argument may now be carried a step further. Since no more than one response can be associated with a stimulus at the same time, competition of responses at recall is impossible in principle. In the example above, B cannot be a competing response during the recall of C since the probability of B was reduced to 0 during the acquisition of A-C.

It is instructive to spell out the implications of this view for negative transfer and interference. Consider the A-B, A-C paradigm. The assumption that multiple associations of varying strength are not possible entails the following deductions: (1) Associative interference during the acquisition of A-C will be eliminated completely after the first correct anticipation of C since the first occurrence of C signals the displacement of B as an associate to A. (2) Proactive inhibition must be ruled out as a mechanism of forgetting. As indicated above, once B has been displaced by C, B cannot function as a competitor at recall. (3) By the same token, retroactive inhibition in the recall of B must always be 100 per cent if C has been given correctly at least once.

These implications of the concept of unitary association must be faced squarely. However improbable they may appear, they follow from the assumption that response probabilities are limited to the values of 0 and 1. It is hardly necessary to point out that the empirical evidence on negative transfer and interference is overwhelmingly in opposition to these deductions from all-or-none theory. For example, proactive inhibition is an established fact, retroactive inhibition is rarely complete, and interlist intrusions often recur intermittently during the relearning of a list. It is difficult to conceive of these basic facts of interference as artifacts inherent in the conventional groups-by-trials designs. All-or-none theory is likely to remain in serious trouble unless and until it can be made consistent with the facts of intertask interference.

In any event, it is clear that according to the hypothesis of unitary association forgetting which is produced by interference must occur on an all-or-none basis. Either a response is displaced by another response or it is not. If retention losses do not obey the all-or-none rule, e.g., if items that have been forgotten are recovered without intervening reinforcement, such incomplete forgetting cannot be attributed to interference. If forgetting is, indeed, incomplete, all-or-none theory is forced either to discard interference as a mechanism of forgetting or to supplement the hypothesis of unitary association with additional assumptions specific to retention.

Summary of Basic Issues. While many of the facts of acquisition are consistent with both an incremental and an all-or-none conception of associative strength, there are three empirical issues on which the two positions are in conflict. (1) Does any learning occur on the trials preceding the first correct response? An incremental position implies that it does whereas an all-or-none position must hold that it does not. (2) Is retention a function of the degree of overlearning? The answer is yes according to incremental theory, and no according to all-or-none theory. (3) Does forgetting occur on an all-or-none basis or can the degree of retention vary continuously? The conception of association as unitary implies that forgetting conforms to the all-or-none principle just as acquisition does. On the assumption that multiple associations of varying strength can be in competition with each other, incremental theory implies continuous variation in the degree of retention.

The experimental problems which we have identified are essentially the same as those considered by Estes (1960). As the issues are examined, it becomes clear that the differences between the two positions are far-reaching and encompass the characteristics of acquisition, transfer, and retention. There is, of course, a considerable body of evidence bearing on the points at issue. However, as Estes has pointed out, much of the available evidence consists of group trends and yields little information about performance of individual learners and about the "fate" of individual items from trial to trial. The empirical questions which flow from the current disagreement about the nature of association require an examination of the fine grain of the learning process. We shall turn next to some of the experimental studies which were designed to make such an examination possible. Before doing so, however, we must consider briefly some problems of definition and measurement which arise in the interpretation of studies of one-trial learning.

PROBLEMS OF DEFINITION AND MEASUREMENT

Associative Strength and Response Probability. Associative strength is a theoretical construct about which we make inferences on the basis of observed relationships between the conditions of practice and measures of response. It is essential that the rules of inference used by a given investigator be made explicit. There is a variety of theoretical positions—some more formal than others—which can be classified as incremental and which do not necessarily agree on these rules. However, Hull's (1943, 1951, 1952) conceptualization of habit strength ($_sH_R$) makes explicit some of the assumptions which are likely to be made by incremental theorists. (1) Habit strength is only one of the determinants of performance: $_sH_R$ interacts with other variables in determining $_sE_R$. (2) Observable responses occur only if and when the magnitude of the reaction potential exceeds a threshold value ($_sL_R$). Since reaction potential is a function of habit strength, no observable reactions will occur until habit strength has reached the value required for attainment of the reaction threshold. (3) The magnitude of the effective reaction potential oscillates from moment to moment. Observable responses will occur only on those occasions on which the effective reaction potential exceeds the threshold value. The higher the "true" value of the reaction potential the less likely it is that its momentary value will fall below the threshold of evocation (Hull, 1943, chap. 18).

For purposes of the present discussion, the critical implication is that the failure of a correct response to appear after one or more reinforcements does not compel the conclusion that habit strength has remained at zero. If the reaction potential has remained sufficiently below threshold, the probability of correct responses may approach zero even when allowance is made for momentary oscillation. Such an interpretation need not make the incremental position invulnerable to disproof. However, on the assumption of a threshold of response evocation a test of the hypothesis of incremental growth may require the determination of a functional relationship between the number of reinforcements and the changes in response probability. Such an analysis can be carried out for individual items and thus yield information which is relevant to the present issue.

Response Measures. Since changes in habit strength must be inferred from stimulus-response relationships, the choice of response measure becomes an important decision. In theories such as Hull's it is assumed that habit strength can manifest itself in a number of different ways, e.g., by changes in response probability, latency, and resistance to extinction. To the extent that these measures change at different rates, the functions relating them to habit strength must differ from each other. In verbal learning, recognition scores rise more rapidly than do recall scores. A common interpretation of this finding is that recognition requires a lower degree of associative strength than does recall. Thus, different measures are used to make inferences about the same underlying process, but they are assumed to be differentially sensitive to the changes in this process.

The question now arises with respect to what measure of response associative strength changes in an all-or-none fashion. If one assumes that different measures of learning are functions of the same associative process, all these measures should be perfectly correlated and obey the all-or-none rule. This conclusion follows from the principle that associative strength is at maximum if it is not zero. As soon as the shift from zero to maximum has occurred, any measure which can ever change as a function of practice must do so at once and to the fullest possible extent. Any two measures which do not covary perfectly in an all-or-none fashion cannot be determined by the same associative process. Such a conclusion would apparently have to be drawn about the relationship between response probability and latency, recall and recognition, etc.

In considering the problem posed by the relationship among different measures of learning, Estes comments that "information about concomitant changes in other variables would have no logical bearing upon conclusions pertaining to the one actually chosen for analysis in a given experiment" (1960, p. 220). He goes on to suggest that the all-or-none principle has to be tested separately for recall, recognition, latency, and so on. This position is logically defensible but reduces the theoretical usefulness of the concept of association. If concomitant changes in different measures of learning have no logical bearing upon one another, they obviously cannot be referred to a common associative process. Thus we would have to have as many definitions and laws of association as there are distinguishable measures of associative learning. Unless one accepts such a "pluralistic" conception of association, the observed lack of correlation among different measures of learning poses a serious empirical problem to all-or-none theory.

Independent Variables—Repetition and Reinforcement. To permit a decision between the incremental and all-or-none interpretations, the experimental arrangements must be such as to preclude mastery of the total learning task, e.g., correct anticipation of all the items in a list, after a single trial. Complete mastery in one trial would be consistent not only with the all-or-none position but could also be regarded as the limiting case of incremental growth under maximally favorable conditions. Unless some items are failed, it would be impossible to determine whether associations can vary in strength.

Given an experimental arrangement which produces less than complete mastery after a single trial, it is not critical for the present argument how one chooses to conceptualize the conditions of learning. One may describe the operations which produce successive improvements in performance as repetitions or reinforcements, depending on his theoretical predilections. In either case one can ask the question whether these operations produce gradual increments in associative strength or merely provide opportunities for increasing numbers of new associations to be acquired on an all-or-none basis. In short, neither the incremental nor the all-or-none position is necessarily tied to any specific assumptions about the necessary conditions of learning. The area of disagreement can be limited sharply to the quantitative development of the changes produced by practice. Thus, it is not altogether unreasonable that investigators with such radically different theoretical orientations as Rock and Estes appear to converge on a common view about the nature of associations.

We turn now to a review of the experimental investigations which have been stimulated by the recent critical reappraisals of the classical conception of associative strength.

ROCK'S STUDIES AND THE DROP-OUT METHOD

Rock's Studies. Rock's experiments were designed to determine whether any learning occurs on the trials prior to the first occurrence of the correct response. For this purpose a control group learning a list of paired-associates under standard conditions was compared with an experimental group for which all items missed on a given trial were replaced by new ones. Under the experimental condition each pair had to be learned in a single trial whereas the control condition permitted gradual acquisition. Whatever increments in associative strength occurred on unsuccessful trials would benefit the control group but not the experimental group. In the first of the experiments using this procedure single letters and double letters were used as stimuli and numbers as responses. For each subject a list of 12 pairs was drawn at random from the available pool of items. Replacements for the experimental subjects were also drawn at random from the remaining pool of items. Study trials and test trials were alternated until the criterion of one perfect recitation was reached. Since there was no difference between the experimental and control group in speed of learning to criterion, Rock concluded that the establishment of associations occurs in one trial and is not aided by repetition. In a second experiment lists of eight paired nonsense syllables were used. Again the subjects in the drop-out condition reached criterion no more slowly than did the members of the control group. Only the first experiment provides evidence which has a direct bearing on the hypothesis of one-trial associative learning. The results of the second experiment can be readily eliminated from consideration on both theoretical and empirical grounds.

Control of Response Learning. The failure to find a difference in favor of the control group in the experiment with nonsense syllables is surprising even on the assumption of one-trial learning. The mastery of a list of nonsense pairs requires the learning of unfamiliar response units as well as the association of these units with the appropriate stimulus terms. The control group which learns a constant set of items should have a considerable advantage in the response-learning stage if not in the associative stage of acquisition. Rock's results suggest the improbable conclusion that both response learning and association occur simultaneously on an all-or-none basis.

It appeared likely, therefore, that these results were due to artifacts inherent in Rock's procedure. Since Rock used a slow rate of presentation—each pair was exposed for three seconds, with a five-second interval between successive pairs—uncontrolled rehearsal is one probable source of error. In a recent study using nonsense syllables Lockhead (1961) reduced the rate of presentation to .75 second and obtained a highly significant difference in favor of the control group. The question also arises whether the drop-out procedure encouraged the experimental subjects to concentrate on a few pairs during each study trial and to ignore the rest. Such selective rehearsal would effectively shorten the list to be learned on any one trial. A reduction in the length of the list would, of course, be beneficial to learning, especially with difficult unfamiliar materials. This interpretation is supported by the results of a study by Postman (1962) in which all subjects were required to spell each stimulus and response term aloud during the study trials. Under these conditions the experimental subjects learned consistently and significantly more slowly than the control subjects. These results do not, of course, disprove the one-trial hypothesis or provide positive evidence for the incremental interpretation. Since the one-trial hypothesis concerns only the associative stage of learning, the use of materials which are known to require a substantial amount of response learning defeats the purpose of Rock's design.

In the case of word-number pairs, the role of response learning is minimized, and speed of acquisition may be assumed to reflect the rate at which associations are established. These materials were used in several investigations of the drop-out method subsequent to that of Rock. While there is some variation in the empirical findings, the amount of disagreement is not serious. Some studies, such as those of Clark, Lansford, and Dallenbach (1960) and Wogan and Waters (1959), fully confirm Rock's results. In four different experiments reported by Underwood, Rehula, and Keppel (1962) the standard control group consistently surpassed the experimental group but the differences were small and of borderline statistical significance. In contrast to the findings with nonsense syllables, procedural variations have only minor effects on the basic results obtained with word-number pairs. In the study of Clark, Lansford, and Dallenbach an increase in the rate of presentation over that used by Rock not only failed to give the control subjects an advantage but actually appeared to produce a difference in the opposite direction. In the experiments of Underwood, Rehula, and Keppel, the relative difference between the experimental and standard control groups did not vary appreciably as a function of exposure rate; the results remained comparable whether subjects merely observed the items on the study trials or read them aloud. Finally, the findings of Reed and Riach (1960) show that variations in instructions produce only marginal effects.

Item Selection. When response learning is eliminated, purely procedural artifacts such as uncontrolled rehearsal cannot account for Rock's results. We shall consider next a source of bias which is inherent in the experimental design itself—the opportunity afforded by the drop-out procedure for the selection of easy items. Since only missed pairs are removed from the list, it is possible and, indeed, likely that the substitute items are easier than those they replace. To the extent that such selection occurs, the task of the experimental subject is easier than that of the control subject. We shall not consider the first attempts at an evaluation of this bias (Rock and Heimer, 1959; Clark, Lansford, and Dallenbach, 1960), which cannot be considered conclusive. A discussion of these studies has been presented elsewhere (Postman, 1962). We shall limit ourselves instead to the findings of Underwood, Rehula, and Keppel (1962) who not only present clear-cut evidence for the systematic selection of items but also give a detailed analysis of the ways in which this bias operates in experiments using the drop-out method.

A precise assessment of item selection requires the use of two control groups rather than one. One control group (C1) learns the list presented initially to the experimental subjects whereas the other control group (C2) learns the list on which the experimental subjects reach criterion. A comparison between the two control groups provides a direct measure of the amount of effective item selection which has occurred during the drop-out procedure. This comparison is conservative since it will detect only those differences in difficulty which are not idiosyncratic. The extended design was used in the experiments of Underwood et al. The main findings and conclusions are as follows:

1. There is considerable consistency among subjects in the selection of items, and the final lists are significantly easier than the initial lists. The probability that a pair will be retained in the experimental list is predicted reliably by two independent indices of difficulty: (a) the proportion of correct responses given on the items in C1 and (b) ratings of the difficulty of the items given by an independent group.

2. The effects of item selection on the relative performance of an experimental and control (C1) subject depend on the difficulty of the initial list. If the initial list is easy, substitute items are likely to be more difficult than those they replace, and the experimental subject is at a disadvantage. When the initial list is difficult, however, new pairs are likely to be easier than those which were missed, and the opportunity for item selection favors the experimental subject. In agreement with this analysis, control (C1) subjects reach criterion substantially faster than the experimental subjects when the initial list is easy but not when it is difficult. Thus, only about half the subjects can contribute to the overall difference between the drop-out condition and C1.

3. When pairs are selected at random, the initial lists will vary widely in difficulty, and the opportunities for effective item selection will differ correspondingly from list to list. As a result, the mean differences in learning speed between the two control groups are likely to be of marginal significance. This is precisely the pattern of differences which was obtained.

This analysis leaves no doubt but that the drop-out procedure introduces a significant amount of item selection. It is also clear that the distribution of list difficulty in any given experiment will influence the observed differences between the drop-out and constant procedures. As Underwood et al. point out, minor contradictions among experiments are to be expected since the distributions of list difficulty are likely to vary. What is more important, however, the demonstrated bias inherent in the drop-out procedure precludes a decision between the one-trial and incremental interpretations. Our final evaluation of Rock's studies brings us back to the status quo ante. The facts are still consistent with both interpretations.

ESTES' "MINIATURE EXPERIMENTS"

The RTT Design. The experiments using the drop-out method leave open the question of whether any learning occurs prior to the first correct response. The "miniature experiments" developed by Estes (1960) are designed to provide an answer to the same question by a much simpler and more economical set of operations. The basic logic leading to the choice of experimental operations and measures is as follows. Let a group of subjects be given a single reinforced trial on a paired-associate item, with reinforcement simply defined as the paired presentation of the stimulus and response member. Suppose that this reinforcement increases the probability of a correct response from 0 to .50. Two interpretations of this result are possible: (a) The probability of a correct response has increased from 0 to .50 for each subject, or (b) the probability of a correct response has remained at 0 for half the subjects, and has increased from 0 to 1 for the other half of the subjects. These alternative interpretations follow from the incremental and all-or-none conceptions of associative strength, respectively. The argument is readily extended to the case in which more than one item is presented to the subjects; i.e., the probabilities would be as stated for each item learned by each subject. A decision between these alternatives is made possible by the introduction of a second test immediately following the first test without an intervening reinforcement, i.e., by use of an RTT paradigm. On the incremental assumption, correct responses on the second test should be equally likely after correct and incorrect responses on the first test, i.e., $C_2:C_1$ (correct on test 2, given a correct response on test 1) should be equal to $C_2:N_1$ (correct on test 2, given an incorrect response on test 1). On the all-or-none assumption, the probability of $C_2:C_1$ should be 1, and that of $C_2:N_1$ should be 0. If there is forgetting between test trials, $C_2:C_1$ may fall below unity but will remain substantially higher than $C_2:N_1$, which must be 0.

Conditional Response Probabilities. Certain assumptions implicit in this argument must be clearly recognized before the empirical evidence is considered.

1. As stated thus far, the argument takes no account of individual differences in learning ability among subjects and in difficulty among items. For an individual item, the prediction that $C_2:C_1 = C_2:N_1$ follows from the incremental hypothesis only if there are no individual differences in learning ability among subjects. If the increment in associative strength is higher for those who give a correct response on test 1 than for those who do not, then $C_2:C_1$ must be expected to be greater than $C_2:N_1$. In the example above, if the probabilities for successful and unsuccessful subjects are assumed to be .75 and .25, respectively, the predicted probabilities of $C_2:C_1$ and $C_2:N_1$ would also be .75 and .25. Exactly the same argument applies to differences among individual items, and of course, when the proportions of correct responses are summed over subjects and items. It is clear that the mere finding that $C_2:N_1$ is

reliably smaller than $C_2:C_1$ would not permit a decision between the incremental and all-or-none interpretations. However, the incremental hypothesis does imply that the associative strength for all items should be greater than zero after one reinforcement. Hence the critical question is not whether $C_2:C_1 > C_2:N_1$ but whether $C_2:N_1$ is actually zero.

2. Inferences about the distribution of associative strengths are based on the pattern of response probabilities observed on successive trials. If the conditional probabilities, $C_2:C_1$ and $C_2:N_1$, are to be used for this purpose, account must be taken of any changes in associative strength which occur between the first and second test trials. Specifically, if correct responses are strengthened by their occurrence on the first test trial, the probability of $C_2:C_1$ will increase relative to that of $C_2:N_1$. Similarly, if overt errors are strengthened by their occurrence on the first test trial, the probability of $C_2:N_1$ is reduced relative to that of $C_2:C_1$. Both types of learning are known to occur on test trials (Estes, Hopkins, and Crothers, 1960), and their effects will summate to inflate the observed differences between $C_2:C_1$ and $C_2:N_1$. Differential forgetting between test trials will also be reflected in the conditional probabilities. Thus, if weak items are forgotten faster than strong items, the difference between the two conditional probabilities is again increased. In fact, if $C_2:N_1$ is found to be equal to zero, this result may occur either because the initial associative strength was zero, or because it was reduced to zero by forgetting. These considerations add to the difficulty of interpreting differences between conditional probabilities. In apparent recognition of these difficulties, a different method of evaluating the results of RTT experiments has recently been proposed by Estes (1961). This new analysis will be discussed below after a consideration of the experiments which focused on the analysis of conditional probabilities.

3. The pattern of response probabilities is used to make inferences about *absolute* as well as relative associative strength. Thus, when $C_2:N_1$ is found to be zero, or near zero, it is concluded that the associative strength of items N_1 is zero. As we indicated earlier, this conclusion does not necessarily follow when a threshold of response evocation is assumed. The inference that the associative strength of missed items is zero can be made only if $C_2:N_1$ can be shown to be independent of the number of prior reinforcements.

Considerable caution is clearly required in the interpretation of conditional probabilities obtained in experiments using the RTT paradigm. Some of the available data will now be considered.

Results of RTT Experiments: Estes, Hopkins, and Crothers. Conditional probabilities are used as the major dependent variable in two experiments reported by Estes, Hopkins, and Crothers (1960). In experiment I, lists of eight paired-associates were used, with consonant syllables as stimuli and the numbers 1 through 8 as responses. For four of the pairs in the list the order of events was RTT, and for the remaining four pairs it was RTRT, i.e., all items were used on the first practice trial and on both test trials, but half the pairs were omitted on the second practice trial. Subjects were instructed to guess on the test trials if not sure about a number. Each subject learned two lists in succession.

With response frequencies pooled over subjects and lists, nearly 50 per cent of the items were correct on the first test trial after one reinforcement. On the second test trial, the proportion $C_2:C_1$ was .71, and the proportion $C_2:N_1$ was .09. The latter proportion is lower than would be expected on the basis of chance guessing (.125). It is concluded that acquisition of correct responses was on an all-or-none basis but that there was more retention loss than can be attributed to guessing shrinkage.

The question arises, of course, of whether the results can be attributed to differences in item difficulty. If C_1 items were considerably easier than N_1 items, a substantial difference in conditional probabilities would be expected. The authors consider this objection but reject it on the basis of the fact that for twice-reinforced items (RTRT) the proportion of $C_2:N_1$ is .46, which compares favorably with the effects of the first reinforcement on the full population of items. Thus it is argued that sets of items for which the proportions of correct responses are about the *same* after one and two reinforcements, respectively, must be equal in difficulty. We do not believe that such a conclusion is justified. In fact, a considerable difference in difficulty is indicated, especially in view of the fact that only four of the eight items in each list were presented to the subject on the second practice trial, i.e., the second reinforcement occurred under more favorable conditions of learning than the first. Thus, the observed difference between conditional probabilities may well have been a function of item selection.

The second experiment of Estes *et al.* was concerned with the course of retention from one test to the next as a function of the prior conditions of reinforcement. An elaboration of the earlier design was used. The conclusions of major interest are (a) retention did not vary with the number of preceding reinforcements (one versus two); (b) retention of both correct and incorrect responses did increase with the number of preceding tests; (c) retention losses did not occur on an all-or-none basis; i.e., when a correct response was followed by an incorrect one, the probability of its recurrence on a later trial remained above chance. It was hypothesized, however, that such response shifts did not represent forgetting but instead may be attributed to fluctuations in the stimulus context from series to series.

The finding most directly relevant to the hypothesis of one-trial learning is that retention from one test to the next is no greater after two reinforcements than after one. This result cannot, however, be considered decisive for two reasons: (a) The level of retention after one reinforcement was extremely high (.90), so that there was little room for improvement as a function of additional reinforcements; (b) each subject learned 12 successive lists, and the differences between one and two reinforcements may have been masked by massive transfer effects. A more extensive variation in the number of reinforcements with naïve subjects is required to obtain conclusive evidence on the relationship between overlearning and retention in this situation. The fact that retention losses do not occur on an all-or-none basis is at variance with the hypothesis of unitary association and requires the introduction of new assumptions about contextual effects if that conception is to be maintained.

Results of RTT Experiments: New Evidence. It is clear that differences in difficulty among items complicate the interpretation of results obtained in RTT experiments. (When items are summed over subjects, differences in learning ability produce an equivalent problem; both types of bias may be conveniently discussed under the heading of item selection.) Just as in the case of the drop-out procedure, items which are learned on the first trial are likely to be easier than those which are not. Even if the failed items develop some associative strength, they may remain too far below the threshold of evocation to appear as correct responses on subsequent tests.

We may come closer to a decision between the all-or-none and incremental interpretations if we consider the changes in $C_2:N_1$ as a function of the number of reinforced trials preceding the first test. According to the all-or-none interpretation, this value should remain at zero. Regardless of the number of preceding reinforcements, an item failed on the first test trial must be assumed to have zero associative strength and hence should not occur as a correct response on subsequent test trials. According to the incremental interpretation, and on the assumption of a threshold of response evocation, the value of $C_2:N_1$ should change significantly as a function of the number of prior reinforcements. If each reinforcement produces increments in associative strength, more and more items should approach or exceed the threshold as practice continues. Failures on test trials will continue as long as the range of strengths over which individual items oscillate includes values below the threshold. However, as the number of reinforcements increases, it should become more and more probable that an item which failed to exceed the threshold on one test trial will do so on a subsequent test trial. Thus, the value of $C_2:N_1$ should increase as a function of the number of reinforcements. The rate of increase should reflect the rate of associative growth; i.e., it should be faster for easy than for difficult items.

The exact form of the function relating the proportion $C_2:N_1$ to the number of prior reinforcements will depend, of course, on the distribution of item difficulty within a list. An inversion in the function may occur if the distribution of item difficulty is extremely skewed so that a majority of the responses has reached asymptotic strength whereas a few items still remain far below the threshold. However, if there is variation in item difficulty, the proportion $C_2:N_1$ should change significantly as a function of the number of prior reinforcements. Manipulation of the number of reinforcements over an extensive range will also make it possible to obtain clear evidence on the relationship between overlearning and retention from one test to the next.

Two experiments investigating performance on successive tests as a function of the number of preceding reinforcements were recently completed in the Berkeley laboratory.[1] The learning materials were lists of 20 paired-associates, with two-digit numbers as stimuli and highly familiar one-syllable words as responses. In Experiment I different groups of subjects were given one, two, four, or six reinforcements (presentations of paired stimulus and response terms) prior to a series of five successive test trials. The pairs were presented at a four-second rate on the study trials, and a four-second anticipation interval was used on the test trials. The interval between successive study and test trials was 20 seconds. There were 36 subjects in each of the groups. Experiment II was designed to check the temporal stability of the effects produced by increases in the number of reinforcements. The materials and procedure were the same as in Experiment I except that (a) a 20-minute interval was introduced between the first and second tests, and (b) only two groups were used which received one and four reinforcements, respectively.

We shall consider the results of Experiment I first. The numbers of correct responses on the first test increased directly with the number of reinforcements, from 16 per cent after one reinforcement to 67 per cent after six. There was considerable agreement from group to group with respect to the relative frequency with which different items were given correctly; i.e., the items in the list varied reliably in difficulty.

Figure 8-1 shows the cumulative numbers of new recalls on Test Trials 2 to 5. Only responses which had been missed on Test I and were given correctly for the first time on a given subsequent test are included. The absolute frequencies of such new correct responses rise to a peak after four reinforcements and then show some decline after six reinforcements. Since the opportunities for new recalls declined steadily, the rises in absolute frequency indicate clearly that shifts from incorrect to correct responses become more likely as the number of reinforcements is in-

[1] This research was supported by a grant from the National Science Foundation.

creased. New responses are added steadily on successive Test Trials, with the separation among groups remaining essentially unchanged.

The changes in the percentages of $C_2 : N_1$ which can be used for comparisons with earlier findings are shown in Figures 8–2 and 8–3. Separate functions are shown for easy and hard items as well as for the entire

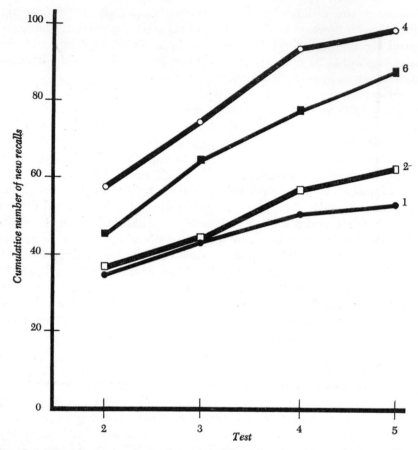

FIG. 8–1. Cumulative numbers of new recalls on Test Trials 2 to 5 after different numbers of reinforcements (Experiment I).

population of items in Figure 8–2. Figure 8–3 presents a parallel comparison of fast and slow subjects. The separation into easy and hard items was based on the probability of a correct response on Test 1, and the breakdown into fast and slow subjects on the total number of correct responses on Test 1. The over-all percentage of shifts from an incorrect to a correct response increases steadily with the number of reinforcements. Thus the prediction derived from incremental theory is confirmed. The values of $C_2:N_1$ are consistently higher and grow more rapidly for the easy than the hard items. The easier an item, the more rapidly it approaches the reaction threshold and the more likely it is that failure on a first test will be followed by success on a second test as a result of oscillation. These considerations also account for the fact that the function for fast subjects lies above that for slow subjects; i.e., the average

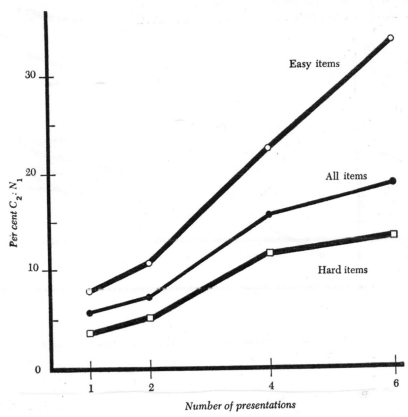

FIG. 8–2. Percentages of $C_2:N_1$ as a function of item difficulty and number of reinforcements prior to the first test (Experiment I).

rate of approach to the reaction threshold is more rapid for the former than for the latter. It should be noted, however, that the increases in the percentage of $C_2:N_1$ are negatively accelerated for the fast learners and positively accelerated for the slow learners. This difference in the shape of the functions may be attributed to an interaction between learning ability and item selection. At the highest levels of reinforcement, the items missed by the fast learners are likely to be the most difficult ones in the list whereas a wider range of difficulty will be represented among the failures of the slow learners. At that stage in learning, the average increment in associative strength produced by each new reinforcement is greater for the slow than for the fast subjects.

The question arises whether the rises in $C_2:N_1$ are simply due to an increase in guessing efficiency. It may be argued that as practice continues the responses in the list become increasingly available to the subject and guessing is more and more restricted to unlearned items. Several internal analyses make this interpretation untenable.

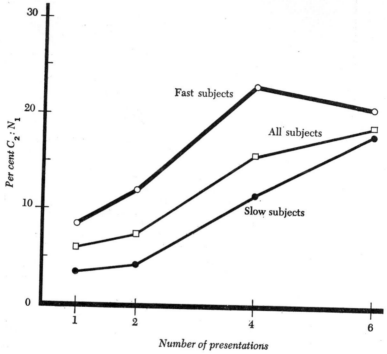

FIG. 8–3. Percentages of $C_2:N_1$ as a function of the number of reinforcements for fast and slow learners.

1. If new correct responses are merely successful guesses, they should be retained no better than new intra-list errors. A comparison was, therefore, made of the repetitions on Test 3 of correct responses and overt errors which were first given on Test 2. The results are shown in Table 8–1. There is a very large and consistent difference in the percentage of repetitions in favor of new correct responses. Since this difference does not show any decline as a function of the number of reinforcements, it appears quite unlikely that the rises in the proportion $C_2:N_1$ were inflated by an increasing number of successful guesses.

2. If subjects restrict their guesses increasingly to unlearned items as learning continues, the probability that $C_2:N_1$ responses had appeared as overt errors on Test 1 should also increase with the number of reinforcements. As Table 8–2 shows, the percentage of $C_2:N_1$ responses which had been given as overt errors on Test 1 decreases steadily with the number

Table 8–1

Per Cent Repetitions on Test 3 of $C_2:N_1$ Responses and of Errors Given for the First Time on Test 2

Number of reinforcements	$C_2:N_1$	New errors
Experiment I		
1	71.4	22.2
2	78.4	16.1
4	77.2	22.2
6	75.6	26.7
Experiment II		
1	87.0	27.8
4	81.2	25.5

Table 8–2

Per Cent $C_2:N_1$ Responses Which Were Also Errors

Number of reinforcements	Test 1	Test 2
Experiment I		
1	45.7	22.9
2	35.1	21.6
4	21.0	10.5
6	13.3	11.1
Experiment II		
1	31.8	4.5
4	14.0	6.1

of reinforcements. Thus, as learning progresses it becomes less rather than more likely that the proportion of new recalls is inflated by guessing. The finding is not unexpected since subjects' ability to recognize and reject incorrect responses should increase with practice.

3. As Table 8–2 shows, the percentage of $C_2:N_1$ responses which appear as overt errors on Test 2 also declines as a function of the number of

reinforcements. Repeated guesses are more likely to produce chance successes early than late in learning.

Our analyses offer no support for the assumption that increasingly efficient strategies of guessing are in any way responsible for the steady rise in the percentage of $C_2:N_1$. Quite on the contrary, there is every indication that $C_2:N_1$ responses are less and less likely to be represented in the subject's guessing repertoire as practice progresses.

The percentages of recall from one test to the next are shown in Table 8–3. The percentages $C_2:C_1$ increase steadily as a function of the

Table 8–3

Percentages of Items Recalled on Adjacent Tests and Percentages Correct on Test 3 as a Function of Prior Recalls

Number of reinforcements	Recall				Recovery	
	$C_2:C_1$	$C_3:C_2$	$C_4:C_3$	$C_5:C_4$	$C_3:N_2C_1$	$C_3:N_2N_1$
Experiment I						
1	71.3	84.5	89.2	93.3	31.4	1.9
2	81.2	93.2	92.9	94.0	30.8	1.3
4	86.3	89.5	92.7	90.6	42.9	6.1
6	90.1	91.4	94.6	94.5	52.1	11.5
Experiment II						
1	79.7	93.4	92.4	96.2	29.2	2.1
4	90.8	92.9	96.5	96.1	41.0	11.5

number of reinforcements; i.e., there is a pronounced relationship between degree of learning and retention. The convergence of the groups on the later tests may be attributed to the learning which occurred on successive test trials. The present results, obtained with naïve subjects, do not bear out the conclusion of Estes *et al.* that retention is independent of the number of reinforcements.

Retention losses did not occur on an all-or-none basis. Table 8–3 shows for each of the groups the proportions $C_3:N_2C_1$ (correct on test 3, given incorrect on test 2 and correct on test 1). These values are considerably higher than the proportions $C_3:N_2N_1$ and increase as a function of the number of reinforcements. Both these findings are contrary to the implications of the concept of unitary association.

The results of Experiment II are consistent with those of Experiment I. It will be recalled that in Experiment II a 20-minute interval was interpolated between the first and second test trials. As Figure 8–4 shows, the absolute number of new recalls was again substantially larger after one than four reinforcements although the opportunities for shifts from incorrect to correct responses were considerably fewer in the latter case. Table 8–4 lists the percentages of $C_2:N_1$. As in Experiment I, the percentages increase with the number of reinforcements and are higher for

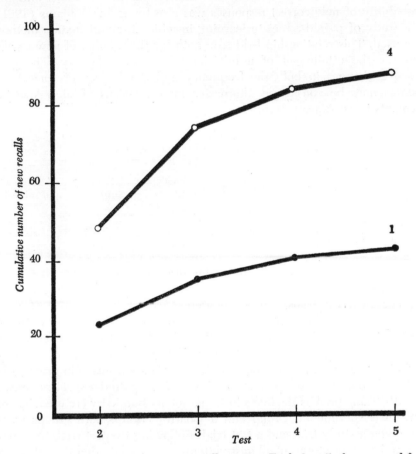

FIG. 8–4. Cumulative number of new recalls on Test Trials 2 to 5 after one and four reinforcements (Experiment II).

easy items and fast learners than for hard items and slow learners. The analyses designed to evaluate the changes in guessing efficiency agree with those in the first experiment (Tables 8–1 and 8–2). As Table 8–3 shows, retention during a 20-minute interval ($C_2:C_1$) is substantially greater after four reinforcements than after one. Finally, retention losses again do not occur in an all-or-none manner, and the probability that a forgotten item will be recovered increases with the degree of original learning. In summary, the two experiments agree in showing that the proportion of new recalls and the amount of retention from one test to the next increase with the number of reinforcements. These findings are in full agreement with the predictions derived from incremental theory and clearly at variance with an all-or-none interpretation.

A direct relationship between the number of presentations and the probability of new correct responses was also found by Williams (1961) in a study of paired-associate learning in which the anticipation method was used. This relationship held true both for the number of new recalls and for the attainment of a criterion of response latency. The progressive changes in both the frequency and the latency of correct responses may be considered alternative manifestations of successive increments in associative strength.

Table 8–4
Percentages of $C_2: N_1$ in Experiment II

Number of reinforcements	Easy items	Hard items	Fast subjects	Slow subjects	All items and subjects
1	5.9	2.2	5.8	2.2	3.8
4	19.8	16.2	32.5	11.7	17.5

Transfer Effects. It follows from the all-or-none hypothesis that there should be no transfer from learning trials which result in failure to subsequent learning trials. An association which has remained at zero strength obviously cannot influence the course of subsequent learning. On the incremental assumption, on the other hand, transfer effects may be expected even if the correct response has not been given. A study made in the Berkeley laboratory by Miss Marian Schwartz (in press) was designed to test these predictions. Lists of 18 paired-associates drawn from the same pool as the items in Experiments I and II were used. There were an Experimental Group and a Control Group. Both groups were first given a study trial and a test trial. Following the test trial, the stimulus and response terms of all missed items were re-paired in the list of the Experimental Group whereas the unlearned items were left intact in the list of the Control Group. Both groups were then given an additional study trial and two successive test trials. On the first of these tests the number correct on the critical items was significantly greater for the Control Group than for the Experimental Group. On the second test trial, the proportions $C_2: C_1$ and $C_2: N_1$ were higher for the Control Group than for the Experimental Group. The magnitudes of these differences are comparable to those obtained in Experiment I between the groups given one and two reinforcements. Thus, the results show that learning trials which result in failure may nonetheless influence the rate of subsequent improvement. The operations of the present experiment do not make it possible to decide to what extent the observed differences are due to positive transfer effects under the control condition and negative transfer effects under the experimental condition. Neither of these effects would, however, be consistent with the all-or-none interpretation.

Two experiments by Underwood and Keppel (1962) equally support the conclusion that associative strength is built up on trials which fail to produce a correct response. In the first investigation an Experimental Group was given a study trial and a test trial on a list of 11 paired-associates, with bigrams as stimuli and single letters as responses. All items that were missed on the test trial were immediately presented again for a second study and test trial. The same critical items were presented to a Control Group which had, however, been exposed to an entirely different list on their first study and test trials. In agreement with the prediction of incremental theory, the Experimental Group recalled more critical items than did the Control Group. However, the possibility could not be ruled out that the Control Group was at a disadvantage because of interference from the first list of unrelated items although the analysis of overt errors gave no indication of such an effect.

A second investigation was, therefore, carried out in which the procedure of re-pairing the stimulus and response terms of missed items was used. The stimuli were again 11 bigrams with the digits 1 through 11 as responses. For one Experimental Group (E1) the treatment was the same as in the earlier experiment whereas for another Experimental Group (E2) the stimulus and response terms of the failed items were re-paired prior to the second study and test trials. According to incremental theory, associative tendencies built up during the first study trial should favor the performance of group E1 and produce negative transfer for group E2. In the recall of the critical items group E1 surpassed group E2 but the difference was not significant. Further analysis showed that the re-paired items were significantly easier than those which had been missed and were left intact. Such a systematic difference in item difficulty was to be expected since items which are failed are *ipso facto* selected for difficulty. The fact that in spite of this bias against it, group E1 performed as well if not better than group E2 is consistent with an incremental interpretation and certainly lends no support to the one-trial hypothesis.

Reanalysis of RTT Results: Joint Probabilities. As was mentioned earlier, Estes (1961) has recently presented a new mathematical analysis of the RTT paradigm with a view to providing precise tests of the incremental (linear) model. This analysis shifts from a consideration of conditional probabilities such as $C_2:N_1$ to an evaluation of the joint probabilities of correct and incorrect responses on successive test trials on the assumption that these probabilities can vary continuously. The basic form of the argument is as follows. Let the probability of a correct response (p_1) on Test 1 be equal to θ, and the probability of an incorrect response (p_0) be equal to $1 - \theta$. Since no reinforcements are given between test trials, it may be assumed that the probabilities remain the same on Test 2. On this assumption, the joint probabilities of correct and incorrect responses are those shown in the first column in Table 8–5. The prediction which is critical for purposes of the present discussion is that $p_{10} = p_{01}$. Estes goes on to show that this requirement does not change even if account is taken of differences in item difficulty (or

Table 8–5
Proportions of Different Combinations of Responses in RTT Experiments

Predicted*	Estes*	Observed							
		Experiment I†				Experiment II†		Schwartz	
		1	2	4	6	1	4	Exp.	Controls
$p_{11} = \theta^2$	.238	.114	.258	.438	.606	.136	.562	.106	.196
$p_{10} = \theta(1 - \theta)$	.147	.046	.060	.069	.067	.035	.057	.049	.051
$p_{01} = (1 - \theta)(\theta)$	.017	.049	.052	.079	.062	.032	.067	.044	.061
$p_{00} = (1 - \theta)^2$	.598	.792	.630	.414	.265	.797	.314	.800	.691

* From Estes, 1961, p. 74.
† 1, 2, 4, and 6 refer to number of reinforcements prior to tests.

differences in learning ability among subjects). If there are subsets of items (or subjects) which vary with respect to the values of θ, the requirement that $p_{10} = p_{01}$ would hold for each of these subsets and hence for the total population of items. A similar argument shows that the requirement does not change if learning on test trials is assumed. Thus, some of the sources of ambiguity in the interpretation of conditional probabilities are removed.

The second column in Table 8–5 shows the values of observed proportions obtained by Estes in a recent experiment. In this experiment, the RTT design was used, but it should be noted that the critical items were introduced, "one per trial, into a larger list, the composition of which changed from trial to trial in an unpredictable (from the subject's viewpoint) manner" (Estes, 1961, p. 75). Clearly p_{10} is not equal to p_{01}, and it appears that the incremental model cannot handle the data. If it is assumed that there are individual differences in retention loss (for items or subjects), the requirement that $p_{10} = p_{01}$ no longer holds. However, the obtained near-zero value of p_{01} could be predicted only if learning were close to perfect or forgetting almost complete. Since neither of these assumptions is reasonable, in the light of the other proportions, Estes considers the empirical results incompatible with the predictions from the incremental model. The data appear to favor an all-or-none model supplemented by an assumption of imperfect retention.

Let us suppose that the assumptions underlying the analysis of joint probabilities are valid. It then becomes important to determine over what range of conditions the empirical facts fail to meet the requirements of the incremental model. The predicted equality of the proportions p_{10} and p_{01} also fails to hold in the studies reported in Estes' earlier papers (Estes, 1960; Estes, Hopkins, and Crothers, 1960). In the remaining columns of Table 8–5 we present the appropriate proportions obtained in our recent experiments. There are eight independent determinations of these proportions—four groups in Experiment I, two groups in Experiment II, and two groups in Miss Schwartz's experiment. In each of these eight cases the observed proportions p_{10} and p_{01} are very nearly equal or differ only by a very small amount. This uniformity is especially noteworthy since different degrees of learning and different experimental procedures are represented. Thus, the requirements of the incremental model are clearly met by our data.

It is not possible at this time to offer a satisfactory explanation of the discrepancy between Estes' findings and our own. From what has been reported, it is clear that there are important differences in materials and procedures. The conditions of intra-list and interlist interference deserve especial attention since Estes used counterbalanced designs in some of his studies and a continually changing list in the most recently reported experiment. It is clear that the empirical inadequacy of the incremental model is still far from being a generally established fact. The discrepancies in experimental findings must be resolved before a final decision about the model is made.

CONCLUSION

Examination of the available evidence has failed to convince us that the incremental conception of associative strength has been challenged decisively. The results of Rock's studies have been shown to suffer from a fatal methodological flaw and can therefore be considered as inconclusive. There are compelling grounds for questioning both the generality and the interpretation of Estes' findings. Our own studies using the RTT paradigm give consistent support to the incremental interpretation.

The methodological obstacles to a clear-cut test between the incremental and all-or-none positions remain formidable. A persistent difficulty appears to stem from the problem of item selection which has intruded itself into all the current experimental procedures aimed at a decision between the opposing points of view. This fact is not surprising since experimental analysis has focused on the question of whether learning occurs prior to correct performance. This question reflects the crucial point of disagreement between the incremental and all-or-none positions. Empirical answers have, perhaps inevitably, been based on comparisons among items which are acquired at different rates under constant conditions of practice. Thus, item selection was entailed by the formulation of the experimental questions. The resulting bias has often made it difficult, if not impossible, to arrive at a clear-cut interpretation of the facts. Standardization of materials for difficulty may help, but norms of extremely high reliability will be required if precise quantitative predictions about the rate of associative growth are to be tested. Deductions from a particular conceptual model about the probable or possible consequences of item selection are not in the long run a satisfactory substitute for experimental control over this variable. The development of new designs which avoid the problem of item selection altogether would constitute a major methodological step toward the resolution of the present issue.

The discussion has also been hampered by the fact that deductions from highly specific models have been used to test the implications of the incremental conception in its broadest sense. For example, the analysis of joint probabilities in the RTT experiment follows from the premises of the linear model in statistical learning theories. The relationship between this analysis and the deductions which follow from such incremental theories as Hull's remains to be explored. As we have emphasized, the concept of response threshold has not been considered in the derivation of predictions which are said to follow from incremental theory. Yet this concept is not only of central importance in Hull's theoretical system but is assumed explicitly or implicitly by many investigators who accept an incremental interpretation of associative growth but are not committed to any formal theoretical model. The incremental position which is part of the warp and woof of much of contemporary learning theory takes too many forms to be testable by a single experimental paradigm. Theories die hard, and crucial experiments are rarely successful in psychology. To the extent that the current controversy has led to an increasingly careful examination of the details of the learning process, it has served a useful purpose.

REFERENCES

Clark, L. L., Lansford, T. G., & Dallenbach, K. M. (1960) Repetition and associative learning. *Amer. J. Psychol.*, **73**, 22–40.

Estes, W. K. (1960) Learning theory and the new "mental chemistry." *Psychol. Rev.*, **67**, 207–223.

Estes, W. K. (1961) New developments in statistical behavior theory: Differential tests of axioms for associative learning. *Psychometrika*, **26**, 73–84.

Estes, W. K., Hopkins, B. L., & Crothers, E. J. (1960) All-or-none and conservation effects in the learning and retention of paired associates. *J. Exp. Psychol.*, **60**, 329–339.

Hull, C. L. (1943) *Principles of behavior*. New York: Appleton-Century.

Hull, C. L. (1951) *Essentials of behavior*. New Haven, Conn.: Yale University Press.

Hull, C. L. (1952) *A behavior system*. New Haven, Conn.: Yale University Press.

Lockhead, G. R. (1961) A re-evaluation of one-trial associative learning. *Amer. J. Psychol.*, **74**, 590–596.

Postman, L. (1962) Repetition and paired-associate learning. *Amer. J. Psychol.*, **75**, 372–389.

Reed, J. C., & Riach, W. D. (1960) The role of repetition and set in paired-associate learning. *Amer. J. Psychol.*, **73**, 608–611.

Rock, I. (1957) The role of repetition in associative learning. *Amer. J. Psychol.*, **70**, 186–193.

Rock, I., & Heimer, W. (1959) Further evidence of one-trial associative learning. *Amer. J. Psychol.*, **72**, 1–16.

Schwartz, M. (in press) Transfer from failed pairs as a test of one-trial vs. incremental learning. *Amer. J. Psychol.*

Underwood, B. J. (1954) Speed of learning and amount retained: A consideration of methodology. *Psychol. Bull.*, **51**, 276–282.

Underwood, B. J., & Keppel, G. (1962) One-trial learning? *J. verb. Learng. and verb. Behav.*, **1**, 1–13.

Underwood, B. J., Rehula, R., & Keppel, G. (1962) Item selection in paired-associate learning. *Amer. J. Psychol.*, **75**, 353–371.

Underwood, B. J., & Richardson, J. (1956) The influence of meaningfulness, intralist similarity, and serial position on retention. *J. Exp. Psychol.*, **52**, 119–126.

Williams, J. P. (1961) A test of the all-or-none hypothesis for verbal learning. Ph.D thesis, Yale University.

Wogan, M., & Waters, R. H. (1959) The role of repetition in learning. *Amer. J. Psychol.*, **72**, 612–613.

COMMENTS ON PROFESSOR POSTMAN'S PAPER[1]

George A. Miller

HARVARD CENTER FOR COGNITIVE STUDIES

A few weeks ago I saw an advertisement that described the current "information explosion" and suggested that International Business

[1] The preparation of these comments has been supported by funds given to Harvard University for the Center for Cognitive Studies by the Ford Foundation, the Carnegie Corporation, the National Science Foundation, and the National Institute for Mental Health. The author is grateful to Dr. Nancy C. Waugh for numerous discussions of the issues here considered.

Machines would muffle it by high-speed data processing. I hope they do. My shelves and files are already so full I don't know where to put all the shrapnel that comes my way. I cannot really feel sorry that so many more people are now competent to write books and articles, but I am sorry that I can't read fast enough to keep up with them all.

In this dilemma, which we all face, there seems to me no alternative—IBM notwithstanding—but to narrow progressively one's range of interests as the years go by and attractive young research problems grow into impossibly fat fields that fill whole wings in the library. For these topics-we-should-know-about-but-can't-follow-firsthand we must rely increasingly on outside help—on abstracts, reviews, summaries, and conferences such as this.

I have found that one of the best ways to keep in touch with more than I can read is to exploit my friends. I tell them what I am working on and thinking about, they say what it reminds them of, and if they mention something unfamiliar, I try to find out about it. This is a good system if you are lucky enough to have the right kind of friends. And you need to know them well enough that you can trust their judgment. That is to say, you have to feel that if you personally looked at all the articles and did all the research they have done, you would arrive at the same conclusions they did.

When I try to define my own interests, in order to decide what I will pursue for myself and what is better delegated to friends, the core of it seems to have something to do with communication in general, and with linguistic communication in particular. As everyone today realizes, there is a psychological price we pay to communicate with our fellow men. We accept their categories, their ways of splitting the world up into things and events, their ways of labeling and evaluating. The fact that we invest so much time and faith in linguistic communication has many important effects on all our other psychological processes.

It is obvious, perhaps, that anyone who has this as the core of his interests must keep informed about verbal learning. Verbal learning, however, is not my first love, and as the field grows progressively larger and more technical I feel more and more an outsider. I make these personal remarks by way of introduction, because you should know that I have no special competence or familiarity either with this general field or with this specific research topic. All I can offer you is a point of view.

One of the friends I rely on to keep me *au courant* in verbal learning is the author of the present paper. In the twenty years I have known Leo Postman I have felt an ever-growing respect and affection for him and for his integrity as a scientist, and I arrive at the task of criticizing his ideas with a certain amount of embarrassment. Since he is one of my major sources of information, it would be impertinent, not to say reckless, for me to take issue with him. So let me begin by saying that I endorse all he says in his paper. If Postman says that one-trial learning is nonsense, then it is nonsense and that is all there is to it. Clark Hull is still our leader.

I must confess, however, that this disposal of the issue saddens me. Estes is another friend whose judgments I am accustomed to rely on; when two of my friends disagree this way, it endangers the very foundations of my parasitic policy. But more than that, I had felt a certain freshness in this new approach, and I am sad that we have no place for it.

In the interests of objectivity, of course, you should recognize that my sadness may have a personal tinge. Several years ago W. J. McGill and I considered what might happen in verbal learning if correct recalls strengthened an association, but failures to recall had no effect at all (Miller and McGill, 1952). If I understand him correctly, I believe this is the position that Rock thinks his data support. But Postman feels this some-or-none approach is almost indistinguishable from an incremental theory plus a threshold, so McGill and I, along with Rock, escape the major thrust of his criticism. His argument is aimed much more directly at the kind of all-or-none hypothesis Estes has recently been considering. My regret, therefore, is not inspired by any personal loss.

There is one puzzling aspect to Postman's success in disposing of the all-or-none theory. I could not help but wonder how intelligent, conscientious psychologists could have been so taken in by a theory he demolishes so completely. After studying his refutation, however, I think I know one reason for its great force. Postman has taken the most extreme, the strictest possible version of an all-or-none theory and has permitted it no ancillary laws to soften its black-and-white contours. The stark simplicity of the theory he considers is quite striking; it eases greatly the problem of disproving it. There is no reason to think he destroyed a straw man, however. Or, if the man was made of straw, it was Estes, not Postman, who set him up.

Now, since I agree entirely with Postman's conclusions, I should probably stop and let the group discussion take its course. But I feel a social obligation to say something more. Consequently, I have—perhaps unwisely—let myself speculate about how an all-or-none theory might be saved and armored against the criticisms that are so devastating to the more extreme versions.

Let me describe for you a class of all-or-none theories that I will call *junk box theories,* since that name is ugly enough to be safe from kidnappers. Those of you who have worked around a shop know what I mean by a junk box; it holds all those odds and ends of nails and washers and coat hangers and sealing wax—junk, in short—that you have no use for just now but that may come in handy some day. There is one property of the junk box that you should note, namely, that either an object is in the box or it is not in the box. No object can be partly in the box and partly somewhere else.

Consider now how you find something in the junk box. You look in, and if it is something you have put there recently, you find it near the top. If you don't see it, you shove things around a bit. Notice that you may not find it even when it is there. Or, if there are several identical items in the box, you may find what you want very quickly. Thus it makes perfectly good sense to talk about a retrieval probability different from 0 or 1, even though the item's presence in the box is an all-or-none affair. And it makes equally good sense to talk about variations in the search time, or latency, required to find something.

In short, therefore, I see nothing illogical or untidy about an all-or-none theory that is pluralistic, to use Postman's fortunate term. It is a very strong and optimistic assumption that the various measures—latency, recall probability, recognition probability, resistance to extinction or to forgetting, etc.—all are nothing but different ways to measure a single underlying variable. Postman's criticism that response measures are not in fact perfectly correlated should be aimed at monistic conceptions of association, not at all-or-none conceptions.

The question of which measure of learning you use is quite relevant to the conclusions you draw about one-trial learning. For example, Nancy C. Waugh has recently done an experiment (unpublished) dropping out paired-associates as soon as they were recalled for the first time; the Waugh procedure is the exact opposite of the Rock procedure. Although it is approximately true that, as Rock should predict, every trial looked like a first trial from the point of view of a *recall* measure, casual reports indicated that the subjects were quite good at *recognizing* which pairs were new, which had been seen before. Something had certainly been learned during the unsuccessful presentations, but whatever it was did not add much $_sE_R$.

As a matter of fact, monistic storage systems would seem to be the exception, rather than the rule. Storage devices usually have at least two different kinds of problems: how to get a new item in, and how to find an old item later. (Or, to use an older terminology, the problems are first to lay down the trace and later to communicate with it.) Junk boxes, libraries, warehouses, telephone systems, filing cabinets, etc., all share these two distinct aspects. It is difficult to believe that our nervous system has unified these two separate processes of verbal learning and recall in such a way that all performance measures would inevitably reflect a single magnitude, $_sE_R$, somewhere in the system.

Newell, Shaw, and Simon (1958) have used list structures to organize a computer's memory when they use it to simulate human cognitive processes. A list is a symbolic junk box; any set of symbols can be collected there. And the order of the items on the list is a plausible, nonprobabilistic analogue of a habit-family hierarchy. Items high on the list can be found sooner than low items, yet the all-or-none character of items on the list is still preserved.

In order to illustrate in the briefest way the kind of theory that can be developed on this foundation, I want to mention EPAM I (Elementary Perceiver and Memorizer). This is a theory that Feigenbaum and Simon (1959) developed to account for the serial position curve in rote serial memorization. The theory has four basic postulates that can be paraphrased as follows:

M0: The central processing mechanism operates serially and is capable of doing only one thing at a time.

M1: Processing an item on a serial list of items requires a substantial time.

M2: The central processing mechanism has a temporary memory of a very limited form.

M3: Items with unique features are processed first and serve as anchor points.

In commenting on these "macroprocessing postulates," Feigenbaum (1959) writes, "M0 establishes a serial processer, capable of doing only one thing at a time; this creates a need for deciding the order in which items will be processed, i.e., an attention focus, and M3 establishes a mechanism for determining this order. M2 provides a temporary storage while the processes in M1 are permanently fixating the item."

The four postulates are all psychologically plausible and can be investigated individually. M0 and M2 taken together are necessary conditions for the phenomenon of attention, a phenomenon that has become increasingly interesting to both experimental psychologists and neurophysiologists during the past decade. M2 calls for exactly the kind of short-term memory that Lloyd Peterson has described in his contribution to this conference. It seems to me entirely consistent with Peterson's own experiments to assume that counting backward interrupts rehearsal and prevents the processing called for in M1. What that processing might be, of course, is the central problem of associative learning. Postulate M3 leaves the features that determine uniqueness for further definition; Feigenbaum and Simon assume, quite reasonably, that the terminal positions on the list are unique. But one would also expect that other items could be made unique by printing them in red (Von Restorff, 1933), or by making some items much easier to learn (McGourty, 1940), or by explicit instructions (Raffel, 1936), etc.

These four postulates describe what can be conveniently called a strategy for rote memorization. Feigenbaum and Simon were able to demonstrate that any device that satisfies these postulates will develop a serial position curve of the general form we have learned to expect (McCrary and Hunter, 1953). They wrote a computer program to comply with M0-M3 and so verified their predicted result. M3 makes the first and last items into anchor points; other items build slowly out from them, thus generating the usual serial position curve. Anyone who has puzzled over Hull's explanation based on Lepley's hypothesis about the inhibition of delay should be pleased by the elegant simplicity of Feigenbaum and Simon's account. The implication of EPAM I is that a serial position curve does not reflect any deep or fundamental properties of human memory, but is a simple consequence of the strategy most people will adopt when confronted with this particular problem.

On the basis of this initial success, Feigenbaum went on to EPAM II, which included "microprocessing postulates" that described what he thought might be going on during the fixation process called for in M1. I will not try to develop these; it would take too long and other postulates might well be substituted for the ones that Feigenbaum chose. But I should remark that some of his assumptions have features in common with some of the abstract ideas presented here by Underwood, but expressed in a far more concrete form to make them intelligible to the computer. (A computer is a completely flexible instrument that will do whatever you program it to do; I do not wish to leave an impression that computer simulation commits the user to any particular psychological theory—incremental, all-or-none, or anything else.)

Notice, incidentally, that the Feigenbaum and Simon theory assumes that subjects will rehearse a few items and let the others go unnoticed on each trial. Postman's experimental demonstration that if you interfere with a rehearsal strategy, you destroy the Rock effect is strong evidence that many people do follow an EPAM I strategy of memorization. Postman refers to this rehearsal strategy as an artifact, but if Feigenbaum and Simon are on the right track it may well be the most important fact of all.

If you pause to consider M0-M3, you may notice that I have worded them to make no explicit reference to rote memorization. In particular, they could describe the process of copying equally as well as the process of memorizing. In that case M0 is satisfied because we can write only one thing at a time; M2 can be satisfied if the situation is such that we can only copy a limited amount of material before we must refer back again to the original text. If we could just create an experimental situation satisfying M1 and M3, too, we should be able to produce a serial position curve for copying.

Two of our graduate students at Harvard, Charles Harris and John McMahon, have verified this speculation in an informal experiment. They used double syllables as items and speeded up a memory drum in order to make the writing time substantial by comparison with the exposure time, thus satisfying M1. And they required their subjects to reconstruct the list in the correct order, thus creating a need for serial order and for anchor points, so M3 was also satisfied. Under these conditions, the number of presentations required before each syllable was copied in its correct slot showed the traditional serial position curve. It should be noted, incidentally, that writing leaves an all-or-none trace. The letters are not written a little more heavily each time around; they are either written or not written.

If one accepts EPAM I as a plausible explanation of the serial position curve, the crucial question, of course, concerns the nature of the processing that goes on when information is transferred from a short-term to a long-term storage system, as postulate M1 assumes. Feigenbaum has proposed one plausible set of microprocesses. Others might be phrased in terms of the consolidation of traces, or the integration of responses, or a search for mediators, or a striving after meaning, or the formation of conditioned reflexes, etc., or in terms of some combination of these. This is the question to which our experimental ingenuity should be addressed.

In my opinion, the issue of incremental versus all-or-none theories might better be formulated as a question: When the processing (whatever it is) is interrupted, can it later be resumed at the same point, or must it be started over afresh? If it can be resumed with little loss, the learning will look incremental. If interruption destroys all that has been done—as it might if we were, say, searching for some explicit mediator—then the learning will fit better into an all-or-none description. According to this view, the basic problem is to determine which kinds of processing are interruptable, and to develop techniques for determining which kind of processing a subject is doing in any particular experimental task.

One of Postman's strongest criticisms of the extreme all-or-none theory is this: If A is associated with B with a probability of 1.0, then A is associated with everything else with a probability of 0. This restriction to a single bond is clearly intolerable, both on empirical and logical grounds. It is not, however, inescapable. Junk box systems, such as the Newell, Shaw, and Simon theory of list structures, seem to avoid this problem yet remain in the realm of all-or-none theories. The stimulus is the name of the list; the several responses are the items, as ordered, on the list.

It should also be noted that in many experimental situations S and R may not themselves be unitary, integrated psychological units. Some associations among their component parts may first be necessary before they can be associated with each other. And so we must assume that a package of associated elements—a cluster or a chunk—can itself function as an element that can be associated with some other package of associated elements. That is to say, the associations a subject forms are probably numerous and *hierarchically organized.* To continue the metaphor, we can have junk boxes filled with junk boxes. This process of forming associations between associations, rather than between stimuli and responses, is quite characteristic of complex associative learning and serves to distinguish it from simple S-R learning. But this point is more forcefully made in the paper on mediation contributed to this conference by James Jenkins.

A learner is not finished when he has formed a single, simple bond from S to R. The learning process is far more complicated than that. If we want to know what could be going on in an all-or-none system during overlearning, a first guess might be that we are forming hierarchical patterns of associations. In the terms used by Kevin Lynch (1960) to describe the images people have of their cities, memory systems become progressively more rigid as more and more paths are learned between one part and another. Professor Olson, whose detour behavior Wallace Russell described, was not following a simple chain leading strictly from S's to R's; he must have had some supraordinate, associative structure imposed upon his image of his city, something that kept him oriented toward the postponed parts of his itinerary. Long after we are able to get along in a minimal way we go on adding new associations, making our associative structures ever stronger, more rigid, and more resistant to forgetting. Once we allow ourselves the luxury of these higher-order associations, most of the criticisms Postman aims at the extreme version of the all-or-none theory seem to lose their destructive force.

In his conclusion Postman remarks that theories die hard. Sometimes I suspect that they never die. They don't even fade away. They just become uninhabited. For the time being, however, both of the theories we have been comparing here seem well populated by vigorous, opinionated exponents. The future looks interesting indeed.

REFERENCES

Feigenbaum, E. A. (1959) An information processing theory of verbal learning. *Rand Report P-1817.* Santa Monica, Calif.: RAND Corporation.

Feigenbaum, E. A., & Simon, H. A. (1959) A theory of the serial position effect. *CIP Working Paper No. 14,* Carnegie Institute of Technology, Graduate School of Industrial Administration, Pittsburgh.

Lynch, K. (1960) The image of the city. Cambridge: Technology Press & Harvard University Press.

McCrary, J. W., & Hunter, W. S. (1953) Serial position curves in verbal learning. *Science*, 117, 131–134.

McGourty, M. C. (1940) Serial position effects in learning as a function of interfering associations. M.A. thesis, University of Iowa. Cited by J. A. McGeoch & Irion, A. L. (1952) *The psychology of human learning.* (2nd ed.) New York: Longmans.

Miller, G. A., & McGill, W. J. (1952) A statistical description of verbal learning. *Psychometrika*, 17, 369–396.

Newell, A., Shaw, J. C., & Simon, H. A. (1958) The elements of a theory of human problem solving. *Psychol. Rev.*, 65, 151–166.

Raffel, G. (1936) Two determinants of the effect of primacy. *Amer. J. Psychol.*, 48, 654–657.

Restorff, H. von. (1933) Über die Wirking von Bereichsbildungen im Spurenfeld. *Psychol. Forsch.*, 18, 299–342.

SUMMARY OF CONFERENCE DISCUSSION

Several questions were directed to points of the Feigenbaum-Simon model as described by Miller in his discussion. Brown and Underwood asked why the terminal positions in a list were considered to be unique, rather than other positions. Miller said the justification was perceptual. Melton pointed out that the model assumes that the subject chooses not to study each item in a serial list to an equal degree on each trial; yet in serial learning studies attempts are made to control this aspect of the subject's behavior. A number of other comments expressed concern about the methods used in the experiments by Waugh and by Raffel.

To a question by Wickens, Miller referred to M2 as a memory-span process; certain materials are held in memory briefly and then discarded. Noble suggested that if the Hunter-McCrary results are predicted by EPAM I this is a prediction of results expressed in percentages; he wondered about the generality of EPAM I, referring especially to the problem of individual differences. Melton added that the properties of items which are unique could vary from person to person. Miller said, in reply, that Feigenbaum had predicted the learning curve for this situation.

Although Miller seemed to agree with Postman's criticisms of the one-trial theorists on the basis of the effects of repetition and overlearning, he did say that he thought there are multiple "routes" between one element and other elements, not just one. This, of course, would depend on the extent to which the stimulus or stimulus complex was unchanged from trial to trial. Postman pointed out that such a conception leads to a linear model, yielding an incremental curve. Miller said he meant a model like that of a nerve, composed of many fibers, each of which works on an all-or-none basis. Such a model could be a theory of $_sH_R$.

Considerable attention was paid to the point that latencies of a response could continue to improve even after the probability of occurrence of the response was constant at 1.00, which shows that responses with equal probabilities of occurrence can have very different latencies. Peterson referred to data reported by Postman and Kaplan (1947). Goss mentioned Moylan's (1959) and Shrader's (1960) data taken over several trials with a single response to a single stimulus and Musgrave's (1962) data taken over several trials with two responses to several stimuli. Jenkins referred to some evidence found by Laberge (1961) in a two-choice discrimination situation. All these data show that latency continues to decline with trials past the point at which the response always occurs. Deese pointed out the generality of this kind of finding, referring to Marbe's law. Goss similarly referred to this point as made in a paper by Spence (1954).

Postman expressed further concern about Estes' suggestion that only one measure (e.g., probability of response) need be a source of concern. Postman finds this difficult to accept and to understand in theoretical terms. Miller said that Estes' position is more extreme on this than his would be but still argued, as he did in his discussion, that the relations of latency to other measures need not be high. Most of the participants seemed to believe latency and accuracy or latency and frequency of occurrence should be correlated though not perfectly.

Mandler pointed to the correlation between associative frequency and latency, but Miller raised the point of response competition (varying across the frequency range) in this connection. Murdock suggested that the use of compound stimuli could permit the study of the competition problem. Peterson thought the data of Barnes and Underwood (1959) were relevant here; after response competition the first-list responses are no longer available. Underwood, however, said the unavailability of responses in that study was a gradually increasing effect, and Deese pointed out that to some extent the responses were still available even at the end of second-list learning.

Postman returned to the point that EPAM I learns gradually and wondered how this could be. Miller replied that in the learning processes only an amount of information "just enough" (at some point in time) for adequate stimulus discrimination and S-R association is stored. The greater the interitem similarity, the more information will be stored. Later-learned items similar to previously learned items cause additional discriminative and associative information to be stored. Postman questioned the associative mechanism of EPAM I. Miller said that in the model an associative link is a list of cues to a response. The cues are stored with the internal stimulus image. When the stimulus is recognized, the cues can be discriminated to select the response.

Jenkins observed that alternative formulations of a simulation model can structure the stimulus, the response, and their relationship quite differently, with no observable difference so far as output behavior is concerned. Miller said that this would be untrue if the behavior were examined in detail, but Jenkins referred to the frequent use of abstract properties such as serial position curves in which specific behavioral characteristics are not examined. Miller's reply to this included the point that serial position curves are not merely abstractions derived from serial learning data but are obtained in other experimental procedures not involving learning (such as experiments on list copying).

Shepard reemphasized the need for explicitness in the formulation of S-R models. He argued that the all-or-none models proposed by Estes and by Feigenbaum at least have the virtue of being explicit enough to be susceptible to disconfirmation. True, Postman's results raise serious doubts about the adequacy of Estes' model, and Feigenbaum's model may be wrong too. But the question still remains as to whether "incremental" S-R formulations can do a better job of accounting in detail for Rock's results. He expressed the view that as soon as S-R theorists invoke such a mechanism as item selection they are already retreating into the safety and invulnerability of vagueness unless they also supply a precise statement of the rules presumed to govern such selection.

Shepard went on to suggest that variations in the extent to which evidence for one-trial learning is found in different studies may depend in part upon the nature of the stimuli. As evidence for one extreme where associations are almost certainly formed very slowly and gradually, he cited an experiment by Rothkopf (1960) in which the stimuli were patterns of dancing lights. Although there were only three S-R pairs to be learned, subjects in Rothkopf's best group were still only getting about 70 per cent correct after as many as 48 presentations of each of the three pairs.

Postman, commenting on Shepard's earlier point, indicated that Underwood, Rehula, and Keppel had accounted for Rock's findings in terms of the distribution of item difficulty. But Shepard asserted that, if, as he thinks, subjects *select* the easier items, their learning is presumably based on more than an automatic, incremental building up of S-R bonds.

There was a good deal of concern for the meaning of such stimulus selection. Brown pointed to variation in attention, similar to that perhaps arising in sentences, because information is not distributed evenly across the sentence. Noble said that attention is trainable, and Shepard remarked that if attention is a factor, its role must be worked out in detail. Noble was concerned with the meaning of such a phrase as "the subject decides to attend." Is it an act of "will"? Shepard said he meant that it is plausible to think that machinery can be built to function isomorphically with the statement about which Noble asked. He finds it difficult to find such isomorphic relations with the S-R model.

Mandler observed that terms such as input and output are not identical with S and R as theoretical terms, but S-R formulations of the concepts of stimulus and response are changing. This is seen in the contrast between the present discussion of one-trial learning and the one at the last conference. Mandler expressed the conviction that while one-trial learning may not hold, as a general principle, there are conditions under which it almost always occurs.

There was some discussion of the term trial for which several definitions can be given. Rehearsal by the subject should not be consistent with the status of a single trial. Deese wondered if the concept of a functional trial would turn out to be necessary.

The discussion concluded on the note that recent neurophysiological findings (cf. Hernandez-Peon, Scherrer, and Jouvet, 1956), such as the discovery of gamma efferents, can bring attention back and at a peripheral level (Wickens, Deese) whereas a few years ago attention would have required central processes (Wickens). A number of other experiments were cited to show the increasing, recent concern with attention (cf. Broadbent, 1957), but Goss, citing the experiment by Eckstrand and Wickens (1954), said this would have been no surprise to early S-R theorists like Watson.

REFERENCES

Barnes, J. M., & Underwood, B. J. (1959) "Fate" of first-list associations in transfer theory. *J. Exp. Psychol.*, **60**, 216–221.

Broadbent, D. E. (1957) A mechanical model for human attention and immediate memory. *Psychol. Rev.*, **64**, 205–215.

Eckstrand, G. A., & Wickens, D. D. (1954) Transfer of perceptual set. *J. Exp. Psychol.*, **47**, 274–278.

Hernandez-Peon, R., Scherrer, R. H., & Jouvet, M. (1956) Modification of electric activity in the cochlear nucleus during "attention" in unanesthetized cats. *Science*, **123**, 331–332.

Laberge, D. L. (1961) Generalization gradients in a discrimination situation. *J. Exp. Psychol.*, **62**, 88–94.

Moylan, J. J. (1959) Stimulus generalization in projective test (Rorschach) behavior. *J. Pers.*, **27**, 18–37.

Musgrave, B. S. (1962) The effect of nonsense-syllable compound stimuli on latency in a verbal paired-associate task. *J. Exp. Psychol.*, **63**, 499–504.

Postman, L., & Kaplan, H. L. (1947) Reaction time as a measure of retroactive inhibition. *J. Exp. Psychol.*, **37**, 136–145.

Rothkopf, E. (1960) Habit strength and intralist interference in identification learning. *Amer. Psychologist*, **15**, 444–445. (Abstract)

Shrader, W. K. (1960) Stimulus generalization with inkblot stimuli in a novel test context. Unpublished M.S. thesis, University of Massachusetts.

Spence, K. W. (1954) The relation of response latency and speed to the intervening variables and N in S-R theory. *Psychol. Rev.*, **61**, 209–216.

BRIEF NOTES ON THE EPAM THEORY OF VERBAL LEARNING[1]

E. A. Feigenbaum and H. A. Simon

UNIVERSITY OF CALIFORNIA, BERKELEY, AND CARNEGIE INSTITUTE

OF TECHNOLOGY

We have been asked briefly to sketch the EPAM (Elementary Perceiver and Memorizer) model. If these notes are overly succinct, clarification will be found in the references.

Model and Method. EPAM is a theory of the information-processing activity underlying verbal learning behavior. The precise formulation of the model is given in an information-processing language for a computer. The computer is then used as a tool for generating the remote consequences of the information-processing postulates in particular experimental conditions. EPAM is a closed model in the sense that it can be treated as a subject in learning experiments. The experiments are not run "live" but are simulated using programs to simulate an experimenter, the apparatus, and the stimulus environment. Such simulated experiments yield a stream of verbal behavior from EPAM fully equivalent in nature to the "raw data" which an experimenter takes from his subject in a live experiment. Of course, the degree to which this behavior looks like human behavior in the same experiments is the fundamental question of model validation.

EPAM I. EPAM contains a set of "macroprocesses" which deal with the organization of the total learning task, and a set of "microprocesses" which learn the individual items. (The macroprocesses are referred to as EPAM I, the complete model as EPAM II.) That such a factorization of the learning activity is useful and valid is argued in another place (Feigenbaum and Simon, 1962).

The fundamental assumptions of EPAM I are as follows:

1. Any given stimulus item requires a definite amount of processing time before it is learned. For items of the same average difficulty, this time is relatively constant. Thus, the total time to learn n items is given approximately by $T_n = Kn$. (It is postulated that *time*, rather than *number of exposures* per se, is the critical variable.)

---

[1] These notes were contributed after the conference at the invitation of Professor Postman (Ed.).

2. There exists an immediate memory of extremely limited size, which provides "temporary storage" for stimulus items undergoing processing. (The effect of this is to postulate an "information bottleneck.")

3. In the face of immediate memory constraint, subjects not otherwise instructed adopt an anchor-point strategy for organizing the learning task. Items at perceptually unique anchor points are learned first. An item, once learned, becomes an anchor point for further learning. (This postulate determines the order in which items are attended to for learning. It is all-or-none attention in that a new pair of items will not be attended to until the previous pair is considered adequately learned.)

EPAM I yields predictions of macrophenomena of serial learning. In particular, we have shown that it predicts the McCrary and Hunter serial position curves better than any other existing theory (Feigenbaum and Simon, 1961c, 1962).

EPAM II. The function of the macroprocesses is to focus the attention of the microprocesses successively on the stimulus-response item pairs which comprise the learning task. For any pair, the primary learning process is as follows: Learn to discriminate the S item from all items in the set already learned; do the same for the R item; finally, construct an association between S and R.

The microprocesses perform four principal functions:[2]

a. Recognize an external stimulus as one about which some information has already been memorized

b. Add new stimulus items to the memory by building discriminations (tests) that allow the new item to be distinguished from the stimuli previously learned

c. Associate (internally) two stored items, say x and y, by storing with x some cue information about y

d. Respond to an external stimulus X with a response, Y, by retrieving the cue to the response, and then retrieving the response using the cue

Thus EPAM has two performance processes, enabling it to respond with material already learned: the discrimination process (a), which recognizes the stimulus, and the response process (d), which finds the appropriate response associated with the stimulus and produces it. EPAM also has two learning processes: the discrimination learning process (b), which elaborates the structure of discrimination tests it applies to stimuli, and the association learning process (c), which associates response cues with stimuli.

The central memory structure, which the performance processes use and the learning processes construct, is the *discrimination net*. It is a net of

[2] The following discussion is adapted from an earlier paper (Feigenbaum and Simon, 1961b).

associations at whose terminal nodes are stored *images* of encodings of external stimuli. At the nonterminal nodes of the net are stored *tests* which examine particular features of the encodings. The internal image of a stimulus is retrieved by sorting the encoding of the stimulus down through the tests of the net to the appropriate terminal. In learning a set of stimuli, the net is grown to a size that is just large enough (roughly) to discriminate among the different stimuli that have been presented to the system.

Association of a response, *y*, to a stimulus, *x*, is accomplished by storing a small amount of the information about *y* (an incomplete *cue image* of *y*) along with the image of *x*. The system determines by trial and error how much information must be stored as a cue to retrieve the response from the net when the association is made.

EPAM responds to a stimulus by sorting it in the discrimination net, finding the associated response cue, sorting that cue in the same net, finding its image, and using the response image to produce the response.

Results. Study of the behavior of EPAM in an initial set of about a hundred simulated experiments shows that a variety of "classical" verbal learning phenomena are present. Referring to traditional labels, these include serial position effect, stimulus and response generalization, effect of intra-list similarity, types of intra-list and interlist errors, oscillation, retroactive inhibition, proactive effect on learning rate (but unfortunately not proactive inhibition), and log-linear discriminative reaction time. Further experiments, especially those involving inhibition phenomena and transfer phenomena, are now in progress.

REFERENCES

Feigenbaum, E. A. (1959) An information processing theory of verbal learning. RAND *Report P-1817*. Santa Monica, Calif.: RAND Corporation.

Feigenbaum, E. A. (1961a) The simulation of verbal learning behavior. *Proc. West. Joint Computer Conf.*, **19**, 121–132.

Feigenbaum, E. A., & Simon, H. A. (1962) A theory of the serial position effect. *Brit. J. Psychol.*, **53**, 307–320.

Feigenbaum, E. A., & Simon, H. A. (1961b) Performance of a reading task by an elementary perceiving and memorizing program. *RAND Report P-2358*. Santa Monica, Calif.: RAND Corporation.

Feigenbaum, E. A., & Simon, H. A. (1961c) Comment: The distinctiveness of stimuli. *Psychol. Rev.*, **68**, 285–288.

Chapter 9

IMMEDIATE MEMORY: DATA AND THEORY[1]

Lloyd R. Peterson

INDIANA UNIVERSITY

It is the aim of this paper to suggest some relationships between immediate memory and learning experiments. An approach will be sketched which starts with generalizations based on behavioral evidence from simple verbal situations. These principles will then be combined in an attempt to account for certain aspects of more complex verbal learning phenomena. The approach will be found to make use of concepts already present in contemporary analyses of learning. Thus learning will have provided a way of looking at immediate memory, and it is hoped that this approach will in turn contribute to the understanding of traditional learning problems.

DECAY THEORY

The initial point to be made about immediate memory is that the term is not in its literal sense descriptive of the experimental operations by which it is measured. When a series of digits, letters, or words is presented and then tested for recall without any appreciable lapse of time, it is only the last item in the series that has occurred immediately before the test. If the instructions specify that recall is to be attempted in order of presentation, then the test is not immediate even for that last item. This consideration has led to interpretation of memory span in terms of a trace decay theory. Stimulation sets up some kind of memory trace in the nervous system which decays rapidly over a short period of time. As the series of items presented is lengthened, the time interval between presentation and recall of the individual members becomes longer. As a result the trace becomes weaker, and probability of correct recall decreases.

Empirical evidence that retention functions change over intervals measured in seconds is not lacking. The negative time error related to

[1] The author has been supported in his investigations of short-term retention by grants G-2596 and G-12917 from the National Science Foundation.

the interval between successive presentations of stimuli in psycho-physical experiments has been cited as evidence for trace decay (Koffka, 1935; Woodworth and Schlosberg, 1954, pp. 226ff.). Strength of classical conditioning in relation to the interval separating presentation of the conditioned stimulus from presentation of the unconditioned stimulus provides another type of evidence (Woodworth and Schlosberg, 1954, pp. 570ff.).

Verbal experiments in which time rather than number of items is the independent variable have not been numerous, but forgetting has been shown to occur within a few seconds when rehearsal is minimized (Pillsbury and Sylvester, 1940; Brown, 1958). A systematic investigation relating retention of individual consonant syllables to time has been made by Peterson and Peterson (1959). Subjects counted backward during the retention interval. A rapidly decreasing retention function was found. Keppel and Underwood (1961) have suggested that the course of forgetting in the latter experiment may have been influenced by the use of the same subjects in repeated tests, so that proactive interference might account for the rapid forgetting.

As a check on this possibility, the data from several experiments testing retention of trigrams of low association value have been combined for the analysis summarized in Table 9–1. Beginning with what have

Table 9–1
Stage Analysis of Proportions of Syllables Recalled

Tests	Retention interval, seconds						
	1	3	6	9	12	15	18
3–8	.85	.52	.47	.17	.21	.08	.08
9–14	.96	.79	.44	.50	.25	.12	.08
45–50	.97	.81	.57	.25	.25	.08	.08

been previously treated as practice trials, the first two tests for each subject have been excluded to ensure that the instructions were understood. The next two blocks of six tests and a block of six tests which was the final block in some of the experiments were analyzed separately. A small improvement in recall occurs in the second block of tests, but there is no appreciable difference between the second and eighth blocks. There is no indication of proactive interference.

Conrad (1960) has noted that in tests of memory span there is no deterioration in performance over a session. Neither did he find any difference in correct recalls when the interval between tests was varied from 15 to 40 seconds, although serial intrusion errors decreased as the interval lengthened. Apparently an interval of 15 seconds between tests is sufficient to minimize proactive effects with single presentations of items. The influence of previous items within a series or a list is a different matter, as will be noted later.

The relative absence of proactive interference has important methodological implications. Economy is served by using the same subjects in many comparisons. More important, functional relationships can be investigated more adequately. The dangers of assuming that a group curve is of the same form as that for an individual subject are well known. If it can be established that under certain conditions proactive effects are minimal, then functions can be based on data from single subjects.

The rapid deterioration of performance over short intervals of time is an empirically established fact. The nature of the events producing the deterioration is not established. Theorists differ as to whether some normal physiological process results in decay of a memory trace or whether intervening events produce interference. If intervening events are responsible, is there an interaction of traces during the interval? Does rehearsal act to postpone decay of a trace or is the trace strengthened? Is it possible to distinguish a short-term memory trace from a long-term trace? The use of the word "trace" in all these contexts indicates that the term may be used to mean nothing more specific than some kind of neural aftereffect of stimulation.

THE STIMULUS TRACE

The beginnings of answers to some of the previous questions may be obtained by analysis of available data on short-term verbal memory. Three aspects of retention invite separate discussion. The first of these will be called the *stimulus trace* for purposes of reference.

The concept of the stimulus trace was incorporated into a basic postulate of Hull's general behavior system (1952, chap. 4). Quantification was made on the basis of studies varying the interval between conditioned stimulus and unconditioned stimulus in eyelid conditioning. However, Hull applied the concept to rote learning studies, suggesting that the idea of stimulus generalization on traces enabled the theorist to conceptualize both forward and backward remote associations as simultaneous associations (1952, p. 117).

It seems reasonable that the aftereffect of verbal stimulation is a more complex phenomenon than that in the case of nonverbal stimulation. It may be misleading to call the aftereffect of verbal stimulation a stimulus trace, since well-defined responses capable of rapid repetition without observation may result. Jane Mackworth (1959) has distinguished between two stages in the development of the memory trace, a perceptual trace and a verbal trace. Her suggestion is based on a continuing task which required memorization of cues seen previously. It was found that when the subject was required to remember only one or two stimuli back, the use of unlabeled lights as cues resulted in better performance than the use of labeled lights. However, the advantage was with the labeled lights when memory of three or four lights back was required. Thus the first brief aftereffect of stimulation was interpreted as a direct representation of the stimulus. This was transformed into a more enduring verbal trace. The verbal trace that made possible the longer memory feats, through rehearsal or reverberation, presumably produced interference when only brief retention was required.

Support for the distinction between a nonverbal and a verbal effect is also provided by latency data obtained by Peterson and Peterson (1959). Latencies for recall of consonant syllables were measured from the signal stopping the intervening activity (counting backward) to completion of a correct recall. Over half the correct recalls required more than 2.5 seconds, and some latencies were over 10 seconds. These latencies did not suggest the identification of a stimulus trace. There was a probabilistic quality to this recall that suggested a recurring event decreasing in frequency of occurrence. Failure of recall in one short interval was often followed by success in the next. The probabilistic nature of recall was similar to recall in a learning task.

We suggest that the aftereffects of verbal stimulation include the production by the subject of a response, neural and perhaps peripheral, which results in an associative effect from a single stimulation. When nonverbal stimulation is not easily labeled, as in psychological experiments where the subject has no clearly defined frame of reference, the term *stimulus trace* may be an appropriate designation for the decaying aftereffects of stimulation. Similarly, in animal conditioning experiments it may be appropriate to measure such a trace. However, in the majority of human verbal studies, what we have called the stimulus trace is hopelessly confounded with other effects.

A class of verbal experiments which does provide information about a decaying stimulus trace is that which simultaneously stimulates two sensory channels with different messages. The two ears have been used most frequently, although eye and ear have also been combined. Broadbent (1956) found that when subjects were stimulated by a different series of three digits to each ear, the digits in corresponding positions of each series arriving simultaneously, subjects were often able to reproduce all six digits. However, when the rate of presentation was one digit per half second per ear, recall was almost invariably ordered in such a way that all of the digits from one of the ears were given before any of the digits from the other ear. Even when instructed to alternate between ears, subjects could not usually do so at that rapid rate. At a slower rate alternation was possible. Broadbent interpreted this to mean that a shift of attention from one ear to the other required an interval of time greater than that available at a fast rate of presentation. Therefore, the subject attended to one ear, while items arriving at the other ear were stored temporarily. Digits from this temporary storage were later identified by attending to their remaining traces. Recall was typically poorer for the ear attended to last.

The trace identified in this case would seem to be uncomplicated by the usual accompaniments of verbal stimulation. Interfering events prevent the message to the unattended ear from immediately reaching the neural mechanism involved in the processing of verbal stimulation. This mechanism, like the speech musculature, would seem to be able to handle only one verbal item at a time. This interpretation is supported by Moray's (1960) variation of the experiment in which the same rapid rate of presentation was used, but arrival of the digits was staggered such that no two digits arrived at precisely the same moment. Under these conditions, alternation of recall between the ears was equally as efficient as recalling all of the message from one ear first. With staggered presentation it would seem that all of the digits can reach the more advanced neural mechanisms without interference, and hence no switching of attention is required.

Another experiment by Broadbent (1957) investigated the decay of this simple trace. Six digits were presented to one ear to be recalled first. Two digits were also presented to the other ear under varied conditions of timing, but always to be recalled last. In one condition these latter two digits were simultaneous with the first two digits to the six-digit-ear. In two other conditions they were simultaneous with the middle two digits or with the last two digits. It was found that these two digits recalled last were recalled best when they were also presented last.

ASSOCIATIVE ASPECTS OF IMMEDIATE MEMORY

One question of interest concerning the stimulus trace is whether any associative effect may be involved. Moray (1959) presents some negative evidence in this respect. The experiment was one in which the subject shadowed a message, that is, he repeated aloud a message presented to one ear, while another message was being presented simultaneously to the other ear. Subjects were found to be unable to report the content of a verbal message to the unattended ear. Even when that message consisted of a short list of words repeated a number of times, the words could not be recognized in a test after a 30-second delay.

The capacity of the subject to produce his responses in order of presentation could be regarded as an indication of the operation of some associative mechanism. Conrad (1959) has noted that in the traditional immediate memory experiment 50 per cent of all errors are errors of transposition; that is, the correct digits are recalled but in the wrong order. He notes that subjects who make few errors in general have a higher proportion of transposition errors than subjects who make many errors. What the mechanism is for ordering recall is not clearly established, but it is subject to failure. It may be that in the usual immediate memory test associations are formed between items presented adjacently and that order is thus preserved. If this is true of a series of items passing normally through the nervous system, it could be true also of the stimulus trace. It is difficult to account for correct recall order in simultaneous stimulation experiments without postulating some such mechanism.

An experiment by Gray and Wedderburn (1960) using simultaneous stimulation indicates that recall can alternate between ears in accordance with preexisting sequential dependencies and result in performance as efficient as when ordering is by arrival at a given ear. Three-word sentences were used, a word being presented simultaneously with a digit, and the words alternating between ears. Alternation in recall was best when subjects were instructed to group words into sentences. The alternation should perhaps be assigned to the recall period rather than to the original time of stimulation. In any event it appears that previously established serial dependencies can offset the serial ordering produced in the stimulus trace.

Whatever the magnitude of a possible associative effect during the initial stimulus trace phase, the aftereffects of verbal stimulation might be expected to involve associative mechanisms at some later stage. A contrary opinion has been stated by Brown (1958) who suggests that rehearsal only postpones the onset of decay of the trace. The point was investigated by Peterson and Peterson (1959) who had subjects repeat consonant syllables 0, 1, or 3 times before counting backward. The slope of the retention curve for syllables was found to be a function of number of repetitions. Analysis of the serial dependencies among letters within the items was made by computing the mean dependent probabilities of a letter being correct, given that the preceding letter was correct. These dependent probabilities were found to increase with repetition of the syllable and to decrease with time. It was considered that these dependent probabilities reflected a serial associative aspect of immediate memory. The proportion of correct recalls of first letters was also computed in each of the conditions of the experiment. This proportion was found to increase with repetition, and a second associative aspect of retention was considered to be reflected by this increase. The question may be raised as to whether this second characteristic is independent of the first. Certainly the two were highly correlated in the experiment under discussion. Conceivably the increase in recall of individual letters could account for the increases in the serial dependencies. However, an examination of the probabilities that a letter was correct, given that the preceding letter was incorrect, showed that these probabilities were much lower than the probabilities of a correct letter following a correct letter. Furthermore, at the three- and nine-second intervals the differences between correct, given correct, and correct, given incorrect, increase with repetition as shown in Table 9–2. Since there is evidence of serial learn-

Table 9–2

Probability of a Correct Letter Given a Correct Preceding Letter Minus the Probability of a Correct Letter Given an Incorrect Preceding Letter

Repetitions	Retention interval, seconds		
	3	9	18
0	.53	.32	.41
1	.41	.42	.37
3	.61	.51	.37

ing, and since it is difficult to see how this serial effect could account for the increased occurrence of first letters with repetition, there is reason to consider that two associative factors were working concurrently.

Before proceeding to the description of operations designed to test empirically the independence of these two factors, let us define some labels in order conveniently to refer to these aspects of retention. We suggest that there are important differences in the nature of the antecedent events to which the (neural?) response to verbal stimulation is being associated. One class of events is related to specific cues introduced by the experimenter, and a strengthening of the conditional relationship between these cues and responses of the subject will be called *cue learning*. The increasing sequential dependencies among the letters in the study in which consonant syllables were repeated reflect one type of cue learning. Increasing dependencies between pairs of words in learning of a list will be considered to be another variety of cue learning. A second class of events is unspecified, largely beyond the control of the experimenter. These may be related to the general situation in which the subject finds himself as well as to characteristics which the subject himself brings into the situation. Strengthening of conditional relationships between these unspecified events and responses of the subject will be called *background conditioning*. Thus, in the previous experiment, the occurrence in recall of first letters will be considered to reflect background conditioning. Both aspects of the associative process will be assumed to have in common the strengthening of conditional relationships through contiguous occurrence of neural events, although the view that is held of the nature of associative learning is not crucial to the definitions that have been made.

We suggest that recall is determined by the combined influence of the two classes of antecedent events just described. We propose to show, first, that the two types of associative learning involved are not perfectly correlated, and second, that there are a number of verbal experiments that can be better understood through a recognition of these two associative aspects of retention.

An experiment in which the effect of cue learning on recall of single items outweighed background conditioning is reported by Peterson, Peterson, and Miller (1961). Low-association-value nonsense syllables, high-association-value nonsense syllables, and three-letter words were presented in a memory drum. Subjects counted backward during a six-second interval. The proportion of syllables recalled was directly related to meaningfulness, although there were no differences in reading of the items. Analysis of the serial dependencies in recall of the individual letters showed that these increased with meaningfulness. However, there was not a clear-cut trend in the case of the first letters of syllables. First letters of high-association-value syllables were not recalled as well as those of low-association-value syllables, although first letters of words were recalled with greater frequency than either of the other types of item. The sequential dependencies between letters in recall presumably reflected cue learning established in the past history of the subjects. This cue learning appeared to determine the difference in recall found in this study.

Another experiment has been reported in which background conditioning appeared to be the dominant factor in recall (Peterson and Peterson, 1960). The spacing interval separating two presentations of the same verbal item was varied. The 24 subjects counted backward during intervals between presentations, as well as during the six seconds from second presentation to recall. Each subject was tested 12 times at each of the intervals shown in Table 9–3. The nonsense syllables of low association value appeared equally often at each interval over the group. Spacing intervals were equally represented in irregular order within each block of four tests. Other details were similar to the previous experiment.

The results of the experiment are summarized in Table 9–3. Proportions of nonsense syllables recalled correctly increased as the spacing interval increased. Proportions of first letters correctly recalled increased in like manner. In both cases analyses of variance resulted in F's significant at the .05 level. In both cases the end points of the ordered series were significantly different at the .01 level by two-tailed t test. On the other hand, the differences among serial dependencies were negligible.

The study is described to support the point that the correlation between background conditioning and cue learning need not be unity in a particular experimental situation. However, the relationship found between spacing and recall is of interest for its own sake, since it seems to run counter to simple trace decay. The possibility that rehearsal is producing the effect should be considered. The same counting task used during the spacing interval has separated presentation and recall in a

Table 9–3
Recall as a Function of Spacing between Presentations

Measure	Spacing interval, seconds			
	1	3	6	11
Nonsense syllables	.66	.67	.74	.77
First letters	.79	.80	.85	.89
Dependent probabilities	.91	.91	.93	.93

number of studies and has been followed regularly by a marked decrement in recall which would not lead one to suspect rehearsal behavior. If rehearsal occurred, the wrong response was being rehearsed as often as the right response. Subjects were admonished to count faster during the eight practice tests, if they did not approximate one number (three digits) per second. Further evidence was obtained from a stage analysis of the data. Presumably, as the subject became more familiar with the counting task, rehearsal might become easier. Two counting tasks were used. If the subject counted by three during the first half of the experiment, then he counted by four during the second half. Thus, if the spacing effect was due to rehearsal, it should have been greater during the second and fourth quarters than during the first and third quarters of the session. An examination of the data showed that the opposite was true. For both measures, recall of syllables and recall of first letters, the difference related to the spacing interval was somewhat greater in quarters 1 and 3.

An explanation along the lines of Estes' fluctuation theory (1955) is an intriguing possibility, although that theory was formulated to account for distribution effects over longer intervals than those of short-term retention studies. An adaptation of Estes' formulation might follow these lines. Assume a background of neural events which fluctuate in time. A response becomes conditioned to those events occurring contiguously with it. However, those events occurring at any one time constitute a sample of the total population of possible events. Probability of recall is proportional to the proportion of conditioned events present at time of recall. Probability of recall will decrease with time because the sample at recall differs from presentation as the interval separating presentation from recall. However, the proportion of conditioned events in the population will increase as the two samples differ, since an event once conditioned remains so until conditioned to some other response. Hence, if counterconditioning can be avoided between presentations, more efficient background conditioning should be obtained with spaced than with massed presentations. Application to the present experiment assumes, then, that during the counting activity the events related to nonsense syllables are not sampled and thus not conditioned to anything else. The random recurrence of fluctuating antecedent events seems consistent with the wide variability in latencies of correct responses which was noted previously. The above interpretation has the virtue of parsimoniously explaining both performance decrement between presentation and test and performance facilitation as time between presentation and repetition increases.

A systematic account of the molecular basis of forgetting must await further experimentation. The empirical basis for defining two associative aspects of retention does not depend on the adequacy of the preceding excursus into fluctuation theory. Short-term retention studies of individual verbal items have furnished illustrations of the working of two associative principles. Their operation in other verbal situations will now be suggested.

MEMORY SPAN

A return to consideration of recall of a series of digits after a single presentation suggests an interpretation of the presentation as a single learning trial. This interpretation may aid in harmonizing certain findings which otherwise seem contradictory.

A decay theory suggests that rate of presentation and recall should be directly related to recall. With a fast rate there should be less decay of the trace, and hence better recall should result. Conrad (1957) has tested this prediction and found evidence to support it. Eight-digit numbers were presented and recalled at the rates of 30 digits per minute or 90 digits per minute. Recall was better at the faster pace.

In contrast to this, consider the work of Pollack, Johnson, and Knaff (1959). Running memory span was measured by interrupting random sequences of digits with a signal for recall of as many of the last digits as possible. As rate of presentation increased from .5 digit per second to 4 digits per second, the digit span decreased.

The discrepancy would be understandable if rate of presentation were inversely related to rate of learning. This has been found to be the case in list learning, and there seems to be no reason why it should not be true of a single presentation of a series of digits. It is probably only during recall that slowing of the rate will lead to poorer recall. Thus, Pollack *et al.* did not control rate of recall. With unpaced recall the slower rate of presentation produced better learning on the single trial and hence better recall. Pollack *et al.* suggested that subjects rehearsed at the slower rates. This is reasonable in view of the finding that the decrease in span with increasing rate of presentation was greatest with messages of known length. Presumably with a message of known length considerations of strategy suggested that items near the end of the series be rehearsed. Such strategy could be used with less effectiveness when the message was of uncertain length, though it could not be ruled out.

IMMEDIATE FREE RECALL

The interaction of two associative aspects of retention can be seen in those experiments in which a list of words is read and the subject writes down in any order as many words as he can remember. When the words are presented in a random order, the items from the end of the list are recalled first and with greatest frequency over a group of subjects (Deese and Kaufman, 1957). The superior strength in recall of this latter half of the list would be predicted on the basis of background conditioning of the responses. But the influence of cue learning is also present in the form of preestablished associations between words. Deese (1959a) correlated an index of prior associative strength between items with number of words in recall. The interitem associative strength was measured by tabulating frequencies of responding with another item in the list when an item from the list was presented as a stimulus. In over 18 lists this index of associative strength showed a high correlation with number of words recalled. When a word was recalled, it appeared to act as a cue for other words in the list. Deese (1959b) has also examined intrusions to determine the cue value of words recalled. On the basis of word-association norms he found that the probability of particular words occurring as intrusions in recall was highly correlated with the average frequency with which those words occurred as associations to words from the list.

Murdock (1960) has studied the number of unrelated words recalled after a single presentation as a function of presentation rate and length of the list. The finding that number of recalls is directly related to presentation time per item suggests consideration of the first presentation as a trial of learning. Efficiency of list learning has generally been found to be related to presentation rate. The finding that number of items recalled beyond the memory span is a linear function of the length of the list at first glance suggests a simple interpretation in terms of probabilities. If each item has a certain probability of recall after one presentation, then the mean number recalled is the sum of the probabilities of the individual items. The more probabilities summed, the larger number you should get. However, this interpretation neglects the recency factors which have been emphasized in this paper. The longer the list, the greater the interval separating presentation of items in the earlier part of the list from recall. Thus on the basis of recency, the probability of recall of an item from the first part of the list should decrease as the list becomes longer. But the likelihood of finding pre-established associations between items in the list increases as the list becomes longer. Thus, the combination of these two opposed effects may result in an apparently linear relationship.

The effect of the cue aspect of recall is further seen in manipulations of sequential dependencies among words in the list. Deese and Kaufman (1957) have shown that frequency of recall as a function of position during presentation changes as a function of the degree of approximation of sequential structure to English. As the sequential dependencies in the Miller and Selfridge (1950) lists increased, the recall of initial words increased much more markedly than recall of last words. The result was that the initial items were recalled most frequently with English text, and the final items only a little more frequently than the middle items. This seems to be related to the finding that order of recall was significantly correlated with order of presentation of textual material. Thus, the effect of recency is lessened when order of recall is changed. It is noteworthy that the sequential dependencies introduced by use of the Miller-Selfridge lists are not a simple function of associations between adjacent items. In the higher-order approximations words far removed from a particular word determine its occurrence, and of course this is true of English text. Hence, the effect of cues in recall is a combined effect of cues preceding at different time intervals. This same notion of the present being determined by complex past events is a possible explanation of the primacy effect found within a series of items. As the series progresses, the stimulus situation includes more and more items recently strengthened. With this increasingly complex stimulus situation, the associative strengthening through contiguity between adjacent items decreases. This of course accounts only for the first portion of the serial position function. Some other factor is required for the later portion of the function. The recency factor is a likely possibility in the case of free recall of unrelated words.

PRIMING

Word associations can be considered to reflect preestablished cue learning. However, there have been studies suggesting that recent background conditioning may influence responses in association tests. Storms (1958) found that reading a list of words just before a word-association test increased the probability that stimuli in the word-association test would elicit words from the prior list as responses. Storms notes that this effect may sometimes be mistakenly interpreted as due to backward association.

Segal and Cofer (1960) report a confirmation of Storms's finding. They have explored further the variables influencing what they call the "priming" phenomenon. They observed priming under a variety of instructional conditions. Priming was found to be related to the already existing associative strength between the word-association cue and the priming word. The strongest priming was obtained when this associative strength was of an intermediate value. It would seem that the effect is not very strong, and if there are other associations which are much stronger than that with the priming word, the effect of the latter will be overwhelmed. Similarly, if there is a very strong association to the priming word, not much will be added by priming. The finding that the effect of priming decreases with time is consistent with the present interpretation.

PERCEPTION

The influence of background conditioning can be seen apart from cue learning in a study of Goldiamond and Hawkins (1958). Subjects responded to a brief flash of light in which there was no verbal message. Prior to this recognition test they had been trained on a set of low-association-value nonsense syllables. Subjects had responded to individual pairs of nonsense syllables with differential frequency. After a 10-minute break, they were instructed to try to recognize the items they had seen previously as the items were projected subliminally on the screen. This test showed a logarithmic relationship between frequency of occurrence of nonsense syllables in training and frequency of response to the flash of light. Since no specific cues were present in the flash, only the background conditioning influenced recognition. The effect of this priming over a 10-minute interval suggests that its influence is largely masked by specific cues in studies such as Segal and Cofer (1960).

Another aspect of perception related to the present analysis is the influence of the time interval between exposure and verbal response in tachistoscopic studies. Lawrence and LaBerge (1956) compared the effect of order of recall when cues for order were presented before exposure with the effect of presenting cues for order after exposure. The same effect was obtained in both cases, with better identification for items recalled first. They concluded that there was no need to postulate a selective effect of instructions on perception in their situation. Instructions determined what was identified first, and what was identified first was identified best from considerations of recency.

PAIRED-ASSOCIATES

The use of unique cues to signal recall is related to the cue learning aspect of memory that has been discussed. Murdock (1961) has briefly reported a study in which immediately after a single presentation of a series of pairs of associates recall was tested by showing the first member of a pair. Recall was an inverse function of the number of intervening pairs. Lloyd, Reid, and Feallock (1960) used the class name of an object to cue recall of the name of the object. Words of various classes were presented in a series at a three-second rate, and errors were found to be related to the average number of items the subject had to remember over a sequence. In both studies number of items was confounded with time.

Paired-associate list learning is different from the above studies in that a recall score is averaged over the list and intervals are measured from the end of a complete presentation of the list to the beginning of another presentation. Keppel and Underwood (1961) have reported a variation in which the list was presented once and the stimulus members were presented alone for a recall test. The stimuli were numbers, and the responses were two-letter combinations of low, medium, or high meaningfulness. Retention was tested by inserting various intervals from zero to five minutes between the end of presentation of the list and the beginning of test for recall. Their results are of particular interest because their retention curves did not decrease monotonically with time. A reminiscence effect was found for low and medium meaningfulness conditions. Keppel and Underwood suggest that the decay functions found by Peterson and Peterson (1959) and Murdock (1961) result from these investigators' using the same subjects repeatedly in many conditions of the experiment. Proactive interference may thus hide the true shape of the forgetting curve.

The author has run a number of short-term retention studies using paired-associates, both in cases where counting filled the interval between presentation and test, and also in cases where other pairs filled this interval. In a number of instances comparison was made of the initial stage of the subjects' first experimental session and the last stage of the session. In none of these comparisons was decreased recall found at the end of the session, but in several there was a slight increase over the session. Note that Murdock found evidence for proactive interference within his sequences (1961). The first item in a series was recalled best, a phenomenon demonstrated under many circumstances and which is found in the Keppel and Underwood study. This is the important locus of proaction in studies of short-term retention.

An analysis of the Keppel and Underwood study in terms of individual pairs is indicated. Their zero interval is zero only for the last pair in the list, and then only if the last pair is tested first. It would not appear that this last pair was tested first, and proportions of correct recall at the zero interval were below .50 for all conditions. In Murdock's study recall after no intervening pairs was above .90. The author has found in unpublished studies, where perception of the stimulus material was ensured by having the subject read aloud, that recall close to 1.0 can be obtained at a zero interval. Hence, list learning would seem to have depressed the retention function. Reminiscence cannot occur after the zero interval when measuring from individual pairs because retention is already near its maximum.

The reminiscence phenomenon found by Keppel and Underwood can be interpreted in terms of the two associative aspects of retention outlined previously. Recall is a function, not only of the stimulus member being shown, but also of background events. Immediately after completion of presentation of the list, the last response is strongest in terms of background conditioning. The next last response is second strongest, and so on. Thus, if a cue is given for a response originally presented near the beginning of the list, there will be strong interference from responses presented near the end of the list. However, when an interval of time elapses before recall, the strength of the last responses as influenced by background events will have decreased to approximately that of the earlier items, since decrease in strength is greatest just after presentation. There will then be less interference and the response of the subject will be influenced to a greater extent by the cue presented by the experimenter. Keppel and Underwood comment that it was an increase in recall of the first two items that produced the reminiscence phenomenon. The present analysis is related to McGeoch's (1942) explanation of reminiscence in terms of differential forgetting.

Underwood and Schulz (1960) call attention to a selective mechanism in list learning related to recency considerations. It is known that early in learning errors stop appearing from outside the set designated by the experimenter as responses to be used in the experiment. The subject has learned what the responses are before he can correctly associate them to the cues provided. In terms of the present interpretation these responses are conditioned to background events. Their availability increases as they are repeatedly presented. This selective mechanism would seem to be reducible to what the present paper calls background conditioning.

CONCLUDING REMARKS

The suggestion has been made by various authors that two types of memory be distinguished, short-term storage and long-term storage. The present analysis suggests on the basis of behavioral evidence that it is useful to distinguish three aspects of memory, all of which normally work together in short-term verbal retention. The *stimulus trace* is very brief and serves only for very short-term storage. The *background conditioning* and *cue learning* aspects of associative memory are considered to function in both short-term and long-term storage. The background conditioning factor, in general, is of more temporary influence than cue learning. However, the influence of background conditioning may extend over relatively long periods, as in the proactive interference that Underwood (1957) has found from lists learned previously.

The preceding analysis of immediate memory pools insights into the learning process contributed by many investigators. Conrad (1959) has suggested that only information theory and neurophysiological theory offer any systematic explanation of the phenomena found in immediate memory. The present paper has outlined a third alternative. The approach to immediate memory by way of learning would appear to have some advantages over approaches stated in the language of information theory or neurophysiology. Information theory offers little more than a technique of measurement. It could be incorporated into the present approach to the extent that its coding of antecedent events is found to relate lawfully to behavioral events. Broadbent (1958) has found it of some help, although its usefulness seems limited (Miller, 1956).

Neurophysiological accounts of immediate memory have a speculative characteristic that limits their usefulness. While the approach of Hebb (1949), for instance, is interesting and runs parallel to the present account at various points, it is of necessity farther removed from the events it seeks to explain. Physiological events can only be related to verbal behavior in a gross manner. For fine-grain analysis of the antecedent events for particular instances of verbal utterances, normal stimulation of the sense organs is at present the only satisfactory technique.

REFERENCES

Broadbent, D. E. (1956) Successive responses to simultaneous stimuli. *Quart. J. Exp. Psychol.*, 8, 145–152.

Broadbent, D. E. (1957) Immediate memory and simultaneous stimuli. *Quart. J. Exp. Psychol.*, 9, 1–11.

Broadbent, D. E. (1958) *Perception and communication.* New York: Pergamon.

Brown, J. (1958) Some tests of the decay theory of immediate memory. *Quart. J. Exp. Psychol.,* **10,** 12–21.

Conrad, R. (1957) Decay theory of immediate memory. *Nature,* **179,** 831.

Conrad, R. (1959) Errors of immediate memory. *Brit. J. Psychol.,* **50,** 349–359.

Conrad, R. (1960) Serial order intrusions in immediate memory. *Brit. J. Psychol.,* **51,** 45–48.

Deese, J. (1959a) Influence of inter-item associative strength upon immediate free recall. *Psychol. Rep.,* **5,** 305–312.

Deese, J. (1959b) On the prediction of occurrence of particular verbal intrusions in immediate recall. *J. Exp. Psychol.,* **58,** 17–22.

Deese, J., & Kaufman, R. A. (1957) Serial effects in recall of unorganized and sequentially organized verbal material. *J. Exp. Psychol.,* **54,** 180–187.

Estes, W. K. (1955) Statistical theory of distributional phenomena in learning. *Psychol. Rev.,* **62,** 369–377.

Goldiamond, I., & Hawkins, W. F. (1958) Vexierversuch: The log relationship between word-frequency and recognition obtained in the absence of stimulus words. *J. Exp. Psychol.,* **56,** 457–463.

Gray, J. A., & Wedderburn, A. A. I. (1960) Grouping strategies with simultaneous stimuli. *Quart. J. Exp. Psychol.,* **12,** 180–184.

Hebb, D. O. (1949) *The organization of behavior.* New York: Wiley.

Hull, C. L. (1952) *A behavior system.* New Haven, Conn.: Yale University Press.

Keppel, G., & Underwood, B. J. (1961) Short-term retention of paired-associate lists. Paper read at Midwest. Psychol. Ass., Chicago.

Koffka, K. (1935) *Principles of Gestalt Psychology.* New York: Harcourt, Brace.

Lawrence, D. H., & LaBerge, D. L. (1956) Relationship between recognition accuracy and order of reporting stimulus dimensions. *J. Exp. Psychol.,* **51,** 12–18.

Lloyd, K. E., Reid, L. S., & Feallock, J. B. (1960) Short-term retention as a function of the average number of items presented. *J. Exp. Psychol.,* **60,** 201–207.

McGeoch, J. A. (1942) *The psychology of human learning: An introduction.* New York: Longmans.

Mackworth, J. F. (1959) Paced memorizing in a continuous task. *J. Exp. Psychol.,* **58,** 206–211.

Mandler, G. (1954) Response factors in human learning. *Psychol. Rev.,* **61,** 235–244.

Miller, G. A. (1956) The magical number seven, plus or minus two: Some limits of our capacity for processing information. *Psychol. Rev.,* **63,** 81–97.

Miller, G. A., & Selfridge, J. A. (1950) Verbal context and the recall of meaningful material. *Amer. J. Psychol.,* **63,** 176–185.

Moray, N. (1959) Attention in dichotic listening: Affective cues and the influence of instructions. *Quart. J. Exp. Psychol.,* **11,** 56–60.

Moray, N. (1960) Broadbent's filter theory: Postulate H and the problem of switching time. *Quart. J. Exp. Psychol.*, **12**, 214–220.

Murdock, B. B. (1960) The immediate retention of unrelated words. *J. Exp. Psychol.*, **60**, 222–234.

Murdock, B. B. (1961) Short-term retention of single paired-associates. *Psychol. Rep.*, **8**, 280.

Peterson, L. R., & Peterson, M. J. (1959) Short-term retention of individual verbal items. *J. Exp. Psychol.*, **58**, 193–198.

Peterson, L. R., & Peterson, M. J. (1960) The effect of spacing repetitions on short-term retention. *Amer. Psychologist*, **15**, 450. (Abstract)

Peterson, L. R., Peterson, M. J., & Miller, A. G. (1961) Short-term retention and meaningfulness. *Canad. J. Psychol.* **15**, 143–147.

Pillsbury, W. B., & Sylvester, A. (1940) Retroactive and proactive inhibition in immediate memory. *J. Exp. Psychol.*, **27**, 532–545.

Pollack, I., Johnson, L. B., & Knaff, P. R. (1959) Running memory span. *J. Exp. Psychol.*, **57**, 137–146.

Segal, S. J., & Cofer, C. N. (1960) The effect of recency and recall on word association. *Amer. Psychologist*, **15**, 451. (Abstract)

Storms, L. H. (1958) Apparent backward association: A situational effect. *J. Exp. Psychol.*, **55**, 390–395.

Underwood, B. J. (1957) Interference and forgetting. *Psychol. Rev.*, **64**, 49–60.

Underwood, B. J., & Schulz, R. W. (1960) *Meaningfulness and verbal learning.* New York: Lippincott.

Woodworth, R. S., & Schlosberg, H. (1954) *Experimental psychology.* Rev. ed. New York: Holt, Rinehart & Winston.

COMMENTS ON PROFESSOR PETERSON'S PAPER

Arthur W. Melton
UNIVERSITY OF MICHIGAN

Professor Peterson has given us a thoughtful and stimulating contribution to the literature on immediate memory. Perhaps his most important contribution, from my point of view, is his concerted effort to relate the phenomena of immediate memory to the phenomena of repetitive learning and long-term retention which have been studied so assiduously and profitably during these last fifty years. Naturally, I am for this reason also in sympathy with his conclusion that this research strategy is more promising than escape into neurophysiological theory, while not denying that the latter should be pursued as a parallel strategy by those qualified to do so. Nevertheless, I find myself in disagreement with some of the principal details of his position, and in agreement with others.

But neither the agreements nor disagreements should cloud our vision to the fact that Peterson has given us an important new method for the study of short-term memory. I refer, of course, to the Peterson and Peterson (1959) idea for studying the recall of single verbal messages over intervals of time measured in seconds and when the message is well below the memory (and perception) span of S and thus has 100 per cent recallability immediately after presentation. As I shall attempt to show later, a proper and systematic employment of this method may well play a key role in the attempt to integrate our knowledge about "immediate" memory and our knowledge about repetitive learning and long-term memory.

This comment leads me to make two further introductory comments, one about the definition of what we are talking about—immediate memory—and the other about methods for studying such memory processes.

It seems to me about time that we abandoned the concept of immediate memory in favor of one that is descriptively and operationally more adequate. Traditionally, immediate memory has referred to the recall of an experience or "message" immediately after a single presentation of it. The referent was usually the result of a memory-span test. Strictly speaking, however, the term is appropriate only when the message is sufficiently simple to be encoded simultaneously in a single moment of experience and read out in a single response. If the message is presented sequentially, as is a necessity in the auditory memory-span method (except for the limited simultaneity used by Broadbent, 1954), and/or recalled in a sequence of responses, as in auditory- and visual-span methods, the immediate recall is possible only for the last element of the message if it is recalled first. This latter condition is, of course, not even permitted in the usual memory-span test.

Even greater ambiguity as well as inappropriateness pertains to the assumption that immediate memory relates to the recall of something that has been experienced only once in exactly the form in which it is to be recalled. In connection with a number of problems of learning, we are being plagued by our loose definition of a "repetition," but studies of immediate memory in the traditional sense and studies of one-trial learning have as a crucial common difficulty the definition of a repetition. Clearly, a three-second visual presentation of a three-consonant message is not the same, repetitionwise, as a one-second presentation; nor is the serial presentation of auditory digits at a two-second rate the same, repetition-wise, as the presentation of those digits at a one-second rate. So, logically and in practice, it is recognized that immediate memory does not necessarily have to do with recall after a single presentation, when the latter is operationally defined as the minimal duration required for complete and accurate perception.

The only alternative concept I have to suggest is that of short-term memory. It has the heuristic advantage of a ready, meaningful abbreviation (STM), and specifies only the *principal* independent variable of interest—the relative brevity of the time interval before testing for retention. It does not imply a particular method of measurement of retention—it is as applicable to measures of recognition memory, reconstruction memory, or perhaps even to various savings methods, as it is to recall. It does not imply that only one repetition has occurred, and thus permits—even requires—the kinds of studies of STM as a function of frequency of repetition that have been performed by Peterson and Peterson (1959) and by Hellyer (1962), and of STM as a function of the spacing of repetitions in time that have been performed by Peterson and Peterson (1960), with the rate of forgetting over intervals up to 27 seconds as the dependent variable. In like manner, the concept of STM is as readily applied to one Millerian "chunk," such as a single consonant or word, as to 2, 3, 4, . . . , 7 ± 2, . . . , n chunks, and thus encompasses not only studies of the subspan range of chunks but also the span and the supraspan range of chunks such as involved in Murdock's (1960) studies of immediate free recall. In short, the term STM places no artificial restrictions on the conditions of presentation, the length or character of the message, or the test for retention, but leaves these quite properly for empirical determination and theoretical integration. It replaces an implied dichotomy (Hebb, 1949) with an implied continuum, and leaves to data and theory the responsibility for showing that discontinuity in fact exists.

Not the least advantage of the term STM is the implication, on operational grounds, that STM is continuous with retention measured after longer intervals of time, for complex multiple-unit tasks (serial and paired-associate lists) after various frequencies of repetition, and under various conditions of preceding and interpolated activity. What to call the latter? Here we face the same dilemma faced by investigators of classical conditioning in the case of "simultaneous" CRs and "delayed" CRs where the continuum of time intervals between the onset of the CS and the onset of the overlapping UCS needed some handy labels. There the consensus seems to be that CS-UCS intervals less than five seconds are simultaneous CR conditions and CS-UCS intervals longer than five seconds define delayed CR conditions. I believe we can in like manner reduce the confusion as to what we are about if we define STM as memory over intervals up to five minutes, and LTM as memory over intervals beyond five minutes. In using this definition, I am not bothered —and, in fact, I consider it an advantage—that performance changes in successive trials in most rote learning and skill learning studies would be classified as STM measures, and that the performance changes over the first five minutes of rest after any level of learning of any task, i.e., where we usually search for "reminiscence" effects, would likewise be considered in the context of STM. But the main point is that the concept of a continuum must be preserved while one realizes the convenience of specifying which end of the continuum is of primary interest in a specific class of investigations.

But perhaps the most important consequence of an agreement to employ the term STM, rather than immediate memory, is that it would (a) reflect a rapidly growing usage of the term, and (b) encompass the proliferation of methods for studying retention over very short intervals of time in both discrete and continuous tasks. To this the term immediate memory is clearly inappropriate. Within the last five years we have witnessed not only an extraordinary growth of interest in STM capacities of the human S, perhaps related to widespread recognition that these capacities represent not only an extraordinary capability but also a major liability of the human operator in man-machine systems, but also a remarkable inventiveness of investigators in devising procedures for investigating STM. Apparently, the limitations and relative sterility of the traditional memory-span technique for answering questions about STM were widely and almost simultaneously recognized. One inventive approach was to modify the memory-span technique. Thus, Broadbent adapted the memory-span technique to the problems of attention in relation to short-term storage by his two-ear (Broadbent, 1954) and his eye-ear (Broadbent, 1956) modifications of the traditional single-channel technique; Klemmer (1961), Anderson (1960), and others adapted the technique to problems of selective recall from within a single message by poststimulus cuing of recall, and Averbach and Coriell (1961) and Sperling (1960) did the same sort of thing with the perceptual span in order to free it from the limitations placed on it by the "readout" time involved in the memory span; and Pollack, Johnson, and Knaff (1959) used studies of the "running memory span" to permit generalizations about STM in the short-term storage of continuous messages. At about the same time, Yntema and Muesser (1960) and Lloyd, Reid, and Feallock (1960) devised tasks in which STM was measured by cued recall in essentially continuous series of events, and this method has since been adapted to the more traditional paired-associate learning by Murdock (1961a), Peterson, Saltzman, Hilner, and Land (1962) and Peterson and Peterson (1962). Of course, these latter techniques have much in common with what is done from trial to trial in standard paired-associate learning where the order of presentation and test of the pairs varies from trial to trial and also with methods used years ago by Thorndike (1932); but with the important difference that in the recent studies the interval between presentation and test for a particular item, and the number of other items in "storage" at the time of test, is the manipulated variable, and the speed or accuracy of recall is therefore the dependent variable. An analogous method for measuring short-term recognition memory has been introduced by Shepard and Teghtsoonian (1961), with striking evidence for the deterioration of recognition memory over intervals up to 4 to 5 minutes, and obvious potential for significant contributions to our understanding of this form of memory.

As indicated earlier, of great promise seems to be the technique introduced by Peterson and Peterson (1959) for measuring the retention of single subspan messages over short intervals of time. Perhaps this is because it can be adapted to the ultimate simplification of the analysis of STM without confounding by overlapping messages in storage. This goal is approximated in Murdock's (1961b) use of it to measure the forgetting of a single word over intervals up to 18 seconds. A closer approximation will be achieved when contamination of observations by proactive inhibition from preceding items of the same class has been eliminated, as will be pointed out later. However, I do not mean to imply that one of these methods for studying STM is necessarily superior to another. On the contrary, each has certain capabilities for the analyses of the determinants of STM, and certain limitations. Nevertheless, the ones most appealing to me are those that permit the manipulation of duration of presentation, frequency of repetition, intervals between repetitions, the time relations between stimulus and response elements, and the length, complexity, and developmental history of the to-be-remembered unit, while permitting variation in the number of units that are being contemporaneously stored. These techniques are, it seems to me, most likely to provide the data that will reveal the continuity, or discontinuity, of STM and LTM.

STIMULUS TRACE VS. MEMORY TRACE

Obviously, one of the first reactions to the suggestion of a continuum of processes for STM and LTM is the question whether or not we have an initial discontinuity between the stimulus trace and the memory trace. I see no basis for rejection of this dichotomy, but I suspect that considerable confusion surrounds the distinction. It seems to me necessary to accept the notion that stimuli may affect for a brief time the sensorium and the directly involved CNS segments, but that they may not get "hooked up" or encoded and thus may not become a stimulus component of an association or memory trace. Thus, a filtering or attention operation may be required to channel the incoming signal to some variety of coding operation available to S (and also to preselect among coding operations on the basis of external or self-instructions) before the stimulus can become part of a viable memory trace. If one then assumes, as does Broadbent (1958), that there is a limited channel capacity for this encoding operation (his P system), it is clear that there must be a distinction between sensory traces and memory traces, and that there must be more in the momentary experience than can be encoded into a report of it, assuming that the stimulus traces are of quite short duration.

The recent work of Averbach and Coriell (1961) and Sperling (1960) clearly indicates that there is briefly preserved in the visual system much more than S can report, i.e., that the sensory span is much greater than dependence on a report of what has been seen, which *requires* sequential encoding and reporting, has led us to believe. When a 16-letter array was presented to Ss for 50 milliseconds by Averbach and Coriell, 4 to 5 letters could be reported; but when S was cued with respect to the letter to be reported (by a bar marker that appeared simultaneously with the array, or at the offset of the array), Ss could report 12 to 13 letters. As might be expected from a decay interpretation of this sensory trace, the bar marker cue for which letter was to be reported first became less effective the longer the interval between the array offset and the cue, until, at 200- to 300-millisecond intervals, it gave no higher frequency of report than the uncued report (ca. 4 to 5 letters). The further specification of this short-term visual storage was achieved by a technique of "erasure" of the cued letter by another symbol or grid which occurred at various intervals after the simultaneous presentation of the array and cue. The results with the grid eraser showed that reports of the cued letter could be made only with very low accuracy (ca. 4 to 17 per cent in different Ss) when the erasing grid occurred at the offset of the letter array and bar marker (i.e., 50 milliseconds after onset); but the accuracy increased, again to the limit established by the memory span, as the erasing grid was delayed by longer intervals up to about 200 milliseconds. This appears to be clearly a function of storage in the visual system prior to encoding into memory, since the erasure is effective if four or more letters are in the array; but it is not effective if a single letter is presented and erased. Also, it is suggested that this is a visual system storage, rather than retinal per se, because it is reported that the erasure effect may be gotten when the stimulus and marker are presented to one eye and the erasing grid to the other.

My interpretation of these data is that there is a temporary storage of information in the sensory system that is preassociational and pre-memorial, that this storage does in fact exhibit rapid decay (Averbach and Coriell estimate the duration to be 270 milliseconds), and that this must be clearly distinguished from the problem of short-term memory, which assumes as a pre-condition that the stimulus has in fact been responded to. This position does not, of course, deny the possibility (perhaps certainty) that the rate of encoding of information from this short-term visual buffer storage and the sensitivity of this encoding process to characteristics of the array may well vary as a function of a number of factors.

The purpose of all this is to introduce the examination of three questions: (a) Is this short-term sensory (STS) system storage what Hull's (1952) stimulus-trace concept referred to? (b) Is it the same as Mackworth's (1959) perceptual trace, as distinguished from the verbal trace? (c) Is it the same as Broadbent's (1958) S system? With respect to the first question, I agree with Peterson that the stimulus trace notion, as applied to the time relations between CS and UCS in conditioning experiments, may well be the same as a rapidly decaying short-term sensory storage, such as represented in the Averbach and Coriell study, but that the long-duration "stimulus traces" required for the interpretation of remote associations in verbal learning and for trace-conditioned responses belong to the category of memory traces, i.e., encoded, integrated, reacted-to stimuli. Hull's difficulty here is, I suspect, just another example of our problem with the concept of stimulus.

As for Mackworth's distinction between perceptual traces and verbal traces, it seems to me that she is describing the relative efficiency of two varieties of memory trace which are distinguished on the basis of the rate of encoding. In the case of the task with only the spatial positions of lights as cues, a more primitive and highly overlearned encoding system was in operation; when position plus letter labels were present the Ss attempted to use a dual coding system and the second was not as well habituated (there was no well-established location-symbol compatibility) and slowed down the processing into memory. Since it is also known (Brainerd, Irby, Fitts, and Alluisi, 1962) that different letters and different subsets of letters have different processing times, as reflected in disjunctive reaction times, it may also be suggested that it should be possible to obtain a set of letter cues that, after extended practice on letter-position correlation, would permit as rapid rates of response as the spatial cues alone when the STM requirement is low. In short, I suspect that there is no fundamental dichotomy between perceptual traces and memory traces, but rather a continuum of rates of encoding sensory information into memory traces based on previous experience and the compatibility of the experience with such previous experience.

As for Broadbent's (1958) S and P systems and their relations to STM and LTM, it will be remembered that he conceives of the S system as having two modes of operation in relation to P. He suggests that the mode of operation used may depend on the stage of practice or familiarity with the situation. Figure 9–1 shows his two modes of operation of S and P, and the system my own thinking would suggest. Figure 9–1a (the unpracticed mode) is a simple diagram of the relationship between what Broadbent calls the S system and the P system, and what I have called the STS and the encoded, perceived event which is associative and therefore an event for which there is a memory trace. There is no disagreement. However, Figure 9–1b is his schematic for a mode of operation of the S and P systems, which assumes (a) that information may go directly into the P system, as well as through the S system, and (b) that, in addition, encoded (P) events may be recirculated through the S system by rehearsal. The latter is introduced particularly to account for the span of immediate memory and the role that rehearsal may play in postponing deterioration in STM. My own schematic (Figure 9–1c)

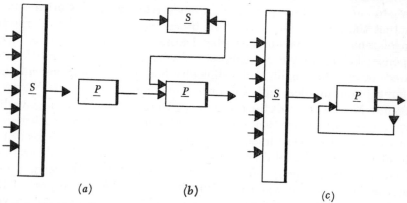

(a)   (b)   (c)

Fig. 9–1. Conceptualizations of the relationship between the sensory and perceptual (memorial) stages.

keeps the STS system free of this recirculation through it (except for objectively identifiable instances of self-stimulation such as echolalia). But more importantly, it locates the recirculation process within the P system, on the grounds that such rehearsal or "inner repetition" acts on the strength of a memory trace to renew it, and strengthen it, just as another repetition of the stimulus in the environment strengthens the memory trace *if* it gets into and through the STS as the "same" event. Actually, a number of readings of Broadbent (1958) fail to convince me that we are in any fundamental disagreement on this point; but from my point of view the distinction between the S and P systems is the distinction between the STS storage, which is not properly identified as a part of memory because it is not yet associational, and the encoded experience, which is in the memory store with a frequency of one but by inner repetition may be given higher frequencies of occurrence without necessarily involving the STS system again. Once this distinction is made, I can then accept the principle of decay as a reasonable hypothesis about

STS, while rejecting it as a reasonable hypothesis about STM, as well as LTM.

DECAY, AND SHORT-TERM MEMORY VS. LONG-TERM MEMORY

The extension of my last remark leads necessarily to a consideration of the decay interpretation of STM, the dichotomy of STM and LTM, and eventually to Peterson's distinction between "background conditioning" and "cue learning." At one time the disuse interpretation of forgetting, in both STM and LTM, was quite generally held, and the active factor associated with the passage of time without reuse was presumed to be some intrinsic decay, deterioration, or homeostatic process in the nervous system that sought a return to the equilibrium disturbed by the new association. This notion, as it applied to LTM, was thoroughly discredited by McGeoch (1932), on the grounds that a principle of reproductive interference plus a principle of stimulus change (context) could more adequately account for forgetting. Postman (1961) has brought together the extensive developments of theory and data on the interference theory since McGeoch's paper, and has assumed, quite properly, that interference is the principal alternative interpretation of LTM.

With the revival of interest in STM has come a revival of the decay theory, but now limited to STM. Perhaps Hebb's (1949) duplexity theory of memory is the most explicit on this point. He postulates an STM process which is transient and subject to decay and which gets transformed into LTM by repetition, or reverberation, or both. LTM is persistent, i.e., permanent, and nonavailability of LTM is a matter of interference. Just why an encoded event with a frequency of 1 should, when lost, have its loss ascribed to decay, while an encoded event with a frequency of 2, 3, 4, . . . , n should have its loss attributed to interference, I cannot understand, and I can find no compelling evidence for the decay hypothesis about STM.

There are, however, some compelling data for the hypothesis that STM operates in much the same fashion as LTM with respect to the rate of forgetting as a function of critical variables in the situation. But before examining these, it should be clear that the frequency of 1 for STM is assumed to be a frequency of 1 for an event involving connectedness, even though only through contiguity with another event, i.e., an event in the P system. In the case of human STM, the *fact* that it is an associational process is revealed by the common operation of all learning studies; namely, a pretest (usually assumed) would not elicit either the specific responses or their ordering in recall, and after one "presentation" they are present and ordered in recall in a systematic way.

My principal reasons for being skeptical about the decay theory of

STM are (a) evidence that STM and LTM are a continuum, (b) evidence that the *rate* of short-term forgetting is a function of the complexity (number of chunks) in the event to be remembered, and (c) inferential evidence that the observed forgetting in STM is accounted for by interference factors.

The principal evidence for the continuum of STM and LTM come from the effects of frequency on the rate of forgetting of single verbal units. Peterson has described the findings of Peterson and Peterson (1959) regarding the effects of repeating the presented three-consonant unit 0, 1, or 3 times before beginning the backward counting prior to the attempt to recall. The slope of the retention curve was clearly a function of the number of repetitions. Hellyer (1962) has repeated and extended this portion of the Peterson and Peterson study with some minor variations in procedure and shows that 1, 2, 4, and 8 repetitions of a single three-consonant unit before a number-filled interval of 3, 9, 18, and 27 seconds gave extraordinarily regular decreases in slope of the retention curve as frequency of repetition increased. While this may not be surprising, it is a critical observation, especially if one holds that rehearsal only postpones decay of the trace. If, as seems to be the case, the resistance of an item to forgetting progressively increases as a function of frequency of repetition, the basic continuum of STM and LTM has been established.

For my second reason, I must call on data from a splendid series of experiments by Murdock (1961b) in which the Peterson-Peterson method was used. First, he repeated the Peterson and Peterson (1959) study with 3 consonant units and their procedure, and got remarkable agreement between the slope of his retention curve over intervals up to 18 seconds and theirs. Then he repeated the experiment with single common words as the memory unit, and then again with word triads, i.e., three unrelated common words. The results of his experiments and the original Peterson and Peterson (1959) experiment are shown in Figure 9–2. Clearly, the slope of the retention curve for one word is much less than the slope of the retention curve for three-consonant units or three-word units, and the slopes in the latter two instances are not significantly different. This means, I believe, that the slope of the STM retention curve is a function of the number of chunks in the to-be-remembered unit, even though that number is well below the memory span. One might even generalize these results to suggest that a complete family of STM retention curves, varying only in the rate parameter, would be obtained for different numbers of chunks in the to-be-remembered unit up to the number that can be encoded from the STS system from a single simultaneous presentation. In any event, it appears that the number of different encoded elements has a very important role in determining the rate of forgetting. I find it difficult to account for this in terms of decay, and very reasonable to account for it in terms of intra-unit interference.

My third argument for a continuum of STM and LTM, and against a special postulate of decay for STM, gets quite involved in association theory, most of which it is not my proper function to develop. However, a brief statement, not fully defended, is perhaps appropriate, if for no other reason than that it permits me to take issue with Peterson's argument that his experimental technique (i.e., Peterson and Peterson,

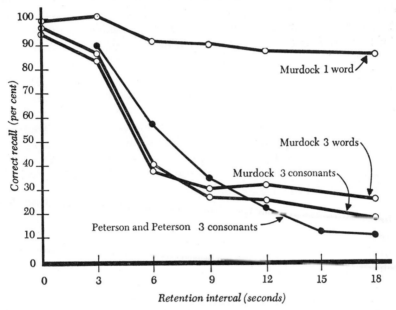

FIG. 9–2. Percentages of correct recall of various types of memory units as a function of the time interval filled with counting backward: Data on three-consonant units, one-word units, and three-word units from Murdock (1961b); data on three-consonant units from Peterson and Peterson (1959).

1959) does not involve proactive inhibition (PI). But first, I must anticipate later remarks about his distinction between background conditioning and cue learning by saying that, in my opinion, no theory of forgetting can get along without a principle of context, such as formulated by McGeoch (1932) and used by every student of stimulus generalization and transfer. This principle asserts that recall is a function of the completeness of reinstatement of the original stimulating conditions. A variant and elegant, but incomplete, formulation of this notion of context is the molecular all-or-none theory of association by Estes and Burke (1953). If one assumes some dependence of recall of an encoded item on the total internal and external stimulus set, and if one assumes further that there is continuous change in such background stimulation, then such changes alone should cause some forgetting over time, and more, the greater the time except as such stimuli may be recycled by internal or external rhythms. The reason I make this point here is that an interference theory does not need to predict perfect and permanent retention of a single experience when all interference has been eliminated; it needs only to predict that forgetting not accounted for by stimulus change.

Murdock's (1961b) very slow rate of forgetting of a *single word* under the conditions of Peterson and Peterson's (1959) experiment suggests that the stimulus-change factor may be of rather minor importance over periods as brief as 30 seconds, especially since there was some opportunity for PI from preceding words in the test series and for retroactive inhibition (RI) from the counting backward. So, it may be suggested that the marked forgetting shown in the case of three-consonant units or three-word units must in a nondecay theory be accounted for principally by a combination of (a) proactive inhibition (PI), intra-unit interference (II), and retroactive inhibition (RI). In the studies described in Figure 9–2, RI may be assumed to be relatively constant and of unknown amount since, to date, there have been no systematic studies of different ways of filling the retention interval. The II, which has been discussed earlier as one basis for the relationship between rate of forgetting and the number of chunks in the to-be-remembered unit, needs no further comment. There remains, however, the question whether PI also makes a contribution.

Peterson believes that his data fail to show an effect of PI within his type of experiment. On the contrary, I suspect it has a quite powerful effect, or at least that new experiments must be done to determine directly its effect. Peterson's chief evidence against a PI factor is that, after he eliminates the first two practice trials and then analyzes his data for blocks of six trials (trials 3 to 8, 9 to 14, 45 to 50), he finds an improvement rather than a deterioration of performance over blocks. It seems to me that this is not a proper test for PI, on several counts. In the first place, in so far as there was a practice effect, the matter is indeterminate, since the practice effect and PI would work in opposite directions on performance; and we have no way of predicting what effect PI would have relative to practice effects. In the second place, it may be hypothesized that general PI gets established very quickly, in fact, as soon as S has seen one or two 3-consonant units and recognizes the set of possible stimuli represented by them (Underwood and Schulz's "selector mechanism," 1960). Specific PI, i.e., the interference resulting from the specific preceding consonant units, would be expected to reach a steady state after only one or a very few trials because of the rapid short-term forgetting of each such unit. Only a trial-by-trial analysis for the first few trials of such an experiment could hope to reveal the presence of PI if it operated in the fashion described.

That specific PI does occur in this type of experiment under some conditions is clearly shown by the data of Murdock (1961b). In his experiment II, where one word was to be recalled when it was preceded by 0, 3, 6, 9, or 12 other words and followed by counting backward for 0, 3, 6, 9, 12, or 18 seconds, there were 324 extra-list intrusions, i.e., words from elsewhere than the list containing the item to be recalled. Of these, 98 (30 per cent) were words that had been correct on one of the preceding trials, 58 of these 98 were from the immediately preceding trial, and 13 were from the trial before that. It is, I believe, especially significant that such substantial amounts of specific PI could show through such massive amounts of intra-list and other extra-list intrusions.

As for the Conrad (1960) data, which Peterson cites in support of his no intertrial PI thesis, I find them unconvincing. The remarkable fact seems to me that he was able to find some evidence for intrusions based on the serial positions of digits in eight-digit sets presented sequentially. Even so, he found only 32 more than expected when he used a 15-second interval between trials and only eight more than expected with the 25-second interval; and the number correctly recalled at the 15-second interval *was* four less (230/384 versus 234/384) than with the 25-second interval, i.e., in the direction expected if intrusions blocked recall. The experiment needs to be redone with a larger set of elements to choose from in constructing successive series, in order to avoid the ambiguities introduced by the occurrence of the intruding digit in another position within the list being recalled.

My conclusion is that STM measurements such as Peterson and Peterson make, and which I consider quite crucial to the thesis of a continuum of STM and LTM, are not demonstrably different from LTM gained through repetition, at least in so far as there is involvement of PI, intra-list interference, and RI. But, of course, many more (and more systematic) experiments need to be done to show this and to demonstrate the interrelations of interference factors, frequency, and rate of forgetting.

BACKGROUND CONDITIONING AND CUE LEARNING

My final comment relates to Peterson's distinction between background conditioning and cue learning. The distinction clearly has some merit, since he is able to relate it to (a) the distinction between free recall and cued recall, and (b) the distinction between the associative phase of learning and the response-integration phase of learning (Underwood and

Schulz, 1960). Both of these latter distinctions are now so well established in our thinking about learning, especially verbal learning, that any new classification that correlates with them must have some degree of acceptability.

Nevertheless, I have two critical comments to make about this new classification. The first is a matter of data, and may well be answered by new data showing that Peterson's claims for less than perfect correlation between the indices of background conditioning and cue learning in his type of STM experiment are valid. I am not, however, convinced by the data he presents.

He attempts to justify the distinction by showing that variables do not affect in the same way the index of background conditioning, which is the frequency of recall of the first letter of a compound verbal memory unit, and the index of cue learning, which is the serial dependency in the recall of the memory unit. The first experiment cited is that of Peterson, Peterson, and Miller (1961). Here he says that the proportions of items correctly recalled and the sequential letter probabilities increase as one goes from low-association-value nonsense syllables to high-association-value nonsense syllables, and increase further as one goes to three-letter words, but that more first letters are recalled with low-AV syllables than with high-AV syllables. The actual frequencies of correct first letters recalled were .77, .73, and .86, respectively. This difference between the low- and high-AV syllables is simply not significant, and cannot be used as evidence for a lack of high correlation between the index of background conditioning and cue learning. (It may be noted that his hypothesis of less than perfect correlation between the indices runs the risk of accepting sampling errors as evidence for his hypothesis.)

The other alleged evidence for this lack of correlation comes from the Peterson and Peterson (1960) study. Here, the completely correct items and the first-letter recalls increased regularly with the spacing interval between repetitions, but the sequential dependencies showed slight and nonsignificant variation (.91, .91, .93, and .93). In this case, I am disinclined to accept the null hypothesis with respect to the index of cue learning when the poorest learning condition gives a sequential probability of .91, if for no other reason than that the beneficial effect of spacing had to operate against an obvious ceiling effect. But there is, I suspect, a better reason, and that is that such high sequential probabilities must mean that very few Ss made partial responses (i.e., single-letter responses or two-letter responses). The frequency of such partial responses in memorization of three-letter units is heavily influenced by instructions to S regarding the recall process, and it may be that Ss also self-instruct themselves differently regarding the acceptability of partial (single- or two-letter) responses as a function of the nature of the memory unit (nonsense syllable or word). In any event, one must infer that these specific Ss inhibited a response unless they had all elements. Said in another way, it is reasonable to expect that the sequential probability measure can be made to shift around quite radically, depending on the instructions to S. In short, it seems that Peterson has not given us compelling evidence for the distinction between background conditioning and cue learning.

My other comment on the distinction between background conditioning and cue learning is that I fear it will muddy the waters of stimulus analysis in our studies of learning even more than they now are. As I understand Peterson, he says that recall in his STM experiment is jointly determined by background conditioning and cue learning, and that these are "two types of associative learning" (p. 343). For this distinction between types to be valid, it must be shown (a) that background conditioning does not involve cue learning, and (b) that cue learning does not involve background conditioning. I think that neither of these propositions is sound, and that the distinction is an attempt to make two types of learning out of the cue and context factors that are necessarily involved to some extent in every association or memory trace. Again, I am in the position of attacking a dichotomy on the grounds that it is a continuum, perhaps because I abhor dichotomies (except the one fundamental to procreation and evolution).

In this case, it seems to me that Peterson is distinguishing two points on a continuum of the homogeneity-heterogeneity of weighting of stimulus elements in a stimulus sample that elicits a response, the stimulus sample being that set of stimuli effectively tied to the response on any one trial. In the case of background conditioning, the assumption is being made that the stimulus elements in the sample are homogeneous in weighting, in the manner assumed by Estes and Burke (1953). In the case of cue learning, the assumption is being made that the stimulus elements in the sample are strikingly heterogeneous in weighting, in fact, that there is *a* cue or stimulus element that carries all the weight of determination of the response. It seems to me that our evidence for the effects of context factors (i.e., the *more* homogeneous subset of the stimulus sample) in the case of cue learning (Bilodeau and Schlosberg, 1951) strongly suggests that the cue for recall is a combination of cue and context. I would also suggest that a completely homogeneously weighted set of stimulus elements is a figment of statistical learning theory imagination, and there is always some degree of heterogeneity of weighting (or cueness) in the effective set of stimuli that has an opportunity, through contiguity or otherwise, to get connected to a response.

The analogy drawn by Peterson between cue learning and response integration suggests that an important factor in determining the heterogeneity of the stimulus set that elicits a response is the amount of training or strength of S-R relationship. That is, early in training, and this would certainly be the situation in free recall after a single presentation as in the STM experiments, the effective stimulus to the elicitation of the response is more homogeneous. Late in learning, i.e., after many repetitions of a particular S-R relationship in which *constancy* of an element of the stimulus set from trial to trial has been *forced*, as in the case of letter-sequence habits or word-sequence habits, there is radical heterogeneity of the weighting of elements in the stimulus set, with the constant stimulus element as the principal cue—but not ever the sole cue.

Obviously, this line of criticism of his distinction and this suggestion regarding an alternative conceptualization leads directly to the heart of the problem of the analysis of the stimulus control of responses in isolation, in sequences, and in simultaneous compounds. It is far beyond my capability to develop an adequate alternative formulation, but my experimental and theoretical strategy will certainly be to emphasize the continuum which his conception of background conditioning and cue learning tends to treat as a dichotomy. My strategy is reinforced by the notion that this is the proper approach to discover the continuum of STM and LTM.

SUMMARY

Peterson has provided us with a thought-provoking analysis of short-term memory. His method of experimentation on STM promises to be one of the most useful of the many new methods for examining STM, because of its analytic possibilities. Through the use of this and the other methods for examining the functional characteristics of STM, it is expected that the rigorous continuity of STM and LTM will be demonstrated, that the interference and stimulus-change interpretations of LTM will be found adequate to explain STM, and that this extension of a single theory of forgetting to encompass both LTM and STM will be aided by considering background conditioning and cue learning as points on a continuum, rather than as types of associative learning.

REFERENCES

Anderson, N. S. (1960) Poststimulus cuing in immediate memory. *J. Exp. Psychol.*, **60**, 216–221.

Averbach, E., & Coriell, A. S. (1961) Short-term memory in vision. *Bell Syst. Tech. J.*, **40**, 309–328. (Monogr. 3756).

Bilodeau, I. McD., & Schlosberg, H. (1951) Similarity in stimulating conditions as a variable in retroactive inhibition. *J. Exp. Psychol.*, **41**, 199–204.

Brainerd, R. W., Irby, T. S., Fitts, P. M., & Alluisi, E. A. (1962) Some variables influencing the rate of gain of information. *J. Exp. Psychol.*, 63, 105–110.

Broadbent, D. E. (1954) The role of auditory localization in attention and memory span. *J. Exp. Psychol.*, 47, 191–196.

Broadbent, D. E. (1956) Successive responses to simultaneous stimuli. *Quart. J. Exp. Psychol.*, 8, 145–152.

Broadbent, D. E. (1958) *Perception and communication.* London: Pergamon.

Conrad, R. (1960) Serial order intrusions in immediate memory. *Brit. J. Psychol.*, 51, 54–48.

Estes, W. K., & Burke, C. J. (1953) A theory of stimulus variability in learning. *Psychol. Rev.*, 60, 276–286.

Hebb, D. O. (1949) *The organization of behavior.* New York: Wiley.

Hellyer, S. (1962) Supplementary report: Frequency of stimulus presentation and short-term decrement in recall. *J. Exp. Psychol.*, 64.

Hull, C. L. (1952) *A behavior system.* New Haven, Conn.: Yale University Press.

Klemmer, E. T. (1961) The perception of all patterns produced by a seven-line matrix. *J. Exp. Psychol.*, 61, 274–282.

Lloyd, K. E., Reid, L. S., & Feallock, J. B. (1960) Short-term retention as a function of the average number of items presented. *J. Exp. Psychol.*, 60, 201–207.

Mackworth, J. F. (1959) Paced memorizing in a continuous task. *J. Exp. Psychol.*, 58, 206–211.

McGeoch, J. A. (1932) Forgetting and the law of disuse. *Psychol. Rev.*, 39, 352–370.

Murdock, B. B., Jr. (1960) The immediate retention of unrelated words. *J. Exp. Psychol.*, 60, 222–234.

Murdock, B. B., Jr. (1961a) Short-term retention of single paired-associates. *Psychol. Rep.*, 8, 280.

Murdock, B. B., Jr. (1961b) The retention of individual items. *J. Exp. Psychol.*, 62, 618–625.

Peterson, L. R., & Peterson, M. J. (1959) Short-term retention of individual verbal items. *J. Exp. Psychol.*, 58, 193–198.

Peterson, L. R., & Peterson, M. J. (1960) The effect of spacing repetitions on short-term retention. *Amer. Psychologist*, 15, 450. (Abstract)

Peterson, L. R., & Peterson, M. J. (1962) Minimal paired-associate learning. *J. Exp. Psychol.*, 63, 521–527.

Peterson, L. R., Peterson, M. J., & Miller, A. G. (1961) Short-term retention and meaningfulness. *Canad. J. Psychol.*, 15, 143–147.

Peterson, L. R., Saltzman, D., Hilner, K., & Land, V. (1962) Recency and frequency in paired associate learning. *J. Exp. Psychol.*, 63, 396–403.

Pollack, I., Johnson, L. B., & Knaff, P. R. (1959) Running memory span. *J. Exp. Psychol.*, 57, 137–146.

Postman, L. (1961) The present status of interference theory. In C. N. Cofer (Ed.), *Verbal learning and verbal behavior.* New York: McGraw-Hill.

Shepard, R. N., & Teghtsoonian, M. (1961) Retention of information under conditions approaching a steady state. *J. Exp. Psychol.*, 62, 302–309.

Sperling, G. (1960) The information available in brief visual presentations. *Psychol. Monogr.*, 74, No. 11.

Thorndike, E. L., *et al.* (1932) *The fundamentals of learning.* New York: Teachers College.

Underwood, B. J., & Schulz, R. W. (1960) *Meaningfulness and verbal learning.* Chicago: Lippincott.

Yntema, D. B., & Muesser, G. E. (1960) Remembering the present states of a number of variables. *J. Exp. Psychol.*, 60, 18–22.

SUMMARY OF CONFERENCE DISCUSSION

A major part of the discussion was devoted to consideration of background conditioning and its differentiation from cue learning. One question which Melton raised was whether these two kinds of learning involve different kinds of traces. Though both decay with time, they do so at different rates; and Melton suggested that since the stimulus (for cue learning) is under the experimenter's control, it is relatively constant, whereas the background factors may vary. Further consideration of the background factor included Staats's statement that the experimenter might hold the background factors constant while varying the stimulus proper. In which case, Jenkins suggested, each response might become equally associated with all background elements.

Goss then recalled Logan's analysis (1954) of Hull's V in terms of discrimination between an intra-trial stimulus complex of CS and situational stimuli and an intertrial complex of situational stimuli alone. Melton questioned the validity of Logan's interpretations; Goss replied that he agreed with Logan. To support his position, Melton cited Underwood's conclusion that since the preceding syllable of a serial list is not the stimulus for a particular response, nor is there some rule, there must be variation throughout the presentation of serial lists. Also mentioned by Melton was Voeks's (1954) experiment in which background stimulation was held constant, with consequent perfect or near-perfect occurrence of CRs on trials subsequent to their first occurrence.

In reply, Goss suggested that Voeks had maximized dissimilarity between intra-trial cues including the CS and intertrial cues with consequent rapid conditioning. Also mentioned was Grice and Davis's (1960) suggestion that Voeks's results might be due to activation or facilitation stemming from subjects pressing the telegraph keys.

Peterson was asked by Melton what he thought is the relation of cue learning to background conditioning and as to their different laws. Peterson replied that the only distinction he makes is in terms of the kind of antecedent events being associated in the two cases. Decay means to him only a forgetting curve, and it could include interference. Stimulus fluctuation could be a molecular explanation for some of these decay effects. Peterson indicated uncertainty relative to the roles of these hypothetical processes. However, a distinction can be made between the kinds of antecedent events involved in the two aspects of the associative effect. Melton illustrated these two aspects with the example of the learning of an item such as CJK. J is a cue for K, and C for J, but the background is the cue for C. These are different because, where one letter is the cue for another, well-established habits may be used.

Peterson denied that he assumes different laws in the two cases, and there was comment that the two cases could be the same in principle (Deese), or follow the same law but differ in initial conditions (Shepard). Wickens observed that partial reinforcement could govern the background factors, and regular reinforcement the cue. Goss cited Hull's (1950, p. 309) formulation that incidental or static stimuli extinguish more rapidly than dynamic stimuli.

Peterson said that, instead of assuming different laws, he would rather describe the difference as follows: If the experimenter removes the cue, it cannot be further conditioned; but at the same time this would permit interfering events to decondition background factors more rapidly than the cue.

Underwood presented some data on the background factor from Barnes's (1960) dissertation. From her studies Barnes inferred that associations are formed between background or context cues and response terms in a paired-associate list, and that these associations can be extinguished. In an A-B, C-D paradigm, response B is associated to the context cues. When learning C-D, the D term must now be associated to the same context as B; thus, an A-B, A-C paradigm is formed with A being the context. Under such circumstances the association between the context cues and B may extinguish during the learning of C-D. Barnes's evidence indicated that this did indeed happen. The notion of the context associations and their susceptibility to extinction would also account for the fact that retroactive inhibition may occur with the A-B, C-D paradigm. Furthermore, this notion would also be applicable to the experiments which have shown that when original and interpolated learning are given in drastically different contexts, retroactive inhibition is reduced.

Goss referred to the review of context factors by Musgrave (1960) which brings out data supportive of Barnes's findings. Melton expressed a desire for data on the retention of a single unit when the cue is or is not present in order to define for Peterson's situation the contributions of cue and background factors.

Underwood asked why the background is considered to be more

variable than the cue. Melton answered in terms of experimenter control over the two factors, but Jenkins observed that there is some control over background—the room, the subject's location in it, and the memory drum, for example. Fractionation of this total stimulus complex is needed in the experimental study of short-term memory (Melton). Melton indicated that a tenable hypothesis is that rather than two kinds of traces there are principles of forgetting which are equally applicable to cue and to background stimuli when the functional stimuli in either case are suitably changed. Miller asked about the interpretation of an experiment by Asch, Ceraso, and Heimer (1960) who increased the variability of the background and improved memory. Melton replied that retention would depend entirely on the cue. Deese pointed out that in certain Pavlovian conditioning situations a constant background is used. Dykman, Gantt, and Whitehorn (1956) found it necessary to use a sound-proof box in order to get conditioning of different heart rates to three different intensities of tone stimuli. Brown suggested that classical conditioning is easier if any change predicts the occurrence of the unconditioned stimulus than it is if only one change does.

Jenkins suggested that a useful experimental approach would be to build into subjects a response pool in situations like and also unlike the learning situation (to control for background factors) and then to give the learning trials under varying kinds of stimuli. Postman thought the situation quite different for the case of only one response and the case of more than one response. He felt that with one item (one response) context would be helpful, whereas with two or more items (responses) context would provide interference. Melton observed that human subjects can learn not to respond to background factors under some conditions.

A second major point of the discussion concerned the interpretation of the decay functions as described by Peterson. Melton's discussion claimed that Peterson denies that interference arises from counting and that proaction from prior lists is involved. Melton suggested that the decay of the trace might be accounted for in terms of changes in background factors and Peterson added that proactive effects might arise from factors outside the experiment. Underwood found it difficult to see much interference arising in Peterson's situation but also indicated that it is not known how strongly learned the items are. Peterson indicated that close to 100 per cent retention is obtained at a zero delay interval in cases in which it is certain that the subject has read a pair of meaningful associates. He went on to say that when a single pair of meaningful associates (presented once) was tested after a 16-second interval of counting backward, recall was found to be about 85 per cent correct. Proactive interference from previous presentations combined with retroactive interference from counting did not produce any considerable amount of forgetting. When another pair was added, either immediately before or immediately after the pair later tested, recall dropped to about 50 per cent. Addition of a third pair dropped recall to around 25 per cent.

Peterson went on to suggest that implications for the incremental versus all-or-none controversy follow from short-term retention findings. Whether or not an item has been "learned" depends on the point on the retention function at which you measure learning. Immediately after a single presentation all pairs have been "learned." The longer you wait to make your test, the fewer pairs will be found to have been learned. This line of thought suggests a continuum of response strength rather than a dichotomy between learning and no learning. Peterson described a study in which different intervals (filled with other pairs) were inserted between presentation, first test, and second test. As the interval between presentation and first test increased, the conditional probability of a correct recall on the second test, given a correct recall on the first test, increased. The most likely interpretation seems to be that if the first test is delayed, only the stronger associations are recalled on that first test; and it is these stronger associations that endure to the second test. Peterson did not know of any all-or-none theory that could account for these findings.

REFERENCES

Asch, S. E., Ceraso, J., & Heimer, W. (1960) Perceptual conditions of association. *Psychol. Monogr.* **74**, No. 3.

Barnes, J. M. (1960) "Fate" revisited. Unpublished Ph.D. dissertation, Northwestern University.

Dykman, R. A., Gantt, W. H., & Whitehorn, J. C. (1956) Conditioning as emotional sensitization and differentiation. *Psychol. Monogr.*, **70**, No. 15.

Grice, G. R., & Davis J. D. (1960) Effect of concurrent responses on the evocation and generalization of the conditioned eyeblink. *J. Exp. Psychol.*, **59**, 391–395.

Hull, C. L. (1950) Simple qualitative discrimination learning. *Psychol. Rev.*, **57**, 303–313.

Logan, F. A. (1954) A note on stimulus intensity dynamism (V). *Psychol. Rev.*, **61**, 77–80.

Musgrave, B. S. (1960) The effect of verbal context factors on cloze and commonality scores. Unpublished M.A. thesis, University of Minnesota.

Voeks, V. W. (1954) Acquisition of S-R connections: A test of Hull's and Guthrie's theories. *J. Exp. Psychol.*, **47**, 137–147.

Chapter 10

SUMMARY AND EVALUATION

Delos D. Wickens

THE OHIO STATE UNIVERSITY

Perhaps the only thing I am certain about in this effort of mine to summarize the proceedings of the last three days is that I have your sympathy. And may I assure you, who must listen to me, that you have mine. Now that we understand each other, I'll explain what I have attempted to do.

I attempted first, while scribbling—and later evaluating—my notes on the papers and the discussions, to discover a theme general enough to be recurrent in a number of sessions. Then I sought for themes of lesser generality, but of sufficient breadth to intrude—or should I say emerge?—in a number of papers or discussions. Finally, so far as individual papers are concerned, I've asked and shall try to answer the following kinds of questions: Does a paper close an issue, close it so the topic can be dismissed in the somewhat impermanent sense that is true of any topic in an active science with the comment "Well done"? Does a paper, because of its description of new techniques or conceptual tools, give promise of bringing closure to some area? Does a paper, in whole or part, suggest some new trend of research in the field of verbal learning? And finally I've looked to see if topics that arose in the last meeting of this group—which I regret missing even more now than at the time—have instigated research and theorizing which now lead to a more thorough understanding of the topic. I've given an affirmative answer or found support for all of my queries, and I'll now turn to what appears to be an over-all theme.

It seems to me that time and time again in the discussions and the interpretations we have been divided into friendly, but highly articulate, opposing camps. The symbol on the banner of one of these camps clearly reads S-R, but how the other shall be identified is not so easy to discover. It is not Gestalt psychology, and it certainly isn't structuralism or functionalism of the Chicago tradition, so for want of a more positive name I'll simply call it non-S-R, or should it be anti-S-R?

It is true, as one of the group said earlier, that S-R psychology is not a theory of behavior, rather it's a way of working and thinking; but certainly there adheres to this way of working and thinking certain predilections which are a consequence of the theoretical and methodological commitments of the early S-R theorists. So it was that there were often disagreements between these two camps over such matters as the proper language and concepts to use in describing some phenomenon, the degree and nature of the analysis to be attempted, the method of attack on the problem, and even the kind of problem selected for study. So with much trepidation I'll make an effort to characterize the two groups from now on referred to as the S-R's and the Antis.

There is an intriguing difference in the manner in which a research problem is generated by these groups. The research of the S-R people seems to be theory generated; they seem to look at a domain of behavior and ask at the outset what their theory has to say about the domain. They are interested in extending their theoretical concepts into behavioral domains that are only a very little bit more complicated than those from which the theoretical concepts have been developed. One suspects that they would seldom think of researching in an area unless the theory is suspected by them of having something to say about the behavior in question.

In contrast the Antis seem to be slightly indifferent to extant psychological theory in generating research. Their inspirations seem to stem from the general intellectual *Zeitgeist*, and often enough from developments in disciplines other than psychology. I think in particular of engineering and linguistics. Thus they begin with a problem area of behavior and develop a theory to account for their empirical findings, whereas the S-R workers are prone to devise a behavioral situation in order to test previously established theoretical formulations. You might say of the two groups that one approaches his problem from below and the other from above.

Another dimension in which these two groups may be contrasted is in the degree of freedom of thought which they permit themselves. The S-R's are strong adherents to the law of parsimony; their first impulse is to seek a simple explanation and to apply whenever possible the timeworn concepts of their system to the new areas of behavior rather than to introduce new concepts. The Antis, on the other hand, are quite receptive to using theoretical formulations which are new to psychology and drawn from other disciplines. In short, they permit themselves a greater freedom of conceptual choices for their theory building than do the S-R's.

This restrictiveness of S-R thinking shows up in another way, for

I believe it is generally less speculative unless there is some promise of checking the validity of speculation with existing data. I think the attitude eventuates in a mild reluctance to discuss, at least for any length of time, a topic for which empirical data are sparse. The S-R's would be happy to examine and verbally evaluate means of collecting data on such a topic, but not the form that the data would take.

My final suggested dimension of difference between the two groups is related to the nature of the concepts that they prefer to employ. The thinking of the S-R group seems to be deeply rooted in physiology, associationism, and Pavlovian conditioning. I don't mean to imply that their work is molecular, that they even desire to reduce their concepts to the language of physiology; and I doubt that any of them would ever care to implant an electrode or aspirate cortical tissue. They find plenty of fun and challenge in searching for the laws of molar behavior, but they remain sensitive to the early physiological orientation of psychology that characterized the Chicago functionalists. This sensitivity causes them to prefer a molar language which carries with it some overtones of the activities in the physiological laboratories, a language which is certainly not dependent upon physiological research, but one which is sympatico with it.

The Antis, on the other hand, seem to exhibit an indifference to the discipline of physiology at least in so far as the shaping of their concepts is concerned. It is not, of course, an antagonism which they demonstrate; rather they just seem to have no residual positive sentiment for this physicalistic way of thought. They choose their concepts from whatever discipline seems to offer the most direct and rapid access to a systematization of their data.

It seems not irrelevant to suggest a contrast between these two groups in their attitude toward that new American institution, the computer. The S-R group sees in it a way of processing data, a device that can produce means, sums of squares, correlations, and even t scores if you have the money to pay for it and don't concern yourself about the possible unemployment of graduate assistants. Perhaps there is in this cautious attitude an element of naïveté, but I am no clinician and I'd better eschew speculations about motives. In contrast, the Antis view the computer as the father of a new language, a language which may be used to express behavioral terms, and whose grammatical laws may thereby lead to new insights into behavioral relations. Perhaps the S-R folk view this approach with suspicion because there is so obviously nothing biological about the computer; if it can be shown to behave like man, it is because man created it—at least a little bit—in his own image, or so they may be inclined to think.

I think I've belabored these differences, which I trust are more than fancied, long enough. It's pertinent now to ask what differential attitudes of this sort may mean to progress in the field of verbal learning. The approach of the S-R psychologist is one which leads to extension by modest steps of a presently established theory into new realms of behavior. It is concerned with an evaluation of the predictiveness of an already established theoretical structure, and to a strong degree it is more concerned with theory evaluation than with discovering new facets of behavior. In contrast the Antis have a strong predilection to study some relatively neglected area of behavior or to look at some old area in a new way. They seem less concerned with theory itself, at least in testing the predictiveness of that theory, than they are with systematizing the behavioral facts in some relatively virgin behavioral domain. They are likely to discover new facts of behavior and present new problems which must be integrated into extant theory, but I believe they leave it to the S-R people to test the adequacies or inadequacies of theory for prediction. So as I see it, both of these biases are most necessary for maintaining the growth of the field of verbal learning; for a science must not only develop a predictive system to handle known data, but must also always seek to discover new raw data and to look at old data in a new way.

So now to concepts or topics of a lesser breadth, but which have been referred to several times in the papers and the discussions. I will list two items in this category: the functional stimulus and context cues. These, of course, are not the only psychological concepts which often entered into the discussions and the papers but they are also ones which imply a broadening of the scope of the problems that are becoming the concern of the modern verbal learning theorist.

It is my impression that the concept of the functional stimulus entered into the previous conference only in a tentative and speculative fashion. This time it has been represented by a formal paper, and this quasi-perceptual process—stimulus selection by the subjects—seems to be well integrated into the thinking of S-R theorists among us. Perhaps this liberalization of S-R thought arises because Underwood's paper has shown that this type of problem can be approached analytically and that rules may be discovered which will make it possible for the functional stimulus to be predicted. At any rate the term was used quite freely and in an explanatory fashion in a number of occasions. I recall in particular Cofer's doing so in his discussion of Brown's paper as well as Mandler in his comments on Jenkins's. It seems to me that there was a bold, confident usage of a concept that would have been used apologetically—or belligerently in the form of an abreaction—in circles such as this only a few years back. And it was accepted by the listeners as calmly as it was used.

Context cues and their potential significance for determining performance have long been recognized, and a word or two is usually said about them in learning texts and courses; and thereafter they are forced into the background by more pressing problems. It seems that now they are emerging from relative obscurity to become a recognized source of variance in learning, transfer, and retention studies—thanks most recently to Barnes as well as to the older work of Schlosberg and Bilodeau. Few systematic studies of how context operates have been made, yet the concept proved to be a fruitful one in our discussions. Melton made use of it in his discussion of Peterson, so did Cofer on Brown, and, if set and the effect of context cues have a psychological core in common, we may say that Staats touched upon this topic in his comments upon Russell's article. Next time—for I hope there will be another such stimulating meeting—we may be able to use the term with a more accurate knowledge of its behavioral significance, for at present there are too few systematic studies of its effect.

And now I move to my last category, my reactions to the contents of specific papers. For me they—that is, my reactions—fall into three classes, the first of which is a feeling that the topic at hand is solved or near enough to solution so that it matters little. The second is that the partially solved topic is in good hands and that the route selected will go; and the third is simply that the problem is yet in the formative stage.

In the first of my classes I place two topics, one-trial learning and the effect of m and familiarity upon learning. I knew as I read these papers or listened to their discussion that a couple of topics in my class in learning next Fall were now taken care of most adequately. True, there may be some loose ends here and there, but thanks to the careful and thoughtful integration of the solid body of research already at hand, no one is likely to trip over them. Perhaps I should attempt to identify at least one of these loose ends in each case. In the instance of m, I'll follow Goss who, in his discussion, argued that although the empirical facts of that field are for the most part known, a theoretical formulation encompassing and simplifying the diverse facts is still to be had. Not so much as a loose end perhaps, but certainly as something provocative to think about is Miller's suggestion that one-trial learning may characterize connection formations in the nervous system. It is a most plausible notion, but he made it apparent that neither he nor the rest of us could, after reading Postman, conclude that verbal learning as a molar phenomenon was other than cumulative in characteristic. Perhaps the word learning is, after all, not an appropriate term to apply to events in the nervous system. At any rate, my reaction to both of these papers is pretty well summarized by those letters QED.

My second group may be characterized as containing topics in an area in which methodology has been refined, a fairly large body of data is presently available, but where intellectual closure, though promised by these achievements, appears to be some distance away. In this group I have placed two topics: immediate memory and the mediating response. Both Peterson and Murdock have demonstrated that their methodologies are sensitive to behavior changes in retention occurring within temporal intervals in the order of magnitude of a few seconds. Not only do their results appear lawful but also their methodology is elegant in its efficiency. Melton in his discussion gave promise that an adequate theory might be couched in the familiar terms of context and proactive inhibition, and that, at least so far as the underlying psychological variables are concerned, a union between long-term and short-term retention may be possible. Somehow I always feel we have made progress when we identify—or at least suspect we identify—common psychological mechanisms in phenotypically disparate events.

I suppose the mediating response is a sort of Kilroy of the neobehaviorists; he is never seen but he is everywhere. It is assumed to have a physiological being, yet our evidence for it remains only at the intervening variable level in the Meehl and MacCorquodale sense of that term. Unlike immediate memory—a body of data looking for a theory—it is a theory looking for a body of data. I think, because of its status as a theory of long standing and of such great importance to the behaviorists' way of thought, that it has almost become dogma. In fact it is almost as if the theory itself were an empirical body of knowledge for which a theory would some day be developed. This is one reason that I have placed the mediating response in my second category; the other, and perhaps the more cogent one, is that its evaluation is in such good hands, for Jenkins has shown that research can be designed which will probe this theory even at the intervening variable level. The data which he reported have indicated that the theory must contain more complexities if it is to be useful, just as we often find that the empirical data are more complex than we had originally thought.

My third group consists of problems in the formative stage both in so far as theory and empirical data are concerned. Certainly the farthest advanced of these problems is that of recognition. The research that was reported offers convincing evidence that the problem is an exciting one and that this long-neglected topic will have something to say about the processes of learning and perception. This potential importance of the topic was emphasized by Deese in his suggestion that the free-recall situation contains the process of recognition along with the process of production. It would not surprise me to learn that in the future we will identify recognition as a part process in several other more complicated learning situations.

The topic of language learning has been approached by an ingenious experimental method, but it is still at the descriptive level; and I think it will be quite a while before we can handle this highly complex activity, for it seems to me that current verbal learning theory doesn't quite contain in its language the proper terms to handle the very complicated activity of the learning and usage of language.

The problem of set has been with us for a long time, since the very early days of experimental psychology, in fact. Russell's paper raised some long-neglected questions as well as new ones, but I don't think we answered any of them in our discussion. It seems to be a field which contains both much and little, much in the sense that it can be readily demonstrated, little in the sense that we do not as yet seem to know how to approach this problem analytically.

Well now I close. I wish I could summarize our doings in one ringing pithy sentence. But I cannot, and perhaps the reason for it is due not to my own linguistic inadequacy, but rather to the fact that the field of verbal learning is so complicated and variegated that only a Faulkner-type sentence could hope to encompass its many realms. But I will add that I found myself stimulated and richly rewarded even though somewhat fatigued by the long vigil around the conference table.

SUMMARY OF CONFERENCE DISCUSSION

Miller took exception to certain points that were made concerning computers. A computer is not a theory, though it can sometimes be a model. A computer provides a language, the programming language for stating the model; it need not be used solely for arithmetic computations. The programming language can be used profitably in talking about psychological processes; actually, the computer language is as close to S-R terms as it is to any other point of view. It should not be tied closely to any particular point of view, although it has been in the conference.

Deese indicated that the ordering relationship which is implied in verbal associations is a matter which S-R and non-S-R viewpoints have in common. He also objected to the implication that analytic experimentation is the exclusive province of S-R theorists. Admittedly S-R workers tend to analytic experimentation, but the correlation is less than unity. Deese said that he himself, if not an S-R theorist, would still be analytic in his approach, interested in experimental treatment, independent variables, and the study of outputs.

It was observed by Peterson that Hull, the S-R theorist, was interested in developing machines[1] which simulated behavioral processes and was an advocate of the use of mathematics in treating learning problems. Peterson was led, by this example, to wonder about the distinction between S-R and non-S-R theory. Russell expressed the view that such distinctions are disappearing. Shepard, however, stressed that there has seemed to be a difference in strategy of research. According to him, the S-R approach has had, as its principal method, the experimental analysis of behavior and, as its principal goal, the discovery of the important variables and the correlations between them. On the other hand the so-called non-S-R approach emphasizes, as an additional method, the synthesis of behavior and, as an additional goal, the elucidation of the detailed mechanisms underlying the correlations uncovered by experimental analysis.

He went on to say that computers, owing to their complete flexibility, do not in themselves favor one of the two approaches over the other. We have talked too much about the machine itself; it is the program that is fed into the machine that is the crucial thing. This program can just as well incorporate S-R or non-S-R principles, discrete or continuous processes, and so on. The advantage of the computer is not that it supplies us with a theory that is better than present S-R theory, but that it provides us with a tool for discovering exactly what behavior is implied by our theory—whatever its kind. Wickens illustrated what Shepard said with the comment that the program is like writing down the principles of algebra and seeing how they work.

Melton felt the basic point is that there would be no major conflict between S-R people and computer people if certain S-R principles, like stimulus and response generalization, were accepted and worked with by the computer people. Shepard, Melton indicated, when he writes a paper on generalization, sounds like an S-R psychologist. If there is a difference between the S-R and non-S-R worker it is that the S-R person likes to examine in detail the principle, such as stimulus generalization, which is to go in the program. S-R people are always constrained by the notion of dealing with animal behavior, and their interest is in individual, physiological phenomena of an organic character. One could put constructs that are rational into a program and not worry about these fundamental, biological, adapta-

[1] See C. L. Hull & H. D. Baerstein. (1929) A mechanical parallel to the conditioned reflex. *Science*, **70**, 14–15.

tional matters. Hull, for some people, was neither mathematical nor "rational" enough, but his biological background prevented him from being so. Melton felt that programming would be difficult without more detailed knowledge than we have about the phenomena to be programmed.

Mandler described Brown's approach as a naturalistic one and Staats's work as more "rational"; i.e., Staats tries to apply the principles he has to a situation. These differences are not too important. But one problem with the S-R approach is the tradition that its theory and terms will be able to explain anything. As a result the principles, like those of the Ptolemaic system, are shifted loosely to fit a particular case. The intuitive belief, held by many, that S-R principles will be adequate may prevent us from keeping open minds about other principles that might be more useful. On the other hand, S-R theory does show some flexibility. Our discussion of concepts, such as functional stimuli and the reinforcement of rules, is a far cry from the S-R theorizing of ten or twenty years ago.

Staats said he believed the difference between the naturalistic and rationalistic approaches did not lie in the value placed on observation. Observation holds an important place in both methods. The difference lies in what is done *after* observation, when the S-R psychologist tries to use the data to confirm or correct theory.

Mandler commented on some of his own remarks earlier in the conference, saying that he had not meant to imply that the principle of reinforcement does not hold but rather that we must be aware of its limitations and examine all its consequences.

Jenkins and Melton observed that this conference group would be characterized as functionalist.

INDEX